ROME GUIDE

YOUR PASSPORT TO GREAT TRAVEL!

CRITICAL ACCLAIM FOR
OPEN ROAD TRAVEL GUIDES!

*Whether you're going abroad or planning a trip in the United States, take Open Road along on your journey. Our books have been praised by **Travel & Leisure, The Los Angeles Times, Newsday, Booklist, US News & World Report, Endless Vacation, American Bookseller, Coast to Coast,** and many other magazines and newspapers!*

Don't just see the world – experience it with Open Road!

ABOUT THE AUTHOR

Having spent eight years living in and traveling through Italy, Douglas E. Morris has finally put his experiences down on paper. Published in a wide variety of media, Mr. Morris gives you the most accurate, up-to-date, and comprehensive information about restaurants, hotels, and sights.

ACKNOWLEDGMENTS

Many people assisted considerably in the development of this book. My parents, Don and Denise, and my brother Dan were invaluable for their support, information, suggestions, and numerous leads. Special thanks for Salguod Sirrom's editorial and creative assistance.

HIT THE OPEN ROAD - WITH OPEN ROAD PUBLISHING!

Open Road Publishing now has guide books to exciting, fun destinations on four continents. As veteran travelers, our goal is to bring you the best travel guides available anywhere!

No small task, but here's what we offer:

• All Open Road travel guides are written by authors with a distinct, opinionated point of view – not some sterile committee or team of writers. Our authors are experts in the areas covered and are polished writers.

• Our guides are geared to people who want great vacations, great value, and great tips for both standard tourist sights *and* fun, unique alternatives.

• We're strong on the basics, but we also provide terrific choices for those looking to get off the beaten path and *experience* the country or city – not just *see* it or pass through it.

• We give you the best, but we also tell you about the worst and what to avoid. Nobody should waste their time and money on their hard-earned vacation because of bad or inadequate travel advice.

• Our guides assume nothing. We tell you everything you need to know to have the trip of a lifetime – presented in a fun, literate, no-nonsense style.

• And, above all, we welcome your input, ideas, and suggestions to help us put out the best travel guides possible.

ROME GUIDE

YOUR PASSPORT TO GREAT TRAVEL!

DOUG MORRIS

OPEN ROAD PUBLISHING

1st Edition

TABLE OF CONTENTS

CONTENTS

CONTENTS

CONTENTS

CONTENTS

MAPS

CONTENTS

1. INTRODUCTION

If you're looking for great fun, serious relaxation, unparalleled artwork and dazzling museums, ancient civilizations, and world-class accommodations, then Rome is the place for you! Besides all of this, Italian food is arguably the best in the world. And don't forget the great wine.

There is so much to see and do that a trip to Rome can be overwhelming. But with this Open Road guide, your days and nights in Italy will be filled with exciting possibilities. I've given you lots of options to tailor the perfect vacation to your particular needs.

If you're looking for that perfect hotel, I've reviewed a huge number of excellent possibilities for you to choose from in every price range. When you get hungry, Rome Guide offers a wide selection of terrific restaurants, with lots of detail about the different regional cuisines and wines from all over Italy. And you won't want for things to do and sights to see: imperial Roman ruins, awe-inspiring medieval and Renaissance museums, incredible churches and monuments (including the many wonders of Vatican City), fun and varied neigborhoods to wander about and enjoy a relaxing cappucino, and all manner of piazzas, palazzi, fountains, and gardens – all part of the wonderful tapestry of life that is modern Rome!

And if you have more time, I've also included several chapters worth of terrific excursions, including a number of hill towns and beaches not far from Rome, and a few destinations further afield: the quaint isle of Capri in the Bay of Naples; the ancient towns of Pompeii and Herculaneum, preserved through the ages through the volcanic lava flow from nearby Mt. Vesuvius; and extensive coverage of Florence and Venice, Italy's other leading cities.

So read on, and have the trip of a lifetime in Rome!

2. EXCITING ROME!
- OVERVIEW

ROME & CENTRAL ITALY

Central Italy extends north of Rome, but for the purposes of this book I've included it in this region. Although only a small part of the area is composed of lowlands, central Italy plays an important role in farming and in some branches of industry, specifically wine growing. **Rome** and **Florence** are the main tourist cities in Central Italy and they have the best museums, the best churches, and the best sights to see. Even if you're a seasoned Italy traveler you should make a point of visiting either of these two cities to refresh your memory of the historical beauty of Italy.

Looking for a respite from Rome? **Frascati**, a quaint hill town just outside of Rome, may be the answer. Every year they have a bacchanalian wine festival celebrating the pressing of the local wine. If you're in Rome during September you have to visit, since Frascati is only a 30 minute train ride away. And if you come any other time of year and want to stay in a small, peaceful, medieval hill town, with wonderful views over the surrounding countryside (vineyards), wonderful little wine bars, plenty of great restaurants, and a quaint ambiance that will be remembered forever, Frascati is the place for you.

Besides Frascati, I've also icluded some other Rome area excursions, plus some further afield, such as the beautiful island of **Capri**; **Pompeii** and **Herculaneum**, those ancient cities smothered but preserved by the lava and ash of the local volcano; and **Florence** and **Venice**, Italy's other leading cities and major destinations in their own right.

THE ETERNAL CITY: THE BEST OF ROME!

Rome has so many options that it's easy to neglect seeing a certain sight, or taking the time to go to a specific restaurant, or making an effort to visit a particular spot late in the evening to enjoy the ambiance and charm. Even though I've itemized the best places to stay, eat, and see while you're here, if you only have a little time, you have to go to the places listed below while in Rome.

Even if you are the furthest thing from being religious, make the effort to see **St. Peter's** and the **Vatican Museum**. This will take the better part of a day if you do a proper tour. No church is more magnificent and no museum is more complete. All others in Rome and the rest of Italy will pale in comparison.

That night, make sure you get to the **Trastevere** district and sample the atmosphere of **La Canonica**, a converted chapel and now a restaurant that also has many tables spilling out along the street. Reserve a spot inside since this may be your last chance to have a meal in a quaint converted chapel. Try their *Spaghetti alla Carbonara* (with a light cream sauce, covered with ham, peas, and grated parmesan cheese) for primo and for your main course sample the light fish dish, *Sogliala alla Griglia* (grilled Sole). Then sojourn to one of the cafés in the **Piazza Santa Maria in Trastevere**, grab a drink, and savor the evening.

During another day it is imperative that you visit **Piazza Navona** and grab an ice cream at one of the cafés, and either lounge on their terraces or take it with you and sit on the edge of one of the fountains. The best vantage point is on Bernini's magnificent **Fontana Dei Quattro Fiumi** (Fountain of Four Rivers). The four figures supporting the large obelisk (a Bernini trademark) represent the Danube, the Ganges, the Nile, and the Plata Rivers. Notice the figure representing the Nile. It is shielding its eyes from the facade of the church facing it, **Santa Agnese in Agone**, which was designed by Bernini's rival at the time, Borromini. An ancient artistic quarrel comes to life everyday in Piazza Navona.

From there, only a few blocks away is the quaint little **Campo dei Fiori** where you'll find one of Rome's best fruit and vegetable markets every day until 1:00pm, except Sunday. Make sure you get here to shop or just to enjoy the atmosphere of a boisterous Roman market.

Here is where you should also enjoy at least one meal, at **La Carbonara** in the square. Even though the name would lead you to believe that the best dish to get is the *Spaghetti alla Carbonara*, I believe you haven't been to Rome if you neglect to sample their exquisite *Spaghetti alla Vongole Verace* (with a spicy oil, garlic, and clam sauce). If you want to sit outside, you should wait until about 2:00pm, after the debris from the outdoor market has been swept up from the piazza.

Other dishes you should sample are the *penne all'arrabiatta* (literally means angry pasta; it's tubular pasta made with a spicy garlic, oil, and tomato-based sauce), the *tortellini alla panna* (meat filled pasta in a thick cream sauce), and any *abbacchio* (lamb) or *maiale alla griglia* (grilled pork).

In the evening, don't miss the **Trevi Fountain**, all lit up and surrounded by locals and tourists strumming on guitars and drinking wine. It's definitely a party atmosphere. Come here with friends or arrive and meet new ones. For one of your evening meals, there's a place somewhat close by a little past the **Spanish Steps**. If you're here in Spring, stop for a minute and admire the floral display covering the steps.

Then move onto **La Capriciossa** where you can sit in a peaceful little piazza just off the Via del Corso, Rome's main shopping street, while you enjoy your meal. They are known for making excellent pizza (only in the evening) as well as preparing perfect Roman pasta dishes and exquisite meat plates. If you haven't already sampled the *penne all'arabiatta*, do so here, and try the succulent *abbacchio arrosto* (roast lamb), another staple of the Roman diet. And to finish the meal, order a *Sambucca con tre mosce* (literally translated, it means a sweet liquor with three flies, but it actually uses three coffee beans). Remember to bite into the beans as you have the sweet liquor in your mouth. The combination of tastes is exquisite.

There is obviously much more to do in Rome than this, but if you only have a little time, make sure you get to the places mentioned above. Then you can say you were truly Roman for a short while.

EXPERIENCE HISTORY

Home to the ancient world's most powerful empire, Italy is awash in history. Daily life revolves around ruins thousands of years old. Modern buildings incorporate ancient structures into their walls. Medieval streets snake through almost all cities including Rome, Florence, and especially Venice. In Italy you can see the tapestry of history woven directly in front of you. Museums abound with ancient artifacts, beautiful paintings, and stunning sculpture.

You can easily spend an entire trip roaming through museums – or for that matter inside the beautiful churches where you'll see some of the most exquisite paintings and sculptures anywhere on earth!

A FEAST FOR THE EYES!

Even though you could spend an entire trip inside museums or churches, if you decided to do so you would miss out on what makes Italy such a wonderful vacation: its natural beauty, charm, and ambiance. Being in Italy is like walking through a fairy tale. The old winding streets, twisting around the quaint refurbished buildings, leading to a tiny piazza centered with a sparkling fountain all seems like something out of a dream. And you'll find a similar scene in virtually every city you visit in Italy.

FOOD & WINE

But a feast for the eyes is not all you'll get. Italy has, arguably (pipe down, you Francophiles!), the best food you'll find anywhere in the world. In most cases it's simple food, but with a bountiful taste. Take, for example, a Roman favorite: *abbacchio arrosto*. This is a succulent lamb dish slowly cooked over an open flame until perfectly prepared. It is usually accompanied by *patate arrosto*, roast potatoes cooked with rosemary, olive oil, and salt that makes my mouth water just thinking about them.

And since Italy is surrounded on almost all sides by water you can sample any flavor of seafood imaginable. Usually caught the same day, especially in the small towns along the sea, the seafood in Italy will have you coming back for more.

And don't forget the pasta. You'll find all shapes and sizes covered with sauces of every description and variety. Regions are known for certain pasta dishes and when there you have to sample them all. The area around Bologna is known for the production of the best ham in the world, *Prosciutto di Parma*, which is fed from the scraps of the magnificent cheese they make in same region, *Parmiggiano Reggiano*. Both of these foods feature prominently in *spaghetti alla bolognese* – smother mine with the locally made parmesan cheese, *Parmiggiano Reggiano*!

To wash down all these savory dishes you need look no further than the local wine list. Italian wines may not be as full-bodied as French or California wines, but they have an intimate, down to earth, simple taste. Order from the wine list or be adventurous and get a carafe of the house wine, which is usually delicious, and more often than not comes from the local vineyards you saw outside the city as you arrived.

SPORTING ACTIVITIES

If you've noticed your waistband stretching a little from all the wonderful food and wine you've been enjoying, have no fear – Italy has plenty of activities for you to shave off some of those unwanted pounds. Not far from Rome and Venice are wonderfully clear water and beaches all along the **Mediterranean Sea** and the **Adriatic Sea**.

You can go waterskiing, snorkeling, skin diving, sailing or just lie on the beach and sunbathe. Many vacation beaches are topless today, an unheard of activity ten years ago, so you'll be treated to an added adventure either trying it or enjoying it.

There are also many top-level golf courses not far from Rome, Florence, and Venice, plenty of tennis courts, horseback riding in the country, fishing in lakes and sailing in the seas.

3. ROMAN ITINERARIES

If you only have a short period of time in **Rome** and you want to fill it up with the best sights, restaurants, hotels, cafes at which to lounge, and pubs from which you can crawl back to your bed, all you have to do is follow the itineraries listed below. The hotels, sights, and restaurants mentioned are all described in more detail in the *Rome* chapter. Simply refer to this chapter to more fully plan your Roman adventure.

The places listed in these itineraries are among my favorites in Rome, but there were plenty of close calls! So follow my advice if you wish, or plow through my chapter on Rome and find the perfect itinerary for you.

THE PERFECT THREE DAYS
Day One

This is going to be a somewhat slow day since you'll have just arrived and will be slightly jetlagged.

Arrive on direct flight to Rome's Leonardo da Vinci airport at 8:00am.

Take a cab to the **Hotel Locarno** near **Piazza del Popolo**, shower and unpack.

Stop at the cafe next to the excellent restaurant **Dal Bolognese** in the Piazza del Popolo and grab a cappuccino, cafe, or espresso to get you going.

Take the second road on your left, the **Via del Babuino** to the **Spanish Steps**.

Get your picture taken while you lean over and grab a drink from the fountain in front of the steps.

Walk to the top of the steps for the magnificent view over the city.

It should be about lunch time now, so walk back down the steps, cross the street, and take a left into the third street at the edge of the piazza, **Via delle Croce**. Follow this to the end, find an outside seat at the superb local restaurant **Pizzeria La Capricciosa**, in Largo dei Lombardi. Try any of their exquisite Roman pasta specialties: *arrabiata, amatriciana,* or *vongole verace*.

After lunch it should be about nap time. But remember to only take a 2-3 hour nap, wake up right away, take a shower and get out again – otherwise you'll sleep until 10:00pm and be wide awake because jet-lag will have set in.

Now it's time to explore the streets around the **Piazza di Spagna**, **Via della Croce**, **Via del Corso**, **Via dei Condotti** and admire all the different shops.

After shopping/exploring, take a small walk (or short cab ride) to **Piazza Navona**.

Stop at **Le Tre Scalini** and sample some of the world famous Italian *gelato* (ice cream). If you sit at the tables outside the cost will double or triple.

If some liquid refreshment is more your style, exit the Piazza Navona on the other side, cross the **Via Vittorio Emanuele**, visit the **Campo dei Fiori** (where they have a superb market in the mornings which we'll get to in a few days) and stop in at the **Drunken Ship** for some Guiness, Harp, or Kilkenny. Have a few ales for me.

From here you are within striking distance of **Trastevere**, the place for Roman nightlife, across the river. Cross the pedestrian bridge **Ponte Sisto** and make your way to **Piazza Santa Maria in Trastevere**.

If it's too early for dinner (7:30pm or 8:00pm is the beginning time) stop at one of the outdoor cafes and replenish your fluids.

For dinner stop at **La Canonica** just outside of the piazza, Here you should also try one of the typical Roman pasta specialties, *arrabiata*, *amatriciana*, or *vongole verace*; as well as some *sogliola alla griglia* (grilled sole) for seconds.

After dinner, if it's not too late, walk down the long road leading from the Piazza, **Via della Lungaretta**, to the large main road **Viale Trastevere**.

Catch a cab here to either return to your hotel if you're tired, or have the driver drop you off at the **Trevi Fountain**.

Day Two

Today is museum day. Start off at the best in the city, the **Vatican Museum** and the **Sistine Chapel**. This should take you all morning.

Instead of a long sit-down meal, stop at one of the cafes around the museum and St. Peters and order a light snack. My suggestion is the *Medallione*, a grilled ham and cheese concoction that is tasty and filling. You don't order at the counter, you first pay for your order with the cashier (order your drink at the same time), then bring the receipt up to the counter and tell the bartender what you'll have. A good tip to leave is about L500.

After your meal, let's explore **St. Peters**. Guys will need slacks for this adventure and women cannot wear short skirts of tank top-like shirts. Don't forget to walk to the top.

Once done here, which should be later afternoon, let's stop at **Castel St. Angelo** and explore the ancient armaments museum and fortifications of the fortress that protected the Vatican in the past.

Now it's time to go home for a 2-3 hour nap, if you need it.

Dinner tonight is at the nearby **La Buca di Ripetta**, on Via di Ripetta, where you should try either the Lasag*na al Forno, Saltimbocca alla Romana,* or the *Osso buco di Vitello.*

After dinner, if you missed the **Trevi Fountain** last night, go there tonight. It's about a 20 minute walk (if you're staying at the Locarno), or a short cab ride away.

If not, you must return to the **Piazza Navona** to soak up the ambiance there at night with its fountains lit up. Either bring your own bottle of wine and sit at one of the benches or grab a table at one of the cafes and enjoy a beautiful Roman evening.

Day Three

Time to explore some serious ruins. On the way, stop at the market in the **Piazza Venezia**.

From here make your way down **Via dei Foro Imperiali** to the entrance to the Forum on the right hand side. Up ahead you'll see the **Coliseum**, our next destination.

View the Coliseum (take some pictures).

Lunch. Time to hail a cab and go back up the Via dei Foro Imperiali, to Piazza Venezia, then on to **Gino ai Funari** on Via dei Funari. This is a small local place in the Jewish Ghetto that makes the Roman pasta specialties perfectly (*carbonara, amatriciana, vongole verace, and arrabiata*). Or you can try the *conniglio alla cacciatore* (rabbit hunter style made with brandy tomatoes and spices). It is superb.

After lunch, before we go back up the Via di Teatro Marcello to go to the second best museum in Rome – the Campidoglio – since it's so close by, let's pay a visit to the **Isola Tiberina**.

After a quick exploration of this island, let's get to the **Campidoglio**. Remember to find *La Buca della Verita*. This should take most of the afternoon.

When completed, make your way to the **Pantheon** (or back to the hotel if you're tired) and sit at one of the outside cafes and savor the sight of one of Rome's oldest buildings in a quaint medieval square. If it is super hot, sit by the pillars at the entrance of the Pantheon since it is always wonderfully cool there.

Back to the hotel to freshen up for your meal this evening at **La Carbonara** in **Campo dei Fiori**. Remember you were here on Day One at the Drunken Ship? They make the best *spaghetti alla vongole verace* I've ever had.

You can stay in Campo dei Fiori for the whole evening and take in the sights and sounds of one of Rome's most popular nighttime piazzas. Most evenings they have live bands playing. You've already been to the other three great piazzas where you can get a true taste of Roman nightlife: Navona, Santa Maria in Trastevere, and Trevi.

THE PERFECT FOUR DAYS

Follow the above itinerary for the first three days, and add Day Four immediately below.

Day Four

Time to go to church (you don't have to pray if you that's not your thing). To get to these churches you're going to need to take the metro and buses or rely on Roman taxis. Our first stop is **Saint Paul's Outside the Wall**. Get your picture taken in the middle courtyard with one of the trees in the background. When you next return to Rome, do the same thing and trace how long it has been by how far the tree has grown. My family has been doing that for over 40 years now.

From here cab it back into town to **Santa Maria Sopra Minerva**.

Next is **Santa Maria Maggiore** near the train station.

On to **San Pietro in Vicolo** close to the Coliseum.

Located between the Coliseum and San Giovanni in Laterano is our next stop, **Church of San Clemente**.

Our next church is the cathedral of Rome, which isn't St. Peter's, it is **San Giovanni in Laterano**.

Time to get ourselves to Trastevere for a late lunch, and **Sabatini's** is the perfect choice. Here we can sit in their large outdoor terrace on the Piazza and enjoy a fine meal.

Most people don't come to Trastevere to look at churches. They come for the more bacchanalian aspects of the area. But we religious types have first come to see **Santa Maria in Trastevere** in the same piazza as Sabatini's, then the **Church of Santa Cecilia in Trastevere**.

Since you've been traveling all over town, let's return to the hotel for brief siesta, since everything is closed anyway, or stop off at **Babbington's Tea Room** near the Spanish Steps for a "cuppa."

When the stores re-open, let's do some antique shopping on the nearby streets of **Via del Babuino** and the **Via Margutta**, Rome's best for antiques.

If you want to buy a book, stop into the **Lion Bookshop** at Via del Babuino 181.

For dinner try the ever popular **Otello Alla Concordia** at nearby Via Della Croce 81, where you can get some of the most succulent *abbacchio alla griglia* anywhere in Rome.

For an after-dinner vino, sample **Antica Bottigleria Placidi,** a great wine bar on the same street.

THE PERFECT SEVEN DAYS

Follow the above itinerary for the first four days, then add Days Five through Seven immediately below.

Day Five

If you don't feel as if you are able to truly appreciate some of the activities listed above, by all means return and enjoy them today, but before you run off, let's start by waking up early and going back to the **Campo dei Fiori** to see how different it is in the mornings. Here you'll find one of Rome's best food and flower markets. Don't miss it.

For lunch, return back into the city and find this great place located between Piazza Navona and the Spanish Steps, **Orso "80"** at Via dell'Orso 80. Here they make great *spaghetti alla carbonara* as well as the *abbacchio alla griglia*.

Now the fun begins. We're going to a terrific town – **Frascati**. If we are lucky and it's September, we may stumble into their wine festival (and definitely stumble out).

To get to Frascati, go to the train station, buy a ticket, go to track 27, board the small local train (takes 35 minutes and costs L6,500), and savor the scenery along the way.

Enjoy the views, exploring the winding medieval streets and the relative peace and quiet compared to Rome. Don't forget to search out some of the little wine stores. My favorite is **Cantina Via Campania**.

For dinner, let's give the wild and raucous **Pergatolo** at Via del Castello 20 a try. If you're into something more sedate, **Zaraza** at Viale Regina Margherita 21 should be your choice.

Once dinner is done, make your way back to Rome.

After arriving at the train station, let's go to a nearby Irish pub, **The Fiddler's Elbow** on Via dell'Olmata, that serves up fine ales, an authentic atmosphere, English conversation, and a fun evening to end an adventurous day.

Day Six

Let's start off the day at the nearby **Mercato de Stampe**, at Piazza Fontanella, which is open from 9:00am–6:00pm Monday through Saturday. Here you can find maps, stamps, books, almost anything on the intellectual side.

When done here, take a cab or stroll the short distance to the **Piazza Barberini** at the base of the **Via Veneto**.

First we'll stop in the **Palazzo Barberini**, located on the Via Quattro Fontane that leads up the hill from the Piazza. This palazzo is the home of the **National Portrait Gallery**.

After soaking up the art, walk back almost to the piazza to a small street named Via degli Avignonesi. At the end of it you'll find a great little local place, **Trattoria Da Olimpico**. Stop here for lunch.

Once lunch is over go back up the street to the piazza, and start up Via Veneto, the street that embodies the good life – *La Dolce Vita*. Halfway up you'll pass by the **American Embassy** on the right hand side. Stop at one of the cafes just past the embassy for refreshment.

At the top of the street, go through the massive gate, cross the street and enter the beautiful park, **Villa Borghese**. Take a leisurely stroll through the gardens to the **Galleria Borghese** that has portraits, paintings, and sculptures galore.

Back to the hotel.

Dinner tonight is at **Dal Bolognese** in the Piazza del Popolo. Try their *fritto misto*, a fried mix of veggies, cheese, and meat.

End the evening by going to the top of the **Spanish Steps** for a view over the city at night.

Day Seven

Assuming today is a Sunday, you must visit the **Porta Portese** market that lines the Tevere every Sunday. Starting at the **Ponte Sublico**, you'll find all sorts of interesting antiques and junk here. A must visit if you're in Rome on a Sunday.

After the market, and since it is Sunday and everything is closed (that's right, no museums, hardly any shops, etc.) except restaurants, it's time to return to the restaurant you liked best that you tried before. I always do this wherever I travel. It ensures that one of my last meals is going be great, and it makes me feel somewhat like I belong. Go to one with an outside terrace like **La Carbonara** in Campo dei Fiori.

Return to your hotel and pack, and afterwards go for a stroll around your new neighborhood.

End your stroll at the top of the **Spanish Steps** again. Tonight we're going to the terrace restaurant in the **Villa Hassler** for a scenic and romantic last dinner in Rome. Try their specialty *abbacchio al forno*.

4. LAND & PEOPLE

LAND

From the top of the boot to the toe, Italy is a little more than 675 miles (1,090 kilometers) long. The widest part, in the north, measures about 355 miles (570 kilometers) from east to west. The rest of the peninsula varies in width from 100 to 150 miles (160 to 240 kilometers). The peninsula of Italy has a total area of about 116,000 square miles (300,400 square kilometers).

A mountainous country, Italy is dominated by two large mountain systems – the **Alps** in the north and the **Apennines** throughout the peninsula. The Alps, which are the highest mountains in Europe, extend in a great curve from the northwestern coast of Italy to the point where they merge with Austria and Slovenia in the east. Just west of the port city of Genoa, the **Maritime Alps** are the beginning of the chain. Despite mighty peaks and steep-sided valleys, the Alps are pierced by modern engineering marvels of mountain passes that have always allowed commerce between Italy and its northern neighbors to flow freely. More modern highway and railroad tunnels provide year-round access through the mountains.

The Apennine mountain system is an eastern continuation of the Maritime Alps. It forms a long curve that makes up the backbone of the Italian peninsula. The Apennines extend across Italy in the north, follow the east coast across the central region, then turn toward the west coast, and, interrupted by the narrow Strait of Messina, continue into Sicily.

There are numerous smaller mountains in Italy, many of volcanic ancestry, and thankfully many extinct. The two active volcanoes, **Mount Vesuvius** near Naples and **Mount Etna** in Sicily, are the only active volcanoes on the European continent. Maybe that has something to do with the heated Italian temperament?

PEOPLE

The Italian people are considered to be one of the most homogeneous, in language and religion, of all the European populations. The only significant minority group live in the region called **Trentino-Alto Adige**. These Alpine valleys of the north once made up part of the Austrian province of Tyrol, and the several hundred thousand German-speaking residents still refer to their homeland as South Tyrol. The region was incorporated into Italy after World War I, and both Italian and German are official languages in this region. Obviously, the people of the region have developed their own sense of identity – part of, but separate from, the rest of Italy.

One much smaller minority also lives in northern Italy. This group, the **Valdotains**, dwells in the region called **Valle d'Aosta** in the northwestern corner of the country, and also has two official languages, Italian and French.

About 95 percent of the Italian people speak Italian, while members of the two aforementioned groups make up the other 5%. For more than seven centuries the standard form of the language has been the one spoken in Tuscany, the region of central Italy centered around Florence. However, there are many dialects, some of which are difficult even for Italians to understand. Two of these principal dialects, those of Sicily and Sardinia, sound like a foreign language to most Italians. If you have lived in Italy for a while, it is easy to pinpoint the different accents and dialects and pinpoint where someone is from.

ORIENTATION

Lazio, the province that **Roma (Rome)** is in, covers an area of 6,633 square miles, including the provinces of Frosinone, Latina, Roma, and Viterbo, and has a population of over 6 million. Its charms include quaint little seaside resorts nestled in pine groves, pretty lakeside villages, many dominated by castles, and exotic skiing resorts, such as Terminillo, only a few hours drive from Rome's center. Also near the city are many beaches, **Lido di Ostia** being one of the best and most easily accessible.

Other than its encompassing the national capital, Lazio does not get much respect from the average Italian. Northerners lump it together contemptuously with the southern provinces of Campania and Calabria, and the southern Italians consider it a wasteland of swamps and poor mountain regions inhibiting the entrance to most everyone's destination in the area – Roma.

That is precisely Lazio's identity problem. It is completely overshadowed by Rome, but this was not always the situation. Rome was not always the largest and most powerful city in the region. Prior to the Roman Empire, another culture, the **Etruscans**, dominated the area around

Rome. **Cervetri** and **Tarquinia**, north of Rome in Lazio, were two of the richest Etruscan cities. Now they are home to magnificent *Necropoli*, or simply, cities of the dead. The Etruscans took great care in laying their dead to rest in cemeteries set up like actual towns; and those found in Tarquinia and Cervetri are two of the finest. Cervetri is the closest, so this may be the best alternative for a quick day trip.

Besides Rome, the other locations, towns, and cities featured in this chapter include **Vatican City**, **Tivoli Gardens**, **Castel Gandolfo**, **Frascati**, **Ostia Antica**, **Lago di Bracciano** and **Cervetri**. Two specific excursions are featured near Rome, and two are further afield not far from Naples: the ancient ruins of **Pompeii** and **Herculaneum**, devoured in volcanic lava and ash nearly 2,000 years ago.

Finally, you'll find an excursion to the beautiful Mediterranean **Isle of Capri**. If you're looking for great beaches and water sports, Capri is close to unbeatable.

The Eternal City

Rome is the capital of the Republic of Italy, the region of Lazio, and the province of Rome. As such, it has turned into Italy's largest city, with over 5 million people. The **Tiber River** (**Tevere**), Italy's third longest (after the Po and the Adige), dissects the middle of Rome.

For a millennium and a half, Rome was the cultural center of Europe. At the time of the Empire, it controlled territory extending from Scotland to North Africa, and from the Atlantic Ocean to the Persian Gulf. During and after the Renaissance (14th century AD), Rome was also a center of artistic expression. **Michelangelo** spent much time here, working on the Sistine chapel, helping to design St. Peter's, carving the Pieta, and much more. Hundreds of churches were built by the Vatican, and many artists were sponsored to fill them with beautiful works.

Because of this extensive history, dating all the way back to before the time of Christ, Rome has a wide variety of sights to see, which is why many people describe Rome as a living museum. You'll see ancient Roman ruins resting side by side with buildings built 3 to 4 centuries ago, and sometimes these ruins have been incorporated into the design of the 'new' building.

5. A SHORT HISTORY

A short history of the peninsula of Italy is a contradiction in terms. So much has occurred in this narrow strip of land which has affected the direction of the entire Western world that it is virtually impossible to succinctly describe its history in a brief outline. We've had the Etruscans, Romans, Greeks, 'Barbarian' hordes, Holy Roman Emperors, the Papacy (although not the whole time – the seat of the Catholic Church was moved to Avignon, France from 1305 until 1377), painters, sculptors, the Renaissance, Crusaders, Muslim invaders, French marauders, Spanish conquistadors, Fascists, American soldiers, Red Brigades, and much more.

What follows is a brief outline of the major events on the Italian peninsula, concentrating mainly on the Roman Empire, since we've already covered some of the Renaissance in the Art sections. I don't claim to be an historian, only a mere *scrittore di guidi di viaggio*, so please accept this brief historical background for your travel enjoyment.

ETRUSCANS

Long before Rome was even a glimmer in Romulus' and Remus' eye (legend had it that these two were raised by a she-wolf and eventually became the founders of Rome), Italy was the home of a people with an already advanced civilization – the **Etruscans**. This powerful and prosperous society almost vanished from recorded history because not only were they conquered by Rome but also devastated by marauding **Gauls**. At such times, it is assumed that most of their written history was destroyed, and little remains today.

Because of this, and the fact that the language of the inscriptions on their monuments has been only partially deciphered, archaeologists have gained most of their knowledge of the Etruscans from studying the remains of their city walls, houses, monuments, and tombs.

From their research, archaeologists believe that the Etruscans were a seafaring people from Asia Minor, and that as early as 1000 BC they had settled in Italy in the region that is today **Tuscany** and **Lazio** (basically from Rome's Tiber River north almost to Florence's Arno River). Their rule eventually embraced a large part of western Italy, including Rome.

As a seafaring people, the Etruscans controlled the commerce of the Tyrrhenian Sea on their western border. After losing control of Rome, they strengthened their naval power through an alliance with Carthage against Greece. In 474 BC, their fleet was destroyed by the Greeks of Syracuse. This left them vulnerable not only to Rome, but the Gauls from the north. The Gauls overran the country from the north, and the Etruscans' strong southern fortress of Veii fell to Rome after a ten-year siege (396 BC). As was the Roman way, the Etruscans were absorbed into their society, and eventually Rome adopted many of their advanced arts, their customs, and their institutions.

THE ETRUSCAN KINGS OF EARLY ROME

When Greece was reaching the height of its prosperity, Rome was growing in strength. Rome didn't have any plan for its ascension to world domination, it just seemed to evolve. There were plenty of set-backs along the way, but everything fell into place at the right time.

The early Romans kept no written records, and their history is so mixed with fables and myths that historians have difficulty distinguishing truth from fiction. The old legends say that **Romulus** founded the city in 753 BC when the settlements on the seven hills were united, but this date is probably too late for the actual founding of the city. As is the case with many emerging societies, their founders are mythical figures, as was Romulus, but there is some evidence that the kings who followed him actually existed.

Shortly before 600 BC, Rome was conquered by several Etruscan princes. The Etruscans were benevolent conquerors (except for Tarquinius Superbus) and set about improving the Roman lifestyles to match their own. Rome was quite a mess at that time.

The first Etruscan king, **Tarquinius Priscus**, drained the city's marshes, improved the **Forum**, which was the commercial and political center of the town, and also founded a temple to Jupiter. To protect his investment in Rome, he carried on wars with neighboring peoples.

Under **Servius Tullius**, the second Etruscan king, a treaty was made with the Latin cities which acknowledged Rome as the head of all **Latium** (Lazio). This was the beginning of the concept of Rome as the center of the universe. At the same time he enlarged the city and built a wall around all seven hills, parts of which still stand today.

The last of the Etruscan kings of Rome, **Tarquinius Superbus**, was a tyrant who oppressed the people and scorned the Roman religions. His activities started the fires of rebellion that would eventually unseat the Etruscans from Rome.

Even with this oppression, the Etruscans built Rome into the center of all Latium. Impressive public works were constructed, like the huge sewer **Cloaca Maxima**, which is still in use. Trade also expanded and prospered, and by the end of the 6th century BC Rome had become the largest and richest city in Italy.

THE NATIVE ROMAN POPULATION REVOLTS

But in spite of all this progress and development, the old Latin aristocracy wanted their power back. **Junius Brutus** led a successful revolt around 509 BC, which expelled the Etruscans from the city. That was when the people of Rome made themselves a **republic**.

The Etruscans tried and failed many times to regain control of the city. Rome's successful thwarting of the Etruscans allowed the young republic to begin its long history of almost constant warfare and conquest. At the time, it was only a tiny city-state, much like the city-states that were flourishing at the same time in Greece, with a population of roughly 150,000. Who would have thought that this small republic would eventually rule the known world?

ROME'S EARLY REPUBLIC

In the beginnings of early Rome, the **patricians** (Rome's aristocracy) controlled the government and ruled the **plebes** or **plebeians** (common people). Because they were shut out from the government, the plebeians were politically and economically oppressed by their wealthy fellow citizens. The internal history of the republic for the next three centuries is mainly a story of how the plebeians wrested reform after reform from the patricians, and gained more and more control over their existence, as well as the eventual direction of Roman politics.

What forced the plebes to seek their freedom was the shackle of the patrician's oppression. The wealthy patricians continued to expand their land holdings, taking the best property and increasing their herds until they monopolized the public pastures. They also continued the practice of lending money at ruinous interest to the small proprietors, eventually reducing the plebes to abject slavery when they could not pay.

At the same time, the population of Rome was increasing too fast for the land and the primitive farming methods could not support the residents. Also the burden of constant warfare fell most heavily on the plebeians, who had to leave their little farms to fight the state's battles. This didn't allow them to provide for their families or even begin to pay off their debts they incurred to start farming the land.

To right these wrongs the plebeians went on what today would be called a general strike. In 494 BC, they marched out of Rome in a body and threatened to make a new city. At the fear of losing its large labor force, the patricians agreed to cancel all debts and to release people who were in prison for debt. By 350 BC, the plebes gained the ability to participate fully in the Republic's government.

While these important changes were taking place at home, the little city-state had been gradually extending its power. Compelled at first to fight for its very existence against its powerful neighbors (mainly the Etruscans, Aequians, and Volscians), Rome gradually fought its way to the leadership of all the Italian peoples. This dependence on military strength helped pave the way for Rome's conquest of the world.

THE GAULS SACK ROME

Rome's progress in leadership of all of the Latin tribes received a temporary setback in 390 BC, when marauding Gauls advanced through the heart of Italy. They decimated the farmland as they went and captured and burned Rome. After a stand-off, with Romans slowly taking their city back, the Gauls accepted a heavy ransom to depart promptly and returned to the valley of the Po.

Although Rome had been burned, the Etruscans north of Rome had suffered far worse in the invasion and were so weakened that Rome was able to seize their southern possessions. In another century, Rome conquered all Etruscan territories.

ROMAN CONQUEST OF ITALY

Meanwhile, the **Latin League** had begun to dislike the growing power and arrogance of their ally Rome, and attempted to break away from its control; but Rome won the two years' war that followed (340-338 BC). As a warning, some towns were reduced to vassals of the new state, while others were given full Roman citizenship or partial citizenship.

Another strong foe in central Italy still remained to be reckoned with: the **Samnites**, who were also of Italic stock. The truce that was made when the Latin League was feuding was broken a few years later (326 BC), and a wild-fought struggle ensued, with a variety of interruptions, until the decisive battle of **Sentinum** (295 BC), which made Rome supreme over all central and northern Italy.

Southern Italy, still occupied by a disunited group of Greek city-states, still remained independent. Alarmed at the spread of Roman power, the Greek cities appealed to **Pyrrhus**, king of Epirus in Greece who inflicted two telling defeats on the Roman army. He then crossed to Sicily to aid the Greek cities there in eliminating Carthaginian rule. This was a classic example of spreading your forces too thin over an extended battlefield. Encouraged by the arrival of a Carthaginian fleet to combat the Greeks, Rome renewed its struggle for the Greek city-states in southern Italy, and in 275 BC defeated Pyrrhus in the battle of **Beneventum** and a new phrase was born: a Pyhrric victory, where you win a battle but lose the war. Eventually, one by one the Greek cities were taken, and just like that Rome was ruler of all Italy.

KEEPING THE CONQUERED LANDS HAPPY

Rome gradually welded the lands they conquered into a single nation, contented and unified. They could have exploited the conquered cities of Italy for its own interests, but instead made them partners in Rome's future success.

Rome granted many of the conquered cities the privileges of Roman citizenship, in full or in part. As it had done for the Latin cities, they bestowed upon them the status of allies or partners. These new conquests were allowed to govern themselves, and had the right to trade freely with and intermarry with Roman citizens, which would also make the non-Roman a citizen. The people of these cities did not, however, have the right to vote.

Rome also set about establishing colonies of its citizens, who still retained their full civil rights, all over Italy. Almost one sixth of all Italy was annexed and distributed among these colonizing Roman citizens. By encouraging this colonization, a common interest in the welfare of Rome spread throughout the Italian peninsula.

THE PUNIC WARS

These centuries of warfare had developed Rome into a nation of soldiers. Its only remaining rival in the western Mediterranean was the Phoenician colony of **Carthage**, the established sea power of the time. Rome was indisputably the chief land power. At the time Carthage had a policy of sinking any trading vessel of any other city that dared to bid for a share of the rich commerce of the Mediterranean region. Rome could not abide these restrictions, so a series of **Punic Wars** for Mediterranean supremacy began in 264 BC.

The courage and endurance of Rome were tested to the utmost in this long and disastrous series of wars. After the battle of **Zama** (202 BC), Carthage was reduced to the position of a vassal state. In 146 BC, during the **Third Punic War**, because Carthage was again beginning to flex its military and economic might, Rome once more savagely attacked its defeated rival and razed the city.

WORLD DOMINATION

Now Rome was well on its way to world domination. Emboldened with this sudden rise to power, the new generation of Roman statesmen ignored the just policies of their successful predecessors. Most of the conquered lands were administered by governors (**proconsuls**), and citizens were given little chance to become full Roman citizens. These governors ruled like czars, and through the enormous taxes levied on the local populations, tried to amass in their one year of office enough wealth to last them a lifetime.

These taxes also enriched the greedy collectors (**publicans**), who purchased the privilege of collecting the taxes. Incredible amounts of gold, jewelry, and money in the form of taxes poured into Rome from all over the world, and the ancient simplicity of Roman life gave way to luxury and pomp. Morals were undermined, and vice and corruption flourished. (For an example of the debauchery that ensued, try and get a copy of the movie *Caligula* – not a movie for family viewing, but it will give you an insight into what happened to Rome during this time of expansion).

The suddenly enriched official bureaucrats acquired estates by buying up the small farms of the peasants. Even if they kept their land the peasants were too poor to compete with the hordes of slaves who worked the great plantations. Because of this the streets of the capital grew clogged with ruined farmers, along with discharged soldiers and the poor from all over Italy. These people lived on state and private charity, as well as on bribes that were given by political candidates to vote for them in the next election.

THE END OF THE ROMAN REPUBLIC

Once again a conflict began to brew between the aristocracy (formerly the Patricians) and the vast oppressed poor citizens (formerly the Plebes). Men tried to step forward and right the wrongs that were occurring, but each man who did ended up assassinated for his efforts.

To try and maintain a semblance of order a law was forcibly passed that transferred supreme power from the people to the **Senate**. The aristocrats, who became Senators, however, were too corrupt and feeble to hold power, and so the Roman Republic came to an end.

Two brilliant statesmen, **Gaius Julius Caesar** and his great-nephew **Augustus (Octavian)**, helped save Rome by scrapping the old republican framework and remolded the tottering structure into an empire. All power was gradually concentrated in the hands of a single ruler, who was backed by the might of the Roman legions.

TWO CENTURIES OF PEACE & PROSPERITY

With the establishment of the Empire, two centuries of profound peace developed, only broken by small frontier warfare. In the provinces men held power responsibly, possibly because they feared the omnipotent wrath of the emperor, and in Rome literature and civilization flourished. Increasingly the Mediterranean came to resemble one great nation, with paved roads leading from the south of Italy into what are now France and Germany. Even today fragments of Roman roads and ruins still exist in Britain, aqueducts and bridges can be seen in France, Roman wells are still used in the Egyptian oases of the Sahara Desert, and Roman amphitheaters can be visited in the heart of Tunisia.

Roman citizenship was extended to all free men throughout the Empire, and Roman law was administered in every court. The **Roman Peace** (*Pax Romana*) extended over the civilized world. But signs of decay were everywhere.

But the pursuit of a good time continued to obsess the people of Rome. The rich amused themselves by giving splendid feasts. The poor had their circuses where free bread was distributed (you've heard of bread and circuses?). Slave labor had degraded the once sturdy peasantry to the status of serfs or beggars, and the middle class, which once had been the backbone of the nation, had almost disappeared. A welfare mentality overcame the population. Then once again, the Roman governors began to concentrate on sucking the provinces dry instead of keeping abreast of the economic and political climate.

FALL OF THE ROMAN EMPIRE

The strength and discipline of the Roman Empire were being sapped by political decay, economic troubles, and decadent living. At this time, German 'barbarians,' who were a violent people led by warrior chiefs living on the fringes of the empire, began to attack the edges of it in the 4th century AD. They defeated unprepared Roman garrison after garrison. These **Goths**, **Vandals** (so that's where the phrase comes from!), **Lombards**, **Franks**, **Angles**, **Saxons**, and other tribes sacked and pillaged the decadent and crumbling empire. With the fall of the Western Roman Empire in AD 476, this was the beginning of the medieval period called the **Dark Ages**. They were so called because these 'barbarians' let Roman civilization collapse along with its artistic and engineering achievements.

What the 'barbarians' did bring with them, however, that helped shape the future of Western civilization, was their belief that the individual was important, more so than the state. In contrast, the Romans believed in the rule of the state over the people – in despotism. The 'barbarians' gave us a rudimentary form of personal rights, including more respect for women, government by the people for the people, and a system of law represented by the people being governed. Kings and chiefs were elected by tribal councils, which also served as courts of law. In essence, they brought with them the beginnings of democracy. So, in 20-20 hindsight, who was civilized and which system was barbaric?

AFTER THE ROMAN EMPIRE

In AD 330, when the Roman emperor **Constantine** moved the capital to **Constinantinople** (today's Istanbul in Turkey), the Western Roman Empire decayed and was overrun by waves of 'barbarians.' Rival governors fought over fragments of Western Roman territory for centuries.

Even **Charlemagne**, who had conquered the Lombard rulers and had himself crowned emperor of the **Holy Roman Empire** in AD 800, could not stop the disintegration of everything the Roman Empire had built. The Holy Roman Empire was a union between the Papacy and Charlemagne in which management of the empire was shared.

But Charlemagne's Holy Roman Empire fell apart after his death, only to be refounded by the Saxon **Otto I** in 962, bringing Italy into a close alliance with Germany. The Holy Roman Empire ruled over the lands north of Rome into Austria and Germany until 1806. During that time, the Holy Roman Empire took on many shapes, sizes, and rulers. It included at different times France, Germany, Luxembourg, the north of Italy (because the Muslims, and then the Normans had taken control of Italy south of Naples), Austria, Switzerland, and more. It had rulers from the Saxon Line, Franconian Line, Hohenstaufen Line, Luxembourg Line, and the Hapsburg Line. It may have been constantly in flux but it did last over 1,000 years.

While the Holy Roman Empire expanded and contracted, it eventually contracted itself outside of Italy, leaving government to warring city states. Florence, Venice, Milan, and the Papacy became the strongest of the contending powers. They came to dominate the countryside while feudalism declined. They drew their riches from the produce of their fertile river valleys and from profits generated in commerce between the Orient and Europe. This trade flowed in by way of Venice (and eventually) Genoa, and passed through other northern cities on its way across the Alps.

THE ITALIAN RENAISSANCE

Under the patronage of the Papacy and of the increasingly prosperous princes of the city-states (such as the **Medici** of Florence), the scholars, writers, and artists created the masterpieces of literature, art, and science that made the **Italian Renaissance** one of the most influential movements in history. In this period many splendid churches, palaces, and public buildings were built that still inspire awe in Italians and visitors alike. But at the same, these beautiful cities, such as Florence, Pisa, Venice, and Milan, were filled with social strife and political unrest.

PAWN OF STRONG NATIONS

While Italy was torn by struggles between the local rulers and the Papacy, strong nations developed elsewhere in Europe, and the Italy of separate city-states became an area of conquest for the powers struggling for European supremacy. French and Spanish rivalry over Italy began in 1494. **Charles VIII of France** valiantly fought his way through the peninsula to Naples, but by 1544 **Charles I of Spain** had defeated the French three times and had become ruler of Sicily, Naples, and Milan.

For centuries the states of Italy remained mere pawns in other nations' games of power. The city-states passed from one to another of Europe's rulers through war, marriage, death, or treaty. The **Papacy** was, however, usually strong enough to protect its temporal power over the areas in central Italy known as the **States of the Church**, or **Papal States**. The tiny republic of **San Marino** in the northeastern Apennines has remained through the centuries as a relic from this period. Although its 24 square miles are entirely surrounded by Italian soil, it is legally independent of Italy and claims to be the oldest state in Europe.

SPANISH & AUSTRIAN RULE

For some 150 years (1559-1713), Spain was the dominant power in Italy. Then the **Treaty of Utrecht** (1713) ended the **War of the Spanish Succession** and established the Austrian Hapsburgs in place of the Spanish as Italy's paramount power.

As time went by the Spanish began to feel slighted by the amount of land that had been ceded to Austria, so they sought to take back their former possessions. In 1734 **Don Carlos**, son of Philip V of Spain, conquered Naples and Sicily, and ruled the area as **Charles III of Naples**.

During this time, in the 18th century, enormous wealth was held by the few while the masses lived in squalor and ignorance. This disparity was especially noticeable in Italy, where the feudal system lingered on. The peasants were without rights or defenders. They lived in hovels and caves, and as a result crime rates were shocking despite harsh laws and punishments.

Ideas of reform coming from other nations found some response among the intellectuals and the middle class, and the concepts of liberty and equality stirring in France gained many Italian supporters. Many Italians were so blinded with the concepts that they offered assistant to a foreigner, **Napoleon Bonaparte,** as he began his conquest of Italy in the 1790s. As time went by the Italians realized their mistake, and hungered to be free of the yolk of French imperialism.

But even when Napoleon was defeated, most Italian states went back to their former sovereigns. For example, Venetia (Venice) was re-absorbed into Austrian rule, and Naples and Sicily were re-absorbed into Spanish rule. Italy was still a pawn in European politics.

MOVEMENT FOR POLITICAL UNITY

Eventually hatred of foreign rule mounted. With it grew the **risorgimento,** or movement for political unity. Such secret societies as the Carbonari (charcoal burners, the name given from their use of charcoal burners' huts for meeting places), plotted against the Austrians, but the **Carbonari Revolts** were crushed in 1821 and again in 1831 by Austrian troops.

Then the idealistic republican leader, **Giuseppe Mazzini,** organized his revolutionary society, **Young Italy,** and called upon **Charles Albert,** king of Sardinia-Piedmont and a member of the ancient House of Savoy, to head a movement to liberate Italy. By early 1848, revolts had broken out in many regions, and constitutions had been granted to Naples, Piedmont, and Tuscany. When Mazzini drove out the pope and set up a short-lived republic in Rome the French came to the pope's aid, while Austria quelled the revolt in the north. Eventually Charles Albert abdicated his rule in Sardinia-Piedmont in favor of his son **Victor Emmanuel II**.

Under the able leadership of the shrewd diplomat **Count Camillo di Cavour,** the minister of Victor Emmanuel, Sardinia-Piedmont grew strong in resources and in alliances. Cavour had learned that, genuine as was Italian patriotic fervor, Italy would never be unified without help from abroad.

Therefore he cleverly won an alliance with **Napoleon III** of France, and in the spring of 1859 Austria was goaded into declaring war against Sardinia-Piedmont and France. Austria was defeated, and Italy claimed the lands of Lombardy for a united Italy, but the Austrian's allowed France to retain Venetia.

Cavour and Victor Emmanuel lobbied the peoples of Tuscany, Modena, Parma, and Emilia who eventually voted to cast out their princes and join Sardinia-Piedmont. Napoleon III consented to such an arrangement, but only if Savoy and Nice voted to join France. (Politics is too complicated. I'll stick to travel writing).

GARIBALDI TO THE RESCUE

The second step toward a united Italy came the next year, when the famous soldier of fortune **Giuseppe Garibaldi** and his thousand red-shirted volunteers stormed the island of Sicily and the rest of the Kingdom of Naples on the mainland. The people everywhere hailed him as a liberator, and the hated Bourbon king was driven out.

Victor Emmanuel II was proclaimed king of Italy in February 1861, and now only the Papal States and Venetia remained to be joined to the new Italian nation. Venetia was gained in 1866, after Austria was defeated by Prussia in alliance with Italy. The Papal States were now the only ones outside the Italian kingdom, besides San Marino. San Marino was small and isolated, but since they were then about the size of the current region of Lazio and not just the small little walled-in city they are today, the lack of that territory was a very real handicap to Italy.

VATICAN CAPTURED - KINGDOM OF ITALY UNITED

But since French troops still guarded the pope's sovereignty, Victor Emmanuel, being the apt pupil of Cavour (who had died in 1861), did not want to attack the French and perhaps undo all that had been accomplished. Then, miraculously in 1870, the **Franco-Prussian War** forced France to withdraw its soldiers from Rome, at which time Italian forces immediately marched in.

Pope Pius IX, in his infinite wisdom and understanding, excommunicated the invaders and withdrew behind the walls of the Vatican. There he and his successors remained 'voluntary prisoners' until the **Concordat of 1929**, or **Lateran Treaty**, between Italy and the Holy See (Vatican), which recognized the temporal power of the pope as sovereign ruler over Vatican City (all 108.7 acres of it, or about 1/6 of a square mile!). At that time, as many would argue now, the Vatican was afraid of adapting to a modern, changing world, and favored the status quo.

MODERN ITALY - THE BEGINNING

Staggering under a load of debt and heavy taxation, giant steps still needed to be taken for Italy to survive. Leaders of the various regions, always trying to gain an edge, were in constant disagreement – and at times in active conflict. At the same time, citizens used to the ultimate control of despotic rule found it difficult to adopt the ways of parliamentary government. As a result, riots and other forms of civil disorder were the rule in the latter half of the 19th century.

Despite all of these problems, in the typical Italian fashion of functioning despite complete political chaos, an army and navy were developed; railroads, ports, and schools were constructed; and a merchant marine was developed. At the same time, manufacturing started to flourish.

But then, in 1900, **King Umberto I** (son of Victor Emmanuel II) was assassinated, and his son, **Victor Emmanuel III**, rose to the throne. Meanwhile, trying to relive the glory days of the Roman Empire, Italian government officials were attempting to gain territory in Africa for colonial expansion. Eventually on Africa's east coast they obtained two colonies, **Eritrea** and **Italian Somaliland**, and on the north coast of Africa they won **Tripoli** after a war with Turkey (1911-12).

Although having joined with Germany and Austria in the **Triple Alliance** in 1882, in the early 1900s Italy began to befriend France and England. With Austria's invasion of Serbia in 1914, after the assassination of Archduke Ferdinand of Austria, Italy declared its neutrality despite being Austria's ally. In April 1915, Italy signed a secret treaty with the **Allies** (Russia, France, and England), and the next month it stated that it had withdrawn from the Triple Alliance. On May 23, 1915, the king declared war on Austria.

When World War I ended in 1918, the old Austro-Hungarian Empire was broken up. Italy was granted territory formerly under Austrian rule, including "unredeemed Italy" of the Trentino in the north and the peninsula of Istria at the head of the Adriatic.

MUSSOLINI & FASCISM

The massive depression after World War I brought strikes and riots, which were fomented by anarchists, socialists, and Communists. The government of Victor Emmanuel III seemed powerless to stop bands of former servicemen lawlessly roaming the country. In these bands, **Benito Mussolini** saw his opportunity. With his gift of oratory he soon molded this rabble into enthusiastic, organized groups in many communities all over Italy, armed them, and set them to preserving the order that they had destroyed. These bands formed the nucleus of his black-shirted **Fascist** party, whose emblem was the *fasces*, the bundle of rods that had symbolized the authority of the Roman Empire.

The party grew rapidly because Mussolini promised everything to everybody. On Oct. 28, 1922, the **Blackshirts**, meeting in Naples, were strong enough, well enough prepared, and willing to march on Rome and seize the government. The king, fearing civil war and his own life, refused to proclaim martial law, forced the premier to resign, and asked Mussolini to form a government.

Within a few years Mussolini, *Il Duce* (The Leader), had reorganized the government so that the people had no voice at all. Mussolini first abolished all parties except his own Fascist party, and took from the

Chamber of Deputies the power to consider any laws not proposed by him. The king remained as a figurehead because he was revered by the people and had the support of many wealthy and important families. In 1939, he replaced the Chamber of Deputies with the Chamber of Fasces and Corporations, composed of all his henchmen. No semblance of popular rule remained. Mussolini even took control of the provinces and cities by naming the prefects of the provinces and the mayors of the cities.

All opposition was crushed by intimidation or violence. Suspected critics of the regime were sentenced to prison by special courts or were terrorized, tortured, or murdered by Blackshirt thugs. News was censored and public meetings could not be held without the government's permission. The new Fascist state was based on the doctrine that the welfare of the state is all-important and that the individual exists only for the state, owes everything to it, and has no right to protection against it. It was a return to the despotism of the later Roman Empire.

A RETURN TO THE ROMAN EMPIRE!

Mussolini, like other Italian leaders before him, longed to create a new Roman empire and to bring back Italy's lost glory. So, in 1935, with his large army and recently expanded navy, he attacked and conquered the weak, backward, and poorly defended African country of Ethiopia.

In October 1936, at Mussolini's invitation, the **Rome-Berlin Axis** was formed between Italy and Nazi Germany to oppose the power of France and England. Strangely enough, at this time Mussolini was considered the stronger ally of the two. Through its military and economic support of Spain, this alliance between Rome and Berlin helped Franco achieve victory in the Spanish Civil War. (Spain was also the training ground for Germany's shock troops that would eventually march through Poland in a matter of days.) In April 1939, Italy invaded Albania, and at that time Italy and Germany became formal military allies.

But when Germany's program of aggression plunged it into war with England and France on September 3, 1939, Italy at first adopted the position of a non-belligerent. But on June 10, 1940, Italian forces attacked southeastern France in an invasion coordinated with German forces in the north. But they had only gotten involved when it was obvious that France was no longer a threat.

DEFEAT IN WORLD WAR II

Italy, however, lacked the military power, resources, and national spirit for fighting a large-scale war. Within six months, Italian armies met defeat in Greece and North Africa. (A running joke during World War II was that Italian tanks had only one gear: reverse.) Italy then humbly accepted the military assistance of Germany. This soon grew into economic dependence, and Italy was forced to let Germany occupy it and control its home affairs, and Mussolini became a German puppet.

After the Allies invaded and won all Italian territory in North Africa as well as Sicily in July 1943, public unrest forced Mussolini to resign. He was arrested and held under guard. The constitutional monarchy was restored, with Marshal Pietro Badoglio as premier.

The Allies invaded Italy's mainland from Sicily on Sept. 3, 1943, and after what some considered to be a token resistance (the soldiers buried beneath the graves of Anzio might beg to differ), Italy surrendered unconditionally that same day, and on October 13 declared war on Germany. Meanwhile, Mussolini had been freed by German paratroopers and had fled into German-held north Italy, where he established a "Republican Fascist State."

The entire length of the mountainous north became a bitter battleground, but eventually enemy forces surrendered their hold on northern Italy on April 29, 1945. Mussolini, his wife, and his henchmen were subsequently captured by partisans, hung, shot, and for good measure, beaten until they were unrecognizable.

The end of the war found Italy with a large part of its industry and agriculture shattered. During its occupation, the Germans had almost stripped Italy's industry bare by commandeering supplies. Italian factories, roads, docks, and entire villages were ruined by the Allied bombing raids and during the invasion. To make things worse, as the Germans retreated they had wrecked whatever industries and transportation remained.

Even with the Allies contributing substantial quantities of food, clothing, and other supplies, the people were cold, hungry, and jobless. After the war, the United Nations Relief and Rehabilitation Administration gave more aid to Italy than to any other country. Reconstruction lagged, however, because of internal political turmoil, such turmoil becoming something of a theme in postwar Italian poltics.

POSTWAR POLITICAL CHANGES

During the battle for Italy its people were politically restless, and so a variety of parties representing many political views, from the extreme left to the far right, had been born. The more liberal parties demanded an end to the monarchy, but backed by the Allies, Victor Emmanuel III retained his sovereignty until the liberation of Rome in 1944.

On May 9, 1946, Victor Emmanuel III formally abdicated in favor of his son, who reigned for less than one month as **Umberto II**, because on June 2, 1946, the Italian people voted to found a republic. They also elected deputies to a Constituent Assembly to draft a new constitution.

Finally on February 10, 1947, the peace treaty between Italy and the Allies was ready to be signed. The treaty stripped Italy of its African 'empire' of Libya, Italian Somaliland, and Eritrea. The pact also ceded the Dodecanese Islands to Greece, internationalized Trieste, made minor boundary changes with France, and gave about 3,000 square miles to Yugoslavia, including most of the Istrian peninsula.

Italy had to pay $360 million in reparations, and was also forced to restore independence to Ethiopia and Albania. One lone gain was that **south Tyrol**, which Austria had been forced to cede after World War I, remained with Italy, and eventually, in 1954, **Trieste** was given to Italy by agreement with Yugoslavia.

On January 1, 1948, Italy's newly formed constitution became effective. It banned the Fascist party (unfortunately, there are today plenty of political parties in Italy that go by another name but informally call themselves *Fascisti*) and the monarchy. Freedom of religion was also guaranteed, but Catholicism remained the state religion.

But a constitution alone cannot recreate a country. Italian leaders had the double task of creating a stable parliamentary system of government while at the same time restoring the economy. (They still haven't solved the first problem.) The main economic hindrance was the poverty-stricken south contributing little to the improving economy of the north. As a result there were many riots and moments of intense civil unrest.

LAND REFORM

The south was so poor because much of central and southern Italy, Sicily, and Sardinia were among the last aristocratic European strongholds of large-scale landowners. The estates of these landowners covered many thousands of acres and employed only small numbers of laborers, mostly at harvest time. These landless peasants, who had no work during much of the year, lived in nearby villages and small towns and barely made ends meet all year. These citizens either stayed peaceful, contributed to civil unrest, or emigrated to find better employment and living conditions.

In the early 1950s, the Italian parliament passed special land reform laws that divided large private estates into small farms and distributed them to the peasants. The new owners were given substantial government support for their first years on the land, and the previous owners received cash compensation. Thousands of new small farms were created in this way during the 1950s, and farm production, as a result of the land reform and other measures, rose quickly.

The Italian government not only invested large sums of money in land reform but at the same time also started to develop the southern infrastructure to help the farmers. New roads were built to help carry produce to market, and new irrigation systems, needed during the long, dry summers, were constructed. Warehouses and cold storage facilities for farm products were provided, and the government also helped to introduce new crops.

Flower growers in the Netherlands began to send seeds to southern Italy, where they could start growing early while the fields of Holland might still be covered with snow. In spring, Italian growers would ship the young plants back north for final growth. As a result of these changes, farming in central and especially southern Italy began to bounce back.

CHAOS MIXED WITH STABILITY

Even with the south's new-found prosperity, Italy's economic development was mainly due to spectacular gains in industrial production in the north. Then during the mid-1960s, Italy began to suffer from severe inflation. A government austerity program to combat this trend produced a decline in profits and a lag in investments. To add insult to injury, devastating floods – the worst in 700 years – hit the country in 1966, ravaging one third of the land and causing losses of more than $1.5 billion. To make matters even worse, some of the priceless art treasures of Florence were irreparably damaged when the flood waters poured through that city.

In 1971 Italy had its largest economic recession since the country's post-World War II recovery. Strikes affected nearly every sector of the economy as Italian workers demanded social reforms. The problems of inflation, unemployment, lack of housing, and unfavorable balance of payments continued in the 1970s. Nevertheless, the economy showed resiliency for the five-year period ending in 1976 with an increase in gross domestic production.

When Italy was about to pull out of its economic problems, political terrorism escalated, culminating in March 1978, when **Aldo Moro**, leader of the Christian Democratic party and former premier, was abducted in Rome by the **Red Brigades**, an extreme left-wing terrorist group. During the two months that Moro was held, Rome was like an armed camp, with military roadblocks everywhere. Eventually Moro was found murdered and left in the trunk of his car.

In 1980, in Italy's worst natural disaster in more than 70 years, an earthquake killed more than 3,000 persons in the Naples area. As if things could only get worse, in May 1981 a Turkish political dissident tried to kill Pope John Paul II in St. Peter's Square in Vatican City. Also in 1981, a corruption scandal involving hundreds of public servants who were allegedly members of a secret society erupted and brought down the government.

Then for the first time in the 35-year history of the Italian republic, a non-Christian Democratic premier was elected. However, the Christian Democrats regained their power in November 1982, and socialist **Bettino Craxi** served as premier from 1983 to 1987, the longest term of any Italian leader since World War II.

Despite a lack of manufacturing base, Rome is home to a variety of light to medium industries, like manufacturers of food stuffs, paper products, textiles, leather goods, furniture and jewelry. The heaviest industrial segment of the Roman economy is the construction business. With a constant shortage of housing and office space, there is always a need for more construction of new buildings on the outskirts of the city, or reconstruction of older buildings in the center of town.

But film and government are Rome's main industries.

Cinecitta *(movie city)*, for 50 years the legendary Roman movie studio, has been the nerve center of Italy's growing film industry. Located just outside the city center, its sound stages featured such vixen as Gina Lollabrigida and Sophia Loren, and helped produce the magnificent Federico Fellini's *La Dolce Vita*. Cinecitta even made the grandiose boast that it was Hollywood on the Tiber, since so many foreign filmmakers visited its sets. Gregory Peck and Audrey Hepburn played roles here in *Roman Holiday*, and Richard Burton and Liz Taylor explored the affairs of *Cleopatra* on Cinecitta's sets. And more recently, much of *Il Postino* (The Postman), in the running for an Oscar in 1996, was filmed here, as well as some of Sylvester Stallone's action films.

Today, despite only producing approximately 50-60 films a year, the movie sets on Cinecitta are still the heart and soul of the Italian movie industry, just like Hollywood is for America.

Rome is also the heart of the country's government. Every government agency is located within the city walls, from the Ministry of Finance and Ministry of Defense on Via XX Settembre, to the Ministry of Post and Telecommunications next to the Pantheon. The Prime Minister's offices and those of Parliament also reside here in the Piazza Parliamento off the Via del Corso. The headquarters for all of the major political parties are located here, including the Socialist Party of the Left (formerly the Communist Party) whose socialist coalition gained control of the Parliament in 1996 and look to stay in power for some time, protecting the "jobs for life attitude" that permeates Italy and many European countries.

Another aspect of the Roman economy that is especially strong is tourism. Over 50,000,000 tourists visited Italy in 1994, and 2,250,000 of those visitors were from the US. This industry brings over $200 million into the Italian economy every year and no small percentage of that finds its way to Rome.

6. PLANNING YOUR TRIP

BEFORE YOU GO

CLIMATE & WEATHER

The climate in Italy is as varied as the country itself, but it never seems to get too harsh. Any time is a good time to travel to Italy. Most of the country has a Mediterranean type of climate, meaning cool, rainy winters and hot, dry summers.

The summers are mild in the north, but winters in the north tend to be colder because these regions are in or near the Alps. The Alps protects the rest of Italy from cold northern winds. Because Italy is a peninsula and thus surrounded by water, the entire country tends to be calm and mild except for the south and Sicily. These regions are very hot in the summer, and in the winter, wetter than normal. Winter temperatures along and near the coasts of southern Italy seldom drop to freezing in winter, and summer temperatures often reach 90°F (32°C) or higher.

Winter is the rainy season, when stream beds that remain empty during much of the year fill to overflowing and flash floods are common.

When to Go

With this in mind, anytime is good time to travel to Italy. The climate doesn't vary greatly making Italy a pleasant trip any time of year. Then again I'm biased – I spent eight wonderful years in Italy and I think it's fantastic all year. The busiest tourist season is from May to October, leaving Spring and Autumn as the choice times to have Italy all to yourself.

The sidebar below offers you a breakdown by season of the best regions to visit during those times:

ITALY'S FOUR SEASONS

Spring – *Italy has an early spring. The best places to visit are Florence, around Naples and Sorrento, Sicily, and Rome.*

Summer – *Summer can be a little hot at times, so to cool you down there are plenty of beach resorts along most of Italy's coast, especially in Liguria on the Italian Riviera. But the best place to go is the mountains of Tuscany or the northern regions of Lombardia, Piemonte, or Trentino Alto-Adige. This is not to say that Rome or Venice would not be pleasant, just crowded with tourists and relatively warm.*

Autumn – *This is a pleasant time to visit Rome and other major cities, since they are less crowded and much cooler.*

Winter – *Time for winter sports. You can find ski centers in the Alps as well as the central Appenines near Florence and Rome. Also at this time, the southern regions and Sicily are at their best.*

WHAT TO PACK

One suitcase and a carry-on should suffice for your average week to ten day trip. Besides, there are countless clothing stores from which you can buy yourself any needed item. Also it's advised to pack light so you can move your belongings with ease. In conjunction, you can always find a local *Tintoria* (dry cleaner) to clean any dirty clothes for you, if your hotel does not supply such a service. If you want to do it yourself, it's best to look for a *Lavanderia* instead, your basic coin operated Laundromat.

Remember to pack all your personal cosmetic items that you've grown used to using, since, more than likely, they're not available in Italian stores. The Italian culture just hasn't seemed to grasp the necessity of having 400 types of toothpaste, or 200 types of tampons.

Also important to remember, especially if you're traveling in the winter time, is an umbrella, a raincoat, and water-proof shoes. You never know when the rain will fall in the winter.

PUBLIC HOLIDAYS IN ITALY

Offices and shops in Italy are closed on the dates below. So prepare for the eventuality of having virtually everything closed and stock up on picnic snacks, soda, whatever, because in most cities and towns there is no such thing as a 24 hour a day 7-11. The Italians take their free time seriously. To them the concept of having something open 24 hours a day is, well, a little crazy.

• **January 1**, New Year's Day
• **January 6**, Epiphany
• **April 25**, Liberation Day (1945)

- **Easter Monday**
- **May 1**, Labor Day
- **August 15**, *Ferragosto* and Assumption of the Blessed Virgin (climax of Italian family holiday season. Hardly anything stays open in the big cities through the month of August)
- **November 1**, All Saints Day
- **December 8**, Immaculate Conception
- **December 25/26**, Christmas

Listed below are some dates that may be considered public holidays in different areas of Italy, so prepare for them too:
- **Ascension**
- **Corpus Christi**
- **June 2**, Proclamation of Republic (celebrated on the following Saturday)
- **November 4**, National Unity Day (celebrated on following Saturday)

LOCAL FESTIVAL DAYS & THEIR PATRON SAINTS		
Town	*Date*	*Patron Saint*
Rome	June 29	Sts. Peter and Paul
Venice	April 25	St. Mark
Florence	June 24	St. John the Baptist

MAKING AIRLINE RESERVATIONS

Since airfares can vary so widely it is advised to contact a reputable travel agent and stay abreast of all promotional fares advertised in the newspapers. Once you're ticketed getting there is a breeze. Just hop on the plane and 6-8 hours later you're there. Italy's two main international ariports are Rome's **Fiumicino** (also knowns as **Leonardo da Vinci**) and Milan's **Malpensa**, which handle all incoming flights from North America, Australia, and the United Kingdom.

There are other, smaller regional airports in Bologna, Pisa and Venice that accept flights from all over Europe as well as the Untied Kingdom, but not from North America or Australia. So, if you are only visiting the fairy tale city of Venice and want to fly almost directly there, contact your travel agent and make sure they get you on an airline, most likely British Air, that will allow for a transfer in London and a connection to Venice.

Fares are highest during the peak summer months (June through mid-September) and lowest from November through March (except during peak Christmas travel time). You can get the best fares by booking far in advance. This will also assure you a seat. Getting a non-stop flight to Italy at the last minute is simply an impossibility during the high season. If you are concerned about having to change your schedule at the last minute, and do not want to book far in advance, look into some special **travel insurance** that will cover the cost of your ticket under such circumstances. Check with your travel agent about details and pricing since these, like ticket prices, change almost on a daily basis.

ARRIVALS & DEPARTURES

FLYING TO ITALY

Alitalia is Italy's national airline. As you probably know, most international carriers have amazing service, pristine environments, serve exquisite food and overall are a joy to travel – but to be honest Alitalia is not one of them. If you're up for the adventure of the chaos of Italy's system (take their frequent lack of a government, for example) at 30,000 feet, try flying Alitalia. As another example of Alitalia's disorganization, they are the only major airline in the U.S. without their own toll-free number. Despite their problems Alitalia does have the most frequent direct flights from North America to Italy.

Below is a list of some other major carriers and their flights to Italy:
• **Air Canada**, *1-800-776-3000*. Flights from Canada to London or Paris, then connections on another carrier to Rome or Milan.
• **American Airlines**, *1-800-433-7300*. Direct flights from Chicago to Milan.
• **Delta**, *1-800-221-1212*. Direct flights from New York to Rome or Milan.
• **British Airways**, *1-800-247-9297*. Connections through London's Heathrow to Rome, Milan, Bologna or Venice.
• **United**, *1-800-241-6522*. Direct flights from Washington Dulles to Milan.
• **Northwest**, *1-800-2245-2525*. Flights to Amsterdam connecting to KLM and onto Rome or Milan.

GETTING TO & FROM THE AIRPORTS IN ROME

The Italian transportation system is the complete opposite of their airline: on-time, goes everywhere, and is clean and comfortable.

Rome has a dedicated **train** to wisk you directly to the central train station, where you can get a taxi to your hotel (doing it this way will be much less expensive than taking a taxi straight from the airport and just about as convenient). From the train station, you can also hop on the **Metro** or a **city bus** to take you near your hotel.

When you are departing the country remember to have at least L15,000 on hand to pay the airport tax.

Rome Fiumicino (Leonardo da Vinci) Airport
· **Direct Link** – A new train service is now available from the airport
directly to **Stazione Termini** (Rome's Central Railway Station). The
trip costs L12,000 and takes 30 minutes). There are 15 trips each day
in both directions, basically one train every hour. The trains are air-
conditioned.
· **Metropolitan Link** – Train service from the Airport to **Stazione Tiburtina**
stopping at the following stations: Ponte Galleria, Muratella, Magliana,
Trastevere, Ostiense, and Tuscolana. Departures are every 20 minutes from 6:00 am to 10:00 pm. Trip takes about 45 minutes. Trains
are air-conditioned.

Rome Ciampino Airport
Dedicated airport buses can be caught outside of the **Agnina Underground Station**. Time to airport: 15-25 minutes, depending on traffic.

PASSPORT REGULATIONS

A visa is not required for US or Canadian citizens, or members of the
European Economic Community, who are holding a valid passport,
unless s/he expects to stay in Italy longer than 90 days and/or study or
seek employment. While in Italy, you can apply for a longer stay at any
police station for an extension of an additional 90 days. You will be asked
to prove that you're not seeking such an extension for study or employment, and that you have adequate means of support. Usually permission
is granted almost immediately.

VACCINATIONS

No vaccinations are required to enter Italy, or for that matter, to re-
enter the U.S., Canada, or any other European country.

CUSTOMS REGULATIONS

Duty free entry is allowed for personal effects that will not be sold,
given away, or traded while in Italy: clothing, books, camping and
household equipment, fishing tackle, one pair of skis, two tennis racquets,
portable typewriter (I suppose they mean a portable computer now),
record player with 10 records, tape recorder or Dictaphone, baby
carriage, two still cameras with 10 rolls of film for each, one movie camera
with 10 rolls of film (I suppose they mean 10 cassette tapes now),
binoculars, personal jewelry, portable radio set (may be subject to small
license fee), 400 cigarettes, and a quantity of cigars or pipe tobacco not
to exceed 500 grams (1.1 lbs), two bottles of wine and one bottle of liquor,
4.4 lbs of coffee, 6.6 lbs of sugar, and 2.2 lbs of cocoa.

This is Italy's official list, but they are very flexible with personal items. As well they should be, since technology is changing so rapidly that items not listed last year could be a personal item for most people this year (i.e. Sony Watchmans, portable video games, etc.)

REGISTRATION BY TOURISTS

This is usually taken care of within three days by the management of your hotel. If you are staying with friends or in a private home, you must register in person at the nearest police station within that three day period. Rome has a special police information office to assist tourists, and they have interpreters available. *Tel: 461-950 or 486-609.*

DIPLOMATIC & CONSULAR OFFICES IN ITALY

These are the places you'll need to contact if you lose your passport or have some unfortunate brush with the law. If such situations occur, remember that the employees of these offices are merely your government's representatives in a foreign country. They are not God. They cannot do everything in the blink of an eye, but they will do their best to remedy any unfortunate situation in which you may find yourself.

Embassies
- **US**, *Via Veneto 119A, 00187 Roma, Tel. (06) 46741*
- **Canada**, *Via GB de Rossi, 00161 Roma, Tel. (06) 445-981*
- **Ireland**, *Largho del Nazereno, 00187 Roma,Tel. 06/678-25-41*
- **South Africa**, *Via Tanaro 14, 00187 Roma, Tel. 06/841-97-94*
- **United Kingdom**, *Via XX Settembre 80A, 00187 Roma, Tel. (06) 475 5441 and 475 5551*
- **Australia**,*Via Alessandro 215, 00187 Roma, Tel. 06/852-721*
- **New Zealand**, Via Zara 28, 00187 Roma, *Tel. 06/440-2928 or 440-40-35*

US Consulates
- *Lungarno Amerigo Vespucci 38. 1 50123 Firenze, Tel. (055) 239-8276*
- *Piazza Portello 6, 16124 Genova, Tel. (010) 290-027*
- *Via Principe Amedeo 2/10, 20121 Milano, Tel. (02) 290-045-59*
- *Piazza della Republica, 80122 Napoli, Tel. (081) 583-8111*
- *Via Vaccarini 1, 90143 Palermo, Tel. (091) 343-546*

Canadian Consulates
- *Delegation du Quebec, Via XX Settembre 4, 00187 Roma, Tel. (06) 488-4183*
- *Via Vittor Pisani 19, 20124 Milano, Tel. (02) 669-7451 and 669-4970 (night line)*

UK Consulates
- *Via San Lucifero 87. 09100 Cagliari, Tel. (070) 66 27 55*
- *Palazzo Castelbarco, Lungarno Corsini 2, 50123 Firenze, Tel. (055) 21 26 94, 28 41 33 and 28 74 49*
- *Via XII Ottobre 2, 16121 Genova, Tel. (010) 48 33-36*
- *Via San Paolo 7, 1-20121 Milano, Tel. (02) 80 34 42*
- *Via Francesco Crispi 122. 08122 Napoli, Tel. (081) 20 92 27, 63 33 20 and 68 24 82*
- *Via Marchese di Villabianca 9, 90143 Palermo, Tel. (091) 33 64-66*
- *Via Rossini 2, 14132 Trieste, Tel (040) 6 91 35*
- *Corso M. d'Azaglio 60. 10126 Torino, Tel. (011) 68 78 32 and 68 39 21*
- *Accademia 1051, R301 00 Venezia, Tel. (041) 272 07*

ACCOMMODATIONS IN ITALY

HOTELS - WHAT TO EXPECT

Don't be surprised by the excessive hotel taxes, additional charges, and requests for payment for extras, such as air conditioning. Sometimes these taxes/service charges are included in room rates; check upon arrival. Remember to save receipts from hotels and car rentals, as 15% to 20% of the value-added taxes (VAT) on these services may be refunded since you're a tourist. *For more information, call I.T.S. Fabry at 803-720-8646.*

The Italian Government Tourist agency rates all of the hotels in Italy with a star basis, so we will continue their system. A five star deluxe hotel (*****) is the best, a one-star hotel (*) is the least desirable and usually the least expensive too. The term *Pensione* is in the process of being phased out, and is being replaced by hotels with a designation of one-star (*), two-stars (**), or three stars (***).

Hotel Prices

The prices that are listed sometimes include a range, for example L100,000-150,000. The first number in the range indicates what the price is during the off-season, the second price is the going rate during high season. If there is no range that indicates that the hotel either doesn't raise their rate for the off-season, or they are not open during that time.

HOTEL RATING SYSTEM

The star rating system that the Italian Tourist Board officially uses has little to do with the prices of the hotels, but more to do with the amenities you will find in them. The prices for each category will vary according to the locale, so if it's a big city, a four star will be super expensive; if it's a small town, it will be priced like a three star in a big city.

This is what the ratings basically mean by star category:

*****Five star, deluxe hotel: Professional service, great restaurant, perfectly immaculate large rooms and bathrooms with air conditioning, satellite TV, mini-bar, room service, laundry service, and every convenience you could imagine to make you feel like a king or queen. Bathrooms in every room.

****Four star hotel: professional service, maybe they have a restaurant, clean rooms not so large, air conditioning, TV-maybe satellite, mini-bar, room service, laundry service and maybe a few more amenities. Bathrooms in every room.

***Three star hotel: a little less professional service, most probably do not have room service, should have air conditioning, TV and mini bar, but the rooms are mostly small as are their bathrooms. Bathrooms might not be in every room.

**Two star hotel: Usually a family run place, some not so clean as higher rated hotels. Mostly you'll only find a telephone in the room, and you'll be lucky to get air conditioning. About 50% of the rooms have either a shower/bath or water closet and sometimes not both together. No amenities whatsoever, just a place to lay your head.

*One star hotel: Here you usually get a small room with a bed, sometimes you have to share the rooms with other travelers. More often than not the bathroom is in the hall. No air conditioning, no nothing. Definitely for budget travelers.

RENTING VILLAS & APARTMENTS

One of the best ways to spend a vacation in Italy is in a rented villa in the country or in an apartment in the center of town. It makes you feel as if you actually are living in Italy and not just passing through. Staying in "your own place" in Italy gives your trip that little extra sense of belonging.

The best way to find a place of your own in Italy is to contact one of the agencies listed below that specialize in the rental of villas and apartments in Italy:

• **At Home Abroad, Inc.**, *405 East 58th Street, New York, NY 10022. Tel: (212) 421-9165, Fax: (212) 752-1591.*

• **Astra Maccioni Kohane** (CUENDET), *10 Columbus Circle, Suite 1220, New York, NY 10019. Tel: (212) 765-3924, Fax: (212) 262-0011.*

• **B&D De Vogue International, Inc.**, *250 S. Beverly Drive, Suite 203, Beverly Hills CA. Tel: (310) 247 8612, (800) 438-4748, Fax: (310) 247-9460.*

• **Better Homes and Travel**, *30 East 33rd Street, New York, NY 10016. Tel: (212) 689 6608, Fax: (212) 679-5072.*

• **CIT Tours Corp.**, *342 Madison Ave #207, New York, NY 10173. Tel. (212) 697-2100, (800) 248-8687, Fax: (212)697-1394*

- **Columbus Travel**, *507 Columbus Avenue, San Francisco, CA 941S3. Tel- (415) 39S2322, Fax: (415) 3984674.*
- **Destination Italia, Inc.** (Excluive U.S. Representative for Cuendet & Cie spa). *165 Chestnut Street, Allendale, NJ 07401. Tel: (201) 327-2333, Fax: (201) 825-2664.*
- **Europa-let, Inc.** *92 N. Main Street or P.O. Box 3537, Ashland, OR 97520. Tel: (503) 482-5806, (800) 4624486, Fax: (503) 482-0660.*
- **European Connection**, *4 Mineola Avenue, Roslyn Heights, NY 11577. Tel: (516) 625-1800, (800) 345 4679, Fax: (516) 625-1138.*
- **Four Star Living, Inc.**, *640 Fifth Avenue, New York, NY 10019. Tel: (212) 518 3690, Fax: (914) 677-5528.*
- **Heaven on Hearth**, *44 Kittyhawk, Pittsford, NY 14534. Tel: (716) 381-7625, Telefax (716) 381-9784.*
- **Hidden Treasure of Italy**, *934 Elmwood, Wilmettw IL 60091. Tel. (708) 853-1313. Fax (708) 853-1340*
- **Hideaways International**, *P.O. Box 1270, Littleton, MA 01460. Tel: (508) 486-8955, (800) 8434433, Fax: (508) 486-8525.*
- **Home Tours International**, *1170 Broadway, New York, NY 10001, Tel; (212) 6894851, Outside New York 1-800-367-4668.*
- **Interhome Inc.**, *124 Little Falls Road, Fairfield, NJ 07004. Tel: (201) 882-6864, Fax: (201) 8051 742.*
- **International Home Rentals**, *P.O. Box 329, Middleburg, VA 22117. Tel: (703) 687-3161, (800) 221-9001, Fax: (703) 687-3352.*
- **International Services**, *P.O. Box 118, Mendham, NJ 07945. Tel: (201)545-9114, Fax; (201) 543-9159.*
- **Invitation to Tuscany**, *94 Winthrop Street, Augusta, ME 04330. Tel: (207) 622-0743.*
- **Italian Rentals**, *3801 Ingomar Street, N.W., Washington, D.C. 20015. Tel: (202) 244-5345, Fax: (202) 362-0520.*
- **Itallan Villa Rentals**, *P.O. Box 1145, Bellevue, Washington 98009. Tel (206) 827-3964, Telex: 3794026, Fax: (206) 827-2323.*
- **Italy Farm Holidays**, *547 Martling Avenue, Tarrytown, NY 10591. Tel: (914) 631-7880, Fax: (914) 631-8831.*
- **LNT Associates, Inc.**, *P.O. Box 219, Warren, Ml 48090. Tel: (313) 739-2266, (800) 582 4832, Fax: (313) 739-3312.*
- **Overseas Connection**, *31 North Harbor Drive. Sag Harbor, NY 11963. Tel: (516) 725-9308, Fax: (516) 725-5825.*
- **Palazzo Antellesi**, *175 West 92nd Street #1GE, New York NY 10025. Tel. (212) 932-3480, Fax: (212) 932-9039*
- **The Parker Company**, *319 Lynnway, Lynn MA 01901. Tel. (617) 596-8282, Fax: (617) 596-3125.*
- **Prestige Villas**, *P.O.BOx 1046, Southport, CT 06490. Tel: (203) 254-1302. Outside Connecticut (800) 336-0080, Fax: (203) 254-7261.*

- **Rent a Home International, Inc.**, *7200 34th Avenue. N.W.. Seattle, WA 98117. Tel: (206) 789-9377, (800) 488-RENT, Fax: (206) 789-9379, Telex 40597.*
- **Rentals In Italy**, *Suzanne T. Pidduck (CUENDET), 1742 Calle Corva, Camarillo, CA 93010. Tel: (805) 987-5278, (800) 726-6702, Fax: (805) 987-5278.*
- **Rent-A-Vacation Everywhere, Inc.** (RAVE), *585 Park Avenue, Rochester, NY 14607. Tel: (716) 256-0760, Fax: (716) 256-2676.*
- **Vacanze In Italla**, *P.O. Box 297, Falls Village, CT 06031. Tel: (413) 528-6610, (800) 533-5405, Fax: (413) 528-6222.*
- **Villas and Apartments Abroad, Ltd.**, *420 Madison Avenue. New York, NY 10017. Tel. (212) 759-1025. (800) 433-3021 (Nationwide), (800) 433-3020 (NY).*
- **Villas Internatlonal**, *605 Market Street, Suite 610, San Francisco, CA 94105. Tel: (415) 281-0910, (800) 221-2260, Fax: (415) 281-0919.*

HOME EXCHANGE

*A less expensive way to have "a home of your own" in Italy is to join a **home swapping club**. These clubs have reputable members all over the world. All you'd need to do is coordinate travel plans with a family in a location you'd like to stay in Italy, and exchange houses. Think of how much money you'd save.*

*The best one that we know is **Vacation Exchange Club**, PO Box, Key West FL 33041, Tel. 305/294-3720, 800/638-3841, Fax: 305/294-1448.*

YOUTH HOSTELS

Youth Hostels (*ostelli per la gioventu*) provide reasonably priced accommodations, specifically for younger travelers. A membership card is needed that is associated with the youth hostel's organization, i.e. a student ID card. Advanced booking is a must during the high season since these low priced accommodations fill up fast. Hundreds of youth hostels are located all over Italy. Contact the Tourist Information office when you arrive in the city to locate them.

7. BASIC INFORMATION

BUSINESS HOURS

From October to June, most shops in Rome are open from 9:00am to 1:00pm and from 3:30pm to 7:30pm, and are closed all day Sundays and on Monday morning. Then from June to September, when it really starts to get hot in Rome, the morning hours remain the same, but the mid-day siesta time is slightly extended to 4:00pm and sometimes 4:30pm, which then pushes closing time back to 7:30pm or 8:00pm. In conjunction with the Sunday/Monday mornings closed, shops also close for half days on Saturday. Is that clear?

Food stores, like an *alimentari*, generally are open from 8:30am to 1:30pm (so stock up on your picnic supplies before you need them) and from 5:00pm to 7:30pm, and during the winter months they are closed on Thursdays.

Bank Hours & Changing Money

Banks are open Monday through Friday from 8:30am to 1:30pm and some do reopen from 2:30pm or so to 3:30pm or so. Some exceptions to that rule are:
• **American Express**, *Piazza di Spagna 38, Tel. 67-64-1. Open weekdays 9:00am to 5:30pm, and Saturdays from 9:00am to 12:30pm.*
• **Banco Nazionale del Lavoro**, *Via Veneto 11, Tel. 475-0421. Open 8:30am to 6:00pm Monday through Saturday.*
• **American Service Bank**, *Piazza Mignanelli 15. Open 8:30am to 6:30pm Monday through Saturday.*

Besides banks, there are plenty of exchange bureaus around (*casa di cambio*). One that is open until 9:00pm on weekdays, and until 2:00pm on Saturdays, is in the **Stazione Termini**. But use this as a last resort since the lines are always horrendously long.

Another option, if all else is closed, is to simply change your money at your hotel or any of the four star hotels that line the Via Veneto. You won't get the best rate but at least you'll have money.

CURRENCY

The current rate of exchange is **US $1= 1,660 lire** and Can$1 =1,180 lire. In this book, I have shown lire prices as follows: L1,660.

You cannot bring in any currency that totals more than 20 million lire (approximately $12,000) without declaring it at the customs office. This is also the same amount of money that can be legally exported from Italy without declaring it.

If you arrive in Sicily without Italian currency, the airports have banks and monetary exchange offices *(Ufficio di Cambio)*. Remember to keep your receipts from your monetary exhanges, because at some banks, when you want to change lire back to your native currency, you will need to show proof that you first exchanged your currency for Italian currency.

The monetary unit in Italy is the **lira** (leer-ah), the plural is **lire** (leer-ay). Notes are issued for 1,000, 2,000, 5,000, 10,000, 50,000, and 100,000 lire. Coins come in 50, 100, 200 and 500 lira denominations.

US DOLLAR/ITALIAN LIRE EXCHANGE RATES
US$1 = 1,660 lire

Lire	100	500	1,000	5,000	10,000
US Dollars	6¢	30¢	60¢	$3.01	$6.02

CANADIAN DOLLAR/ITALIAN LIRE EXCHANGE RATES
CDN$1 = 1,180 lire

Lire	100	500	1,000	5,000	10,000
Canadian Dollars	4.26¢	21.3¢	42.6¢	$2.14	$4.27

NOTE: The currency situation vis-avis the US and Canadian dollar is constantly floating. Please check the paper or a bank for the current rates of exchange.

DOCTORS & DENTISTS
English-Speaking

In case of need, the **American Embassy** *(Via Vittorio Veneto 119, Tel. 06/467-41)* will gladly supply you with a recommended list of English-speaking doctors and dentists (That's why I can't supply it here, they wouldn't give it to me because I hadn't had an accident!).

An English-speaking hospital, **Salvator Mundi**, is at *Viale della Mura Gianicolensi, Tel. 500-141*. I had my tonsils out here so it can be trusted.

EMBASSIES & CONSULATES

- **United States**, *Via Veneto 199, Tel. 06/467-41*
- **Canadian Embassy**, *Via Conciliazione 4D, Tel. 06/68-30-73-16*
- **United Kingdom**, *Via XX Settembre 90, Tel. 06/482-5441*
- **Australia**, *Via Alessandro 215, Tel. 06/852-721*
- **New Zealand**, *Via Zara 28, Tel. 06/440-2928 or 440-40-35*
- **Ireland**, *Largho del Nazereno, Tel. 06/678-25-41*
- **South Africa**, *Via Tanaro 14, Tel. 06/841-97-94*

FESTIVALS IN ROME

- **January 1**, Candle-lit processional in the Catacombs of Priscilla to mark the martyrdom of the early Christians.
- **January 5**, Last day of the Epiphany Fair in the Piazza Navona. A carnival celebrates the ending.
- **January 21**, *Festa diSant'Angese*. Two lambs are blessed then shorn. Held at Sant'Agnese Fuori le Mura.
- **March 9**, *Festa di Santa Francesca Romana*. Cars are blessed at the Piazzale del Coloseo near the church of Santa Francesca Romana.
- **March 19**, *Festa di San Giuseppe*. The statue of the saint is decorated with lamps and placed in the Trionfale Quarter, north of the Vatican. There are food stalls, sporting events and concerts.
- **April**, *Festa della Primavera* (festival of Spring). The Spanish Steps are festooned with rows upon rows of azaleas.
- **Good Friday**, The Pope leads a candlelit procession at 9pm in the Coliseum.
- **Easter Sunday**, Pope gives his annual blessing from his balcony at noon.
- **April 21**, Anniversary of the founding of Rome held in Piazza del Campidoglio with flag waving ceremonies and other pageantry.
- **May 1**, *Festa del Lavoro*. Public Holiday
- **First 10 days of May**, international horse show held in the Villa Borghese at Piazza di Siena.
- **May 6**, Swearing in of the new guards at the Vatican in St Peter's square. Anniversary of the sacking of Rome in 1527.
- **Mid-May**, Antiques fair along Via dei Coronari
- **First Sunday in June**, *Festa della Repubblica* involving a military parade centered on the Via dei Fori Imperiali. It's like something you'd see in Moscow during the Cold War.
- **June 23-24**, *Festa di San Giovanni*. Held in the Pizza di Porta San Giovanni. Traditional food sold: roast baby pig and snails.

- **June 29**, *Festa di San Pietro*. Festival to Saint Peter. Very important religious ceremony for Romans.
- **July**, *Tevere Expo* involving booths and stalls displaying arts and crafts, with food and wine lined up along the Tiber. At night there are fireworks displays and folk music festivals.
- **July 4**, A picnic organized by the American community outside Rome. Need to contact the American Embassy *(46741)* to make reservations to get on the buses leaving from the Embassy.
- **Last 2 weeks in July**, *Festa de Noiantri* involving procession, other festivities, feasting and abundance of wine all in Trastevere.
- **July & August**, Open air opera performances in the Baths of Caracalla.
- **August 15**, *Ferragosto*. Midsummer holiday. Everything closes down.
- **Early September**, *Sagra dell'Uva*. A harvest festival with reduced price grapes and music provided by performers in period costumes held in the Roman Forum.
- **Last week of September**, Crafts show held in Via del'Orso near Piazza Navona.
- **Early November**, Santa Susanna Church Bazaar. Organized by the church for the Catholic American community to raise money for the church. Great home-made pies and cookies as well as used books and clothes. Auction of more expensive items held also.
- **December 8**, Festa della Madonna Immacolata in Piazza di Spagna. Floral wreaths inlaid around the column of the Madonna and one is laid at the top by firefighters.
- **Mid-December**, Start of the Epiphany Fair in the Piazza Navona. All throughout the piazza a fair filled with food stands, candy stands, toy shops opens to the public. Lasts a week. A must see.
- **December 20-January 10**, Many churches display elaborate nativity scenes.
- **December 24**, Midnight Mass at many churches. I recommend the one at Santa Maria Maggiore.
- **December 25**, Pope gives his blessing at noon from his Balcony at St. Peters. The entire square is packed with people.
- **December 31**, New Years Eve. Much revelry. At the strike of midnight people start throwing old furniture out their windows into the streets, so be off the streets by that time, or else your headache from the evening's festivities will be much worse.

LAUNDRY

- **Uondo Blu**, *Principe Amadeo 70, near Termini Station*. Coin operated laundry open until 1am. If you need clean clothes, this is the only place to come that is inexpensive. Otherwise it's the wash-in-the-sink-and-let-them-dry-for-days routine.

GOLF

In the summer you can also enjoy some excellent **golf** courses. Located all over Italy, except for the poor south, there are plenty of accessible courses around the main tourist areas of Rome, Milan and Florence (see regional chapters for more information). You can also find courses around the many seaside resort areas that dot Italy's coastline.

Since Constatino Rocca choked in the Ryder Cup in 1994 for the whole world to see, and when in the British Open in 1995 made that miraculous putt after chili dipping his chip (he eventually lost to John Daly), Italian golf has started to get recognition. Maybe not the kind of recognition it wants but nonetheless, the *cognoscenti* have begun to discover some gems of courses all over Italy. It's only natural that a country filled with such natural beauty would provide superb golf.

PAPAL AUDIENCES

General audiences with the Pope are usually held once a week (Wednesday at 11am) in Vatican City. To participate in a general audience, get information through the **North American College** *(Via dell'Umita 30, tel. 672-256 or 678-9184)*, the American seminary in Rome. Catholics are requested to have a letter of introduction from their parish priest. During the audience women should dress modestly, with arms and head covered, and dark or subdued colors are requested. Men are asked to wear a tie and a jacket.

During the latter part of the summer, because of the heat in Rome, and now moreso for tradition, the Pope moves to his summer residence at **Castel Gandolpho** in the Alban Hills about sixteen miles southeast of Rome. Audiences are also regularly held there.

PETS

If you're bringing your precious pooch (unfortunately your dog will have to be on a leash and wear a muzzle in public in Italy) or kitty into Italy with you, you must have a veterinarian's certificate stating that your pet has been vaccinated against rabies between 20 days and 11 months before entry into Italy, and that your pet is in overall good health. The certificate must contain the breed, age, sex, and color of your pet and your name and address. This certificate will be valid only for 30 days. The specific forms that the vet needs to fill out are available at all Italian diplomatic and consular offices.

Parrots, parakeets, rabbits, and hares are also subject to health certification by a vet, and will also be examined further upon entry into Italy. Also Customs officials may require a health examination of your pet if you have just come from a tropical region or that they suspect the pet to be ill. All this means that they can do whatever they want whenever they want, so it might be wise to leave your pet at home.

POSTAL SERVICE

You can buy stamps at tobacconists (they are marked with a "T" outside) as well as post offices. Mail boxes are colored red. Post offices are open from 8am to 2pm on weekdays. The two exceptions to this are: the **main post office** (Palazzo delle Poste) at Piazza San Silvestro, which is open Monday through Friday from 8am to 9pm, and Saturday from 8am to noon; and the branch at **Stazione Termini** that keeps the same hours.

AIR MAIL PRICES	
Postcards to US and Canada	*1100 lire*
Letter (up to 20 grams)	*1250 lire*
Each additional 20 grams	*400 lire*
Aerograms for all countries	*850 lire*

RELIGIOUS SERVICES
Church Ceremonies in English
• **All Saints'** (Church of England), *Via del Babuino 153b, Tel.06/679-4357. Sunday Mass 8:30am an 10:30am*
• **St. Andrews** (Scottish Presbyterian), *Via XX Settembre 7, Tel. 06/482-7627. Sunday mass at 11:00am*
• **St. Patrick's** (English Speaking Catholic), *Via Boncompagni 31, Tel. 06/465-716. Sunday ass at 10:00am*
• **St. Paul's** (American Episcopal), *Via Napoli 58, Tel. 06/488-3339. Sunday Mass 8:30am and 10:30pm (sung)*
• **San Silvestro** (English speaking Catholic), *Piazza San Silvestro, Tel. 06/679-7775. Sunday Mass at 10:00am and 5:00pm. Weekdays Mass at noon*
• **Santa Susanna** (American Catholic), *Piazza San Bernardo, Tel. 06/482-7510. Sunday Mass at 9:00am, 10:30am, and noon. Weekdays at 6:00pm*

SAFETY

Italian cities are definitely much safer than any equivalent American city. You can walk most anywhere without fear of harm, but that doesn't mean you shouldn't play it safe. Listed below are some simple rules to follow to ensure that nothing bad occurs:

• At night, make sure the streets you are strolling along have plenty of other people. Like I said, most cities are safe, but it doesn't hurt to be cautious.

• Always have your knapsack or purse flung over the shoulder that is not directly next to the road. Why? There have been cases of Italians on motor bikes snatching purses off old ladies and in some cases dragging them a few blocks.

• Better yet, have your companion walk on the street side, while you walk on the inside of the sidewalk with the knapsack or purse.

• Better still is to buy one of those tummy wallets that goes under your shirt so no one can even be tempted to purse-snatch you.

That's really all you should need, but always follow basic common sense. If you feel threatened, scared, or alone, retrace your steps back to a place where there are other people.

STAYING OUT OF TROUBLE

Staying out of trouble is paramount, because in Italy you are guilty until proven innocent, unlike in the states where it's the other way around. And most importantly, if arrested you are not simply placed in a holding cell. The Italian officials take you directly to a maximum security prison and lock you up.

And that's where you'll stay for as long as it takes your traveling partners to figure out where you are, bribe your case to top of the local judge's pile, and have your case heard. That whole process can sometimes take months.

So if you like your drinks strong and your nights long, remember to keep your temper in check. And don't even think about smuggling any banned substance into the country, or God forbid, buying something illicit when you're in Italy. If you are approached to buy some hashish or something else, simply say politely, *No Grazie* (no thank you) and walk away.

TAXIS

Taxi service is widely available in all major cities in Italy, and a little less so in smaller cities such as Pisa or Lucca, and almost non-existent in remote towns and villages. Rates are comparable to those charged in your basic American city. Generally taxis locate themselves in special taxi stands located at railway stations and main parts of the city, but many are out cruising the streets for fares. At these taxi stands are usually telephones that you can call directly from your hotel, but remember, in Italy, if called, the meter starts at the point of origin, so you'll be paying the cabby to come pick you up.

Fares will vary from city to city, but basically when you get in the cab there will be a fixed starting charge, approximately 2,800 to 6,400 lire, and a cost per kilometer, approximately 1,000 to 1,250 lire. Some extra charges may come into play, like the **nighttime supplement** (between 10:00pm and 6:00am), a **Sunday** and **public holiday supplement**, as well as a **per item luggage charge**. All of these vary from city to city.

There is fierce taxi-cab competition in Italy. Some private citizens dress up their cars to look like cabs, so only take the yellow, metered cabs.

TIME

Italy is six hours ahead of Eastern Standard Time in North America, so if it's noon is New York it's 6:00pm in Rome. Daylight savings time goes into effect each year in Italy usually from the end of March to the end of September.

TIPPING

Hotels

A service charge of 15-18% is usually added to your hotel bill, but it is customary to leave a little something else. The following figures are simply guidelines:

- **Chambermaid**: 1,000 lire per day
- **Concierge**: 3,000 lire per day; additional tip necessary for additional services
- **Bellhop or Porter**: 1,500 lire per bag
- **Doorman** (for hailing or calling you a cab): 1,000 lire
- **Room Service Waiter**: 1,000 lire minimum and a little more depending on the amount ordered

Restaurants

A service charge of around 15% is usually automatically added to all restaurant bills. But if you felt the service was good, it is customary to leave between 5-10% more for the waiter. Also, it is not a requirement that you receive an official receipt, so if you need one please ask.

In cafes and bars, if the bill does not already include a gratuity (and most will so be sure to check) a 15% tip is expected even if you don't eat a meal. Two hundred lire is normal if you're standing at the counter drinking a soda, cappuccino, etc. If you have an alcoholic beverage, something to eat, etc. at the counter, the tip should be 500 lire or more.

Theater Ushers

Yep – they get 1,000 lire or more if the theater is very high class.

Taxis

Give the cabbie 10% of the fare, otherwise they just might drive away leaving you without your luggage. (Just kidding).

Sightseeing Guide & Driver

Give 2,000 lire minimum per person for half day tours, and 2,500 minimum per person for full day tours.

Service Station Attendant
Give 1,000 lire or more for extra service like cleaning your windshield, or giving you directions while also filling up your tank.

TOUR COMPANIES
- **American Express**, *Piazza di Spagna 38, Tel. 06/676-41*
- **Wagon-Lit**, *Via Gradisca 29, Tel. 06/8-54-38-86*
- **Thomas Cooke Travel**, *Piazza Barberini 21A 06/482-81-82*

TOURIST INFORMATION & MAPS
You can buy maps and guide books at most newsstands and bookstores. This may be necessary even though the tourist offices give away free maps for the subway, buses, as well as an extensive map of the streets of Rome. Most of the time, especially in high season, they are out of all of the above. And in Grand Italian Fashion, nothing gets done about it. So newsstands are your only recourse.

Below are some sources for tourist information:
- **American Express**, *Piazza di Spagna 38, Tel. 06/676-41*
- **Rome Provincial Tourist Board** (**EPT**), *Via Parigi 5, Tel. 06/488-3748*
- **EPT Termini**, *between tracks #2 and 3, Tel. 06/487-1270*
- **EPT Fiumicino**, *just outside customs, Tel. 06/601-1255*
- **Italian Government Travel Office** (ENIT), *Via Marghera 2, Tel. 06/ 49711*
- **Enjoy Rome**, *Via Marghera 2, Tel. 06/446-3379 or 444-1663*
- **Centro Turistico Studentesco e Giovanile**, *66 Via Nazionale, Tel. 06/ 467-91*

WEIGHTS & MEASURES
Weights

Italy	*14 grams*	*Etto*	*Kilo*
US	*1/2 oz*	*1/4 lb*	*2lb 2oz*

Liquid Measure

Italy	*Litro*
US	*1.065 quart*

Distance Measure

Italy	*Centimeter*	*Meter*	*Kilometer*
US	*2/5 inch*	*39 inches*	*3/5 mile*

8. ARRIVALS & DEPARTURES

BY AIR

Most travelers will arrive at **Rome's Fiumicino (Leonardo da Vinci)** airport that handles most incoming flights from North America, Australia, and the United Kingdom. If you are arriving from other points in Europe you may arrive at Rome's **Ciampino** airport.

Rome's Fiumicino has a dedicated **train** to whisk you directly to the central train station (**Termini**). To get to the train at the airport simply follow the signs (**Treno**) right after you get through customs. After you leave the arrivals building you'll see the train station about fifty feet in front of you across the street and up a ramp. The trip costs L12,000 and takes 30 minutes. There are 15 trips each day in both directions, basically one train every hour. The trains are air conditioned. From the Termini train station you can get a taxi from the taxi stand outside in front of the station, hop on the Metro, or a take city bus to get close to your hotel.

There is also a **Metropolitana** service from the airport to **Stazione Tiburtina** stopping at the following stations: Ponte Galleria, Muratella, Magliana, Trastevere, Ostiense, and Tuscolana. Departures are every 20 minutes from 6:00 am to 10:00 pm. The trip takes about 45 minutes, and trains are air conditioned.

You can also spend the equivalent of a night in a hotel on a **taxi** ride directly to your hotel. This choice can sometimes take longer depending on the traffic situation at and around the airport. Your best bet is to take the train to Termini station and catch a cab there.

If you are renting a car, you will get explicit directions from your rental company. See the *Renting a Car* section below for more complete information. If they neglect to give you directions, get on the large road – **SS 201** – leading away from the airport to the **GRA** *(Grande Raccordo Anulare)*, which is Rome's beltway and is commonly known as the **Anulare**, going north. Get off at **SS 1** (**Via Aurelia**) and follow this road all the way into town.

If you arrive at Rome's **Ciampino**, there are dedicated airport buses that leave for the **Agnina Underground Station** every half an hour. They take 15 minutes to get into town. Taking a **taxi** from here also costs an arm and a leg but not nearly as much as from Termini, since this airport is closer to Rome. If you rent a car, simply take **Via Appia** all the way into town. For the scenic view get on the **Via Appia Antica** a kilometer or so after passing the **GRA**.

BY CAR

To get into Rome you will have to either get on or pass by the **GRA** *(Grande Raccordo Anulare)* which is Rome's beltway and is commonly known as the **Anulare**. If arriving from the north you will be using **Via Cassia** (which can get congested), **Via Flaminia**, **Via Salaria** or the fastest route, the **A1** *(Autostrada del Sole)*, which will dump you onto the GRA.

If arriving from the south, the fastest route is the **A2**, also referred to as the *Autostrada del Sole*. A more scenic route is along the **Via Appia**.

Sample trip lengths on the main roads:
• **Florence**: 3 1/2 hours
• **Venice**: 6 1/2 hours
• **Naples**: 3 hours
• **Bari**: 13 hours

BY TRAIN

When arriving by train, you will be let off at Rome's **Termini** station. From here you can catch a **taxi** at the row of cabs outside the front entrance, walk down to the **Metro** and catch a train close to your destination, or hop on one of the **buses** in the main square just in front of the station.

Termini is a zoo. Packed with people from all over the world, queuing up to buy tickets, trying to cut in line to get information, and in some cases looking for unprotected belongings. Don't leave your bags unattended in any train station in Italy. The Tourist information office is located near the train tracks *(Tel. 06/487-1270)*. You can get a good map here and make a hotel reservation. The railway information office faces the front entrance along with the taxis and buses. If you're planning a trip, you should come here to find out when your train will be leaving. All attendants speak enough English to get by.

Sample trip lengths and costs for direct *(diretto)* trains:
• **Florence**: 2 1/2 hours, L35,000
• **Venice**: 5 hours, L56,000
• **Naples**: 2 hours, L25,000
• **Bari**: 12 hours, L70,000

9. GETTING AROUND ROME

BY CAR

Are you nuts? Unless you are from Boston and used to aggressive driving tactics, driving a car to get around Rome is a crazy idea, considering that the public transportation system is so good and that virtually everything is within walking distance. Now if you want to rent a car for a day trip at the beach at Lido di Ostia or another excursion, that's another story. But even in those circumstances, you can still get to those destinations and most others by train from Stazione Termini.

So think twice about renting a car, because Italian drivers are like nothing you've ever seen.

Renting a Car

Cars can be rented at **Fiumicino** or **Ciampino airports**, booked in advance by a travel agent, or rented at many offices in the city, especially at **Termini Station**. Try the following places:

- **Avis**, *Main Office, P Esquino 1c, Tel. 06/478-001 or 478-011. Open Monday through Friday 9am-1:30pm and 2:30pm-6:00pm. Their office at Termini Station is open Monday-Saturday 7:00am-8:00pm, and Sundays from 8:00am-11:00pm (Tel. 06/470-1219). Their office at Fiumicino is open every day from 7:30am-11:00pm (Tel. 06/601-551).*
- **Budget Rent A Car**, *Main Office, Via Ludovisi. Tel. 06/482-0966 or 482-0927. Open Monday through Friday 9am-1:30pm and 2:30pm-6:00pm. The office at Fiumicino airport is open Monday-Saturday 7:00am-8:00pm, and Sundays from 8:00am-11:00pm (Tel. 06/6501-0347 or 06/652-9133. The office at Ciampino holds the same hours (Tel. 06/7934-0137).*
- **Hertz**, *Main Office is on the Via Veneto #156. The phone number is 06/321-6831 or 06/321-6834. It's conveniently located in the underground garage that can be accessed from either the Piazza di Spagna Metro stop or the Via Veneto. In and of itself it's something that should be seen and walked through while you're in Rome. The office is open Monday - Saturday 7:00am-8:00pm and Sun day 8:00am-1:00pm. The office number at Termini station is 06/474-6405; at Fiumicino it's 06/602-448; at Ciampino it's 06/7934-0095.*

The fees usually include the costs for towing, minor repairs, and basic insurance, but you should ask. Also most firms require a deposit equal to the daily cost of the rental, which is usually between L200,000 and L300,000. The minimum age usually is 21 and you must have had a drivers license for at least a year. Rules and regulations will vary according to company. Standard industry business practices haven't hit Italy yet.

BY MOPED

If you are looking for a new experience, a different way to see Rome (or any city in Italy), try renting a moped. Walking, riding a bicycle, driving a car, taking the bus, or riding in a taxi cannot come close to the exhilaration of riding a moped.

A moped gives you freedom. A moped gives you the ability to go from one corner of Rome to another, quickly. Riding a moped makes you feel in tune with the flow of the city. With no plan, no sequence, no itinerary, no boundaries, you can go from the tourist areas to a part of Rome tourists rarely see. You can find monuments and markets in Rome you would never have seen if not on a moped. It makes you feel a part of the city, and this familiarity gives you the confidence to widen your explorations.

Now that I've built it up, think hard about renting a moped. As with cars, a moped is even more dangerous since you have nothing to protect you. Only if you feel extremely confident about your motorcycle driving abilities should you even contemplate renting a moped. This isn't the Bahamas where everyone's polite. The Romans will just as soon run you over as make way for you.

Personally, I find a moped to be the most fun way to get around Rome. They're inexpensive, quick, easy to maneuver, and practical since parking is virtually impossible for a car. But, granted, I have had my accidents. Once, as I was speeding between cars who were stopped at a light, a pedestrian walked in front of me and POW, next thing you know I'm wrapped around a pole. And then there was the time a public bus decided that he had the right of way in a circle and casually knocked me down. Anyway, only if you're *un po pazzo* or very brave should you attempt to rent a moped.

Renting a Moped

• **Scooters for Rent**, *Via Della Purificazione 66, Tel. 488-5685. Open 9:00am-7:30pm, seven days a week.* A centrally located moped rental, just off the Piazza Barberini. After the steep climb up this street, you will definitely want a moped. This is a small, quaint little rental outfit that, to the best of my knowledge, were the first to start renting mopeds to tourists many years ago. The people here are fun, helpful, and friendly.

• **I Bike Rome di Cortessi Ferruccio**, *Viale Galappatoio, near Via Veneto. Tel. 06/322-5240. Open Monday-Saturday 9:00am-1:00pm and 4:00pm-8:00pm, and Sundays 9:00am-8:00pm.* They rent from the same underground parking garage (connecting the Piazza di Spagna Metro Stop and the Via Veneto) as does Hertz. Maybe that's why you get a 50% discount with a Hertz card.

• **St. Peter's Moto**, *Via di Porto Castello 43, Tel. 06/687-5719. Open Monday-Saturday 9am - 1:30pm and 3:30pm-9:30pm.*

• **Scoot-A-Long**, *Via Cavour 302, Tel. 06/678-0206. Open Monday-Saturday 9:00am-7:00pm, Sunday 10:00am-2:00pm and 4:00pm-7:00pm.*

MOPED CAUTION & RATES

*If you cannot ride a bicycle, please do not rent a moped. The concept is the same, one vehicle just goes a little faster. Also, start off renting a 50 cc (**cinquanta**), not a 125 cc (**cento venti sei**). With more than twice the engine capacity, the 125 cc is a big difference, and in the traffic of Rome it's best to start slow. But if you insist on riding two to a moped, then a 125 cc is necessary. It's the law. (Not that any Italians abide by it). Also you need to be at least sixteen years old to rent a moped, but you don't need a motorcycle license. Just hop on, and ride away ... but don't let Mom and Dad know about it.*

A sizable deposit (around L200,000+) is required for each moped. The deposit will increase based on the size of moped you want to rent. Your deposit can be cash in any currency, travelers cheques, or on a credit card. This is standard procedure for all rental companies. Do not worry, you'll get your money back. Daily rates are between L50,000 and L80,000. Renting for a more extended period can be a better bargain. Rates should be prominently posted.

BY BICYCLE

Bicycles make getting from one spot in Rome to another quicker and easier, but if you haven't been on one in awhile, trying to re-learn on the streets of Rome is not a good idea. And don't even think about having children younger than 14 try and ride around Rome unattended. Not only could they get lost very easily, but the traffic laws are so different they may not be able to adapt very well.

I've seen older teenagers fare very well, especially around the Trevi Fountain, Spanish Steps area. Letting your kids do this gives them a sense of freedom, but reinforce to them how careful they have to be.

Renting a Bike

All four places listed above that rent mopeds also rent bicycles on a daily or hourly basis. The cost for en entire day varies from place to place, and year to year, but the latest price is L25,000 per day and L8,000 per hour, except at the one below, which is only L20,000 a day and L5,000 per hour.

• **Bici e Baci**, *Via Principe Amadeo 2B, Tel. 06/474-5389.* Run by a beautiful and animated Italian *signorina* with bubbling brown eyes who insisted I refer to her as *Laura delle Biciclette* (Laura of the bicycles). Her effervescence is in the name of her business *(Bici e Baci)* which means "Bikes and Kisses." I only got a bike this time. Maybe next time I'll get a kiss. Her rates (for the bicycles) are L5,000 for an hour and L20,000 for a day.

BY TAXI

Taxis are the best, and also the most expensive, way to get around Rome. They are everywhere so flagging one down is not a problem. But since they are so expensive I wouldn't rely on them as your main form of transportation. Use them as a last resort, when you start to get tired from walking. Also have a map handy when a cabby is taking you somewhere. Since they are on a meter, they sometimes decide to take you on a little longer journey than necessary. And also watch out for the fly-by-night operators that don't have a licensed meter. They will really rip you off.

The going rate as of publication was L3,500 for the first 2/3 of a kilometer or the first minute (which usually comes first during the rush hours), then it's L300 every 1/3 of a kilometer or minute. At night you'll also pay a surcharge of L3,000, and Sundays you'll pay L1,000 extra. If you bring bags aboard, say for example after you've been shopping, you'll be charged L500 extra for each bag.

Besides having to rely on flagging down a cab, there are strategically placed **cab stands** all over the city. The ones that will benefit you as a tourist the most are probably the ones in Piazza del Popolo, Piazza della Republicca, Piazza Venezia, and at Piazza Sonino just across the bridge in Trastevere.

BY BUS

At all bus stops, called **fermatas**, there are signs that list all the buses that stop there. These signs also give the streets that the buses will follow along its route so you can check your map to see if this is the bus for you. Also, on the side of the bus are listed highlights of the route for your convenience. Nighttime routes (since many of them stop a midnight) are indicated by black spaces on newer signs, and are placed at the bottom of the older signs. (Italians just aren't as compulsive as we are about changing everything at once. They seem to ween the population into everything more slowly.)

In conjunction the times listed on the signs indicate when the bus will pass the *fermata* you're at during the night so you can plan accordingly.

Riding the bus during rush is like becoming a sardine, complete with the odor, so try to avoid the rush hours of 8:00am to 9:00am, 12:30pm to 1:30pm, 3:30 to 4:30pm, and 7:30pm to 8:30pm. Yes, they have an added rush hour in the middle of the day because of their siesta time in the afternoon.

The bus fare costs L1,000 and lasts for one hour. Despite the convenience and extent of the Roman bus system, which helped me get anywhere I wanted to go in Rome for a long time, since the advent of the Metro I recommend taking the underground transport since it is easier, quicker, less crowded, and more understandable.

ATAC Bus Tours & Bus 119
If you are a hardy soul, take the no-frills *Giro di Roma* tour offered by **ATAC**, the intra-city bus company *(Tel. 06/469-51)*. This three hour circuit of the city leaves from the information booth in the middle of the **Piazza Cinquecento** in front of the train station daily at 3pm and at 2:30pm on Saturday, Sundays and holidays. For your L15,000 fee they give you a free map and a semi-guided tour in a kind of half-Italian half-English monologue that lets you see many parts of the city for cheap.

If you really want to be a native, the **regular bus #119** takes you to some of Rome's classic sights. It starts in the Piazza Augusto Imperatore and takes you by the Pantheon, Piazza Colonna, Via del Tritone, Piazza di Spagna, and the Piazza del Popolo. This is a regular bus route, and I know it doesn't sound too exciting, but it takes you through the heart of old Rome and is an inexpensive alternative to a guided bus tour (only L1,000).

You can buy these 1 hour bus tickets and other longer versions at all *tabacchi* in the city. They are indicated by the large "T" sign in the front of their stores.

Bus Passes
If you are staying in Rome for an extended period of time and need to use the buses frequently since your hotel or destinations are not on a Metro line, you can buy one of the following bus tickets:
• **Weekly Ticket** *(Biglietto Settimanale): L24,000*
• **Monthly Pass** *(Bonamente Mensile): L50,000*

By Metro
The Roman *Metropolitana* (**Metro**) has two lines (Linea A and Linea B) that intersect in the basement of Termini station. You'll find these and all other stations marked with a prominent white "M" inside a red square

up on a sign outside. **Linea A** is probably the most used by the tourists since it starts at Ottaviano, near St. Peters, and has Piazza del Popolo, Piazza di Spagna, Piazza Barberini, and Piazza della Repubblica as stops. **Linea B** comes in a close second since it takes you to the Coliseum, the Circus Maximus, and the Piramide (which really isn't the greatest sight in the world, but I always return since my family members have been getting their picture taken in front of the Piramide since the 1950's).

Buses used to be the way to get around Rome, quickly, efficiently, and inexpensively, but now it's the Metro. A fare only costs L1,500 and lasts for 75 minutes or a return trip within the time allotted. Which means you can make two trips on the Metro, in less than an hour and 15 minutes, for only about a dollar.

The Metro can get quite crowded around the Stazione Termini and during rush hours. Sardine-like is the best way to describe it, otherwise rides are very pleasant. Always be on the look out for pickpockets – at least that's what the signs in the Metro cars tell you to do.

Take the Metro to the Beach!

If you're interested in going to the beach or visiting the ruins at Ostia Antica, take the Linea B Metro to the Magliana stop and transfer to the train that will take you there. You'll have to pay a new fare, since the Metro and the train systems are different animals.

HOW TO BUY A METRO TICKET

Walk down the steps into the subterranean caverns of the Roman Metro, then buy the ticket at the ever-present ticket booths in any station. To get to the trains you stamp the ticket in an ugly bright orange machine. The stamp received from these hideous looking devices marks the start of your 75 minutes. When you get back on the system just stamp your ticket again. Simple.

*If it's late at night, the ticket booths are usually closed so you'll have to use one of the ever-present ticket machines in all stations. Simply have L1,500 ready, or close to it in bills or coins. Then a touch tone screen awaits your commands. Press the upper left image on the screen to indicate to the machine you want a 75 minute ticket. Then insert your bills or coins as indicated (the machines do not like **Gettone**, the coins that used to be used exclusively for the telephones, and which are about the same size as a L200 coin), and presto your ticket and change (if any) will appear.*

10. FOOD & WINE

FOOD IN ITALY

Most Italian food is cooked with fresh ingredients making their dishes healthy and satisfying. There are many restaurants in Italy of international renown, but you shouldn't limit yourself only to the upper echelon. In most cases you can find as good a meal at a fraction the cost at any *trattoria*. Also, many of the upper echelon restaurants you read about are only in business because they cater to the tourist trade. Their food is good, but the atmosphere is a little hokey.

The traditional Italian meal consists of an **antipasto** (appetizer), pasta or soup course, **il secondo** (main course usually meat or fish), salad, and dessert (which can be cheese or fruit). As you will notice in each regional chapter, I target those restaurants that are superb, and most are not well known to the tourist trade.

Most North Americans think that there is one type of Italian food, and that's usually spaghetti and meatballs. They don't know what they are missing. Region by region Italy's food has adapted itself to the culture of the people and land. In Rome, don't miss the roast lamb if you're a meat eater; in Florence, you have some of the best steaks in the world; and in the south, the tomato-based pastas and pizzas are exquisite.

ROMAN CUISINE

"Italian Food" is definitely a misnomer, because each region of Italy has its special dishes, and in most cases so do each province and locality. As a rule, Roman cooking is not refined and is considered a poor man's cuisine. The food is basic, simple, and enjoyable. Gone are the days of the Roman Empire's lavish banquets.

Authentic Roman dishes today are often based on rudimentary ingredients, such as tomatoes, garlic, hot pepper, and parmesan cheese, and the results are magnificent. Some favorite dishes, like brains, tripe, oxtail, and pig's snout, never seem to find their way onto the plate of squeamish foreigners like myself. Instead we get treated to the omnipresent pasta and grilled meats.

Besides these staples, Romans enjoy the harvest of seafood from the shores just 15 miles from their city, and prepare excellent grilled seafood dishes and the famous *spaghetti alla vongole verace* (spicy clam sauce), as well as other pastas brimming with other fruits from the sea. The Roman countryside provides exquisite fresh greens and vegetables, which arrive daily at their open air markets. Also in never-ending supply are the local cheeses, *pecorino*, made from sheep's milk, and plump *mozzarella* balls, generally made from the milk of water buffaloes.

The Jewish ghetto has made a lasting impression on Roman cuisine. The most memorable dish to come from there is the *carciofo alla giudia*, a small artichoke flattened and fried. What I'm trying to say is that it is very difficult not to eat well in any one of Rome's 5,000-plus restaurants.

In case you didn't know, lunch hour is usually from 1:00pm to 2:00pm, and dinner any where from 7:30pm to 10:00pm. So enjoy your meal and remember to take your time. Meals are supposed to be savored, not rushed through.

TRADITIONAL ROMAN FARE

You don't have to eat all the traditional courses listed below. Our constitution just isn't prepared for such mass consumption, so don't feel embarrassed if all you order is a pasta dish or an entrée with a salad or appetizer.

Antipasto - *Appetizer*
• **Bruschetta** – garlic bread brushed with olive oil
• **Antipasto Misto** – Mixed appetizer plate. Differs from restaurant to restaurant
• **Tomate, Mozzarella ed olio** – Tomato and mozzarella slices covered in olive oil with a hint of basil

Primo Piatto - *First Course*
Pasta
• **Spaghetti alla carbonara** – Spaghetti tossed with bacon, garlic, peppers, grated cheese, and a raw beaten egg
• **Bucatini alla matriciana** –Thin tubes of pasta with red pepper, bacon, and pecorino cheese
• **Penne all'arrabbiata** – Literally means angry pasta. It is short ribbed pasta tubes with a hot and spicy tomato base, garlic and parsley sauce (this is my favorite, but if your stomach can't handle spicy food, steer clear of this delicacy)

- **Fettucine all'burro** – fettucine with butter and parmasan
- **Spaghetti alla puttanesca** – Litrerally translated it means whore's spaghetti! So named because the ingredients, peppers, tomato, black olives and garlic, are so basic that prostitutes could quickly create a meal between tricks

Zuppa – *Soup*
- **Stracciatella** – a light egg–drop soup
- **Pasta e ceci** – a filling pasta and chick pea soup
- **Zuppa di telline** – soup made from tiny clams

Second Piatto - *Entrée*
Carne – *Meat*
- **Abbacchio** – Milk–fed baby lamb. Can be grilled (alla Griglia), sautéed in a sauce of rosemary, garlic, onions, tomatoes, and white wine (alla Cacciatore), or roasted (al Forno)
- **Saltimbocca alla romana** – veal fillets that are covered in sage and prosciutto and cooked in butter and white wine
- **Pollo alla cacciatore** – same dish as the lamb above but replaced with chicken
- **Pollo all romana** – Chicken stewed with yellow and red dell peppers
- **Pollo al diavolo** – so called because the chicken is split open and grilled over an open fire and flattened by a weight placed on top of it. I guess it's what Romans think hell would be like.
- **Fritto misto** – a selection of mixed deep–fried meats and seasonal vegetables
- **Lambata di Vitello** – Grilled veal chop
- **Porchetta** – Tender suckling pork roasted with herbs
- **Maile arrosto can patate** – Roasted pork with exquisite roast potatoes

Pesce – *Fish*
- **Soliola alla griglia** – Thin sole lightly grilled
- **Ciriole** – Small tender eels dredged from the Tiber
Contorno – *Vegetable*
- **Carciofi alla guidia** – Jewish–style artichokes, pressed flat and fried. Usually served with a an anchovy garlic sauce
- **Peperonata** – Stewed red and yellow bell peppers
- **Patate arrosto** – Roasted potatoes that usually come with a grilled meats but can be ordered separately
- **Insalata Mista** – mixed salad. You have to prepare your own olive oil and vinegar dressing. American's lust for countless types of salad dressings hasn't hit Italy yet

GLOSSARY OF ITALIAN EATERIES

Bar – *Not the bar we have back home. This place serves espresso, cappuccino, rolls, small sandwiches, as well as sodas and alcoholic beverages. It is normal to stand at the counter or sit at a table when one is available. You have to try the* **Medallione,** *a grilled ham and cheese sandwich available at most bars. A little 'pick-me-up' in the morning is* **Café Corretto,** *coffee corrected by the addition of* **grappa** *(Italian brandy) or Cognac.*

Gelateria – *These establishments offer* **gelato** *- ice cream - usually produced on the premises. Italian gelato is softer than American but very sweet and rich.*

Osteria – *Small tavern-like eatery that serves local wine usually in liter bottles as well as simple food and sandwiches*

Panineria – *A small sandwich bar with a wider variety than at a regular Italian bar, where a quick meal can be gotten. One thing to remember is that Italians rarely use condiments on their sandwiches. If you want mustard or such you need to ask for it.*

Pasticceria – *Small pasty shops that sell cookies, cakes, pastries, etc. Carry-out only.*

Pizzeria – *A casual restaurant specializing in pizza, but they also serve other dishes. Most have their famous brick ovens almost directly in the seating area so you can watch the pizza being prepared. There are many featured excellent pizzerias in this book.*

Pizza Rustica – *Common in central Italy. These are huge cooked rectangular pizzas displayed behind glass. This pizza has a thicker crust and more ingredients than in a regular Pizzeria. You can request as much as you want, since they usually charge by the weight, not the slice. Carry-out only.*

Rosticceria – *A small eatery where they make excellent inexpensive roast chickens and other meats, as well as grilled and roasted vegetables, mainly potatoes. Sometimes they have baked pasta. Carry-out only.*

Trattoria – *A less formal restaurant where many local specialties are served.*

Ristorante – *A more formal eating establishment, but even most of these are quite informal at times.*

Tavola Calda – *Cafeteria-style food served buffet style. They feature a variety of hot and cold dishes. Seating is available.*

RESTAURANT LISTINGS IN THIS BOOK

On the next page, you'll find a sample listing in our *Where to Eat* chapter. The number preceding the name of the restaurant tells you where to find it on the restaurant map (see Chapter 12):

2. CAMPARONE, *Piazza in Piscinula 47. Tel 06/581-6249. Closed Mondays. Credit cards accepted. Dinner for two L75,000.*

This restaurant owns the entire block, starting with the bar/café on the left, this restaurant in the middle, and the pizzeria/birreria on the right. The outside seating at the restaurant is the best pace to enjoy a Trasteverian evening. Their food includes an excellent rendition of *osso bucco alla romana.* They do it with *fungi* (mushrooms). Mmm, good. They are mainly known for their grilled meats and some of their pastas.

The restaurant listings indicate which credit cards are accepted by using the following phrases:
• **Credit cards accepted** = American Express, Visa, and Diners Card
• **All credit cards accepted** = Everything imaginable is accepted, even cards you've never heard of
• **No credit card accepted** = Only cash or travelers checks (if a listing is left without an indication, that means that no credit cards are accepted.)

Each review will also give a ballpark price for a dinner for two in Italian lire. For example: "Dinner for two L80,000." With the exchange rate at roughly $1=L1,600, this example the dollar price would be $50 for the meal. This price includes three courses per person and a bottle of house wine with the meal. In most cases you will get by with one course. Thus the actual price you will pay will be less than indicated.

WINE

Italy is also famous for its wines. The experts say the reds are not robust enough, and the whites are too light, but since I'm not an expert, I love them, one and all. Most importantly, to get a good bottle of wine, you don't have to spend a fortune either. You can find some excellent wines straight out of wine vats in small wine stores in every city in Italy. In any restaurant, all you'll need to order is the house wine to have a satisfying and excellent wine. (*Vino di casa*: House Wine. *Roso*: Red. *Biancho*: White).

Romans prefer 'local' wines from the **Castelli Romani** area: **Frascati**, **Marino**, **Velletri**, etc. These are soft, well-rounded simple white wines that most anyone can appreciate. They do well in countering the aggressive flavors of the Roman food.

In most restaurants you can also get better known wines such as Chianti, Orvieto, Verdiccio, Pinto Grigio, and Barolo, but the best bet if you're not a wine expert is to simply try the house wine of the restaurants you visit. You will find this to be not only less expensive but usually as enjoyable as a more expensive bottle.

The house wine can be ordered in liters *(un litro)*, halves *(mezzo litro)*, or quarters *(quarto do un litro)*.

But if you're a connoisseur, or simply want to try a wine for which a certain Italian region is known, in the sidebar below you'll find a selected list of wines and their regions (if you like red wine, try the **Chianti**, and if it's white you prefer, try **Verdicchio**).

ITALIAN WINES BY REGION

PIEMONTE – *Barolo (red, dry)*, *Barbera (red, dry)*, *and* *Asti Spumanti (sweet sparkling wine)*

LOMBARDIA – *Reisling (white, dry)*, *Frecciarossa (rose wines)*

TRENTINO-ALTO ADIGE – *Reisling (white, dry)*, *Santa Maddalena (red, semi-dry)*, *Cabernet (red, dry)*

VENETIA – *Soave (white, dry)*, *Valpolicella (red, dry or semi-sweet)*

LIGURIA – *Cinqueterre (named after a section of Liguria you must visit. Cinqueterre is five small oceanside towns inaccessible by car or train, you have to walk. They're simply gorgeous.)*

EMILIA ROMAGNA – *Lambrusco (red,semi-sparkling, several kinds going from dry to sweet)*, *Sangiovese (red, dry)*, *Albano (white, dry or semi-sweet)*

TUSCANY – *Chianti (red, dry; look for the Chianti Classicos. They're the ones with a black rooster on the neck of the bottle)*

MARCHE – *Verdicchio (white, dry)*

UMBRIA/LAZIO – *Orvietto (white, dry)*, *Frascati (white, dry or semi-sweet)*, *Est Est Est (white, slightly sweet)*

ABRUZZI – *Montepulciano (red, dry)*

SARDINIA – *Cannonau (red, dry to semi-sweet)*

SICILY – *Etna (red and white, wide variety)*, *Marsala (white,dry or sweet)*

CAMPANIA, APULIA, CALABRIA, BASILICATA – *Ischia (red and white, several varieties)*, *San Severo (red, dry)*

SAMBUCA LIQUEUR

You have to try the Sambuca, an anise-flavored after dinner drink, served with three coffee beans. It's called *Sambuca con tre mosce*, Sambuca with three flies. If you blur your vision a little they do look like flies floating in the drink. When sipping this small drink get one of the beans in your mouth and chew on it. It's bitter taste compliments the sweetness of the liqueur perfectly.

The best brand of Sambuca is **Molinari**, and the next is **Romana**, which is better known in the States because of the company's aggressive marketing campaign.

ORDER LIKE A NATIVE:
READING AN ITALIAN MENU

Here are a few choice words to assist you when you're ordering from a menu while in Italy. Usually, the waiter should be able to assist you, but if not, this will make your dining more pleasurable. You wouldn't want to order octopus by surprise, would you?

ENGLISH	ITALIAN	ENGLISH	ITALIAN
Menu	*Lista or Carta*	Teaspoon	*Cucchiaino*
Breakfast	*Primo Colazione*	Knife	*Cotello*
Lunch	*Pranzo*	Fork	*Forchetta*
Dinner	*Cena*	Plate	*Piatto*
		Glass	*Bicchiere*
Table setting	*Coperto*	Cup	*Tazza*
Spoon	*Cucchiao*	Napkin	*Tovagliolo*

Antipasto

ENGLISH	ITALIAN	ENGLISH	ITALIAN
Soup	*Zuppa*	Broth	*Brodo*
Fish Soup	*Zuppa di Pesce*	Vegetable soup	*Minestrone*
Broth with beaten egg	*Stracciatella*		

Pasta

ENGLISH	ITALIAN	ENGLISH	ITALIAN
Ravioli with meat stuffing	*Agnolotti*	Egg noodles	*Fettucine*
Large rolls of pasta	*Cannelloni*	Potato-filled, ravioli-like pasta	*Gnocchi*
Thin angel hair pasta	*Capellini*	Thin pasta	*Vermicelli*
Little hat pasta	*Capelletti*	Macaroni-like pasta	*Penne*

Eggs	*Uova*		
soft-boiled	*al guscio*	hard boiled	*sode*
fried	*al piatto*	omelette	*frittata*

Fish	*Pesce*		
Seafood	*Frutti di mare*	Eel	*Anguilla*
Lobster	*Aragosta*	herring	*Aringa*
Squid	*Calamari*	Carp	*Carpa*
Mullet	*Cefalo*	Grouper	*Cernia*
Mussels	*Cozze/Muscoli*	Perch	*Pesce Persico*
Salmon	*Salmone*	Clams	*Vongole*

Octopus	*Polpo*	Bass	*Spigola*
Oysters	*Ostriche*	Mixed fried fish	*Fritto Misto Mare*

Meat *Carne*

Spring Lamb	*Abbachio*	Lamb	*Agnello*
Rabbit	*Coniglio*	Chicken	*Pollo*
Small Pig	*Porcello*	Veal	*Vitello*
Steak	*Bistecca*	Breast	*Petto*
Pork	*Maiale*	Liver	*Fegato*
Cutlet	*Costellata*	Deer	*Cervo*
Wild Pig	*Cinghiale*	Pheasant	*Fagione*
Duck	*Anitra*	Turkey	*Tacchino*

Methods of Cooking

Roast	*Arrosto*	Boiled	*Bollito*
On the Fire/ Grilled	*Ai Ferri Alla Griglia*	Spit-roasted	*Al Girarrosto*
Rare	*Al Sangue*	Grilled	*Alla Griglia*
Well Done	*Ben Cotto*	Medium Rare	*Mezzo Cotto*

Miscellaneous

French fries	*Patate Fritte*	Cheese	*Formaggio*
Butter Sauce	*Salsa al burro*	Tomato and Meat Sauce	*Salsa Bolognese*
Tomato Sauce	*Salsa Napoletana*	Garlic	*Aglio*
Oil	*Olio*	Pepper	*Pepe*
Salt	*Sale*	Fruit	*Frutta*
Orange	*Arancia*	Cherries	*Ciliege*
Strawberry	*Fragola*	Lemon	*Limone*
Apple	*Mela*	Melon	*Melone*
Beer	*Birra*	Mineral Water	*Aqua Minerale*
Orange Soda	*Aranciata*	7-Up Like	*Gassatta*
Lemon Soda	*Limonata*	Juice (of)	*Succo (di)*

Wine *Vino*

Red	*Roso*	White	*Bianco*
House wine	*Vino di Casa*	Dry	*Secco*
Slightly Sweet	*Amabile*	Sweet	*Dolce*
Local Wine	*Vino del Paese*	Liter	*Litro*
Half Liter	*Mezzo Litro*	Quarter Liter	*Un Quarto*
A Glass	*Un Bicchiere*		

11. WHERE TO STAY

Hotels in Italy are strictly controlled by a government rating system that categorizes them from "no star" hotels to "four star deluxe" hotels. Each and every hotel must prominently display their official ranking for all visitors to see.

These ratings have little or nothing to do with price. They only indicate what types of facilities are available. The stars do not indicate what level of service you will receive, how clean the hotels are, whether management is surly or sweet. Even in hotels with the same rating, the quality of facilities is unequal. Below are the star rankings (see Chapter 6, *Planning Your Trip*, for more details on accommodations and ratings).

You'll find the stars listed at the end of the italicized basic information section (name of hotel, address, phone, price, cards accepted, etc.) before the review itself begins for each hotel.

*Minimum facilities. Probably no rooms with private bath. No air conditioning. No TV. No phones in the room. Boarding-room style accommodations, unless the hotel is on the cusp of being recognized as a two star.

**Comfortable room with a telephone, many with a private bath. No air conditioning. No TV. Maybe a breakfast served in the mornings. You may, however, have TV and air conditioning if the hotel is bucking for three star status.

***All rooms will have private baths, a color TV, CNN (i.e. satellite TV), air conditioning, a lobby bar, maybe a restaurant, and will be as comfortable as a four star, except with smaller rooms and public areas, but also with much lower prices.

****This is a first class hotel and will have every comfort you expect to find in a regular North American hotel. There are some very small four star hotels that can make your stay in Italy much more intimate and romantic.

*****Four star deluxe hotel. These places have everything you could possibly imagine and more. The place where the jet-set stays.

NO HOTEL RESERVATIONS!

*If you get to Rome without a reservation and arrive at the train station, there is a free service located at the end of **track #10** that will get you a room. There is no fee, but you usually do have to pay them for the first night's stay up front. They call ahead and book your room, give you a map, and show you how to get to your badly needed bed. It's a great service for those who like to wing it or arrived in Rome on a whim. Sometimes the lines are long, so be patient.*

Near Termini Station

1. ALBERGHO IGEA, *Via Principe Amedeo 97, 00184 Roma. Tel. 06/ 446-6913. Fax 06/446-6911. Mastercard and Visa accepted. 42 rooms, 221 doubles, 21 singles, all with shower and WC, air conditioning, and TV. Single L90,000; Double L120,000; Triple L160,000. Breakfast L8,000 per person. ***

Currently in the process of remodeling some of the rooms but will be completed by 1996. The rooms are large, clean, and with full bath facilities, air conditioning and TV in each room, it can't be beaten for the price. The lobby is large and spacious, completely covered in white marble making it a pleasant place to relax; and the staff is friendly, knowledgeable, and professional. So why only the two stars and low price? They're still remodeling and to get three stars you need a mini-bar in the room. Also, they're around the train station which has a reputation for being not so hospitable.

Granted there's not much to do around the station, and the restaurants are better almost anywhere else in the city, but if you want a lot of amenities for a low price, stay here.

2. HOTEL ADLER, *Via Modena 5, 00184 Roma. Tel. 06/488-0940. Fax is same number. Mastercard and Visa accepted. 16 rooms, 10 with bath. Single L85,000; Double L96,000-124,000; Triple L132,000-165,000. Breakfast Included. ***

Located near the Via Nazionale, but off on a side street, this hotel offers a good location for shopping as well as sightseeing. The rooms are spartan but clean, and the staff is wonderfully helpful. Most of them speak more English than the normal tourist does Italian, so you can make yourself understood. They have a person at the desk all night long to let you take care of those late night phone calls from your loved ones. One good feature is a small terrace overlooking an interior courtyard that is not that pretty but is cool and calming and makes you feel a part of Italian life. Check out some of the other two stars before you stay here, but if need be you will be happy here.

3. HOTEL ASTORIA GARDEN & MONTAGNA, *Via Bachelet 8/10, 00187 Roma. Tel. 06/446-9908. Fax 06/445-3329. 30 rooms, 23 with bath. Single L56,000-67,000, Double L97,000-121,000; Triple L134,000-174,000.* **

You cannot beat the prices at this place. A single with a bath for L67,000. Oh, that feels good. This has got to be the best kept secret in Rome in terms of price. But the decor and ambiance are great also. Better than their neighbor Hotel Select that charges through the roof. This place is a little darker, but has more character and their outside enclosed garden doesn't glare out onto an ugly building. This place has loads of old-world charm to spare ... downstairs. But upstairs they have modernized all the rooms, which makes for great comfort.

4. HOTEL BRITANNIA, *Via Napoli 64, 00184 Roma. Tel. 06/488-3153. Fax. 06/488-2343. 32 Rooms all with private baths. Air conditioning. Parking Available. American Express, Diners Club, Mastercard, and Visa accepted. Single L220,000; Double L240,000; Triple L275,000. Breakfast included. Children up to ten share parents rooms for free.* ****

Located just north of the Via Nazionale, this is a small efficiently run hotel with a slightly modern decor downstairs. The rooms tend towards a neo-classic ambiance. The rooms aren't the largest in the world but you have all you could want at your fingertips: TV, phone, air conditioning, minibar, sun lamps. Downstairs you can relax at the comfortable American style bar and mingle with the other guests in the evening. Situated near a Metro stop for easy access to all parts of the city.

5. DIANA, *Via Principe Amedeo 4, 00185. Tel. 475-1541 187 rooms all with private baths. All credit cards accepted. Single L155,000; Double L265,000; Triple L348,000. Suites L275,000. Breakfast, Lunch or Dinner costs an extra L40,000.* ***

Located near Stazione Termini and the opera, this is a comfortable well run three star hotel with plain but attractive decor. The rooms are rather large by Roman standards with all the amenities associated with a hotel in its class. The lobby and common areas are an eclectic mixture of marble floors and columns with subtle lighting and paintings.

There is an American style bar with intimate little glass tables that seem straight out of *La Dolce Vita*. It's comfortable and cozy, a good value for your money. Also, they have special rates for groups of 20 or more that will make your stay very cheap if you're arranging for a group. Call for details.

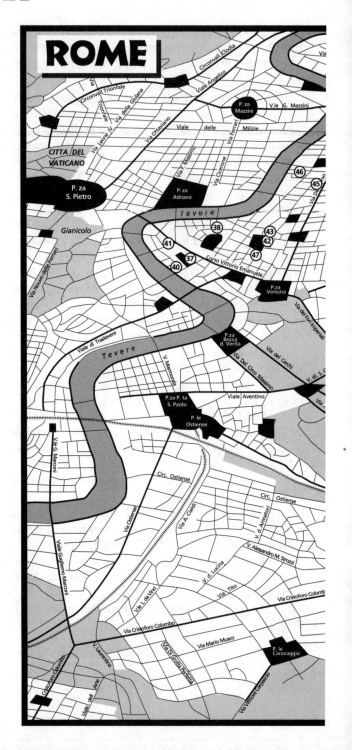

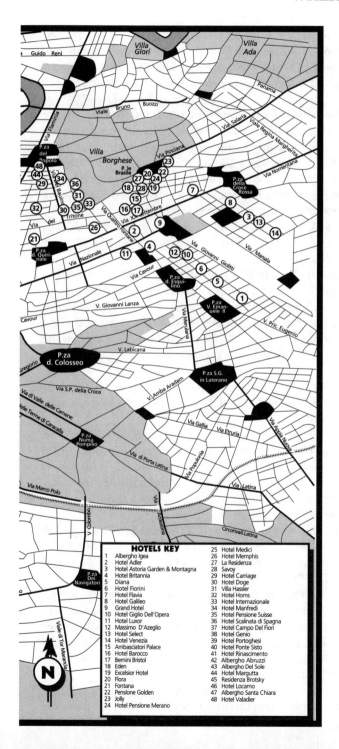

HOTELS KEY

1	Albergho Igea
2	Hotel Adler
3	Hotel Astoria Garden & Montagna
4	Hotel Britannia
5	Diana
6	Hotel Fiorini
7	Hotel Flavia
8	Hotel Galileo
9	Grand Hotel
10	Hotel Giglio Dell'Opera
11	Hotel Luxor
12	Massimo D'Azeglio
13	Hotel Select
14	Hotel Venezia
15	Ambasciatori Palace
16	Hotel Barocco
17	Bernini Bristol
18	Eden
19	Excelsior Hotel
20	Flora
21	Fontana
22	Pensione Golden
23	Jolly
24	Hotel Pensione Merano
25	Hotel Medici
26	Hotel Memphis
27	La Residenza
28	Savoy
29	Hotel Carriage
30	Hotel Doge
31	Villa Hassler
32	Hotel Horns
33	Hotel Internazionale
34	Hotel Manfredi
35	Hotel Pensione Suisse
36	Hotel Scalinata di Spagna
37	Hotel Campo Del Fiori
38	Hotel Genio
39	Hotel Portoghesi
40	Hotel Ponte Sisto
41	Hotel Rinascimento
42	Albergho Abruzzi
43	Albergho Del Sole
44	Hotel Margutta
45	Residenza Brotsky
46	Hotel Locarno
47	Albergho Santa Chiara
48	Hotel Valadier

6. HOTEL FIORINI, *Via Principe Amadeo 62, 00184 Roma. Tel. 06/ 488-5065. Fax 06/488-2170. American Express, Diners Club, Mastercard and Visa accepted. 16 rooms, 15 with bath. Single L110,000-135,000; Double 150,000-170,000. Add 35% for each extra person. A sumptuous buffet breakfast included with fruits, cheeses, meats, bread, sweet rolls, coffee, and tea.* **

Even though this hotel is located near the train station and is on the fifth floor, the appeal of this place is not dimmed. The streets it's on is a parade of food, clothing, and shoes stores, as well as outside cafés, bars, and restaurants. After you've taken all you can out of Rome, you can quietly relax in their clean airy rooms, watch a little TV or amble down to their Bar/Breakfast room for a nightcap and a conversation with some other guests. The beautiful proprietor Roberta is charming and friendly.

7. HOTEL FLAVIA, *Via Flavia 42, 00184 Roma. Tel 06/488-3037. Fax 06/481-9129. No credit cards accepted. 30 rooms all with bath. Single L100,000; Double L130,000; Triple L190,000.* **

Located near the Via Veneto and parallel to the Via XX Settembre, this place would be priced higher if (a) they weren't located on the second floor and (b) the building they're in didn't seem to be always under reconstruction. The entrance area is small, as is the breakfast and guest rooms, but for your money you can't ask for much more. You also get the amenities of a three star like mini-bar, TV, direct dial phones, etc., for the price of a two star.

8. HOTEL GALILEO, *Via Palestro 33, 00185 Roma. Tel. 06/444-1205/ 6/7/8. Fax 06/444-1208. Single L139,000; Double L198,000. All credit cards accepted. 80 rooms all with bath. Breakfast included.* ***

They have a lovely garden terrace on the first floor where you can have your breakfast or relax in the end of the day. There are four beautiful floors in this hidden treasure. The only drawback is that the entrance is down a driveway that leads to a garage. But once you're inside everything is transformed to cater to all your needs. The prices are so low for a three star, I think, because of the driveway situation.

9. GRAND HOTEL, *Via Vittorio Emanuele Orlando, 00185 Roma. Tel. 06/4709. Fax 06/474-7307. Single L370,000; Double L550,000; Suites L1,500,000. Extra bed costs L85,000. Continental or American Breakfast is extra (can you believe it?).* ****

Located between the Piazza della Repubblica and Piazza San Bernardo, near the American speaking church in Rome, Santa Susanna, this top-class luxury hotel has everything you'd ever need. There is a hairdresser service, beauty salons, and saunas. The hotel used to be located in one of the most fashionable quarters but it has long since lost its chic. Nonetheless that doesn't detract from the ambiance of opulence.

The rooms and suites are palatial, some with 16 to 17 foot ceilings. You'll feel like a prince or princess too when they serve you afternoon tea downstairs at 5pm. If tea is not your style, there's a very relaxing but expensive American-style bar.

10. HOTEL GIGLIO DELL'OPERA, *Via Principe Amadeo 14, 00184 Roma. 62 rooms all with bath. Tel. 06/484-401 or 488-0219. Fax 06/487-1425. Single L200,000; Double L250,000.* ***

Close to the opera, this hotel appears as if it houses some of the performers. If you like the longhaired chic crowd that always looks just right, this is the place to stay. The rooms are all attractive in a neo-classic style. The lounge area is large and is perfect for the look they're going for. Also they have a small and intimate area that serves as a bar in the evenings. You'd better know music to get involved in the conversations. Breakfast is served in a spartan, white, brightly lit room off the lobby.

11. HOTEL LUXOR, *Via A. De Pretis 104, 00184 Roma. Tel. 06/485-420, 06/481-5572. Fax 06/481-5571. 27 rooms all with bath. Single L170,000; Double L230,000.* ***

They offer individual discounts if you tell them you want one – up to 25% or so, they told me. Don't tell the Italian Government. Anyway ... this is a small hotel off the Via Nazionale that is small, as you'll see when you enter, but comfortable. The proprietor and her husband will do almost anything to make you happy. It has all the amenities of a three star hotel and you'll just love the classic beds and armoires. Centrally located, near a Metro for all your sightseeing pleasure.

12. MASSIMO D' AZEGLIO, *Via Cavour 18, 00184 Roma. Tel. 460-646. 200 rooms, all with private baths. Single L260,000; Double L350,000.* ****

Located near Stazione Termini, this hotel opened in 1875 and still continues in its old fashioned ways, which give the place its charm. They have all the modern amenities to be rated a four-star in Italy, but the look and feel of the place is 1950s. The best part is the *Cantina* restaurant downstairs that looks like a wine cellar. There are lots of nooks and crannies. For the money, stay on the Veneto or another better located place, but do come and visit, especially the restaurant.

13. HOTEL SELECT, *Via V. Bachelet 6, 00187 Roma. Tel. (06)6994-1349. Fax 06/6994-1360. American Express, Mastercard and Visa accepted. 19 rooms all with bath. Single L195,000; Double L225,000; Triple L300,000.* ***

Located just off the Piazza Indipendenza this hotel has a pleasant outside garden except for the building it faces. Still, a good place to relax after touring. The lobby lounge and bar are also a good place to lift up your feet for a while. The rooms are made to seem larger with the mirrors strategically placed on the armoires; each room has the necessary amenities for a three star. Quiet and calm, but for the money I'd stay next door at the Hotel Astoria (see above) with the same accommodations (save for the rooms without a bath) for a much lower price.

14. HOTEL VENEZIA, *Via Varese 18, 00184 Roma. Tel. 06/445-7101. Fax 06/495-7687. American Express, Diners Club, Mastercard and Visa accepted. 61 rooms all with bath. Single L135,000; Double L180,000; Triple, L245,000.* ***

If you have to or simply desire to stay near the Stazione Termini, this is the place to stay. For a three star the prices are so low and the service so high at this wonderful hotel you can't go wrong. Located on a side street away from all the noise, ask for a room on the fifth floor with a balcony (all singles). Here you can relax and enjoy the wonderful Roman evenings. The rest of the rooms are just as nice. Some have showers to cater to Americans, others have a bath for the Japanese.

The hotel caters also to business customers as well as visiting professors (the University of Rome is just around the corner) and there's an office with computer, printer, copier, and fax machine for your use. They're contemplating the introduction of e-mail service also. You'll love the 16th century altar that serves as buffet table for breakfast and bar at night, as well as the 16th century table that centers their conference room. Say hello to the charming, beautiful, and ever hospitable owner and operator, Patrizia Diletti, for me when you get there.

Trevi Fountain/ Via Veneto area

15. AMBASCIATORI PALACE, *Via Vittorio Veneto 62, 00187 Roma. Tel. 06/47-493. fax 06/474-3601. 103 rooms and 8 suites, all with private bath. All credit cards accepted. Single L350,000; Double L460,000; Suite L700,000. Buffet breakfast L21,000 extra.* *****

Virtually in the center of the Via Veneto, this hotel deserves its luxury rating since it has impeccable service, palatial rooms, and a top class restaurant *La Terrazza* to complement its fine ambiance. Your every need can be taken care of her: massage, evening companion, theater reservations, travel arrangements, etc. If you're looking for deluxe treatment at a deluxe price, look no further.

16. HOTEL BAROCCO, *Piazza Barberini 9 (entrance on Via della Purificazione 4), 00187 Roma. Tel. 06/487-2001/2/3, 487-2005. Fax 06/485-994. 28 rooms all with bath. Single L280,000; Double L380,000.* ****

If you're looking for an intimate four-star experience and don't want to get lost in the crowd at the Excelsior or the Eden, this is the place for you. All rooms are elegantly furnished with enough space for you to relax. If that's not good enough go on up to their roof terrace where you can bring your drink from the downstairs bar and soak in the Roman night. Centrally located with the Trevi Fountain, Spanish Steps, Via Veneto all around the corner. A great place to spend an entire vacation, or simply the last night of a long one.

17. BERNINI BRISTOL, *Piazza Barberini 23, 00187 Roma. Tel. 06/ 488-3051. Fax 06/482-4266. 124 rooms all with private baths. Single L315,000; Double L440,000; Suite L1,100,000. Continental Breakfast Buffet L25,000. VAT excluded.* *****

The hotel is located in the Piazza Barberini at the foot of the Via Veneto facing Bernini's Triton Fountain. This is another hotel that deserves its luxury rating. Perfectly located for shopping and sightseeing, you can get to the Spanish Steps and Trevi Fountain in minutes. The upper rooms have grand views as does the attractive roof garden, which is a great place to unwind after a long day. The rooms are not furnished with the faux antique look as are other deluxe hotels, they are more modern and seemingly more comfortable.

18. EDEN, *Via Ludovisi, 49, 00187 Roma. Tel. 06/474-3551. Fax 06/ 482-1584. 100 rooms all with private baths. Single L390,000; Double L550,000, Suites L1,100,000. Continental breakfast is L28,000 extra, buffet breakfast is L43,000.* *****

Located west of Via Veneto in the exclusive Ludovisi section, the Eden is a long-established top ranked hotel. It has a high class of service and amenities virtually unmatched the world over. Located off the crowded Via Veneto is an advantage since it makes your stay at the Eden much quieter. The terrace restaurant where you can have your breakfast, lunch, or dinner has a beautiful view of the city and the Villa Borghese. Also available is a complete gym for working out with everything from cardiovascular equipment to free weights. The Eden is truly luscious.

19. EXCELSIOR HOTEL, *Via Vittorio Veneto 125, 00187 Roma. Tel. 06/4708. Fax. 06/482-6205. All 244 doubles, 38 singles, and 45 suites have private baths. Single L 320,000; Double L480,000, Suite L1,200,000. An extra bed costs L90,000. Continental breakfast is L27,000 extra and American breakfast is L42,000.* *****

This superb hotel is located on the east side of the Via Veneto not far from the walls that lead to Villa Borghese. All rooms and common areas are done up with ornate moldings and elegant decorations. A truly palatial experience. They have a world renowned restaurant, *La Cuppola*, as well as a piano bar at night. You can do anything and get anything here, even rent the CIGA corporate jet!

20. FLORA, *Via Vittorio Veneto 191, 00187 Roma. Tel. 489-929. Fax 06/ 482-0359. All 8 suites and 167 rooms have private baths. All credit cards accepted. Single L270,000; Double L360,000, Suites L600,000.* ****

Located immediately at the top of the Via Veneto by the old Roman walls, this old-fashioned hotel has first class traditional service. The public rooms are elaborately decorated with antiques, oriental rugs, and soothingly light color schemes. The rooms are immense and some have wonderful views over the walls into the lush greenery of Villa Borghese.

Try and request one of those rooms, since Borghese is beautiful at night. This hotel offers everything you could want: location, service, great rooms.

THE BEST HOTELS IN ROME

You'll find plenty of great hotels when in Rome, but for a truly relaxing stay here is a list of my ten best, so your stay in the Eternal City will be even better.

**Two star hotels

3. HOTEL ASTORIA GARDEN & MONTAGNA, *Via Bachelet 8/10, 16 rooms, 10 with bath. Single L85,000; Double L96,000-124,000.*

37. HOTEL CAMPO DEI FIORI, *Via del Biscione 6, Four singles with shower each L115,000; Nine Doubles with shower each L170,000, 14 doubles without shower each L100,000.*

44. HOTEL MARGUTTA, *Via Laurina 34, 24 rooms all with bath. Single or Double L140,000*

24. HOTEL PENSIONE MERANO, *Via Vittorio Veneto 155, 30 rooms all with bath. Single L95,000; Double L138,00.*

***Three star hotels

46. HOTEL LOCARNO, *Via della Penna 22, 38 rooms all with bath. Single L170,000; Double L250,000; Suite L420,000.*

36. HOTEL SCALINATA DI SPAGNA, *Piazza Trinita Dei Monte 17, Only 15 rooms all have baths. Single L300,000; Double L380,000.*

14. HOTEL VENEZIA, *Via Varese 18, 61 rooms all with bath. Single L135,000; Double L180,000.*

****Four star hotels

16. HOTEL BAROCCO, *Piazza Barberini 9 (entrance on Via della Purificazione 4), 28 rooms all with bath. Single L280,000; Double L380,000.*

31. VILLA HASSLER, *Piazza Trinita Dei Monti 6, 80 rooms all with bath. Single L420,000-450,000; Double L620,000-900,000.*

*****Five star hotels

18. EDEN, *Via Ludovisi, 49, Single L390,000; Double L550,000, Suites L1,100,000. Continental breakfast is L28,000 extra, buffet breakfast is L43,000.*

---

21. FONTANA, *Piazza di Trevi 96, 00187 Roma. Tel. 06/678-6113, 06/679-1056. Single L180,000; Double L250,000. All credit cards accepted.* ***

The location of this hotel is great, but is not secluded or tranquil because it is in the same square as one of Rome's most famous monuments, the Trevi Fountain. You can hear the cascading waters and ever-present crowds far into the night. If you're a heavy sleeper this hotel's location is perfect, but if not try elsewhere. The rooms are sparse but comfortable and since this is a converted monastery, some rooms have been made by joining two monk's cells together. There is also a pleasant roof garden from which you can sip a drink and gaze over the rooftops of Rome.

22. PENSIONE GOLDEN, *Via Marche 84, 00187 Roma. Tel. 482-1659. 12 of the 13 rooms have private baths. All credit cards accepted. Single L140,000; Double L180,000.* **

Kind of an upscale pensione since it has air-conditioning, TV, phone, and mini bar in every room. It's located on the first floor of an old house, on a quiet street off of the Via Veneto. The stark white breakfast room that serves you your mini-buffet in the mornings doubles as the bar/lounge in the evenings. All the amenities of a three star, with the location of a one star at the prices of an upscale two star.

23. JOLLY, *Corso d'Italia 1, 00198 Roma. Tel. 06/8495. Fax 06/884-1104. All 200 rooms have private baths. Al credit cards accepted. Single L315,000; Double L415,000. Breakfast an extra L45,000.* ****

You haven't seen anything like the Jolly. Its ultra-modern, Buck Rogers glass and steel architecture contrasts sharply with the ancient Aurelian wall just across the street. Located just outside of the old wall overlooking the Villa Borghese. Jolly sits in a perfectly serene position. If you like the standards of comfort and efficiency associated with North American hotel chains, and don't mind a rather impersonal modern atmosphere, then this is the hotel for you.

The rooms are relatively small but all their amenities make up for it. Try to get a room with a view of the Borghese Gardens, otherwise you'll end up looking at the Aurelian wall and be woken up by the traffic on the Corso D'Italia.

24. HOTEL PENSIONE MERANO, *Via Vittorio Veneto 155, 00198 Roma. Tel. 06/482-1796. Fax 06/482-1810. American Express, Diners Club, Mastercard and Visa accepted. 30 rooms all with bath. Single L95,000; Double L138,00; Triple L178,000.* **

Another great find. Perfect location on the Via Veneto at rock bottom prices. The only reason the prices are so low is that you have to ride an elevator up to the third floor of a building to get to the hotel. The entranceway is dark and dingy but the rooms are warm and cozy. Everything is spic and span in the bathrooms, and you don't have to worry about remembering to buy your drinks for the evening. They sell beer, soda, and water. If you want to enjoy Rome inexpensively, this is one of the better places from which to do it.

25. HOTEL MEDICI, *Via Flavia 96, 00187 Roma. Tel. 06/482-7319/ 487-1802. Fax 06/474-0767. All credit cards accepted. Single L140,000; Double L200,000; Triple L240,000. Includes breakfast.* ***

The lobby is a little worse for wear but the sedate garden in the back makes up for it. The rooms are spartan and seem to have just made the three star rating, but that doesn't mean they're not comfortable. And the hotel is ideally situated near the Via Veneto and within walking distance of all the major sights. Also, they have a working relationship with three local restaurants to be able to offer you meals at a discount.

26. HOTEL MEMPHIS, *Via degli Avignonesi 36-36A, 00187 Roma. Tel 06/485-849. fax 06/482-8629. 24 rooms all with bath. Single L235,000; Double L300,000. Extra bed costs L90,000. Breakfast is L23,000 extra.* ****

This is a small four star hotel that has begun to develop a reputation worldwide. There are plenty of mirrors everywhere to make the place look bigger. All they did to me was offer me a fright whenever I passed by. It has all the amenities of a four-star and a great location. If you stay here, try the Tube Pub just up the street. Great darts, drinks, and conversation.

27. LA RESIDENZA, *Via Emilia 22-24, 00187 Roma. Tel. 06/488-0789. Fax 06/485-721. Mastercard and Visa accepted. 27 rooms all with bath. Single L248,000; Double L280,000. Full American Buffet breakfast offered.* ***

Wonderfully located just off of the Via Veneto, La Residenza offers well appointed and large rooms, a cozy American-style bar where you can sink into the leather chairs after a few drinks, an intimate roof terrace for those late night escapades, and one of the best buffet breakfasts around. You'll find a few Roman cats strolling around the grounds regally ignoring your presence unless you throw them a scrap of food. The only reason it's not a four star is because its entrance way is a little jumbled looking. Everything inside is perfect.

28. SAVOY, *Via Ludovisi 15, 00187 Roma. Tel. 474-141. All 135 rooms have private baths. All credit cards accepted. Single L320,000; Double L380,000; Triple L650,000; Suite L650,000.* ****

Located in the upscale Ludovisi section west of Via Veneto, this is a comfortable and well run hotel and features an excellent restaurant, offering both a la carte ordering and a superb buffet for quick dining, and a lively but still relaxing bar downstairs. The service is impeccable as it should be and the decor is elaborately expensive. The rooms that face off of the Via Veneto are quiet and comfortable. The location is perfect, especially if you're a spy – the hotel is almost directly across the street from the American Embassy.

Piazza di Spagna area

29. HOTEL CARRIAGE, *Via delle Carrozze 36, 00187 Roma. Tel. 06/ 679-3312. Fax 06/678-8279. American Express, Diners Club, Mastercard, and Visa accepted. 24 rooms all with bath. Single L215,000; Double L270,000; Triple L330,000; Suite L660,000. 30 rooms all with bath. Breakfast included.* ***

Located near the Piazza di Spagna, this elegant little hotel is luxuriously furnished with a variety of antiques but is still quite comfortable. They have a lovely roof garden terrace from which you can have your breakfast or an evening drink. There's not much of a view, but just being above the street level with the open sky above you has a calming effect. The bathrooms are immaculately clean.

30. HOTEL DOGE, *Via Due Macelli 106, 00187 Roma. Tel 06/678-0038. Fax 06/679-1633. American Express, Mastercard and Visa accepted. 11 rooms all with bath. Single L100,000; Double L147,000; Triple L185,000. Breakfast included.* **

The accommodations here are clean and spartan as well as comfortable, and you'll notice the prices are pretty good considering this is one block from the Spanish Steps. It's located on the fourth floor of an apartment building that you enter by walking through the entrance/retail show space of a local sports store. The prices are so low because it doesn't have it's own entrance. A good value for your money in a prime location. Only 11 rooms, so reserve far in advance.

31. VILLA HASSLER, *Piazza Trinita Dei Monti 6, 00187 Rome. 06/678 2651. Fax 06/678-9991. No credit cards accepted. 80 rooms all with bath. Single L420,000-450,000; Double L620,000-900,000. Continental breakfast L30,000 extra. Buffet breakfast L45,000 extra.* ****

In many traveler's opinions, this is the best hotel in Rome. And even if it's not, people come here to see each other and be seen. Located at the top of the Spanish Steps, with its own garage, a relaxing courtyard restaurant in the summer, and an excellent (but expensive) roof garden restaurant with the best view of the city. Remember to request one the nicer apartments facing the church belfry and the Spanish Steps. That's the whole point of staying here: the beautiful view. Even if you don't stay here, come to the restaurant, sample the food, and enjoy the superb view.

32. HOTEL HOMS, *Via Delle Vite 71-71, Tel. 0/679-2976. Fax 06/678-0482. All credit cards accepted. 50 rooms all with bath. Single L155,000; Double L240,000; L320,000.* ***

Located on the same street as the great Tuscan restaurant *Da Mario* and just across from the Anglo-American bookstore, as well as being virtually in between the Trevi Fountain and the Spanish Steps, this hotel has a quaint, pleasant ambiance and decor. Since Via Delle Vite is not well traveled you also escape the traffic noise. The lobby area is dark, but the rooms are light and airy.

33. HOTEL INTERNAZIONALE, *Via Sistina 79, 00187 Roma. Tel. 06/6994-1823. Fax 06/678-4764. American Express, Mastercard and Visa accepted. 42 rooms all with bath. Single L200,000; Double L285,000; Extra bed L90,000. Buffet Breakfast included.* ***

Located just a stone's throw away from the top of the Spanish Steps, you can hardly find a better location at a better price. The building itself is a part of history, having been redone and built upon since the first century BC. The lobby is small and without heart, but don't fret: once you move into your rooms and the other public areas, the antiques and tasteful decorations abound.

34. HOTEL MANFREDI, *Via Margutta 61, 00187 Roma. Tel. 06/320-7676. Fax 06/320-7736. American Express, Mastercard and Visa accepted. 17 rooms all with bath. Single L200,000; Double L280,000; Triple L370,000. American style breakfast buffet with ham, eggs, cheese, fruit etc. included.* ***

If you only stay for the breakfast it's worth it. The prices quoted above are those they offer as a perpetual discount because they do not agree with the rates the Italian Government Travel Service has forced upon them. So when you make your reservations tell them you read it here in this book and you'll receive the prices above.

This cozy, accommodating hotel is located near the Spanish Steps and has all the charm, service, and amenities of a four-star hotel, but it is on the third floor of a local building. They even have VCRs in some rooms as well as movies to rent at the front desk for your convenience. The street they're located on is cute, quiet, and home to some of Rome's best antique stores and at galleries.

35. HOTEL PENSIONE SUISSE, *Via Gregoriana 54, 00187 Roma. Tel. 06/678-3649, 06/678-6172. Fax 06/678-1258. No credit cards accepted. 14 Rooms, only 9 with private baths. Single L85,000-100,000; Double L120,000-150,000; Triple L165,000-200,000. Breakfast included.* **

Located near the Spanish Steps, this long-running and efficiently run small hotel is on two floors of an old building. It used to be part of two buildings but their lease ran out on one (for those of you that remember her before 1990). The rooms are large, spotlessly clean, and comfortably furnished. There is also a public room in which to relax as well as a breakfast room. The staff is superb, especially the matriarch who is a little hard of hearing but will assist you in any way she can, in four languages.

36. HOTEL SCALINATA DI SPAGNA, *Piazza Trinita Dei Monte 17, Rome. 06/679 3006 and 06/679 0896.Fax 06/684-0598 American Express, Mastercard and Visa accepted. Only 15 rooms all have baths. Single L300,000; Double L380,000; Triple 450,000. Suite for 5 people L600,000. Breakfast included.* ***

Just across the Piazza from the Hassler, this used to be a moderately priced, quaint little pensione. But since it received a three star rating its prices have sky-rocketed. Nothing much else has seemed to have changed so the proprietor must be making up for lost time by bringing in all the money he can. The best feature of this hotel is it's location at the top of the Spanish Steps and the superb view of the city from the roof terrace.

The roof is open in the summer months for breakfast, as well as for your own personal nightcaps for the evening. Having a roof terrace makes this place wonderful and will make your stay in Rome so much more pleasant and intimate. *687-5929*

Piazza Navona & Campo dei Fiori area

37. HOTEL CAMPO DEI FIORI, *Via del Biscione 6, 00186 Roma. Tel. 06/687-4886. Fax 06/687-6003. All credit cards accepted. Four singles with shower each L115,000; Nine Doubles with shower each L170,000, 14 doubles without shower each L100,000.* ** *FAX 654 - 5495?*

All the amenities of a three star with the best, I repeat, the best roof terrace in Rome, all at two-star prices. Why? The hotel is on six floors in a sliver building without an elevator. Also there's no air conditioning, which could be a problem in August. But at any other time this is the place to stay in Rome, bar none, if you're on a budget or not.

You have a great location only a few blocks away from the Trastevere area and its nightlife. Here you are in the perfect location to visit the best outdoor market in the city, the Campo dei Fiori, eat at some of the best restaurants (*La Carbonara* in Campo dei Fiori), a great bar/pub nearby (*The Drunken Ship* in Campo dei Fiori), and the best sights just around the corner. You also have the wildest, craziest, friendliest staff, as well as inexpensive prices, and the terrace to beat all terraces. Breakfast is served in a basement dining area, but you are free to bring it to the roof with you. The only real drawback is that it's not near a Metro line, but plenty of buses do pass this way.

38. HOTEL GENIO, *Via Zanardelli 28, Roma 00186. Tel 06/683-2191,06/683-3781. Fax 06/6830-7246. American Express, Mastercard, and Visa accepted. 61 rooms all with bath. Single L150,000-185,000; Double L200,000-270,000 An extra bed costs L70,000. A large breakfast buffet is included.* ***

Located almost in the Piazza Navona you get a great location in the Old City of Rome. Most of the guests are from Scandinavia and Germany. The rooms are well appointed with tasteful paintings, Persian rugs, and cream colored wall coverings. The lobby/common areas seem a little worse for the wear but the roof garden terrace has a spectacular view. This is where you'll be served your breakfast in the morning. A great way to wake up, gazing at the Dome of St. Peter's.

39. HOTEL PORTOGHESI, *Via dei Portoghesi 1, 00186 Roma. Tel. 686-4231. Fax 06/687-6976. Mastercard and Visa accepted. 27 rooms all with bath. Single L130,000; Double L210,000. Suite L230,000-260,000. An extra bed costs L50,000.* ***

Between Piazza Navona and the Mausoleum of Augustus, nestled beside the church of Sant'Antonio, and on a narrow medieval style street, this small hotel's central location is ideal. It may be not be near a Metro line but the restaurants, shops, food stores, small streets, and sights all around it make its location perfect. There are a smattering of antiques all over the hotel to give the place a feeling of old world charm that matches its unique location. The rooms are large and airy but the common areas are a little cramped. Not to worry: there are great restaurants all over the place where you can relax. A great place to stay.

40. HOTEL PONTE SISTO, *64 Via dei Pettinari, 00186 Roma. Tel. 686-8843. Fax 06/6830-8822. All credit cards accepted. Single L152,000; Double L199,000; Triple L241,000. Over 100 rooms all with bath. Breakfast included.* ***

Located close to the walking bridge Ponte Sisto that gives you access to Trastevere, the Renaissance quarter, this is a well situated and finely appointed hotel. The hotel is spartan but very comfortable, and the rooms and common areas are spacious. I especially love the central outside terrace garden with its fountain and palm trees. The perfect place to relax at the end of hard day. Try to get a room on a higher floor so you can have great views from your window. The staff is superbly professional and are fluent in many languages.

41. HOTEL RINASCIMENTO, *122 Via Del Pellegrino, 00186, Rome. Tel. 687-4813. Fax 06/683-3518.. All credit cards accepted. 20 rooms all with bath. Single L128,000. Double L200,000. L72,5000 for an extra be. Breakfast included.* **

Perfectly situated for the sightseer. It's five minutes from the Piazza Navona (where you can get gelato at *Tre Scalini*), Campo dei Fiori (where you can shop for local produce in the mornings), and 10 minutes from the Pantheon and the Vatican (in different directions). There is mostly a German clientele here, but that is changing as we speak. The rooms and bathrooms are clean but a little small. There is a large buffet breakfast served in the mornings.

Piazza del Popolo to the Pantheon
42. ALBERGO ABRUZZI, *Piazza della Rotunda 69, 00186 Roma. Tel. 06/679-2021. No credit cards accepted. 25 rooms on four floors all without bath. 2 bathrooms in every corridor. Single L75,000; Double L100,000.* **

Even though you don't have a private bathroom, you do have a great location at a great price. Besides, there is a sink in every room. This place decided not to upgrade its facilities like the Albergho del Sole (see below) and is content being a small, clean, and comfortable *pensione* for travelers who like to stay cheap. There is no common area, but the rooms are large enough to relax in. If not, the piazza in front of the Pantheon is a great place to kick back with a bottle of wine, or if you're more upscale you can sit at a nearby sidewalk café.

43. ALBERGHO DEL SOLE, *Piazza dell Rotunda 63, 00186 Roma. Tel. 06/78-0441. Fax 06/6994-0689. All credit cards accepted. 62 rooms all with bath. Single LL320,000; Double L450,000; Suite L530,000-600,000.* ********

This is a place that used to be a small well appointed *pensione* that upgraded its rooms prior to the new "star" ratings and voila: we have a four-star hotel. But it did upgrade quite a bit. The clean white walls and delicate furniture attest to the changes made under new ownership. Most of the furniture is of the neo-classic mold but leaning towards almost modern. Some of the rooms have a view over the Pantheon, which can be beautiful but also noisy in the mornings. The service is exquisite and everything conforms to the highest standards, making this a well-located fine little four-star hotel.

44. HOTEL MARGUTTA, *Via Laurina 34, 00186 Roma. Tel. 06/322-3674. American Express Diners Club, Mastercard and Visa accepted. 24 rooms all with bath. Single or Double L140,000; Triple L180,000. #s 50/52 have a terrace L170,000. #59 is great L180,000. Breakfast included.* ******

The prices are great since it's a two star, and it has that rating because there is no TV or mini-bar in the room, and no air conditioning which is a must in August. The hotel has been totally renovated and is as modern as can be. There's a relaxing lounge area and the rooms are all spacious and airy (except in August).

And it's location, ooh la la, right between the Piazza del Popolo and the Spanish Steps. Who could ask for more? That, coupled with the excellence of the accommodations and the low prices, make this place a definite rare gem.

45. RESIDENZA BROTSKY, *Via del Corso 509, 00186 Roma. Tel. 06/361-2339. No credit cards accepted. 24 rooms, 10 with bath. Single with bath 90,000-100,000. Single with out bath L60,000. Double with bath L105,000-115,000. Double without bath L90,000. Triple with bath L140,000-150,000. Triple without bath L125,000. Quad with bath 175,000-185,000. Quad without bath 160,000. L35,000 for each extra person.* ******

This is a dark, dingy little place, but the proprietor is friendly and helpful and he makes sure the place stays clean as a whistle. It's located on the third floor of an apartment building off one of Rome's most famous streets. This is a favorite of students and those who travel on the cheap, where they all gather in the evenings on the roof gardens and share a bottle of wine and the stories of their day. Ah, to be young again.

46. HOTEL LOCARNO, *Via della Penna 22, 00186 Rome. Tel. 06/361-0841. Fax 06/321-5249. American Express, Mastercard and Visa accepted. 38 rooms all with bath. Single L170,000; Double L250,000; Suite L420,000. Breakfast included.* *******

Situated between the Piazza del Popolo and the Tiber River, in a nice neighborhood of stores and galleries, this hotel is perfectly situated for those of you that love to shop. It has a very relaxing American-style bar, spacious common areas, a small garden patio, and a roof terrace where breakfast is served in good weather. On top of all that, the rooms are tastefully decorated to make you feel right at home: not too many faux antiques here. There are excellent restaurants all around, *Da Bolognese* for example, which means you won't have to wander far for your gastronomic pleasures. A little off the beaten path too, so it offers a respite from the hectic pace of Rome.

47. ALBERGHO SANTA CHIARA, *Via Santa Chiara 21, 00186 Roma. Tel. 06/687-2979. Fax 06/687-3144. All credit cards accepted. Single L200,000-225,000; Double L250,000-290,000.* *******

A three star that should be a four star. Once you enter the lobby you feel as if you've been whisked away to a palace. Everything is marble. The ceilings reach to the sky. The rooms are all tastefully decorated and the ones on the top floors get great breezes, if you don't want to use your air conditioning. You also have some good views over the roof tops. The service is impeccable. The place is great. If you want four star accommodations for a three star price, stay here.

48. HOTEL VALADIER, *Via della Fontanella 15, 00187 Roma. Tel. 06/361-0592, 361-0559, 361-2344. Fax 06/320-1558. 50 rooms and suites all with bath. Single L270,000-330,000; Double L370,000-450,000, Suite L400,000-600,000. All credit cards accepted.* ********

The first word that comes to mind is opulent. There is black marble everywhere, and it is doubled by the placement of the many mirrors and shining brass fixtures. But you ain't seen nothing yet. The wood paneling here sparkles, it's so well shined. The rooms are no less ostentatious with lights, mirrors (some on the ceiling ... but only slightly over the bed so don't get too excited), and the ever-present marble. If you want to feel like an oil sheik who has money to burn, spend your stay in Rome here.

The hotel is between the Piazza del and the Spanish Steps, so you're in walking distance to many of the sights and shops.

12. WHERE TO EAT

EXPLAINING THE REVIEWS

The reviews are arranged by neighborhood. Each entry lists a price for dinner for two. This indicates what the cost of a meal would be if two people order two dishes apiece (i.e., a pasta and a meat for one person and an antipasto and a fish dish for the other, etc.) and a liter of house wine.

If you only choose to eat one dish per sitting, the price will be significantly less than what is indicated here. I've also given you a feel for neighborhood sights, so you can combine food with views and sights.

THE BEST RESTAURANTS IN ROME

You'll find plenty of good restaurants in Rome, but for a truly great meal every time, here is a list of my ten best.

1. LA CANONICA, *Vicolo dei Piedi 13, Dinner for two L80,000.*

5. SABATINI I, *Piazza Santa Maria in Trastevere 13, At least L100,000 for two.*

7. TAVERNA DEL MORO, *Via del Moro 43, Dinner for two L55,000.*

10. PIZZERIA LA CAPRICCIOSA, *Largo dei Lombardi 8, Dinner for two L75,000.*

22. OTELLO ALLA CONCORDIA, *Via Della Croce 81, Dinner for two L80,000*

24. LA CARBONARA, *Campo dei Fiori 23, Dinner for two L90,000.*

27. ORSO "80", *Via dell'Orso 33, Dinner for two L85,000.*

32. LA BUCA DI RIPETTA, *Via di Ripetta 36, Dinner for two L70,000.*

33. LA NUOVA COMPANNINA DA ENRICO E VITTORIO, *Piazza delle Coppelle 8, Dinner for two L60,000.*

38. LA CIOTTOLA, *off of the Via Cassia Nuova outside of town on an unnamed dirt road. Tel. 06/267-324. Dinner for two L85,000.*

Trastevere

This is the perfect place for exploring the way Romans actually live. **Trastevere** literally means "across the river," and this separation has allowed the area to remain virtually untouched by the advances of time. Until recently it was one of the poorest sections of Rome, but now it is starting to become gentrified. These changes have not altared Trastevere's charm. You'll find interesting shops and boutiques, and plenty of excellent restaurants among the small narrow streets and *piazzetta* (small squares). The maze of streets is a fun place to wander and wonder where you're going to end up.

This area offers some of the best dining and casual nightlife in town. Here you can sit in a piazza bar, sipping Sambuca or wine and watch the life of Rome pass before your eyes. To accommodate this type of activity, many stores have begun to stay open later.

1. LA CANONICA, *Vicolo dei Piedi 13, just off of the Piazza Santa Maria in Trastevere. Closed Mondays. Major credit cards accepted. Tel. 580-3845. Dinner for two L80,000.*

In the capital of the Catholic world, what better way to dine than in a deconsecrated chapel transformed into one of Rome's most entrancing restaurants. Located across from Rome's only exclusive English language movie theater, *La Pasquino*, at Vicolo del Piede 13, La Canonica's Baroque facade is delicately covered with vines and flowers. In the summer months tables are set outside (and around the corner into the adjacent street) to enjoy this beautiful display and the warm Rome evenings. The best place to sit is inside; it's always cool and you can soak in the atmosphere of a renovated chapel that now has meats, kegs, and bottles hanging from the ceiling.

The menu is dominated by seafood and pasta. My recommendations: *Spaghetti alla Vongole Verace* (spaghetti with spicy clam sauce of garlic, basil, oil, and hot peppers) or the *Spaghetti alla Carbonara* (spaghetti with a light cream sauce, covered with ham, peas, and grated parmesan cheese). For the main course, try the light fish dish of *Sogliala alla Griglia* (grilled Sole). The *Grigliato Misto di Pesce* (mixed grilled fish) is also good and is sold by the *etto*, which is about a quarter of a pound.

2. CAMPARONE, *Piazza in Piscinula 47. Tel 06/581-6249. Closed Mondays. Credit cards accepted. Dinner for two L75,000.*

This restaurant owns the entire block, starting with the bar/café on the left, this restaurant in the middle, and the pizzeria/birreria on the right. The outside seating at the restaurant is the best pace to enjoy a Trasteverian evening. Their food includes an excellent rendition of *osso bucco alla romana*. They do it with *fungi* (mushrooms). Mmm, good. They are mainly known for their grilled meats and some of their pastas.

3. DA CENCIA, *Via della Lungaretta 67, 00153 Roma. Tel. 06/581-2670. Credit cards accepted. Closed Sundays and Mondays for lunch. Dinner for two with wine L75,000.*

They have crowded outside seating in a side area under an awning, but it's perfect for people watching. Inside is small but the tables are spaced a little farther apart. Inside is where you'll find all the locals sitting and savoring the restaurant's fine food.

Try any of their pastas for a primo (*arrabiatta, amatriciana, vongole,* etc.). They are all Roman specialties and are made perfectly. Then move onto the *fritto misto mare* (mixed fried fish) and you won't be disappointed.

4. GINO IN TRASTEVERE, *Via Della Lungaretta 85, 00153 Roma. Tel. 06/580-3403. 06/580-6226. Closed Wednesdays. Dinner for Two L80,000.*

The spacious and bright interior makes you want to sit outside under their awning on the side or in the front by the main road. Wherever you end up the food will be exceptional. One of the proprietors, Paulo, will greet you at the door and make sure everything is perfect all night long. Since it's popular it tends to get crowded, so get there early (7ish) or late (10ish) otherwise you may be in for a wait. But later is better because then you can watch the parade of people pass by on their way to Piazza Santa Maria.

An extensive fish and meat menu is featured: try the *Sogliola alla Griglia* (grilled sole), or the *saltimboca alla romana* (veal shanks in sauce and spices) for seconds. Your primo piatto has to be one of their great Roman pasta dishes like *arrabiata* (tomato-based with garlic and peppers), or *vongole verace* (clams in a spicy oil, garlic, and basil sauce). Or if the desire for pizza hits you, it's great here.

DA MEO PETACA, *Piazza dei Percanti 30. Do Not Go Here.*

This is a real tourist trap. I'm not even going to give you the phone number. If someone asks you to go, or your tour guide has been bribed to take you there, just politely say no and go to any other restaurant in Trastevere.

5. SABATINI I, *Piazza Santa Maria in Trastevere 13, Tel. 06/581-8307 (outside seating) or 06/581-2026 (inside seating with an entrance on side). Closed Wednesdays, and two weeks in August. But at that time their other restaurant is open. No credit cards accepted. Very expensive. At least L100,000 for two.*

Besides the excellent fish dishes here, you can soak up the Trastevere life-style, especially in summer when outside seating is available. At night the floodlights keep the church at the opposite end of the piazza aglow. Try the *spaghetti cozze* (mussels), *zuppa di pesce*, the *spiedino misto di pesce al forno* (mixed grilled fish), and the grilled sole (*sogliola alla griglia*).

If you want to see the fish grilled go to the very back of the restaurant and there they'll be roasting over an open fire, scales and all. (You can

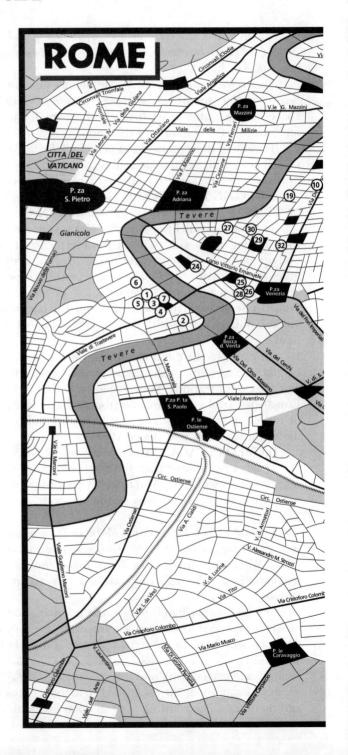

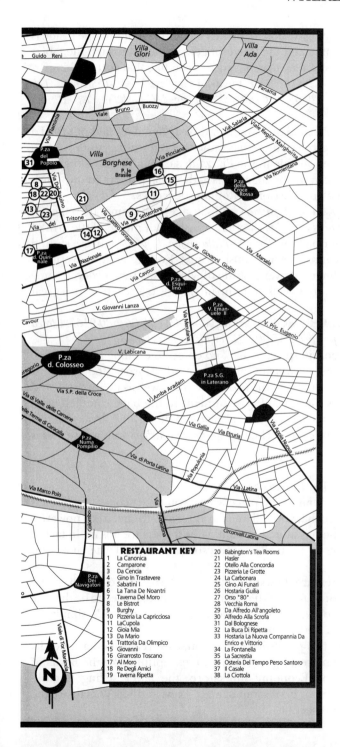

RESTAURANT KEY

1 La Canonica
2 Camparone
3 Da Cencia
4 Gino In Trastevere
5 Sabatini I
6 La Tana De Noantri
7 Taverna Del Moro
8 Le Bistrot
9 Burghy
10 Pizzeria La Capricciosa
11 LaCupola
12 Gioia Mia
13 Da Mario
14 Trattoria Da Olimpico
15 Giovanni
16 Girarrosto Toscano
17 Al Moro
18 Re Degli Amici
19 Taverna Ripetta

20 Babington's Tea Rooms
21 Hasler
22 Otello Alla Concordia
23 Pizzeria Le Grotte
24 La Carbonara
25 Gino Ai Funari
26 Hostaria Guilia
27 Orso "80"
28 Vecchia Roma
29 Da Alfredo All'angoleto
30 Alfredo Alla Scrofa
31 Dal Bolognese
32 La Buca Di Ripetta
33 Hostaria La Nuova Compannia Da
   Enrico e Vittorio
34 La Fontanella
35 La Sacrestia
36 Osteria Del Tempo Perso Santoro
37 Il Casale
38 La Ciottola

watch your meal being de-boned, de-headed and de-tailed). The inside is cozy and comfortable and they have singers walking through the tables serenading the customers, which is nice if you like that sort of thing.

6. LA TANA DE NOANTRI, *Via della Paglia 1-2-3, 00158 Roma. Tel. 06/580-6404 or 06/589-6575. Credit cards accepted. Closed Tuesdays. Dinner for two L75,000.*

Located past Piazza Santa Maria and past the tables laid out for La Canonica, this superb restaurant has rather boring seating inside, but oh so wonderful places outside in the Piazza di san Egidio which they take over at night. You can sit under awnings in the quiet piazza and savor dish after dish of succulently seasoned Roman specialties.

I've had the *pizza con salsiccia* (with sausage) as a primo, then moved onto the *Bracioline di abacchio* (literally translated it means "little arm of lamb"). My partner had the *Tortellini alla crema di funghi* (cheese stuffed tortellini with cream sauce and mushrooms). Even though we were too full to go on, we lingered over a bottle of white wine then ordered some *spaghetti alla carbonara* to close out the night. It was a real feast in a great atmosphere.

7. TAVERNA DEL MORO, *Via del Moro 43, Tel. 06/580-9165. Closed Mondays. Dinner for two L55,000. No credit cards accepted.*

A great inexpensive place to eat and enjoy an evening in Trastevere after you go pick up a novel at Clair Hammond's Corner Bookstore just up the road. Here you'll find the pizza superb, as well as their pasta's and meats. On Fridays they have Egyptian night in the back complete with belly dancers and more. A fun local place. When in the area, give this small, charming place a try. Their *spaghetti alla carbonara* is as great as is their *alla vongole*.

Trevi Fountain & Via Veneto area

The **Trevi Fountain** is the place where you toss a coin at Neptune's feet for a guarantee that you will one day return to Rome. It is a powerful 18th century baroque statue that dominates the square it is in. In fact, it seems overbearing for so small a space, especially at night when it is lit up by floodlights.

All around Trevi are shoe stores and small *pizzerie*. Then you have the **Via Veneto**, backdrop for the 1959 film *La Dolce Vita*. It used to be the chic gathering place for international movie stars but now it's simply an expensive place to stay, shop, and eat.

Besides these two places in this section, the area is modern, hectic, and devoid of many real sights. There are exceptions like the **Baths of Dioclesian** and the **Economy Bookstore**, the latter selling English-language new and used books, but overall, Trevi and Via Veneto are the places to see in this section.

8. LE BISTROT, *Via dei Greci 5, Tel. 967-97704. Open evenings only from 8pm -2am. Closed Sundays and three weeks in August. Dinner for two L80,000.*

If you're interested in trying some good French food during your stay in Italy, give Le Bistrot a try. Even though the name is French, they also have some Italian pasta dishes since the place is owned by an Italian. Furnished in authentic Art Nouveau style. I'm not a big fan of French food but I found the *Soupe a l'oignon* (onion soup) a worthwhile light meal in the early evening.

9. BURGHY, *Via Barberini 2 -16, Tel. 465-107. Closed Sundays. No credit cards accepted. Dinner for two L20,000.*

What used to be The Piccadilly, Rome's version of an American diner, is now a fast food place specializing in – you guessed it – burgers. I normally wouldn't write about this, but if you're dying for a burger and don't want to go to McDonalds out of guilt since you're in Italy, try an Italian version of a fast food burger. You'll be surprised. I tried them and thought they were better than Micky D's, which is not hard to do. Give it a shot if you have that Big Mac Craving.

10. PIZZERIA LA CAPRICCIOSA, *Largo dei Lombardi 8 just off of the Via Del Corso. Telephone numbers: 6794027 / 6794706. Open lunch and dinner (until 1 am). Closed Tuesdays. Dinner for two L75,000. No credit cards accepted.*

Do not be fooled by the name. This is no ordinary pizzeria. This is a large, wonderfully authentic Italian restaurant with over 25 tables inside. At night and on weekends, the restaurant expands into the Largo dei Lombardi. Through a white marble retail arcade are some ruins your kids can play in while you dine in peace. Beside the ruins, La Capricciosa is in a convenient location directly in the middle of Rome's premier shopping area, Via del Corso. So after an evening of shopping, stop in. But remember to bring cash, because La Capricciosa doesn't accept American Express, Visa, or Mastercard.

The beginning feature is a large selection of antipasto with all sorts of prepared vegetables, ham, salami, and mozzarella. Mainly a pasta and pizza restaurant (pizza served only in the evenings), specializing in the gargantuan *Pizza Cappricciosa*. This is a pizza with everything, Italian style. Give it a try. They also make all of the Roman pasta staples perfectly: *arrabiatta, amatriciana*, and *vongole*. One pasta dish that was a little different but really good was the *spaghetti al burro con funghi* (with butter and mushrooms). Try the *mezzo pollo all'diavolo* (half chicken cooked over the flames) if you're in the mood for poultry.

11. LA CUPOLA, *in the Hotel Excelsior, at Via Veneto 125, Tel. 4708. Credit cards accepted. Open 7 days a week. Dinner for two L100,000.*

This is the restaurant in the Hotel Excelsior where I first had *spaghetti al burro* when I was a kid. It's expensive and the French Empire style decorations are ostentatious, but you can have your basic Roman-style dishes, like *penne all'arrabiata, amatriciana,* or *carbonara,* some nouvelle cuisine the chef creates, or anything your little heart desires. If you want to feel like you're part of *La Dolce Vita,* eat here.

12. GIOIA MIA, *Via degli Avignonesi 34. Tel. 06/462-784. Closed Wednesdays. Credit cards accepted. Dinner for two L70,000.*

A small family-run pizzeria which serves excellent *calzone, bruschetta* (garlic bread made with olive oil), and pizza. They can also make you a *crostino* sandwich that they roast in their oven. Another favorite in this restaurant is their roasted or grilled meats. The *abbacchio* (lamb) is great.

13. DA MARIO, *Via della Vite 55, Tel. 678-7381. Closed Sundays and August 5-30. Dinner for two L80,000.*

You can tell the specialty of this restaurant by the stuffed game birds in the window. Da Mario serves unpretentious Tuscan food. I suggest trying the *ribollita* (thick cabbage soup) and the staple of all Tuscan restaurants, the *Bistecca alla Fiorentina,* which is big enough for two. Try all of this with a bottle of the house wine (excellent Chianti) and you should be able to get a meal for a good price. If you order two dishes apiece you'll match the price listed above.

14. TRATTORIA DA OLIMPICO, *Via degli Avignonesi 37. Credit cards accepted Closed Tuesdays. Dinner for two L60,000.*

Located just up the road from the Hotel Memphis, this is a great inexpensive place to eat. The street it's on is not well traveled, so they lure people in to sample their succulent dishes by offering great prices. Their *pizza margherita* (tomatoes and cheese) and other pizzas are made the perfect Roman Way. If you only eat the pizza and have a bottle of wine you could get out of here with only a L30,000 meal.

15. GIOVANNI, *Via Marche 64, Tel. 482-1834. Closed Saturdays and the entire month of August. Credit cards accepted. Dinner for two L150,000.*

Close to the hustle and bustle of the Via Veneto is this good restaurant with an Adriatic flair. The owners are from Ancona and they serve fresh fish brought in from there. The soups in their restaurant are also very good, so if you've had your fill of pasta, come here and try the seafood and soups. I really like the *Calamaretti ai ferri* (small shrimp cooked over and open flame). The house White, from the Verdicchio region is quite good.

16. GIRARROSTO TOSCANO, *Via Campania 29, Tel. 493-759. Closed Wednesdays. No credit cards accepted. Dinner for two L120,000.*

Located in the cellar of a huge building facing onto the Aurelian Wall, this is a first class restaurant that accepts orders until 1am. An ideal place to come back to after a night of revelry if you have a lingering hunger. The food is mainly veal and beef grilled on a spit over an open wood fired oven. Prior to the meats you can indulge in melon, Parma ham and *ovoline* (small mozzarella cheeses). The servings are large and so are the prices, and befitting its location near the Via Veneto the service is excellent.

Beside the food you'll enjoy the rustic atmosphere, with hams hanging in the entrance way along with a table filled with fresh produce. In the dining area bottles of wine line the walls above the tables, and the wood paneling adds to the peasant appeal at princely prices.

17. AL MORO, *Vicolo dell Bollette 13 (off Via del Lavatore), Tel. 678-3495. Closed Sundays and the entire month of August. No credit cards accepted. Dinner for two L110,000.*

The food is excellent in the Roman style, the ingredients are all fresh and of the highest quality, but the prices are a little high, and since this a popular eating establishment you'll need to make reservations. I swear the *Spaghetti al Moro* (a light carbonara sauce with cheese, egg, bacon, and red pepper flakes) is the best I've tasted. They make an excellent *all'arrabiata* (hot and spicy sauce) too. I also enjoyed the *Scampi alla Moro* (broiled Shrimp). Other excellent dishes are the *abbacchio romanesco al forno con patate* (roasted lamb with superb roasted potatoes with a sprinkle of rosemary). The inside front room is dominated by a large picture of Moro himself, long since passed away. The other two rooms have wine bottles surrounding the walls above the tables and are relatively roomy. If you want to sit outside you'll be crowded against a wall on a lightly traveled little *via*. I recommend the inside seating.

18. RE DEGLI AMICI, *Via della Croce 33b, Tel. 679-5380 or 678-2555. Credit cards accepted. Closed Mondays and the last three weeks in June.*

This *trattoria* close to the Spanish Steps has been serving traditional Roman food for years. If you don't want a full meal their antipasto bar will more than suffice. After 7:30pm, you can get one of their excellent pizzas. My favorite is the one named after the restaurant, made with sausage, mozzarella, oregano and tomatoes. The pasta dishes here are also something that shouldn't be missed. Try any of the Roman specialties: *carbonara, amatriciana,* or *arrabiata.*

19. TAVERNA RIPETTA, *Via di Ripetta 158, Tel. 06/6880-2979. Credit cards accepted. Dinner for two L75,000.*

This is small restaurant with a Middle Eastern flair. They have couscous, falafel, shish kebab, and tabule as well as a Roman staple such as *sogliola alla griglia* (grilled sole). This is a good place for a light but filling meal with a twist. Vegetarians should love this place since many of the dishes are meatless.

Piazza di Spagna area

The **Piazza di Spagna** is where it all happens in Rome. You have the best shops, great restaurants, beautiful sights. Stately *palazzos* lining the streets look like an ideal place to live, but today much of the housing has been replaced by offices, shops, boutiques, or restaurants. Only the lucky few can afford an apartment in this location.

This area is home to the **Spanish Steps**, which gets its name from the Piazza, which gets its name from the Spanish Embassy in the square that has been its residence since 1622. The area was adopted by British travelers in the 18th and 19th century, because it was not yet a popular location. Their presence is still here in the form of **Babbington Tea Room**, an expensive but satisfying establishment in the piazza; as well as a plaque commemorating the house where Keats died in 1821. The area used to called *il ghetto degli inglesi* – the English ghetto.

At the beginning of Spring, the steps are laden with banks of flowers that make the whole area look like a garden. This is the only time it's difficult to do what most do at the Spanish Steps ... simply sit down and watch the world go by, with a nice chilled bottle of wine of course.

20. BABINGTON'S TEA ROOM, *23 Piazza di Spagna, Tel. 678-6027. Credit cards accepted. Closed Thursdays.*

Really a place to grab a spot of tea, except in the mornings when they serve massive breakfasts of scones, shepherd's pie, and other British delights (if there is such a thing). This ancient café, with its heavy furniture, musty decor, and creaky floors has been serving customers for several centuries. The service is out of the eighteenth century, but the prices are from the 21st. Expect a cup of tea to cost over $5.

21. HASLER, *Piazza Trinita dei Monti 6, Tel. 678-2651. Credit cards accepted. Open 7 days a week. Dinner for two L120,000.*

If you have the money to spend, the view down the Spanish Steps from the glassed-in and air-conditioned terrace is worth every penny. You can pick out the Castel Sant'Angelo, the Jewish Ghetto's synagogue, the Pantheon, and the Quirinale Palace from the terrace. The food used to be passable, but now its Italian and Continental menu has begun to sparkle. The multilingual waiters will tell you that the *abbacchio al forno* is excellent, and I'd agree. There are many fine dishes on the menu, so you can order anything, but remember it's expensive.

22. OTELLO ALLA CONCORDIA, *Via Della Croce 81. Tel. 679-1178. No credit cards accepted. Closed Sundays. Dinner for two L80,000.*

This is a family-run, formerly small trattoria off of the Via della Croce. It's set off the road, which used to render it unnoticed, but now it seems to be crowded all the time. And with good reason – the food is excellent. You go through a tiny entrance off the main road then through a small shady garden to get to the restaurant. They have now made the garden eating area enclosed in removable glass, so people can eat out here all year round. In the summer it's especially nice.

On the inside the walls are filled with countless oil paintings, many received as trade for a good meal by a struggling artist. The prices are perfect and the food is simple, basic, and good. I loved the *abbacchio arrosto can patate* (roast lamb with grilled potatoes). The pasta dishes are not that good, which is strange for Rome, but if you stick with the meat fishes and vegetables you'll have a great meal.

They open at 7:30pm. Make sure you get there early or else you'll have a wait. The help is surly, but in a typical Roman way.

23. PIZZERIA LE GROTTE, *Via delle Vite 37. Credit cards accepted. Dinner for two L70,000.*

This place has a dark rustic appearance complete with partially wood walls. They are known for their excellent antipasto bar that could fill you up for the rest of the meal. I've had the *spaghetti alla vongole verace* (spicy clam sauce) and the *pollo arrosto* (spit roasted chicken) and loved them both. The food is down-to-earth peasant in the Roman fashion, and mixes well with the decor.

Piazza Navona & Campo dei Fiori area

Piazza Navona is the perfect place to explore Rome's historical tapestry. Just outside Navona in the **Piazza Tor di Sarguinana**, you'll find ancient Roman ruins completely surrounded by the "modern" baroque buildings of Piazza Navona. The square itself has a charm that makes you want to come back over and over again. It is like a living architectural gallery, with its baroque churches and buildings lining the square and the immense statues standing majestic in the square itself.

On a hot day, the fountains here are a visitor's oasis, allowing for needed foot soaking refreshment. But before you take your shoes off and relax your sore feet by soaking them in one of the fountains, stroll to the center of the piazza and take note of the magnificence of Bernini's **Fontana Dei Quattro Fiumi** (Fountain of Four Rivers). Navona is filled with wonders. You'll find some of the ice cream Navona has become famous for, as well as the carnival of life swirling around you. You might see fire-eaters, painters, jugglers, caricaturists, tourists, rampaging Italian children, and much more here. And from mid-December to mid-January, the square becomes a giant Christmas market with booths and stalls selling stuffed animals, toys, handicrafts, and candy that looks like coal.

This Navona area is basically an extension of the Campo dei Fiori area in character. They are both genuinely picturesque and intriguing neighborhoods, with a maze of interconnecting narrow streets and *piazzetta* (small squares), and each has a reputation of becoming a haven for hashish sellers late at night. This commercial aspect goes hand in hand with the Campo die Fiori (literally translated means "field of flowers") flower and produce market every morning. Both areas evoke a feeling of what Rome used to be like many centuries ago, with the centuries-old buildings and the peddlers, carts, and small stores lining the narrow streets.

24. LA CARBONARA, *Campo dei Fiori 23, Tel. 654-783. Credit cards accepted. Closed Tuesdays. Dinner for two L90,000.*

Located in the best piazza for dining, and the food's not bad either. As could be expected, *pasta alla carbonara* is the house specialty so give that a try here. Here it is prepared to perfection with *rigatoni* in a rich peppery sauce of egg, cheese, and bacon. They also make the best *spaghetti alla vongole verace* (spicy clam sauce) I've ever had. The *fritto misto* (lightly fried mixed vegetables and cheese) is excellent since most of the produce comes in directly from the *mercato* in the square. The market can be a problem at early lunch since there are still discarded veggies on the ground where the tables should be. There's no smell, but the sight isn't too appetizing. As always, I loved the *abbacchio alla griglia* (roast baby lamb) and the roasted potatoes.

25. GINO AI FUNARI, *Via dei Funari. Closed Wednesdays. American Express accepted. Dinner for two L65,000.*

Another inexpensive place, this one located in the Jewish ghetto. The decor is simple and basic but the food is good and cheap. They have the basic Roman pastas (*carbonara, amatriciana, vongole verace, and arrabiata*) but I jumped over them to try the *conniglio alla cacciatore* (rabbit hunter style made with brandy tomatoes and spices). It is superb.

26. HOSTARIA GUILIA, *Via della Barchetta 19, Tel. 06/6880-6466. Dinner for two L65,000.*

A beautiful arched interior with brown tiled floors welcomes you to this great find. The dishes are basic but great Roman fare too, like the *Penne all'arrabiata* or the *Spaghetti alla Vongole*. Besides the pasta they have fresh fish and grilled meats. These guys are off the beaten track and their prices are great. Give them a try if you're in the neighborhood.

27. ORSO "80", *Via dell'Orso 33, Tel. 06/656-4904. Credit cards accepted. Closed Mondays. Dinner for two L85,000.*

This is a fine Roman restaurant, a place to come for some classic pasta dishes, good fresh fish, and juicy meats. They bake their breads on-site in their red-brick pizza oven. Basically this is a restaurant with a little bit of everything for everybody. Pasta, pizza, fish, grilled meats, home-made breads, extensive antipasto, etc. I really like the Roman favorite *spaghetti alla carbonara* as well as the *abbacchio alla griglia* (grilled baby lamb). The place always seems to be crowded even though it's large, so try to get there early. Located near Piazza Navona, Pantheon, and Campo dei Fiori.

28. VECCHIA ROMA, *Piazza di Campitelli 18, Tel. 656-4604. No credit cards accepted. Closed Wednesdays. Dinner for two L85,000.*

The setting of the piazza with its Baroque church and three beautiful palazzos makes your meal worthwhile, even if the buildings are covered in grime. This menu changes constantly, but the basics are the wide variety of antipasto (which could be a meal in itself), as well as *agnello* (lamb) and *capretto* (goat) or their grilled artichokes. You have to try the artichoke, since this is the Jewish ghetto and the dish is a local favorite.

Piazza del Popolo to the Pantheon

This historic area shares many of the flavors of the bordering Piazza Navona area. It is filled with a delightful mixture of artisan's shops and modern commercial stores. When you stray off the Via del Corso, this section's eastern boundary, you'll enjoy meandering through narrow streets lined with small shops and boutiques.

The focal point of the area is the **Pantheon**, built almost two thousand years ago by Consul Marcus Agrippa as a pantheistic temple, hence its name. The city's population was centered in this area during the Middle Ages, and except for the disappearance of a large fish market, the area has remained virtually unchanged.

29. DA ALFREDO ALL'ANGOLETO, *Piazza Rondanini 51 Tel. 686-8019, 06/686-1203. Credit cards accepted. Closed Mondays and August 11-15. Dinner for two L100,000.*

A vibrant and noisy trattoria specializing in fish. Try to resist the lure of the innumerable, mouth-watering *antipasti* or you won't have room for the superbly fresh fish, the enormous Mediterranean prawns, or the still live lobsters in the display case awaiting your cooking instructions. This tentatively can be called the best seafood restaurant in Rome. Mushrooms are another Alfredo specialty from late summer to late autumn. I recommend you try any of their seafood dishes, roast meats, or pastas.

There is outside seating on a small piazza as well as air-conditioned inside seating. The decor is simple, with wine bottles lining the shelves set above the tables. Come here for great food and go away satisfied.

30. ALFREDO ALLA SCROFA, *Via della Scrofa 104, Tel. 654-0163. Closed Tuesdays. Credit cards accepted.*

There are photographs of the very rich and famous literally papering the walls. The restaurant has been in business for over half a century and was even frequented by Douglas Fairbanks and Mary Pickford. All the pasta dishes are superb, especially *Fettucine al triplo burro* (with triple butter sauce). The wine list is excellent and so are their house variations. If you like music with your meal, there is a strolling guitarist inside.

31. DAL BOLOGNESE, *Piazza del Popolo 1-2, Tel. 361-1426., 06/322-2799. Closed Mondays and Sunday evenings, and August 9-25. Credit cards accepted. Dinner for two L85,000.*

The cooking is Bolognese in style, which some claim is the best in Italy. Why? Because of the *Parmigianno Reggiano* cheese and the *Prosciutto di Parma*, as well as their affinity for pastas that use one or both of these ingredients. They have a menu in English to help you search through their great dishes. The *fritto misto alla Bolognese*, which includes fried cheeses, meats and vegetables, is great. The *Misto di Paste* (mixed pasta and sauces) was filling enough for two. By ordering this dish you get to sample a variety of dishes while only ordering one. They have outside seating, perfect for people watching, but the intimacy of their inside rooms decorated with a fine collection of modern paintings appeals to me more. Also inside, you don't have to breathe exhaust fumes while you eat.

32. LA BUCA DI RIPETTA, *Via di Ripetta 36, Tel. 678-9528. Closed Mondays and the whole month of August. No credit cards accepted. Dinner for two L70,000.*

This is a very small, friendly trattoria, where you must arrive early if you have not made a reservation. It is popular for its food and the reasonable prices. Also, the jovial *padrone* is in constant attendance. The food is basic, straightforward Roman fare. Try the *Lasagna al Forno, Saltimbocca alla Romana,* and the *Osso buco di Vitello.* The restaurant consists of one room only, its high walls covered with cooking and farming paraphernalia like enormous bellows, great copper pans, etc.

33. HOSTARIA LA NUOVA COMPANNINA DA ENRICO E VITTORIO, *Piazza delle Coppelle 8, Tel. 06/6880-3921. Dinner for two L60,000.*

This is a country restaurant transplanted into the city, with country prices and country accents. I couldn't understand the waiters half the time and I speak Italian. They have outside seating in a little *piazza* that helps you escape the hordes of tourists. If for nothing other than the quaint small *piazza*, come here for a meal. A perfect respite from a day's touring. Try the *vitello arrosto con funghi* (roasted veal with mushrooms) or the *Ossobucco alla Romana.* Did I forget the primo? Yes.

This place makes great meats, but they don't know diddly about pasta. So stick to an antipasto and a secondo.

34. LA FONTANELLA, *Largo Fontanella Tevere 86, Tel. 678-3849. Closed Mondays. Credit cards accepted. Dinner for two 85,000.*

A simple enjoyable restaurant with a distinctive Tuscan flair. Their specialties are game when it's in season. The charm of the restaurant is distinctively old world, with a gleaming wood floor and flowers on every table. Their pastas are also good and they have all the basic Roman staples: *Tortellini alla panna, penne all'arrabiata,* etc.

35. LA SACRESTIA, *Via del Seminario 89, Tel. 679-7581. Closed Wednesdays. No credit cards accepted. Dinner for two L85,000.*

Close to the Pantheon, this restaurant has over 200 places for seating, and offers good food at reasonable prices. The decorations leave much to be desired, especially the garish ceiling and fruit clustered grotto. Come for their pizzas, served both during the day and at night, an unusual offering for an Italian restaurant.

They also serve good cuts of grilled meat, and the pasta is typically Roman also, which naturally makes it good.

36. OSTERIA DEL TEMPO PERSO SANTORO, *Via dell'Oca 43, Tel. 06/322-4841, 6/322-0947. No credit cards accepted. Dinner for two L65,000.*

Great rustic, peasant fare, a stone's throw away from the Piazza del Popolo – and at great prices too. The restaurant is in a small area enclosed by planters in which you can eat your meals on papered wooden tables. This place is not haute cuisine, but it has great pizzas and pastas.

Come here for the Roman specialties *carbonara, arrabiata, and amatriciana.* You can get your pizza with virtually anything on it, just ask. You want salami, they'll put salami.

Outside of Town

Motivating yourself at the end of a tiring day to sample these restaurants may be difficult, but I believe they will be worth your while. The food at each is stupendous, and the settings uniquely Roman, making for a fabulous dining experience!

37. IL CASALE, *Located 10 kilometers outside of Rome on the Via Flaminia. Tel. 06/457-986. Best way to get there is simply hail a cab. Cost for the cab should be around L10,000 each way. Dinner for two L90,000.*

Excellent outdoor dining, especially during the summer months since the restaurant's location offers a respite from the hectic Roman crowds. Housed in a renovated farm house with roaring fires, looking out over expansive grounds, creates a terrific ambiance for a wonderful evening. The grounds are perfect for children to explore while their parents wile away the hours with a good Italian wine after dinner.

An enormous table of antipasto is the perfect first course, since you can help yourself as often as you want. For the main course, grilled meats are the specialty, especially veal, lamb, and beef. All are prepared with exquisite care, and could be the finest servings of succulent meat south of Florence.

My recommendations for a pasta dish are either the *Penne All'Arrabiatta* or *Tortellini alla Panna* (Cheese tortellini in a thick cream sauce.)

Recommendations for meat dishes: *Lambata di Vitello* (Veal Chop), *Lambatta alla Griglia* (Grilled Veal), *Maiale all Griglia* (Grilled Pork), *Miallino all Griglia* (grilled baby pork, more juicy and flavorful than *Miale*).

38. LA CIOTTOLA, *off of the Via Cassia Nuova outside of town on an unamed dirt road. Tel. 06/267-324. Dinner for two L85,000.*

This place is situated down a small, deserted country road and is located in an old farmhouse. It has a great country ambiance and is a perfect escape from the rigors of inner city Rome. The outside seating in the summertime is a great place to spend an afternoon. It can be cold inside in the winter (this is an old farmhouse, remember) so dress for warmth.

Their specialty is *Pasta Strudel* served in a rustic soup-like bowl. If you have room left, try their roasted wild chicken.

13. SEEING THE SIGHTS

There are several approaches to sightseeing in Rome. The chief difficulty, most visitors find, is that there is so much to see in this mammoth and historic city, so that even a month's concentrated touring would only scratch the surface.

If your time is limited, a sightseeing tour, or series of tours by bus, is perhaps the one way you can be sure to see at least the greatest sights in Rome and its environs. There are a variety of tours available through **CIT** (the official Italian company), *located at Piazza della Repubblica 64*; **American Express**, *at Piazza di Spagna 38*; **Thomas Cook**, *Via Vittorio Veneto 9/ 11*; or **Wagon-Lits**, the French travel company, *at Via Boncompagni 25*.

If you have more time, or prefer to set your own pace, the best approach —indeed the only workable approach in Rome — is to choose only what you're really most interested in and not force yourself to visit something that doesn't appeal to you merely because "everybody" goes to see it.

A map of Rome, some walking shoes, and a spirit of adventure are all you need to explore the innumerable *piazzas*, churches, galleries, parks, and fountains of this unique city. If you saunter through the narrow streets of old Rome, behind the **Piazza Navona**, for example, or along the **Via Giulia** or near the **Pantheon**, you'll get many unexpected and revealing glimpses of flowerhung balconies, inner courtyards, and fountains. Here, perhaps more than in the impressive ruins of antiquity, you will get a little of the feeling of this city where civilizations have been built on the ruins of the previous ones for centuries, an ancient city whose vitality seems to be perpetually renewed.

And remember, most, if not all, of these sights follow the Italian siesta system, which means that they will open at 9:00am until 1:00pm, then close from 1:00pm to 3 or 4:00pm. This goes for the museums, sights, monuments, etc. Thereafter they will stay open until 6:00pm or 7:00pm. So plan your tours accordingly. Also, all of the museums, buildings, and monuments will charge a small fee to enter, mostly around L5,000 (or $3.00), so be prepared for that also.

TEN MAGNIFICENT SIGHTS!

The Vatican Museums alone can take you an entire day to work through, so don't believe that you can do all of these places justice in a few short days. Also, when you visit Piazza Navona, Piazza di Spagna, and Trevi Fountain, you will get a different experience depending on the time of day you go. At night each of these places livens up with Italians of all ages strolling, chatting, sipping wine, strumming guitars, while during the day they may only be swarmed by tourists.

Take your time – don't do too much. These ten could easily last you a week.

Sistine Chapel – Site of Michelangelo's magnificent frescoed ceiling and walls.

Vatican Museums – Everything you could imagine including Egyptian, Greek & Roman artifacts, as well as the best collection of paintings and sculpures anywhere in the world.

St. Peter's – The world's largest cathedral, exquisitely decorated.

Castel Sant'Angelo – The fortress that used to protect the Vatican, now houses a wonderful armaments museum.

Imperial and Roman Forums – The center of ancient Roman life. A great place for people of all ages to explore.

Capitalone Museum on the Campidoglio – The second best museum in Rome, with many fine sculptures and paintings as well as the Boca della Verita (Mouth of Truth).

Piazza Navona – In what used to be the place for naval gladiatorial battles is now a lively piazza filled with wonderful fountains, churches, and palazzi as well as good cafés and restaurants.

Piazza di Spagna – Walk to the top and get a great view of the city. Sit by the fountain during siesta and enjoy Rome as it passes you by.

Trevi Fountain – One of the most beautiful fountains in Italy. At night, when lit up it is a magnificent sight..

Saint Pauls Outside the Walls – Location of many buried Saints, some fine sculptures and mosaics.

ANCIENT ROME

THE IMPERIAL FORUMS

Via dei Fori Imperiali. Admission L4,000. Open Tuesday–Saturday, 9:00am–1:30pm and Sunday 9:00am–1:00pm. In the summer they are also open Tuesdays–Saturdays from 4:00pm 7:00pm.

The **Imperial Forums** were built in the last days of the Republic, when the Roman Forum became inadequate to accommodate the ever-increasing population. These forums were used as meeting places for Romans to exchange views, as lively street markets, or as places where official announcements could be proclaimed to the populace. The first was built by Julius Caesar, and those that followed were created by Augustus, Vespasian, Domitian, Trajan, Nerva, and Hadrian. After the fall of the Roman Empire, these places of great import fell into disrepair and during the Middle Ages and the Rennaissance all that was left are the ruins we see today. Gradually, over the centuries, these monumental ruins became covered with soil until they began to be excavated in 1924.

Trajan's Forum

Located below current street level, this is the most grandiose of the Forums of the imperial age. Here you can see one of the finest monuments in these Imperial Forums, **Trajan's Column**, built to honor the Victories of Trajan in 113. It is over 30 meters high and is covered with a series of spiral reliefs depicting the military expoilts of the Emperor against the Dacins in the 1st century AD. At the summit of this column is a statue of St. Peter, placed there by Pope Sixtus V in the 17th century.

Trajan's Market

This is a large and imposing set of buildings attached to Trajan's Forum, where people gathered and goods were sold. In the vast semicircle is where the merchants displayed their wares.

Forum of Caesar

Located to the right of the Via dei Fori Imperiali (the road itself was built in 1932 on the site of a far more ancient road to more adequately display the monuments of Ancient Rome), this was the earliest of the Imperial Forums. It was begun in 54 BC to commemorate the Battle of Pharsalus, and finished in 44 BC. Trajan redesigned many parts of this Forum to meet his needs in 113 AD.

For example, Trajan added the **Basilica Argentaria** (Silver Basilica) that was a meeting place for bankers and money changers. Originally a bronze statue of Julius Caesar stood in the center of this Forum; currently it is located in the Campidoglio.

Forum of Augustus

Built around the time of Christ's birth, this Forum commemorates the deaths of Brutus and Cassius (the traitors who allied agianst Caesar) at the Battle of Philippi in 42 BC. Here you'll find some remains of the **Temple of Mars Ultor**, the god of war, including a high podium and some trabeated (horizontal) columns. To the side of the temple you'll find the remains of two arches of triumph and two porticos.

Forum of Nerva

Constructed in 96 AD, this Forum was generally known as the **Forum Transitorium** since it served as a passageway between the **Forums of Augustus** and **Vespasian**. Here you'll find two large columns projecting up from the walls of the **Temple of Minerva**. Little is left of the Forum of Vespasian, at least anything that is identifiable.

Basilica of Maxentius & Constantine

This large building was begun by Maxentius between 306-312 AD and eventually completed by Constantione. It was used as a court of law and a money exhange, as were all Roman basilicas. It faces the Coliseum and is one of the best preserved of the buildings in the Imperial Forums. In its prime, the building was 100 meters long and 76 meters wide and divided into three naves, most of which remains to this day.

THE COLISEUM

Piazza Colosseo. Admission L8,000. Hours in the summer 9:00am– 4:00pm. In the winter 9:00am–7:00pm. Catch buses 11, 27, 81, 85, 87 or get off at the Colosseo Metro stop.

The **Coliseum** (*Ampitheater Flavium*) remains the most memorable monument remaining from ancient Rome. Its construction bgean in 72 AD by Vespasian on the site of the Stagnum Neronis, a lake near Nero's house, and was eventually dedicated by Titus in 80 AD. It is recorded that at this dedication, which lasted three months, over 500 exotic beasts and many hundreds of gladiators were slain in the arena. These types of spectacles lasted until 405 AD, when they were abolished by the Emperor. The building was severly damaged by an earthquake in the fifth century AD and since then it has been used a a fortress and as a supply source for construction material for papal buildings.

What we see today is nothing compared to what the building used to look like. In its prime it was covered with marble, and each portico was filled with a marble statue of some important Roman. The Coliseum used to be fully elliptical and could hold over 50,000 people. The first tier of seats was reserved for the knights and tribunes, the second teir for citizens, and the third tier for the lower clsses. The Emperor, Senators, Government Officials and Vestal Virgins sat on marble thrones on a raised platform that went around the entire arena.

Today in the arena we can see vestiges of the subterranean passages that were used to transport the wild beasts. They employed human powered elevators to get the animals up to the Coliseum floor. At times the arena was flooded to allow for the performance of mock naval battles.

Arch of Constantine
Piazza Colosseo. Catch buses 11, 27, 81, 85, 87 or get off at the Colosseo Metro stop.

Located near the Coliseum, this monument was built in 315 to commemorate the Emperor's victory over Maxentius at the Ponte Milvio, is comprised of three archways, and is the largest and best preserved in Rome.

Even though this is the Arch of Constantine, the bas-reliefs refer to deeds performed by Trajan, Hadrian, and Marcus Aurelius. The upper reliefs facing the Coliseum represent Marcus Aurelius in his battle with the Dacians, and on the opposite side there are episodes of deeds by Marcus Aurelius and Constantine.

THE ROMAN FORUM & NEARBY SIGHTS
Via dei Fori Imperiali. Tel. 699-0110. Admission L12,000. Open Tuesday–Saturday 9:00am–1:30pm, and Sunday 9:00am–1:00pm. In the summer also open Tuesdays–Saturdays from 4:00pm–7:00pm. Catch buses 11, 27, 85, 97, 181, 186, 718, and 719.

The best way to get an overall view of the **Roman Forum** is to descend from the Piazza del Campidolglio by way of the Via del Campidoglio, which is to the right of the Senatorial Palace. Here you get a clear view of the Forums in the front, with the Coliseum in the background, and the Palatine hill on the right.

In the Roman Forum you'll find the following sights and more:

Arch of Septimus Severus
Built in 203 AD to celebrate the ten years of the Emperor Septimus Severus' reign, it is constructed with three archways and is one of the most imposing sturctures from ancient Rome. Over the side arches are bas-reliefs depicting scenes from victorious battles fought by the Emperor over the Parthians and the Mesopotamians.

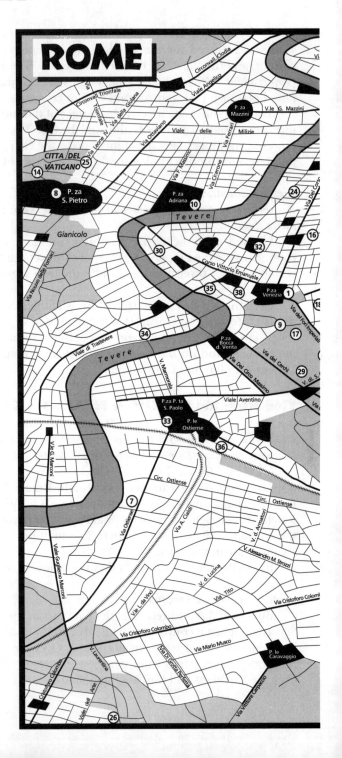

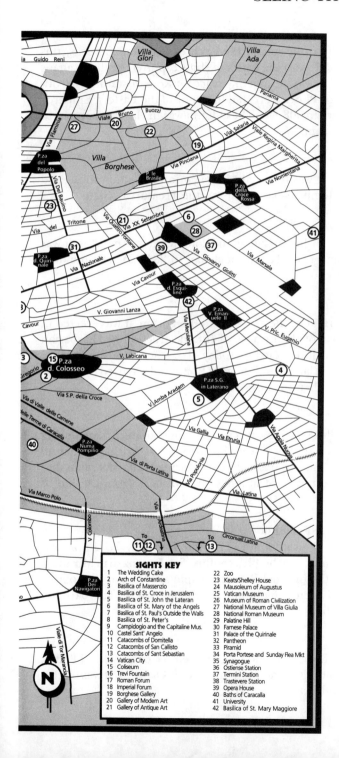

SIGHTS KEY

1	The Wedding Cake
2	Arch of Constantine
3	Basilica of Massenzio
4	Basilica of St. Croce in Jerusalem
5	Basilica of St. John the Lateran
6	Basilica of St. Mary of the Angels
7	Basilica of St. Paul's Outside the Walls
8	Basilica of St. Peter's
9	Campidoglio and the Capitaline Mus.
10	Castel Sant' Angelo
11	Catacombs of Domitella
12	Catacombs of San Callisto
13	Catacombs of Sant Sebastian
14	Vatican City
15	Coliseum
16	Trevi Fountain
17	Roman Forum
18	Imperial Forum
19	Borghese Gallery
20	Gallery of Modern Art
21	Gallery of Antique Art
22	Zoo
23	Keats/Shelley House
24	Mausoleum of Augustus
25	Vatican Museum
26	Museum of Roman Civilization
27	National Museum of Villa Giulia
28	National Roman Museum
29	Palatine Hill
30	Farnese Palace
31	Palace of the Quirinale
32	Pantheon
33	Piramid
34	Porta Portese and Sunday Flea Mkt
35	Synagogue
36	Ostiense Station
37	Termini Station
38	Trastevere Station
39	Opera House
40	Baths of Caracalla
41	University
42	Basilica of St. Mary Maggiore

Rostra

Located directly to the left of the Arch of Septimus Severus, this building was decorated with the beaks of ships captured by the Romans at Antium in 338 BC. It was the meeting place for Roman orators. In front of it is the **Column of Phocas**, erected in honor of the Eastern Emperor of the Roman Empire in 608 AD. The column was the last monument to be erected in the Forum.

Temple of Saturn

Built in 497 BC, it was restored with eight ionic columns in the 3rd century AD. In the temple's basement was the Treasury of State.

Basilica Giulia

Started in 54 BC by Julius Caesar and completed by Augustus, it was destroyed by fire and restored by Diocletian in 284 AD. The building served as a large law court.

Basilica Emilia

Located to the right of the entrance to the Forum, it was erected in 179 BC, and because of the ravages of fire, destruction by "barbarian hordes" and neglect, little remains today. Together with the Basilica Giulia, it was one of the largest buildings in Rome and was used by money-changers and other other business people.

The Curia

Founded by Tullus Hostilius, this was the house of the Senate during the Late Empire. It used to be covered with exquisite marble. Today all that remains are two balustrades called the **Marble Walls of Trajan** that are scultped with bas-reliefs of animals and episodes from the life of Trajan.

Temple of Anthony & Foustina

Built by Antonius Pius in honor of his wife Faustina, the temple was later converted to a church in the 11th century, **San Lorenzxo in Miranda**. All that remains of the original Roman temple are the ten monolithic columns that are 17 meters high, and an elegant frieze. The baroque facade is from the 1600s.

Temple of Caesar

Near the Arch of Augustis and past the Temple of Casot and Pollux you'll find the Temple of Caesar, built in 42 BC by Octavius. It was on this site that Caesar's body was cremated.

Temple of Castor & Pollux

Built in 484 BC and restored by Hadrian and Tiberius. The three Corinthian columns in the podium are from that period of restoration. It was originally built to pay homage to the Gods Castor and Pollux who, according to legend, aided the Romans against their enemies.

House of the Vestal Virgins

The vestal virgins dedicated themselves to maintaining the sacred fires in the nearby **Temple of Vesta**. A portico of two stories adorned with statues of the Vestals surrounded an open court that was decorated with flowerbeds and three cisterns. In the court you can still see the remains of some of the statues and the pedestals on which they sat.

Arch of Titus

Erected to commemorate the vistories of Vespasian and Titus, who conquered Jerusalem. The arch contains bas-releifs of the Emperor and of soldiers carrying away the spoils of Jerusalem. One of the most imposing structures remaining from ancient Rome.

Temple of Romulus

Built by the Emperor Maxentius who dedicated it to his deified son Romulus. A circular building that was converted to a church in the sixth century.

The Palatine Hill

This is one of the seven hills of Rome and was the residence of the Roman Emperors from the Golden Age and Imperial Period. It was here, in 754 BC, that Romulus is said to have founded the city of Rome. Noble families also resided here, leaving behind wonderful architectural relics that have mostly all been excavated today, making the Palatine Hill one of the must-see places when you tour the Forum.

Here are the baths of Septimus Severus, the Stadium of Domitian, the Farnese Gardens, the House of Livia, the Flavia Palace, the House of Augustana, and more. Most of the ruins are covered with grass and wild bushes, making a walk through the ruins a relaxing natural adventure.

BATHS OF CARACALLA

Via di Terme Caracalla, Tel. 575-8626. Admission L8,000. Hours Monday–Saturday 9:00am–3:00pm. Sundays 9:00am–1:30pm. Catch buses 90, 90b, 118 or get off at the Circo Massimo Metro Stop.

Constructed in 217 AD by the Emperor Caracalla, these baths were second in size only to the Baths of Diocletian. They were used until the sixth century when they were destroyed by Gothic invaders. They used to be rich with marble, statues, stuccoes, and more. Today, on cool summer evenings, opera perfromances are held among the ruins of the **Calidarium**, the circular vapor bath area.

BATHS OF DIOCLETIAN

Catch buses 57, 64, 65, 75, 170, 492, and 910 or get off at the Repubblica Metro stop.

These were the most extensive baths of their times. More than 3,000 bathers could be accommodated at one time. They were built by Maximian and Diocletian fromn 196–306 AD. Today the **National Museum** is located within their walls, as is the **Church of Santa Maria Degli Angeli**.

CAMPIDOGLIO

Catch buses 94, 95, 713, 716.

One of the seven hills of Rome. Today it houses the **Capitalone Museum**, **Senatorial Palace**, the **Palace of the Conservatori**, and the **Church of Santa Maria D'Arcoeli** (formerly the Temple of Juno Moneta). To ascend the hill, take the steep stairway that leads to the church, the winding ramp of the Via delle Tre Pile, or from between the two of these by way of the monumental stairs, Cordonate, which were designed by Michelangelo. At the entrance to these stairs you'll find two imposing Egyptian lions and at the top the statues of Castor and Pollux.

Try to visit the museums here, since they are second in magnificence only to Vatican Museums, and are even better in certain exhibits.

CIRCUS MAXIMUS

Catch buses 15, 90, 90b, 94 or get off at the Circo Massimo Metro.

One of the most perfectly conserved monuments of ancient Rome. It was erected in 309 AD by the Emperor Maxentius in honor of his deified son Romulus, whose temple is nearby.

CATACOMBS OF SAINT CALLIXTUS, SAN SEBASTIAN, & SANTA DOMITILLA

Catch buses 118 and 218.

Located next door to one another on the Via Appia Antica south of the city, these tombs were originally an ancient Roman necropolis, then they were used by the early Christians as a meeting place as well as a place of worship, and a haven from prosecution. Here you can visit the **crypts of the Popes**, the crypt of Saint Cecilia, the crypt of Pope Eusebius, as well as frescoes dating back to the 3rd century AD. All three are an eerie reminder of the time before Christianity dominated the Western world.

CHRISTIAN ROME

CASTEL SANT'ANGELO

Lungotevere Castello. Admission L8,000. Open 9:00am–6:00pm. Last entrance time is 1 hour before closing. Catch buses 23, 34, 64, 280, 982.

Also known as the **Mausoleum of Hadrian** since it was built for Hadrian and his successors. For eighty years it was used as a funeral monument where the ashes of the Roman emperors were stored. Subsequently the structure was used as a fortress, a residence for popes and princes, a prison, and as a military barracks.

In the Middle Ages it was transformed into what it is now, the **Papal fortress**. A covered walkway leads from Saint Peter's to the Castel Sant'Angelo and, because of the volatile political siuation in Italy for many centuries, this walkway was used more than once to protect the Pope.

On the summit of the building is the statue of an angel (hence the name of the castle), and rumor has it that in 590 AD, Gregory the Great saw a vision with an avenging angel sheathing its sword at the summit of the castle. He took this to mean the plague that had ravaged Rome was over. To commemorate this event he placed an angel on top of the building. Today the castle houses a museum with one of the best collections of articles of war from the Stone Age to the present ever assembled. There are also some non-descript art exhibits and luxuriously preserved Papal apartments.

SAINT PETER'S

Piazza San Pietro. Hours 9:00am–6:00pm. Catch the Metro to Ottaviano or buses 19, 62, 64, or 492.

Located in the monumental square **Piazza San Pietro**, a masterpiece created by **Bernini** between 1656 and 1667, sits Saint Peter's, the largest church in the world. The square itself is oval and 240 meters at its largest diameter. It is composed of 284 massive marble columns, and 88 pilasters forming three galleries 15 meters wide. Surrounding the square, above the oval structure are 140 statues of saints.

In the center is an oblesik 25.5 meters high with four bronze lions at its base, all of which were brought from Heliopolis during the reign of Caligula (circa 40 AD) and which originally stood in the circus of Nero. It was placed here in 1586. Below the monument you can see the points of the compass and the names of the winds. To reach Saint Peter's you must pass the obelisk and walk up a gradual incline.

The church rises on the site where Saint Peter is buried. The early Christians erected a small oratory on the site of the tomb, but that was destroyed in 326 when Constantine the Great erected the first Basilica on this site. Over the centuries the church began to expand and became incongrously and lavishly decorated, so that by 1452 Nicholas V decided to make it more uniform. He commissioned Bernardo Rossellino to deisgn a new structure. When the Pope died three years late this work was interrupted, but in 1506 Pope Julius II, with the assistance of Bramante, continued the work on a grander scale.

Bramante died before his work could be finished. His successors were Raphael, Baldassare Peruzzi, and utlimately Antonio de Sangalloo the Younger. Eventually, the project was taken over and modifed by **Michelangelo** in 1546. After he died, his plans too were changed by Vignola, Pizzo Ligorio, Giacomo dell Porta, Domenico Fontana, and finally Carlo Maderno, who designed the facade. On November 1, 1626, **Urbano VIII** dedicated the Basilica as we know it today.

The Facade

Rounding off, the **facade** is 115 meters long and 45 meters high, and is approached by a gradually sloping grand staircase. At the sides of this staircase are the statues of **Saint Peter** (by De Fabis) and **Saint Paul** (by Adamo Tadolini). On the balustrade, held up by eight Corinthian columns and four pilasters, are the colossal statues of the Savior and St. John the Baptist surrounded by the Apostles, excluding Saint Peter.

The Interior

The church is more than 15,000 square meters in area, 211 meters long and 46 meters high. There are 229 marble columns: 533 of travertine, 16 of bronze, 90 of stucco, and 44 altars. On the floor of the central nave you'll find lines drawn identifying where other churches in the world would fit if placed in Saint Peter's. Kids love to explore this aspect of the basilica.

There are nine balconies, and from the central one the Pope gives his Christmas and Easter benedictions. There are five doors from which to enter the chruch, but today only the large central one is used.

PROPER ATTIRE, PLEASE!

When you're visiting most museums and monuments in Italy, follow these necessary rules:

__Women:__ don't forget to wear either long pants or a long skirt or dress, and a top with sleeves.

__Men:__ wear long pants and no tank tops.

You will be denied entry to St. Peter's for sure, and to many other sights as well if you're wearing shorts!

Also on the floor, near the front entrance, is a disk of red porphyry indicating the spot where **Charlemagne** was crowned Holy Roman Emperor by Leo III on Christmas Day in 800 AD. To the right of this, in the first chapel, is the world famous *Pieta* created by Michelangelo when he was on 24, in 1500 AD. In the niches of the pilasters that support the arches are statues of the founders of many religious orders. In the last one on the right you'll find the seated bronze statue of Saint Peter. The statue's foot has been rubbed by so many people for good luck that it has almost disappeared.

Just past the statue is the grand **cupola** created by Michelangelo. One of the most amazing architectural wonders of all times, it is held up by four colossal spires which lead to a number of open chapels. Under the cupola, above the high altar rises the famous **Baldacchino** (or Grand Canopy) made by Bernini. It's made from bronze taken mainly from the Pantheon. In front of the altar is the **Chapel of Confessions** made by Maderno, around which are 95 perpetually lit lamps illuminating the **Tomb of Saint Peter's**. In front of the shrine is the kneeling statue of Pius VI made by Canova in 1822.

Throughout the rest of the Basilica you'll find a variety of superb statues and monuments, many tombs of Popes, and a wealth of chapels, not the least of which is the **Gregorian Chapel** designed by Michelangelo and executed by Giacomo della Porta. It is rich in marbles, stuccos, and mosaics, all put together in the creative Venetian style by Madonna del Soccorso in the 12th century.

If you grow tired of the many beautiful works of art and wish to get a bird's eye view of everything, you can ascend into Michelangelo's Cupola either by stairs (537 of them) or by elevator. If you come to Saint Peter's, you should do this.

VATICAN CITY

Piazza San Pietro. Catch the Metro to Ottaviano or buses 19, 62, 64, or 492. City is generally inaccessible except for official business. Can look into gardens from cupola of Saint Peters.

Vatican City sits on the right bank of the Tiber river, in the foothills of the Monte Mario and Gianicolo section of Rome. In ancient Rome this was the site of the Gardens of Nero and the main circus where thousands of Christians were martyred. Saint Peter met his fate here around 67 AD. Today it is the world center for the Catholic Church, rich in priceless art, antiques, and spiritual guidance.

The Vatican (officially referred to as The Holy See) is a completely autonomous state within the Italian Republic and has its own radio station, railway, newspaper, stamps, money, and diplomatic representatives in major capitals. Though it doesn't have an army, the **Swiss Guards**, who are volunteers from the Swiss armed forces, guard the Vatican day and night.

PIAZZAS, FOUNTAINS, MONUMENTS, PALAZZI & GARDENS

PIAZZA NAVONA

Catch buses 70, 81, 87, 90.

The piazza is on the site of a stadium built by Domitian that he used for naval battles and other gladiatorial contests, as well as horse races. The style of the piazza is richly Baoroque, featuring works by two great masters, **Bernini** and **Borromini**. Located in the middle of the square is Bernini's fantastic **Fontana Dei Quattro Fiumi** (Fountain of Four Rivers), sculpted from 1647-51. The four figures supporting the large obelisk (a Bernini trademark) represent four rivers: the Danube, the Ganges, the Nile, and the Plata Rivers.

Besides the statue's obvious beauty, Bernini has hidden a subtle treasure in this sculpture. Notice the figure representing the Nile. Some historians interpret the shielding of its eyes from the facade of the church it is facing, **Santa Agnese in Agone**, as a statement of revulsion. This church was designed by Bernini's rival at the time, Borromini, and Bernini, as the story is told, playfully showed his disgust with his rival's design through the sculpted disgust in his statue. Others claim the revulsion comes from the fact that the church, originally a family chapel for Pope Innocent X's Palazzo Pamphili, was built on the location of an old neighborhood brothel.

To savor the artistic and architectural beauty, as well as the vibrant nightlife of the Piazza, choose a table at one of the local bars or cafés and try some ice cream, grab a coffee, or have a meal. Navona is one of Rome's many gathering spots for people of all ages. You'll find local art vendors, caricaturists, hippies selling string bracelets, and much more. This is a place you cannot miss if you come to Rome.

PIAZZA DI SPAGNA

Catch buses 52, 53, 56, 58, 60, 61, 62, 71, 81 or get off at Piazza di Spagna Metro stop.

This is one of the most beautiful and visited spots in Rome. It is named after the old Spanish Embassy to the Holy See that used to stand on the site. The 137 steps are officially called the *Scalinata della Trinita dei Monti*, and are named for the church which they lead to at the top. But most people just call them the **Spanish Steps**. The fountain in the middle of the piazza is known as the **Barcaccia** and was designed by Pietro Bernini in commoration of the big flood of 1598. To the right is the column of the **Immaculate Conception** erected in 1865 by Pius IX.

The Spanish Steps, besides being the location of fine works of art and architecture, are also a favorite meeting spot for Italians of all ages, and the place can get quite crowded at night. You'll find musicians, artists, caricaturists, palmists, tourists, and many others assembled together making this place perfect for people watching. Grab a bottle of wine (yes, you can drink in public in Italy) and sitby the fountain for an afternoon or an evening and watch the world pass by.

CAMPO DEI FIORI

Catch buses 46, 62, 64.

This is a typically Roman piazza that hosts a lively flower and food market every morning until 1:00pm. Here you'll find the cries of the vendors blending with the bargaining of the customers. A perfect place to see and smell the beauty of Rome. This used to be a square where heretics were burned at the stake and criminals were hanged. The monument in the middle is in memory of Giordano Bruno, a famous philosopher who was burned here in 1600.

This is another place to come at night, since there are plenty of impromptu concerts and a great restaurant, **La Carbonara**, that serves the best *Spaghetti alla Vongole Verace* I've ever had, and a great Irish Pub, **The Drunken Ship**.

TREVI FOUNTAIN

Catch buses 52, 53, 56, 58, 60, 61, 62, 71, 81.

Another meeting place for Italians in the evenings. You'll always find an impromptu guitar solo being performed as well as wine being drunk by many. A great place to hang out in the evenings and make new friends. This is the largest and most impressive of the famous fountains in Rome. It is truly specatacular when it is lit up at night. Commissioned by Clement XII, it was built by Nicola Salvi in 1762 from a design he borrowed from Bernini. In the central niche you see Neptune on his chariot drawn by marine horses preceded by two tritons. In the left niche you see the statue representing Abundance, to the right Health.

There is an ancient custom, or legend, or rumor, that says that all those who throw a coin into the foutain are destined to return to Rome. So turn your back to the fountain and throw a coin over your left shoulder with your right hand into the fountain and fate will carry you back. By the way it is completely illegal, and severely enforced, to walk in the fountain, especially to try and get wine money from the many coins in the pool of the fountain.

PANTHEON

Catch buses 70, 81, 87, 90.

The **Pantheon** is one of the most famous and definitely the best preserved monuments of ancient Rome, located in another piazza frequented by the locals and tourists all day. There some expensive restaurants and cafés/bars to grab a quick meal or drink from around the piazza in which the Pantheon sits. Besides the architectural beauty, the entrance area to the Pantheon is by far the coolest place in Rome during the heat wave of August. So if you want to relax in seemingly air conditioned comfort in the middle of a hot day, park yourself here.

First constructed by Agrippa in 27 BC, it was restored after a fire in 80 AD and returned to its original rotunda shape by the Emperor Hadrian. In 609 AD, it was dedicated as a Christian Church called Santa Maria and the Martyrs, and in the Middle Ages it served as a fortress. A variety of Popes stole its bronze ceiling and melted it into the cannons for Castel Sant'Angelo, as well as for the Baldacchino in Saint Peter's. The building is made up of red and grey Egyptian granite. Each of the sixteen columns is 12.5 meters high and is composed of a single block.

You enter the building by way of the cool and comfortable portal area and the original bronze door, and you can feel the perfect symmetry of space and harmony of its architectural lines. This feeling is somewhat lessened by the fact that the Roman authorities in their infinite wisdom have started charging for entrance to the building, and have placed a ticket booth inside along with a small souvenir stand. Nonetheless, you will still be awed by the marvelous dome (diameter 43 meters) with the hole in the middle.

There are three niches in the building, two of which contain **tombs**: the tomb of **Victor Emmanuel II** (died 1878), one of Italy's few war heros, and the tombs of **Umberto I** (died 1900) and **Queen Margherita** (died 1926), and in another niche the tomb of reknowned artist **Raphael Sanzio** (died 1520).

VILLA BORGHESE

Catch buses 95, 490, 495, 910.

The most picturesque park in Rome, complete with bike and jogging paths (you can rent bikes in the park), a lake where you can rent boats, a wonderful museum – **Galleria Borghese** – lush vegetation, large grass fields, the Roman **zoological park**, a large riding ring, and more.

This is the perfect place to come and relax in the middle of a hard day of touring. Kids of all ages will love to wander all over the park or simply cuddle up together and take a quick siesta.

The Borghese Gardens
This is a great sanctuary just outside the ancient walls of Rome. If you only want an afternoon's respite from the sights of the city, or you're tired of spending your time in your hotel room during the siesta hours, escape to the luscious and spacious **Borghese Gardens**.
To get to the gardens is simple enough: either exit the old walls of Rome through the gates at the Piazza del Popolo or at the top of the Via Veneto. From the Piazza del Popolo exit, the gardens will be on your right through the iron gates just across the busy Piazzale Flaminio. Once you enter you will be on the Viale Washington.
Anywhere to the left of you, after a few hundred meters, will be prime park land. From the Via Veneto exit, cross the major thoroughfare in front of you and you're in Borghese. From here stroll to your right and you will instantly find a pleasant area to picnic or take a small nap for the afternoon.
Borghese houses Rome's **zoo**, several museums (including Galleria Borghese and the Galleria Arte Moderna), playing fields for calcio, a small lake, an amphitheater, and many wooded enclaves to have a wonderfully secluded picnic (look out for those heated Italian couples).

Galleria Borghese
One of Rome's finest museums is in the Borghese Gardens, the **Galleria Borghese**. For those of you that entered the Gardens from Piazza del Popolo, it will be a long hike up the Viale Washington to the lake, and around it to the Viale Dell'Uccelleria (the zoo will be on your left) which leads directly to the Galleria Borghese.
From the Via Veneto it is not quite as long. From where you first entered the gardens, there is a road, Viale Del Museo Borghese, on your right. Take this all the way to the Galleria.
The Galleria Borghese was built by Dutch architect Hans van Santes during the 1820's. It houses a large number of rare masterpieces from many disciplines and countries. There are classical works of Greeks and Romans, along with 16th and 17th century paintings by such notables as Raphael, Titian, Caravaggio, and Antonella da Messina. Sculptures are also featured with works by Lorenzo Bernini, Pietro Bernini, and Houndon.
For more details, see the Galleria Borghese description below under *Museums.*

ROMAN NEIGHBORHOODS

PIAZZA DEL POPOLO

Catch buses 90, 119 or get off at Flaminio Metro stop.

This impressive piazza, and the ascent to the **Pincio**, was designed by G. Valadier at the beginning of the 19th century. The piazza is decorated on its sides with two semi-cycles of flowers and statues, and in the center is the **Egyptian Obelisk** that is 24 meters high and came from Egypt during the time of Ramses II in the 8th century BC. The obelisk was removed from Heliopolis by order of Augustus and initially erected in the Circus Maximus. Then in 1585, Sixtus V had it placed here in its present location.

There are two symmetrical baroque churches at the south end of the piazza flanking the intersection of the Via del Corso. These two churches, **Santa Maria dei Miracoli** (1678) and **Santa Maria in Monesanto** (1675) both have picturesque cupolas that were begun by C. Rainaldi and finished by Bernini and Carlo Fontana.

EERIE ROMAN TRIVIA

There is a movie theater directly next to Santa Maria dei Miracoli that played the first run release of the Exorcist when it came out in the 1970's. During the first showing of the film, the cross on the top of the church dislodged itself from its perch and shattered itself directly in front of the movie theater. No one was hurt. This is a true story.

VIA VENETO

Catch buses 52, 53, 56, 58 or get off at the Barberini Metro stop.

Definitely the most famous and most fashionable street in Rome. It used to be the center of all artistic activities as well as the meeting place for the jet set, but it doesn't quite have the same allure it used to. Nonetheless, it's still a great place to wander up the road, which is flanked by hotels, stores, and cafés.

At the bottom of the street in the **Piazza Barberini**, where you'll find the graceful **Fontana delle Api** (Fountain of the Bees) made by Bernini. Up a little ways on the right you will find the famous Church of Bones, **Santa Maria della Concezione**, which has a macabre arrangement of over 4,000 friars that have died over the centuries in the adjoining convent. The bones are located below the church in the **Cappucin crypt**. Up a little way is the grandiose **Palazzo Margherita**, built by G. Koch in 1890 and now the home of the American Embassy. You'll recognize it by the armed guards hanging around out front.

VIA APPIA ANTICA

Catch buses 118 and 218.

This celebrated of all Roman roads was begun by Appius Claudius Caecus in 312 BC. The road has been preserved in its original chracter as have the original monuments. Originally it was the chief line of communication between Rome and Southern Italy, Greece, and the eastern possessions of the Roman Empire.

Now it is a well travelled picturesque road to the country and the famous Roman/Christian **catacombs**.

TRASTEVERE

Catch buses 44, 75, 170, 710, 718, 719.

This is the perfect place for exploring the way Romans actually live. **Trastevere** literally means "across the river" and this separation has allowed the area to remain virtually untouched by the advances of time. Until recently it was one of the poorest sections of Rome, but now it is starting to become gentrified. Yet these changes have not altered Trastevere's charm. You'll find interesting shops and boutiques, and plenty of excellent restaurants among the small narrow streets and *piazzette* (small squares). The maze of streets is a fun place to wander and wonder where you're going to end up.

During the month of July the *Trasteverini* express their feeling of seperation from the rest of Rome with their summertime festival called **Noiantri**, meaning "we the others," in which they mix drunken revelry with religious celebration in a party of true bacchanalian proportions. *Trasteverini* cling to their roots of selling clothing and furnishings to make ends meet by continuing to hold the **Porta Portese** flea market on Sundays. Today, the goods sold are of much higher quality, especially the antiques, but the event is true Trastevere.

This area offers some of the best dining and casual night life in town. Here you can sit in a piazza bar sipping Sambuca or wine and watch the life of Rome pass before your eyes. To accommodate this type of activity many stores have begun to stay open later. Trastevere is a great place to enjoy for a day or even more, because it is the way Rome used to be.

ISOLA TIBERINA

Catch buses 44, 75, 170, 710, 718, 719.

Halfway across the river going towards Trastevere, this island used to be a dumping ground for dead and sick slaves. Then the Romans had a cult of healing *(aesculapius)* here in the 3rd century BC, and currently half its size is taken up by a hopsital. One of the bridges to the mainland, **Ponte Fabricio**, is the oldest in Rome. This is a good place to cross the Tiber going towards Trastevere if you've been exploring the Jewish Ghetto.

JEWISH GHETTO

Catch buses 780, 774, 717.

Located west of city center, next to the Tiber just across from Trastevere, you'll find the old **Jewish Ghetto** where Rome's Jewish population was forced to live for centuries. To find out more about this period check out the **Jewish Museum** in the **Sinagoga Ashkenazita** *(Tel. 06/687-5051)* that has a plan for the original ghetto, as well as artifacts from the 17th century Jewish community and more.

Besides learning about the history of the ghetto, you can find some of Rome's truly great restaurants here as well as see many ancient Roman buildings, arches, and columns completely incorporated into modern day buildings. It seems as if many structures were better preserved here, since the locals did not have the resources to tear them down and replace them.

PALAZZO BARBERINI

Via Quattro Fontane, 13. Tel. 854-8577. Admission L4,000. Hours 9:00am–7:00pm, Holidays 9:00am–1:00pm. Closed Mondays. Catch buses 95, 490, 495, 910.

Located just off the Piazza Barerbini on the Via Quattro Fontane, this baroque palace was started by Carlo Maderno in 1625 with the help of Borromini and was finished in 1633 by Bernini. The palace is the site of the **National Portrait Gallery**. Besides the wonderful architecture which shouldn't be missed, the gallery has many wonderful paintings such as *Marriage of St. Catherine* by Sodoma, *Portait of a Lady* by Piero di Cossimo, and *Rape of the Sabines* by Sodoma.

PALAZZO FARNESE

Piazza Farnese. Hours 9:00am–Noon. Monday–Thursday. Catch buses 23 and 280.

This palace represents one of the high points of Rennaissance architecture. It was started in 1514 by Antonio da Sangallo the Younger for Cardinal Alessandro Farnese (later Pope Pius III), and was continued by Michelangelo who added the large window, the molding on the facade, the thrid floor of the court, and the sides. It was finally finsihed by Giacomo della Porta. As well as being an architectural wonder, there is a first floor galery of frescoes depicting mythological subjects by the painters Carracci, Domenichino, and Reni.

GIANICOLO

Catch bus 41.

Offering one of the best panoramas of Rome, **Gianicolo hill** is located between Trastevere and the Vatican, across the river from the old city of

Rome. At the terrace of the Piazzale del Gianicolo, you'll find the equestrian statue of Giuseppe Garibaldi and a perfect photo opportunity. The walk may be a little tiring but the view is calming and serene, as is the lush vegetation.

CHURCHES

SAINT PAUL'S OUTSIDE THE WALLS

(San Paolo Fuori le Mura). Via Ostiense. Church open 7:00am–7:00pm. Cloisters Open 9:00am–1:00pm and 3:00pm–6:00pm. From the Piramide stop on the Metro take buses 23, 170, or 673.

Located a mile or so beyond the Porta Paolo, **St. Paul's Outside the Walls** (San Paolo Fuori le Mura) is the fourth of the patriarcal basilicas in Rome. It is second only in size to St. Peter's and sits above the tomb of St Paul's. It was built by Constantine in 314 and then enlarged by Valentinian in 386 and later by Theodsius. It was finally completed by Honorius, his son.

In 1826 the church was almost completely destroyed by a terrible fire and many of its great works of art were lost. Immediatley afterward, its renovation began and today it seems as magnificent as ever. So much so that every time my family returns to Rome we line up just inside the entrance to the *quadroportici* with its 150 granite columns and get our picture taken with one of the palm trees in the background. We've been doing this since the 1950's and in that time the palm in the background has grown from a stubby bush into a gigantic tree. Along with the exterior with its beautiful garden surrounded by the great rows of columns, the palms growing in the center, the gigantic statue of St. Paul, and the facade with mosaics of four prophets (Isaiah, Jeremaih, Ezekial, and Daniel) the interior of the basilica is quite lovely.

The interior is 120 meters long and has four rows of columns and five naves. The columns in the central nave are Corinthian that can be identified by their splendidly ornate capitals. The walls contain Medallion Portraits of the Popes from Saint Peter to Pius XI. On the High Altar still sits the ancient Gothic tabernacle of Arnolfo di Cambio (13th century) that was saved from the fire in 1826. Saint Paul rests beneath the altar in the confessional. The mosaic in the apse, with its dominating figure of Christ, was created by artists from the Republic of San Marino in 1220.

To the left of the apse is the **Chapel of St. Stephen**, with the large statue of the saint created by R. Rainaldi, and the **Chapel of the Crucifix** created by Carlo Maderno. This chapel contains the crucifix which is said to have spoken to Saint Bridget in 1370. Also here is St. Ignatius de Loyola, who took the formal vows that established the Jesuits as a religious order.

To the right of the apse is the **Chapel of San Lorenzo**, the **Chapel of Saint Benedict** with its 12 columns. Look for the cloisters with fragments of ancient inscriptions and sarcophagi from the early Christian era.

SANTA MARIA SOPRA MINERVA

Piazza della Minerva (behind the Pantheon). Hours 7:00am–Noon and 3:30pm–7:00pm. Catch buses 70, 81, 87,90.

Built on the pagan ruins of a temple to Minerva (hence the name Saint Mary above Minerva) this church was begun in 1280 by the Dominican brothers Sisto and Ristoro, who also began the beautiful Santa Maria Novella in Florence. The facade was created during the Rennaissance by Meo del Caprino in 1453.

The interior is divided into three naves, seperated by pilasters with ogival vaulting. You can find many tombs of famous personages of the 15th through the 16th centuries as well as valuable works of art. Saint Catherine of Siena, who died in Rome in 1380, lies beneath high altar. To the left of the altar is the statue of *Christ Carrying the Cross* created by the great Michelangelo in 1521.

Behind the altar are the tombs of Pope Clement VII and Leo X which were created by the Florentine sculptor Baccio Bandanelli. In the Sacristy is a chapel covered with frescoes by Antoiazzo Romano, brought here in 1637 from the house where Catherine of Siena died.

SAN PIETRO IN VICOLO

Piazza di San Pietro in Vicolo. Hours 7:00am–12:30pm and 3:30pm–6:00pm.

Located only a few blocks from the Coliseum, this church was founded in 442 as a shrine dedicated to preserving the chains with which Herod bound St. Peter in Jerusalem. Its single, completely unforgettable work is the seated figure of *Moses* created by the master Michelangelo himself. This statue captures the powerful personification of justice and law of the Old Testament.

In fact, Moses appears as if he is ready to leap to his feet and pass judgement on you. You can almost see the cloth covering his legs, or the long beard covering his face move in the breeze. Because of this one work, this church cannot be missed.

SANTA MARIA MAGGIORE

Piazza di Santa Maria Maggiore. Hours 8:00am–7:00pm. Catch buses 4, 9, 16, 27, 714, 715.

Like St. Paul's Outside the Walls, St. Peter's, and St. John Lateran, this is one of the four patriarchal basilicas of Rome. It is called *Maggiore* since it is the largest church in Rome dedicated to the Madonna. The facade, originally built in the 12th century, but badly tampered with in the 18th century is nothing to look at and so many people pass this church by.

But the interior, in all its 86 meters of simplistic splendor, is interesting and inspiring mainly because of the 5th-century mosaics, definitely the best in Rome, and its frescoes. On the right wall of the Papal Altar is the funeral monument to Sixtus V and on the left wall the monument to Pius V, both created by Fontana with excellent bas-reliefs. Opposite this chapel is the **Chapella Paolina**, sometimes referred to as the **Borghesana** since the sepulchral vaults of the wealthy Borghese family lie beneath it. Here you'll view the beautiful bas-relief monumental tombs to Paul V and Clement VIII on its left and right walls.

SAN GIOVANNI IN LATERANO

Via dei Querceti. Hours 6:00am–12:30pm and 3:30pm–7:00pm. Catch buses 16, 85, 87, and 650.

Another of the great basilicas of Rome, this is the actual cathedral church of Rome and of the whole Catholic world, and not St. Peter's. Bet you didn't know that? The simple and monumental facade of the church, created by Allessandro Galiliei in 1735, is topped by fourteen colossal statues of Christ, the Apostles, and saints. It rises on the site of the ancient palalce of Plautinus Lateranus (hence the name), one of the noble families of Rome many eons ago.

To get inside, you must pass through the bronze door that used be attached to the old Roman Senate house. The interior of the church, laid out in the form of a Latin cross, has five naves filled with historical and artistic objects. In total it is 150 meters long, while the **central nave** is 87 meters long. This central nave is flanked by 12 spires from which appear 12 statues of the Apostles from the 18th century. The wooden ceiling and the marble flooring are from the 15th century.

The most beautiful artistic aspect of the church is the vast transept, which is richly decorated with marbles and frescoes portraying the *Leggenda Aurea* of Constantine. This is here because the Emperor Constantine, after he became converted to Christianity, donated the building to the Catholic church. One piece of historical interest is the table of wood, on which it is said that Saint Peter served mass, which you'll find in the **Papal Altar**.

CHURCH OF SAN CLEMENTE

Via di San Giovanni Laterano. Admission L3,000. Hours to visit the basement 9:00am–1:00pm. Not on Sundays. Catch bus 65.

Located between the Coliseum and St. John Lateran is the beautiful **San Clemente**. One of the better preserved medieval churches in Rome,

ANGLO-SAXON CHURCHES IN ROME

*The largest group of churches in Rome that have remained under foreign protection belongs to the Anglo-Saxon countries. These churches include **San Silvestro in Capite**, St. Isidor, St. Patrick, Santa Susanna, and **Blessed Canadian Martyrs**.*

The English still retain the use of the church of San Silvestro in Capite, the Irish have the churches of St. Isidori and St. Patrick, Santa Susanna is the grandiose national church of the Americans, and the relatively modern Blessed Canadian Martyrs is spiritual home to the Canadian expatriates in Rome.

San Silvestro in Capite *is the most important from an historic viewpoint. Located on a corner of the crowded Piazza San Silvestro, this church is generally accepted to have been built in the 8th century by Popes Stephen III and Paul I, and possibly even earlier.*

The upper section of the building, the oratory, contains the bodies of St. Sylvester and St. Stephen. The church is layed out in a Latin cross and contains sumptuous, baroque, gilded stucco work. The term "In Capite" was added in 1530, when the head of St. John the Baptist was brought to the church from the oratory and placed in a niche in the high altar.

*The national church of the Irish in Rome, **St. Patrick**, stands on Via Boncompagni. The facade is somber and modern, and the interior is simple but contains many fine pictures and beautiful mosaics. **St. Isidori**, the other Irish church, located on the Via degli Artisit, is richly decorated in the grand 17th century style. Built in 1622 by the Spanish reformed Franciscans in honor of St. Isidor, a landowner in Madrid who died in 1170, it was taken over by the Irish Minor Friars in 1624 and redecorated in its current style.*

*Standing in Piazza San Bernardo on the Via XX Settembre is the national church of the Americans, **Santa Susanna**. Having been confirmed in that church, I thought I knew every detail about the fine structure until I started doing more research. It is presumed to be very old, since recent excavations under the foundations uncovered traces of Roman construction of the 3rd century. Of more recent historical significance is the simple well in the adjacent courtyard the church shares with the convent of the Sisters of St. Bernard which is attributed to the master himself, Michelangelo. Inside the paintings, stuccowork and ornaments all retain a colorful but austere 17th century quality.*

*The **Church of the Virgin and Blessed Canadian Martyrs**, built between 1952 and 1955 in a modern Gothic style, is dedicated to the eight Jesuit martyrs who suffered death in Canada during the 16th century. It is simple in nature and design and aesthetically pleasing to the eye, but nowhere near as interesting as its other Anglo-Saxon brethren.*

it was originally built in the fifth century. The Normans destroyed it in 1084 but it was reconstructed in 1108 by Pachal II. Today when you enter you are in what is called the **Upper Church**, a simple and basic basilica divided by two rows of columns. The altar is intricately inlaid with a variety of 12th century mosaics.

The thrill of this church is that all you have to do is descend a set of stairs to the **Lower Church**, which was discovered in 1857, and immediately you have left the Middle Ages and are now surrounded by early Christian frescoes and a small ancient altar. Then you can descend a shorter set of stairs and go to the third level where a small temple and a meeting room still exist from the days when Christians had to practice their religion below ground for fear of prosecution. The temple is of **Mithraic**, a lost religion known for their evil blood rites. Below this level are still more ruins that are in the process of being excavated. This church is perfect for a descent into four different levels of Roman/Christian history.

CHURCH OF SANTA CECILIA IN TRASTEVERE

Via dei Genovesi. Hours 10:00am–Noon and 4:00pm–6:00pm. Catch buses 181, 280, 44, 75, 717, 170, 23, 65.

Normally visitors don't go to Trastevere to visit churches. Instead they are attracted by the more secular delights of this part of Rome. But if you're interested in beautiful churches, **Santa Cecilia** is one to visit in Trastevere; the other is Santa Maria.

Santa Cecilia was founded in the fith century and had a make-over in ninth century as well as the 16th. A baroque door leads to a picturesque court, beyond which is a baroque facade, with a mosaic frieze above the portico, and a beautiful bell tower erected in the 12th century. There are several important works of art to be found in the church, not the least of which is the expressive statue of Santa Cecilia by Stefano Maderno. It represents the body of the saint in the exact position it was found when the tomb was opened in 1559.

Another place of interest to visit on the church grounds is the Roman house where Santa Cecilia suffered her martyrdom by being exposed to hot vapors. There are two rooms preserved, one of them the bath where she died. It still has the pipes and large bronze cauldron for heating water. A great church to visit, not just for the art, but also for the history.

SANTA MARIA IN TRASTEVERE

Piazza Santa Maria in Trastevere 1. Hours 7:00am–7:00pm. Mass at 9:00am, 10:30am, noon, and 6:00pm. Catch buses 181, 280, 44, 75, 717, 170, 23, 65.

A small church in Trastevere, in a piazza of the same name that is the most frequented by locals and tourists alike, making the church one of the most visited. Around this church are some of the best restaurants and cafés in all of Rome, the only dedicated English language theater, a handsome 17th century fountain where hippies hang out at all night long, and the Palace of San Calisto.

This was one of Rome's earliest churches and the first to be dedicated to the Virgin. It was built in the 3rd century and remodeled between 1130-1143. It is best known for its prized mosaics, especially the 12th and 13th century representation of the Madonna which adorns the facade of the church. The romanesque bell-tower was built in the 12th century. The interior is of three naves separated by columns purloined from ancient Roman temples.

On the vault you'll find exquisite mosaics depicting the Cross, emblems of the Evangelists, and Christ and the Madonna enthroned among the Saints (created by Domenichino in 1140). Lower dwon, the mosaics of Pietro Cavallini done in 1291 portray, in six panels, the life of the Virgin.

MUSEUMS

CAPITOLINE MUSEUM

Piazza del Campidoglio. Tel. 6710-2071,Admission L10,000. Hours 9:00am-1:30pm. Sundays 9:00am-1:00pm. Tuesdays and Saturdays also open from 5:00pm to 8:00pm. Closed Mondays. Catch buses 44, 46, 56, 57, 90, 90/ 94, 186, 710, 713, 718, 719.

Actually the **Capitoline Museum** is actually two museums, the **Capitolone** and the **Palazzo dei Conservatori**.

The **Capitoline** is the perfect place to come to see what ancient Romans looked like. Unlike Greek sculpture, which glorified the subject, Roman sculpture captured every realistic characteristic and flaw. There are rooms full of portrait busts dating back to the republic and imperial Rome, where you have many individuals of significance immortalized here, whether they were short, fat, thin, ugly. Here they remain, warts and all. Because of these very real depicitions of actual Romans, and many other more famous sculptures, this museum has to rank second only in importance to the Vatican collections.

Besides the busts, you'll find a variety of celebrated pieces from antiquity including *Dying Gaul, Cupid and Psyche*, the *Faun*, and the nude and voluptuous *Capitalone Venice*. Then in the **Room of the Doves** you'll find two wonderful mosaics that were taken from Hadrian's Villa many centuries ago. One mosaic is of the doves drinking from a basin, and the other is of the masks of comedy and tragedy. Besides these items in the interior, the exterior itself was designed by none other than the master himself, Michelangelo.

The **Palace of the Conservatori** is actually three museums in one, the **Museum of the Conservatori**, the **New Museum**, and the **Pinocoteca Capitolina**. It too was also constructed by a design from Michelangelo. Their draw to me, and most people young at heart, are the largest stone head and stone foot you're ever likely to see. A great place to take a few pictures. These pieces are supposed to be fragments from the statue of Constantine. Wouldn't that have been a sight to see?

You could wander here among the many ancient Roman and Greek scultptures and paintings but remember to see the famous *Boy with a Thorn*, a graceful Greek sculpture of a boy pulling a thorn out of his foot, the *She-Wolf of the Capitol*, an Etruscan work of Romulus and Remus being suckled by the mythical wold of Rome, the death mask bust of Michelangelo, the marble *Medusa* head by Bernini, the celebrated painting *St. Sebastian* by Guido Reni that shows the saint with arrows shot into his body, and the famous Caravaggio work, *St. John the Baptist*.

And don't forget to find *La Buca della Verita*, the mouth of truth. This is one museum you simply cannot miss while in Rome.

NATIONAL MUSEUM - MUSEO DELLE TERME

Baths of Diocletian, Viale di Terme. Admission L2,000. Hours 9:00am–2:00pm. Sundays until 1:00pm. Closed Mondays. Catch buses 57, 64, 65, 75, 170, 492, 910.

If you like sculpture you'll love this collection of classical Greek and Roman works, as well as some early Christian sarcophagi and other bas-relief work. Located in the **Baths of Diocletian**, which are something to see in and of themselves, this museum is easily accesible since it is located near the train station and right across from the Republicca Metro stop. Since there are so many fine works here, you should spend a good half day perusing the items, but remember to start with the best, which are located in the *Hall of Masterpieces*. Here you'll find the *Pugilist*, a bronze work of a seated boxer, and the *Discobolus*, a partial sculpture of a discus thrower with amazing muscle development.

At the turn of the century this collection was graced with the Ludovisi collection, collected by Cardinal Ludovico Ludovisi, and by a number of Roman princes. There are many fine works of art, the most inspiring of which is the the celebrated *Dying Gaul and His Wife*, a colossal sculpture from Pergamon created in the thrid century BC. The collection also contains the famous Ludovisi throne, created in the 5th century BC and is adorned with fine Greek bas-reliefs.

Another must-see in the museum is the *Great Cloister,* a perfectly square space surrounded by an arcade of one hundred Doric columns. It is one of the most beautiful achitectural spaces in Rome, which is something to say. Rumor has it that it was designed and built by Michelangelo in 1565, which may be the case, but since he was so busy many experts believe that it is actually the work of one of his more famous, and possibly intimate pupils, Jacopo del Duca.

GALLERIA BORGHESE

Villa Borghese, Piazza dell'Uccelliera 5. Tel. 845-8577. Admission L4,000. Hours 9:00am-7:00pm. Holidays 9:00am-1:00pm. Closed Mondays. Catch buses 95, 490, 495, 910.

Located in the most picturesque public park in Rome, this is a gallery to visit before or after a nice picnic lunch in the shade of the many trees or by the large man-made lake in the center of the park. On the ground floor of the museum is their sculpture collection, which would be superb if not for the fact that it is located in Rome, but the main draw of this museum is the beauty of the gallery of paintings on the first floor.

Before you abandon the sculptures, take note of the reclining *Pauline Borghese,* created by Antonio Canova in 1805. She was the sister of Napoleon, married off to one of the wealthiest families in the world at the time to ensure poeace and prosperity. She looks quite enticing posing half naked on a lounge chair. Another work not to miss is *David and the Slingshot* by Bernini in 1619. It is actually a self-portrait.

On the first floor there are many great works especially the *Madonna and Child* by Bellini, *Young Lady with a Unicorn* by Raphael, *Madonna with Saints* by Lotto, and countless works by Caravaggio.

MUSEUM OF VILLA GIULIA

Piazza di Villa Giulia. Admission L8,000. Hours 9:00am-7:00pm. Holidays 9:00am-1:00pm. Closed Mondays. Catch buses 19b or 30b.

Located in the Palazzo di Villa Giulia, which was built in 1533 by Julius III. This archaeological museum contains ancient sculptures, sarcophogi, bas-reliefs, and more, and is separated into five sections consisting of 34 rooms.

Items of interest include the archaic statues created in the 5th century BC of a *Centaur,* and *Man on a Marine Monster*; Estruscan clay sculptures of *Apollo, Hercules with a Deer,* and *Goddess with Child*; objects from the necropoli at Cervetri including a terracotta work of *Amazons with Horses* created in the 6th century BC and a sarchophagus of a "married couple," a masterpiece of Etruscan sculpture created in the 6th century BC.

VATICAN MUSEUMS

Viale Vaticano. Tel. 6988-3333. Admission L13,000. Summer hours 8:45am–1:00pm. Winter hours 9:00am–4:00pm. Saturday 9:00am–1:00pm. Closed Sundays. The last Sunday of every month they are open and entrance is free. Catch buses 19, 23, 32, 45, 51, 81, 492, 907, and 991.

Pinacoteca Vaticana

A wonderful collection of masterpieces from many periods, covering many styles from primitive to modern paintings. Look for paintings by Giotto (who was the great innvoator of Italian painting since prior to his work Italian paintings had been Byzantine in style), many works by Raphael, the famous *Brussels Tapestries* with episodes from the Acts of the Apostles created by Pieter van Aelsten in 1516 from sketches by Raphael, and countless paintings of the Madonna, Virgin, Mother and Child, etc.

Pius Clementine Museum

Known mainly as a sculpture museum, it was founded by Pius VI and Clement XIV. You can also find mosaic work and sarcophogi from the 2nd, 3rd and 4th centuries. One mosaic in particular is worth noting, the *Battle between the Greeks and the Centaurs*, created in the first century AD. The bronze statue of Hercules and the **Hall of the Muses** that contain statues of the Muses and the partons of the arts are also worth noting. Here you can also find many busts of illustrious Romans including Caracalla, Trajan, Octavian and more.

In the **Octagonal Court** are some of the most important and the beautiful statuies in the history of Western art, especially the *Cabinet of the Laocoon*. This statue portrays the revenge of the gods on a Trojan priest, Laocoon, who had invoked the wrath of the goids by warning his countrymen not to admit the Trojan horse. In revenge the gods sent two enormous serpents out of the sea to destroy Laocoon and his two sons.

Chiaramonti Museum

Founded by Pope Pius VII, whose family name was Chiaramonti, this museum includes a collection of over 5,000 Pagan and Christian works. Here you can find Roman Sarcophogi, *Silenus Nursing the Infant Bacchus*, busts of Caesar, the Statue of Demosthenes, the famous *Statue of the Nile* with the 16 boys representing the 16 cubits of the annual rise of the Nile, as well as a magnificent Roman chariot recreated in marble by the sculpture Franzone in 1788.

Etruscan Museum

If you can't make it to any of the necropoli around Rome, at least come here and see the relics of a civilization that preceded Ancient Rome.

Founded in 1837 by Gregory XVI, it contains objects excavated in the Southern part of Etruria from 1828-1836, as well as pieces from later excavations around Rome. Here you'll find an Etruscan tomb from Cervetri, as well as bronzes, gold objects, glass work, candelbra, necklaces, rings, funeral urns, amphora and much more.

Egyptian Museum

If you can't make it to Cairo to see their splendid exhibit of material excavated from a variety of Egyptian tombs, stop in here. Created by Gregory XVI in 1839, this musem contains a valuable documentary of the art and civilization of ancient Egypt.

Here you will find sarcophogi, reproductions of portraits of famous Egyptian personalities, works by Roman artists who were inspired by Egyptian art, a collection of wooden mummy cases and funeral steles, mummies of animals, a collection of papyri with hieroglyphics, and much more.

Library of the Vatican

Founded through the efforts and collections of many Popes, this museum contains many documents and incunabula. Today the library contains over 500,000 volumes, 60,000 ancient manuscripts, and 7,000 incunabuli. My favorite are the precious manuscripts, especially the *Codex Vaticanus B* or the 4th century Bible in Greek.

Appartamento Borgia

Named after Pope Alexander VI, whose family name was Borgia, since he designed and lived in these lavish surroundings. (What about that vow of poverty?) From the furnishings to the paintings to the frescoes of Isis and Osiris on the ceiling, this little "museum" is worth a look.

Sistine Chapel

This is the private chapel of the Popes but it is famous for some of the most wonderful masterpieces ever created, many by **Michelangelo** himself. Michelangelo started the ceiling in 1508 and it took him four years to finish it. On the ceiling you'll find scenes from the Bible, among them the *Creation*, where God comes near Adam, who is lying down, and with a simple touch of his hand imparts the magic spark of life. You can aslo see the *Separation of Light and Darkness*, the *Creation of the Sun and Moon*, *Creation of Trees and Plants*, *Creation of Adam*, *Creation of Eve*, *The Fall and the Expulsion from Paradise*, the *Sacrifice of Noah and his Family* and the *Deluge*.

But on the wall behind the altar is the great fresco of the *Last Judgment* by Michelangelo. It occupies the entire wall (20 meters by 10 meters) and was commissioned by Clement VII. Michelangelo was past 60 when he started the project in 1535. He completed it seven years later in 1542. Michelangelo painted people he didn't like into situations with evil connotation in this frescoe. The figure of Mides, with asses' ears, is the likeness of the Master of Ceremonies of Paul III, who first suggested that other painters cover Michelangelo's nude figures. This eventually was done by order of Pius IV, who had Daniele da Volterra cover the most prominent figures with cloth.

These changes were left in when the entire chapel underwent its marvelous transformation a few years back, bringing out the vibrant colors of the original frescoes that had been covered by centuries of dirt and soot.

Rooms of Raphael

Initially these rooms were decorated with the works of many artists of the 15th century, but because Pope Julius II loved the work of Raphael so much, he had the other paintings destroyed and commissioned Raphael to paint the entire room himself. He did so, but spent the rest of his life in the task. Not nearly as stupendous as the Sistine Chapel work by Michelangelo, but it still is one of the world's masterpieces.

Chapel of Nicholas V

Decorated with frescoes from 1448-1451 by Giovanni da Fiesole. The works represent scenes from the life of Saint Stephan in the upper portion and Saint Lawrence in the lower.

The Loggia of Raphael

Divided into 13 arcades with 48 scenes from the Old and New Testaments, these were executed from the designs of Raphael by his students, Giulo Romano, Perin del Vaga, and F. Penni. The most outstanding to see are the *Creation of the World, Creation of Eve, The Deluge, Jacob's Dream, Moses Receiving the Tablets of Law, King David,* and the *Birth of Jesus.*

Grotte Vaticano

The Vatican caves seem to be a well-kept secret even though they've been around for some time. I think that's because you need special permission to enter them, and if you haven't made plans prior to your arrival it is quite difficult to gain access at short notice. To gain permission you need to contact the **North American College** in Rome *(Via dell'Umita 30, Tel. 672-256 or 678-9184).*The entrance to the Grotte is to the left of the basilica of St Peter's where the Swiss Guards are posted. The Grotte were dug out of the stratum between the floor of the actual cathedral and the previous Basilica of Constantine. This layer was first excavated during the Rennaissance. After passing fragments of inscriptions and mosaic compositions, tombstones, and sarcophogi, you descend a steep staircase to get to the Lower Grottos, also called the **Grotte Vecchie** (the Old Grottos).

Here you'll find pagan and Christian necropoli dating from the 2nd and 3rd century. The Grotte are divided into three naves seperated by massive pilasters that support the floor of St. Peter's above. Along the walls are numerous tombs of popes and altars adorned with mosaics and sculpütes. At the altar is the entrance to the **Grotte Nuove** (New Grottos), with its frescoed walls, marble statues, and bas-reliefs.

MUSEO DELLA CIVILITA ROMANA
Get off at the EUR stop on the Metro.
Always wanted to see a scale model of ancient Rome? If so, a perfect replica of Rome during the height of empire in the 4th century BC is in the **Museum of Roman Civilization** in EUR. This piece, called *Plastico*, is an exquisitely detailed plaster model that brings ancient Rome to life. Even if you are not a museum person, this exhibit is well worth seeing. Ideal for kids of all ages.

WALKING TOUR OF MICHELANGELO'S ROME

Even though he was Tuscan born and bred, and is still considered Florence's native son. Rome helped develop **Michelangelo Buonarotti** into the world's greatest artist, and in Rome he spent most of his adult life. Michelangelo specialized in four distinct art forms – sculpture, painting, architecture, and poetry. Rome at that time was a run-down faded city, but it was where Michelangelo became the wonder of his time, and the master of all ages.

The Fabric of Rome in the Mid-Fifteenth Century
At the age of 21, in June 1436, Michelangelo Buonarotti arrived in the city of Rome. The contrasts between Rome, a dirty, noisy, chaotic place, practically in a state of complete disrepair, and Florence, where order, reason, and beauty were cherished and cultivated, were immense. Many tourists today still consider this to be true.

This once vast city had turned to pasture lands outside the Roman walls. Sheep grazed among the ruins of ancient Rome, and the population, which had shrunk to a mere 50,000 from its height of over 1 million inhabitants, was beset with disease and a lack of potable water. But even in this setting Michelangelo blossomed, and Rome is where he created many of his most memorable masterpieces. Uncovering these works from the many corners of Rome can be the highlight of any trip to Italy, and I've laid it out for you in a special walking tour of Michelangelo's Rome.

The Search

For most people, the **Vatican** and **St. Peter's** offer the extent of Michelangelo's influence on Rome. But Vatican City holds just the beginning of the fabric Michelangelo wove into the tapestry of Roman life. It is true that nothing yet conceived can rival the magnificence of the **Sistine Chapel**, which is dominated by Michelangelo's powerful ceiling, made even more so by the recent cleaning that again allow the colors to jump out at you. And you also shouldn't miss the apocalyptic *Last Judgment*, located on the immense wall above the main altar. Every time I return to Rome I visit these two masterpieces to reassure myself that their beauty is not just a figment of my imagination.

These two works seem to epitomize the contrasts of Michelangelo's long career, which seems to coincide with the rise and fall of the Renaissance itself. The *Last Judgment*, begun when Michelangelo was in his 60's, marks the end of his life's work, and the Renaissance's magnificence, while the glorious Sistine ceiling commemorates the peak of excellence.

These two works, coupled with *La Pieta*, located just to the right of the entrance inside St. Peter's, completes for most visitors to Rome the extent of Michelangelo's influence on the Eternal City. Remember to wear long pants, men, otherwise the Vatican guards will not allow you entrance into St. Peter's. By the way, this holds true for most, if not all, monuments and museums in Rome.

Other Works

Michelangelo's Roman tapestry spreads over the entire city. To attempt to see every piece of Michelangelo's work would be virtually impossible, therefore we cover only the most important pieces in this little tour. Get your walking shoes on.

To begin, return to the Vatican, to the art works overlooked by most. The **Vatican Museum** houses two definite musts for any Italian expert and lover. The beautiful sculpture *Apollo Belvedere* should be viewed even if you will be visiting, or have seen, the godlike *David* in Florence. The Apollo's importance stems from the fact that it was Michelangelo's inspiration for his ageless *David*.

Palazzo Farnese

To get to our next destination, cross the **Ponte Vittorio Emmanuelle** and walk down the Corso Vittorio Emmanuelle on the right hand side.

Follow this street, then turn into **Campo dei Fiori** after you pass the Palazzo Della Cancelleria. The Campo dei Fiori was once the site of brutal executions, but now is the home to a beautiful open air market every morning.

Walk through the Campo dei Fiori and you'll find the **Palazzo Farnese** at the other end. Situated in one of Rome's most picturesque quarters, the Palazzo Farnese is one of the most unexplored examples of Michelangelo's work, since it now houses the French Embassy.

The Palazzo was begun in 1514 by Antonio Sangano, The Younger, and was then passed onto Michelangelo's creative genius and imagination to develop the finishing touches. Just prior to overall completion, Michelangelo handed over the reins of design to Giacamo Della Porta, but many of the master's inclusions were left untouched. The most apparent Michelangelo marks are the pieces above the main doorway, but if you have any diplomatic pull (possibly a brother or cousin who happens to be a US Senator) or more realistically try to get a note from your Congressman, you should be able to get yourself inside to see the elegant third floor. A bribe to the French won't help, incidentally, since the French government rents this exquisite building for the incredible fee of only 1 lira a year.

Since it is hard to get inside, go around the left of the building to the **Arch of the Palazzo Farnese** over Via Guilia. This bridge was designed by Michelangelo and connects the Piazza Farnese with its satellite houses that were originally on the river's edge, but now are restricted by the high walls and roadway of the Lungotevere. Michelangelo's plan had been to connect the Palazzo Farnese with its cousin in Trastevere, the Villa Farnesina, by a private bridge. Unfortunately for the French, and the rest of us, the bridge was never built.

On to the Piazza Navona

From here stroll through the aforementioned Campo dei Fiori, across the Via Vittorio Emmanuelle II, onto the small Via Cuccogno and into the elegant **Piazza Navona**. On a hot day, the fountains here are a visitor's oasis, allowing for needed foot-soaking refreshment. But before you take your shoes off and relax your sore feet by soaking them in one of the fountains, stroll to the center of the piazza and take note of the magnificence of Bernini's **Fontana Dei Quattro Fiumi** (Fountain of four Rivers). The fours figures supporting the large obelisk (a Bernini trademark) represent four rivers, the Danube, the Ganges, the Nile and the Plata Rivers; see the story behind this statue in the *Piazza Navona* section above.

Even though this has close to nothing to do with Michelangelo, it is one of the many pieces of Roman history intertwined almost inconspicuously with its present. And it's a good place for a refreshing break. Try the *gelato* (ice cream) at the small *gelateria* a few paces down the small unnamed road to the left of **Le Tre Scalini**, one of Rome's best attractions. True, the *gelato* at Le Tre Scalini is also good, if you are willing to pay an exorbitant price for a small scoop. That's why it's wise to simply walk down the road to a smaller, better, less expensive gelato place. With ice cream in hand you can sit in the piazza, soak your feet if you wish, and partake in the Roman tradition of people watching.

Santa Maria Sopra Minerva

The last stop on today's *passegiatta* involves a short walk to the **Piazza Della Minerva** and the church of **Santa Maria Sopra Minerva**. To get there, leave the Piazza Navona via the exit directly across from Le Tre Scalini. As you exit, bear to your left and go down the Via di Crescene to the piazza directly in front of the imposing **Pantheon**. If you haven't seen the Pantheon yet, stay awhile and go inside. It's a beautiful sight and pleasantly cool in the interior. The Piazza Della Minerva is around the left of the Pantheon.

Santa Maria Sopra Minerva is a combination of an early Renaissance exterior and an austere Gothic interior. Besides displaying splendid frescoes by Fillipino Lippi and elaborate marble tombstones made by Michelangelo of two Medici popes (Leo X and Clement VII, who played large roles in the sculptor's life), the masterpiece of the church to the left of the main altar is Michelangelo's *Christ Bearing the Cross*. This obviously spiritual sculpture epitomizes how much the church meant to Michelangelo, even though some historians claim he was a closet homosexual.

More Buried Treasure

The next day's itinerary is much shorter and begins at the church of **San Pietro in Vincolo** near the Cavour Metro stop. Here you can admire Michelangelo's glowering, biblical figure *Moses*, which emphatically demonstrates the qualities of excellence, perfection, and intensity that make Michelangelo's works so memorable.

From here, grab the Metro at Cavour and take it to Termini. From Termini transfer to Linea A and go one stop to Repubblica. In the **Piazza della Repubblica** is the church of **Santa Maria Degli Angeli**, whose interior was created by Michelangelo out of the ruins of the enormous **Diocletian Baths**. Even though the interior was modified in the 18th century, Michelangelo's creative transformation is still very apparent.

The monumental task of reconstructing a church's interior contrasts well with our next stop, a virtually unknown and infinitely smaller creation. Go up the Via VE Orlando to the **Piazza San Bernardo**, where you'll find the national Catholic church of Americans in Italy, **Santa**

Susanna. Its baroque exterior and interior, rich paintings, stucco work, and ornaments has played host to many a visiting American dignitary, with OJ Simpson and George Wallace balancing out the spectrum. (I got both their autographs when they were visiting. I think OJ's might be worth something now.) Also, in case you were paying attention, as we go through the Piazza San Bernardo, there is a copy of the figure *Moses* we just saw.

The paintings inside Santa Susanna's, though created many years after the life of Michelangelo, and have nothing to do with this tour except to show you some more of Rome's glory, are exquisitely beautiful and can be fully enjoyed with the realization that many casual visitors to Rome never witness their grandeur. What we came to see is not these paintings, but the small **well** in the adjacent courtyard. Surrounded by what was once the convent of the sisters of San Bernardo, this well is one of the smaller threads of Michelangelo's tapestry in Rome.

The architrave (main form and structure) and pilaster (rectangular column work on the well) were created by the master himself. And to think that after Mass every other Sunday, we the parishioners of Santa Susanna would congregate here for coffee and donuts. Isn't Rome magnificent?

ROME'S BEAUTIFICATION PROGRAM

Rome is beginning its beautification process to prepare for the celebration of two thousand years of Christianity. Many plans are in the works, but already the Roman authorities have restored the Spanish Steps and outlawed eating, drinking, or loitering on them. In theory this is wonderful, but in true Italian fashion, just after the newly renovated steps had been opened in December 1995, natives and tourists alike could be seen eating sandwiches and drinking soda while the police looked on passively. But don't try and bring a bottle of wine, a guitar, and some long-haired friends with you. Then the police will intervene.

To open up the city even more to the many admirers from all over the world who will descend to celebrate the beginning of the third millennium, another metro line is being built from the Coliseum to Saint Peter's, traveling under the Old Town of Rome. This will afford quicker access, for those intimidated by taking the bus, to the Pantheon, Piazza Navona, and Campo dei Fiore, as well as the nightlife of Trastevere across the river.

With the fear of further traffic congestion playing on their minds, authorities have also approved a tunnel along the Tiber to bypass Castel Sant'Angelo and Saint Peter's. The entire area is being envisioned as a vast pedestrian paradise, which would completely enhance the beauty that is Rome. So if you're coming to Rome at the turn of the century, be prepared to see a few changes in the eternal city.

LITERARY ROME

For centuries, Rome has been luring artists from all over the world to bathe in its charms, especially writers seeking inspiration for their next tomes. Here you can explore the city and imagine that Virgil, Robert and Elizabeth Browning, Hans Christian Anderson, Henry James, Lord Byron, Mark Twain, Goethe and more all traced the same steps you are taking.

If you are interested in following almost exactly in these famous writers' footsteps, read on, for we are going to trace for you the paths taken, the places stayed and the restaurants/cafes frequented by literati of times gone by.

The perfect place to start is the **Piazza di Spagna**. In the 18th and 19th century this piazza was literally (no pun intended) the end of the line for many traveling coaches entering the city. Near the western end of the piazza, the **Via delle Carrozze** (Carriage Road) reminds us that this is where these great coaches tied up at the end of their long journeys. More often then not, travelers would make their homes in and around this area.

At *Piazza di Spagna #23*, you'll find **Babbington's Tea Room** (see Chapter 12, *Where to Eat*) where Byron, Keats, Shelley, and Tobias Smollett all shared at one time or another some afternoon tea. Across the piazza, *at #26*, is the **Keats/Shelley Memorial** where Keats spent the three months before his death in 1821 at the age of 25. The memorial contains some of Keats' manuscripts, letters, and memorabilia, as well as relics from Shelley and other British writers. Keats and Shelley still reside in Rome, in the **Protestant Cemetery** near the metro stop Piramide. Located on the *Via Ciao Cestio 6*, it is open all day, but visitors must ring the bell for admittance. Next, *at #66 in the piazza*, the grand poet George Gordon (Lord) Byron took lodging in 1817 and performed work on *Child Harolde's Pilgrimage*.

From here, you can explore the **Via Condotti**, Rome's center for consumerism. **Caffe Greco**, *at #86*, is where you could have found Goethe, Hans Christian Anderson or Mark Twain sipping an aperitif a little stronger than what you can find at Babbington's. In 1861, one of the upper rooms were also the lodgings for Hans Christian Anderson of *Ugly Duckling* fame. A little further along, *at #11 Via Condotti*, poet Alfred Lord Tennyson and writer William Thackeray made their home when they visited Rome.

Just off the Via Condotti, *at Via Bocca di Leone #14*, is the **Hotel D'Inghlitera** where Mark Twain scratched many pages for *Innocents Abroad* in 1867 and where Henry James initially stayed during his forays into the Eternal City. Later on, James would reside at the **Hotel Plaza** *at Via del Corso 126* where he began his work *From a Roman Notebook,* which described his exploration of the city, its culture, history, and expatriate social activities.

Further down the Corso, *at #20,* is where the German poet Goethe made his home from 1786 to 1788. Here he penned his immortal travel diary *Italian Journey.* Goethe's old house now contains a small museum of photographs, prints, journals, books, and other material relating to the poet's travels in Italy.

At Bocca di Leone, #13, you'll see where Robert and Elizabeth Browning lived in 1853. This is where Robert got the inspiration for his epic poem *The Ring and the Book,* a tragic tale of the murder of the Comparini family and their daughter Pompilia (who had lived on the Via Bocca di Leone in 1698), by Pompilia's husband, Count Franchescini.

Another famous writer who resided in Rome was the magnificent Charles Dickens, who, *at Via del Babuino 9,* wrote part of his *Pictures From Italy* . If you get a chance, try and read this book, since it brings the Rome of that time to life as vividly as he brought London to life in his many other books.

14. NIGHTLIFE

Rome is filled with many discos, pubs, and *birrerias* (bars) where you can spend your evening hours having wild and raucous times. If that's what you want to do, I've compiled a list of the best places to go. But if you want to do like (most of) the Romans do, seat yourself at a bar/café or restaurant, and savor the beauty that is Rome. Linger in the evening air while recalling the day's events or planning tomorrow's. Slow down your pace. Adapt to the culture. Be one with the Force, and so on. You get the picture.

Anyway, there are a few places in Rome in which you can do just that, become part of the culture. The best is in **Trastevere** at one of the little open air cafés where you can either stay all night sipping a few glasses of wine, or visit after you've had your dinner in one of the restaurants around the piazza (see Trastevere, *Where to Eat*). This is definitely THE best place to go for a night out in Rome.

Another is **Campo dei Fiori**, which also has many cafés and restaurants where you can sit while you watch the life of Rome amble past. The other nightspot is around **Piazza Navona**, of course, where you can admire the fine sculpture, the beautiful people, and the many different life forms comprising the streetlife of Rome.

But if this sedate, appreciative, slow-paced lifestyle is not for your, by all means try one of the following. I found them all perfect for letting off some steam.

BARS & CLUBS

JACKIE O, *11 Via Bon Compagni, Tel. 06/488-5457.*

This place has been famous for years and the fact that it is located just off the Via Veneto makes their prices sky high. The place is a combination, in three different areas, of a piano bar, a disco, and restaurant, so conceivably you can go to dinner, grab an after dinner drink, then dance the night away at the same place. It claims to be Rome's most prestigious and best loved nightclub, with members of the jet set visiting whenever they're in Rome, and from the atmosphere I can see why. Besides the high class but bawdy decor, you can expect discreet and professional service while at Jackie O's.

BIRRERIA LOWENBRAU MUNCHEN, *Via delle Croce 21, Tel. 06/ 679-5569.*

You can eat here if the need for Viennese cuisine creeps up on your stomach (you'll find plenty of German tourists here enjoying the staples from their homeland), but I find it's a perfect place to have the best German beer on tap. It's a festive place to throw down a few pints with your travel partners. They serve their large beers in glass boots which adds to the charm of this *birreria*. In conjunction you're in one of the best nighttime areas in Rome, around the Piazza di Spagna, where you can go for a casual stroll before or after your drinking adventure.

FLAN O'BRIEN'S PUB, *Via Napoli 29/34. Tel. 06/488-0418. Pints L8,000, Half Pints L5,000, Panini L4,000. Open all day from 9:00am to 1:00am.*

There's a café/bar store front on Via Nazionale, but this place is in the back on Via Napoli. Run by Italians, but has the look and feel of a real Irish pub. Definitely not of the same ilk as the one I know by the same name in Boston, since that one is a hole in the wall.

There are two bars, both serving Harp Lager and Stout, Kilkeny, and Guiness on tap. The menu is relatively meager but you can get a *Panino* (sandwich) of ham and cheese, which is good. All wood decor, a little brightly lit, with polished brass fitting, framed pictures of vaguely Irish origin, and stained glass and floral pattern wallpaper. There are tables and plenty of places to pull up a stool, and they play great music by which to enjoy a pint or two. The Hotel Britania just across the street contributes to the flow of people that can truly appreciate its ambiance. It gets fairly crowded on Friday and Saturday nights.

NED KELLY'S, *Via delle Copelle 13. Pints L8,000, Half pints L5,000. Open 12:30am - 3:30pm and 6:00pm - 1:00am.*

As you guessed, this is an Aussie pub. At lunch they serve amazing salads with a beer and mineral water for only L10,000-15,000. If you're a foreign student you get discounts in the evening by buying a membership card for the night, for only L2,000. You'll save that on your first pint. For all of you who know and love the camaraderie and festivities associated with Australian people, you'll want to check this place out. It's located near the Pantheon, so it's in the center of everything and very hard to miss.

THE TUBE PUB, *Via Avignonesi 10A. Pints L8,000. Half Pints L5,000.*
A real hole in the wall – actually a real bottom of the basement. Located just off the Piazza Barberini in the basement of a building down

this dark and dingy street, this place has a lot of character and a dart board to boot. Two separate areas, one near the bar with booths which is frequented by the younger set, and the other with tables frequented by many ex-pats from abroad living in Rome.

NIGHT AND DAY, *Via dell'Oca 50. Pints L8,000. Half Pints L5,000. Open until 5am.*

Yes, it's open until 5am, so put your drinking hat on. They also serve a lovely lunch from 12:30pm until 3:30pm with great salads and shepherd pies. You'll find your Guiness on tap for strength, as well as a nice assortment of local Frascati wines graciously served to you by the owners Stefano and Simone.

FIDDLER'S ELBOW, *Via dell'Olmata 43. Tel. 06/487-2110. Open 7 days a week 4:30pm - 1:15am. Pints L8,000 Half Pints L5,000.*

Located just off the Piazza Santa Maria Maggiore near the train station, this place claims to be Rome's oldest pub, and it sure looks like it. That slightly ratty ambiance helps to give it a truly Irish flavor. The Guiness helps too, as do the crowds of Anglophones. So if you're looking for a taste of home, or just want to hear another English speaking person, "come on down." No food is actually served so if you're hungry you'll have to make do with chips, peanuts, or salami sticks. They also have places in Florence and Venice, so you can have a pint at the "Elbow" throughout Italy.

OLD MARCONI, *Via Santa Prassese 9c, 00184 Roma. Tel. 06/486-636. Open until 1:30am.*

Located near it's brother pub, The Fiddler's Elbow, this one serves fine English fare like fish and chips. You'll find Guiness, Harp, and Kilkeny on tap (pint L7,000, half-pint L4,000), and pleasant company all around. This and Fiddler's are the main hangout for Anglo's in the city, but they'll accommodate a Yank if you've got a sense of humor.

BIRRERIA TRILUSSA, *Via Aruleno Cello Sabino 29P, Tel. 06/7154-2180. Pints L8,000. Half Pints L5,000.*

Located a stone's throw away from the Campo dei Fiori, you can see a few shady characters in here, but all are having fun. So if you want a little adventure, and desire to be a part of the in-crowd in Rome, give this place a try. (But do not buy anything illegal from anyone in there, no matter how nicely they offer. The laws are very strict in Italy, i.e. incarceration for many months before you even go to trial. Here you're guilty until proven innocent). That being said, have a pint for me.

THE DRUNKEN SHIP, *Campo de' Fiori 20/21, Tel. 06/6830-0535. Open 10am - 2:00am. Pints of Guiness, Harp, Kilkenny L6,000.*

Located in one of Rome's best piazzas for night life, the Campo dei Fiori. This is in the opinion of many the only real Irish bar in town. The place has European style and plays American music. The "frat boy types" in the crowd will love their Jello shots and cute American female bartenders. The decor is dark wood and the whole place has slight tilt to it befitting, I suppose, a drunken ship. No outside seating but the inside is fun enough. In the evening, every evening, this little piazza fills up with quite a few counterculture Italians and ex-pats. A fun place to be.

PIPER 90, *Via Taglimanento 9, Tel 06/841-4459 or 06/855-5398.*

This place only really gets going on the weekends with its video screens, live bands, and rockin' DJs. A place to really let your hair own, your body drench with sweat, and your money flow like water.

RADIO LONDRA, *Via di Monte Testaccio. No telephone ... how chique can you get.*

Recommended to me by a wine importer friend, who said it was wild. Well, he was way off base. It's totally insane, and crowded, and loud, and completely out of this world. You have segments of all parts of society here, making for a complete viewing pleasure. If the goings-on inside the inferno gets too hot, you can always sojourn to one of the tables on the terrace. A great place to meet other single people, not necessarily tourists.

MOVIES IN ENGLISH

Look for listings for both of these in local papers or contact each cinema for a list of movies.

PASQUINO, *Vicolo del Piedo 19A, Tel. 06/580-3622.*

Located just off the Piazza Santa Maria in Trastevere, this is the only true English language cinema in Rome since this is all they show. So if you are in need of a little touch of back home, come here and enjoy. Beware of the changing of the reels in inclement weather. Since there is only one projector, they have to change reels when one ends, and when they do they usually open the skylight roof and sometimes forget it's pouring outside.

Despite the possibility of a drenching by coming to the Pasquino, you will probably witness the last remaining true intermission, complete with intermission girls walking around selling popcorn, candy, and ice cream throughout the theater.

ALCATRAZ, *Piazza Merry del Val, Tel 06/588-0099.*

They show English language films that have not been dubbed, but since they also show French, German, Indian, and other films in their original language, they are really a multilingual cinema.

15♦ SHOPPING

As mentioned earlier, store hours are usually Monday through Friday 9:00am to 1:00pm, 3:30/4:00pm to 7:30/8:00pm, and Saturday 9:00am to 1:00pm. This may vary in Milan and/or Turin, where sometimes the lunch break is shorter so shops can close earlier.

The big Italian chain stores are **La Rinascente**, **Coin**, **UPIM**, and **STANDA**. In Coin, UPIM, and STANDA, you will also find supermarkets filled with all manner of Italian delectables. At the end of this chapter I'll make some suggestions about what you could buy at a local Italian *Supermercato* or *Alimentari* (smaller food store) to bring home with you so you can make a fine Italian meal with authentic ingredients!

Besides food and clothing, Italy has a wide variety of handicrafts. Any one of Italy's crafts would be a perfect memento of your stay. Works in alabaster and marble can be readily found in and around Florence, Milan, and Venice. Wood carvings are the specialty of many of the cities in the south, such as Palermo and Messina. Beautiful glasswork is at its best in and around Venice and Pisa. Embroidery and lace work can be found all over Italy, and rugs from Sardinia rival those of most other European countries. Sardinia is also known for its straw bags, hats, and mats, as is Florence.

Exquisite gold and silver jewelry is a specialty of Florence, where, on the Ponte Vecchio, you'll find shop after shop of jewelry stores. In other parts of Tuscany you can find hand-wrought iron work as well as beautiful tiles.

And finally the main fashion centers in Italy are, of course, Milan, Florence and Rome, with Florence specializing in shoes and gloves, and Milan and Rome everything else. Each regional chapter will describe for you specific places to visit to find the most exquisite and authentic regional handicrafts.

GET YOUR TAX REBATE ON PURCHASES

*If you acquire products at the same merchant in excess of L300,000 (about $180), you can claim an **IVA** (purchase tax) **rebate**. You must ask the vendor for the proper receipt (**il ricetto per il IVA per favore**), have the receipt stamped at Italian customs, then mail no later than 90 days after the date of the receipt back to the vendor. The vendor will then send you the IVA rebate. I know it's complicated, but if you spend a fair chunk of money in Italy on clothing or other items, this is a good way to get some money back.*

CLOTHING SIZES

The chart below is a comparison guide between US and Italian sizes. Many sizes are not standardized, so you will need to try everything on in any event.The following conversions should help you out in your shopping quest:

• Women's Clothing Sizes

US	2	4	6	8	10	12	14	16
Italy	36	38	40	42	44	46	48	50

Continued

	18	20	24
	52	54	56

• Women's Shoe Sizes

US	$5_{1/2}$	$6_{1/2}$	7	$7_{1/2}$	8	$8_{1/2}$	9	10
Italy	35	36	37	38	38 $_{1/2}$	39	40	41

• Women's Hosiery Sizes

US	Petite	Small	Medium	Large
Italy	I	II	III	IV

• Men's Suites, Overcoats, Sweaters, and Pajamas

US	34	36	38	40	42	44	46	48
Italy	44	46	48	50	52	54	56	58

• Men's Shirts

US	14	$14_{1/2}$	15	$15_{1/2}$	16	$16_{1/2}$	17	$17_{1/2}$
Italy	36	37	38	39	40	41	42	43

• Men's Shoes

US	6	$6_{1/2}$	7	$7_{1/2}$	8	$8_{1/2}$	9	$9_{1/2}$
Italy	30	40	$40_{1/2}$	41	$41_{1/2}$	42	$42_{1/2}$	43

Continued

	10	10$_{1/2}$		11-11$_{1/2}$			
	43$_{1/2}$	44-44$_{1/2}$		45			

• **Men's Hats**

US	6$_{7/8}$	7	7$_{1/8}$	7$_{1/4}$	7$_{3/8}$	7$_{1/2}$	7$_{5/8}$	7$_{3/4}$
Italy	55	56	57	58	59	60	61	62

• **Children's Sizes**

US	1	2	3	4	5	6	7	8
Italy	35	40	45	50	55	60	65	70

Continued

	9	10	11	12	13	14
	75	80	85	90	95	100

• **Children's Shoes**

US	4	5	6	7	8	9	10	10$_{1/2}$
Italy	21	21	22	23	24	25	26	27

Continued

	11	12	13
	28	29	30

KEY SHOPPING & BARGAINING PHRASES

Italian	*English*
• *Quanto costa?*	*How much is this?*
• *E Troppo*	*That's too much*
• *No Grazie*	*No thank you*
• *Voglio paggo meno*	*I want to pay less*
• *Che lai questo pui grande?*	*Do you have this in a bigger size?*
..... *pui piccolo*	..... *in a smaller size*
..... *in nero*	..... *in black*
..... *in bianco*	..... *in white*
..... *in roso*	..... *in red*
..... *in verde*	..... *in green*

BARGAINING

Most Italian vendors see foreigners as easy marks to make a few more *lire* because they know it is not in our culture to bargain, while in theirs it is a way of life.

The best way to bargain, if the street vendor doesn't speak English, is by writing your request on a piece of paper. This keeps it personal too in case you're embarrassed about haggling over money. Basically while in Italy try to let go of that cultural bias. "When in Rome..." Anyway, you and the vendor will probably pass the paper back and forth a few times changing the numbers before a price is finally agreed upon. And of course, the Italian vendor will be waving his arms about, jabbering away, most probably describing how you're trying to rip him off, all in an effort to get you to pay a higher price. Remember, this is all done in fun – so enjoy it.

ITALIAN SOCCER ATTIRE

If you or someone you know is a soccer nut, you may want to get them a jersey, hat, or scarf from one of the local teams. Most cities and towns in Italy have a soccer team, whether in the **Serie A** *(First Division) or in the three lower divisions. The games are played from September to June and are the best places to get low cost, high quality merchandise.*

Outside of most games vendors are selling everything from key rings to official soccer jerseys, all at a low price. The Italian soccer teams are starting to open their own stores featuring their specially-licensed products, like **Milan Point,** *for one of the teams in Milan, but those prices will be about four times as much as at the stadium.*

WHAT YOU CAN BRING BACK THROUGH CUSTOMS

See *Planning Your Trip* for more detials, but in short you can bring back to the US $400 worth of goods duty free. On the next $1,000 worth of purchases you will be assessed a flat 10% fee. These product must be with you when you go through customs.

You can mail products duty free, providing the total value of each package sent is not more than $50 *and* no one person is receiving more than one package a day. Also, each package sent must be stamped "Unsolicited Gift" and the amount paid and the contents of the package must be displayed. They'll be able to tell you all this again at the post office.

What you can't bring back to North America are any fruits, vegetables, and in most cases meats and cheeses, even if they're for your consumption alone, and even if they are vacuum sealed. Customs has to do this to prevent any potential parasites from entering our country and destroying our crops. Unfortunately, this means all those great salamis and cheeses you bought at those quaint outdoor food markets and had on one of your picnics will not be let back into the North America.

But there are some things you can buy. In most supermarkets you can find salamis and cheeses that have been shrink-wrapped, which customs should let through. Good luck!

ROME'S BEST SHOPPING AREAS

Because the very best of Italian design and craftsmanship are conveniently located in one small area, Rome is one of the finest shopping cities in the world. You can find beautifully made items made from the very best material, and as such this is not the place to look around for cut-price bargains. Leather and silk goods predominate, but Rome is also an important location for jewelry, antiques and general top of the line *pret-a-porte* (ready to wear) fashion.

The main shopping area is a network of small and large streets containing the famous **Via Condotti**. The shopping area boundaries extend over to **Via della Croce** in the north to **Via Frattina** in the nouth, and **Via del Corso** in the west to **Piazza di Spagna** in the east.

Romans, like other Italians, prefer to shop in boutiques, and the Via Condotti area has these quaint little shops selling everything from shirts to gloves. This specialization originates in the craft shops from which the smart shopping village has grown, and generally ensures top quality and personal service. In Italy, **department stores** are the exception rather than the rule, but in this shopping area there are some that warrant a look, like **La Rinascente**, **Standa**, **Upim**, and **Coin**.

To get the instant smile and respect you expect when you shop in most stores in America, you may have to dress the part here in Italy. It's not like in the malls back home where it doesn't matter how you dress; here in Rome the wealthier you look the better assistance you'll get. Unfortunately as tourists we usually leave our best attire back home, but try the best you can. Shorts and tank tops usually will get you no respect at all, particularly if you're shopping on the Via Condotti and Via Borgognona. This holds true, and I can vouch for this personally, if you're shopping on some of the parallel streets like Via Frattina, some of the little cross-streets, and even in Piazza di Spagna or Via del Babuino.

SHOPPING STREETS

Top of the Line Shopping – Via Condotti, Via Borgognona, Via Bocca di Leone

Middle Range Fashion – Via Nazionale, Via del Corso, Via Cola di Rienzo, Via del Tritone, and Via Giubbonari

Antiques – Via del Babuino, Via Guilia, Via dei Coronari.

Food Stores – Via del Croce

Inexpensive Shoes – Fontana di Trevi area

Leather goods and apparel – Via due Macelli, Via Franscesco Crispi

Straw and Wicker Products – Via dei Deiari, Via del Teatro Valle

ITALIAN DEPARMENT STORES

It's always fun to go to supermarkets and department stores in other countries to see what the natives like. Even if you don't buy anything, it's still fun to browse and not be followed around the store, as you would in one of the smaller boutiques by one of the vulture-like owners or staff. Both STANDA and UPIM are designed for the Italian on a budget, while Rinascente is a little more chic.

STANDA, *Viale di Trastevere 60 and Via Cola di Rienzo 173.*

Italy's largest food market, the perfect place to find that food product to bring back to the States with you. Since most of their stuff is vacuum sealed and pre packaged you should not have any problems with customs. Standa also has a large selection of housewares and clothing. This is the combined K Mart and Safeway of Italy, with slightly better quality products.

UPIM, *Via Nazionale 111, Piazza Santa Maria Maggiore and Via del Tritone 172.*

This department store is just like STANDA, except without the food.

LA RINASCENTE, *Piazza Colonna on the Via del Corso and Piazza Fiume.*

This is much more upscale than the other two and has about the same prices as boutiques, and even has some of the vultures hanging around too.

Other shopping districts are less formal, and many of these are worth investigating if you have time, for here is where you'll find the real bargains. **Via del Tritone** and the streets around the **Trevi Fountain**, **Via Cola di Rienzo** across the Tiber and north of the Vatican, **Piazza San Lorenzo** in Lucina and the streets around **Piazza Campo dei Fiori** are all areas where you will find cheaper leather bags and shoes. **Via Veneto** also has more of an international flavor, but boy, is it expensive.

Besides these areas, Rome also has many colorful street markets offering a vast selection of top quality fruit, flowers, vegetables, prosciutto, salami, cheeses, meat and fish, as well as cheap (that's inexpensive and sometimes just plain cheap) clothes. Because of this proliferation of shops and markets, and the Italian penchant for shopping in them, there are few department stores or supermarkets in the city center.

Straight bargaining is an accepted practice in clothes markets, but elsewhere transactions are conducted in a more roundabout way. At food stalls, cheeses and other weighed items have *prezzi fissi* (fixed prices), and in nearly all clothes shops, you can try asking for a *sconto* (discount). Reasons for meriting a *sconto* may be numerous – buying two articles at once is a good example – but if you are bold you will ask for a *sconto* for no good reason at all, and will usually get one. This practice applies to all but the very grandest of shops.

Surprisingly few shopkeepers speak English, but in the larger shops there is usually one person on hand who understands enough to be able to help you. Try to get your shopping done in the morning hours, when the stores are not so busy. At night, traditionally when Italians shop, it is so crowded it is difficult to get assistance.

ANTIQUES

Today, the typical Roman antique can be either a precious Roman artifact or pieces in the baroque and neoclassical style. There are also many French and English antiques masquerading as Italian. One thing that they all have in common is that they are extremely expensive.

The best antique shops in Rome can be found in the **Via del Babuino** and the **Via Margutta**. Other shops can be found on the **Via dei Coronari**, and the **Via Guila**. And don't forget to check out the **Porta Portese** Sunday market *(open 6:30am–2:30pm)*. You'll find some interesting and inexpensive antiques there.

OUTDOOR MARKETS

Many natives buy their vegetables, fruits, flowers, meats and cheeses from one of the many street markets held daily all over the city. Stalls of inexpensive clothing are also available, but there are whole markets devoted specifically to clothing. The food and flower markets are the best, and I advise you not to miss the opportunity to wander through one in the mornings, since they are usually closed in the afternoons.

Here are some of the better markets:

Campo dei Fiori, *Piazza Campo dei Fiori. Open 6am–2pm. Closed Sunday.*

Rome's oldest market held in the cobblestoned square in the center of Rome's old medieval city. You can buy flowers (the name Campo dei Fiori means fields of flowers), fruits and vegetables, all delicately presented under makeshift awnings or giant umbrellas. Surrounding the square are some *Alimentaris* where you can pick up cold cuts, cheeses, and bread for picnics.

Piazza Vittorio Emmanuele, *Open 7am–2pm. Closed Sundays.*

Stretching all the way around this large piazza is the city's largest market. Clothes and leather goods are displayed along the south side, with some fine bargains to be found. The food stalls on the north side are known by their specialization: one stall will sell only fresh tuna, another calves livers, another tangerines. The crowing of the cocks and scuttling of crabs really adds to the atmosphere of this market. You can find some very unusual food in these stalls as well as some exquisite cheeses and salamis.

Porta Portese, *Ponte Sublico. Open 6:30am–2:30pm, Sundays only.*

This flea market stretches along the Tiber from Ponte Sublico (where the Porta Portese is) in the north to the Ponte Testaccio in the south. That's basically south of Trastevere along the river and not even on most maps, but tell a cab driver where you're going and he'll know. The clothes and accessories are inexpensive but of cheap quality, as befits most flea markets. This is a true Roman market and not many tourists venture here, but it's safe, and if you like flea markets, a whole lot of fun.

Via Andrea Doria, *Open 8am–1pm. Closed Sundays and Mondays.*

Filling almost the entire length of the Via Andrea Doria, as well as spilling into many side streets, this is a large and lively food market. The stalls are laid out in artistic arrangements to attract buyers. You can find strings of onions, cheeses, bottled oils, salamis, sausages, cheeses, etc. all laid out perfectly for the customer.

Via Sannio, *Open Monday through Friday 8am–1pm, Sat 8am–7pm. Closed Sundays.*

Most of these clothes sellers move their wares to the Porta Portese on Sundays, so if you can't make it there try to make it here. To get here by Metro, go two stops past the Piazza Vittorio Emmanuele.

Mercato de Stampe, *Piazza Fontanella Borghese, Monday–Saturday 9:00am–6:00pm.*

A small outdoor market based at the end of the square that specializes in old prints, stamps, postcards, assorted books, and knickknacks that could be considered antiques. The prices tend to be high, especially if you're pegged as a tourist, so bargaining is essential.

BOOKSTORES WITH ENGLISH LANGUAGE TITLES

American Book Shop, *Via della Vite 27 & 57, Tel. 583-6942. American Express, Diners Club, Mastercard and Visa accepted. Open Monday 4:00pm–8:00pm, Tuesday–Saturday 10:00am–1:00pm and 3:30pm–7:30pm.*

A small English-language only new bookstore that has almost everything you could want. It's a little pricy but that's to be expected.

Ancora Book Shop, *Via della Conciliazione 63, Tel. 656-8820. American Express, Diners Club, Mastercard and Visa accepted. Monday–Friday 9:00am–1:00pm, and 3:30pm–7:30pm. Saturdays 9:00am–1:00pm.*

Mainly a Catholic religious bookstore, but they have English language titles upstairs as well as a good selection of travel guides.

Anglo-American Bookstore, *Via delle Vite 102. Tel. 06/679-5222. Credit cards accepted. Monday–Friday 9:00am–1:00pm, and 3:30pm–7:30pm. Saturdays 9:00am–1:00pm.*

Located between the Spanish Steps and the Trevi Fountain, this bookstore caters to all manner of bibliophiles and computer nerds too.

As well as a full selection of travel books, paperbacks, history books, etc. They have a multimedia computer center too.

The Corner Bookshop, *Via del Moro 48, Tel. 583-6942. Mastercard and Visa accepted. Open Monday 3:30pm–7:30pm, Tuesday–Saturday 10:00am–1:00pm and 3:30pm–7:30pm.*

Located in Trastevere, this is a relatively new bookstore featuring English-language titles exclusively. Owned by the very knowledgeable, helpful, and friendly Claire Hammond, you can almost always find what you want. They're stocked with hardbacks, paperbacks in non-fiction, fiction, general interest and more. A great place to meet other ex-pats or fellow travelers. Say hello to Claire for me when you see her.

Economy Bookstore and Video Center, *Via Torino 136, Tel. 474-6877. Credit cards accepted. Monday 3:00pm–7:30pm, Tuesday–Saturday 10:00am–1:00pm and 3:30pm–7:30pm.*

The best place to find a novel in English, and now they rent movies too. This mainstay of the English-speaking community for the past three decades has recently moved from Piazza di Spagna to this new location (I almost didn't find it again). They buy and sell second-hand English language paperbacks and have an excellent selection of both new and used books, including everything from fiction to non-fiction, children's, science fiction, best sellers and mysteries. They also carry a complete range of guide books on Rome and Italy.

Lion Bookshop, *Via del Babuino 181, Tel. 360-5837. Credit cards accepted.*

This is the largest English-speaking bookstore for new books. Has a definite Anglo bent to it, while the Economy Bookstore is more for people from across the pond. Since the Economy Bookstore has recently left its abode at the Spanish Steps for a much larger location near the Train station, this is the best English language bookstore in Rome's prime tourist area.

Libreria Internazionale Rizzolo, *Largo Chigi 15, Tel. 679-6641. Credit cards accepted.*

The largest store of Italy's largest bookstore chain. It has a great selection of artistic and cultural books. On the ground floor and in the basement there is also an adequate selection of guidebooks and paper-backs in English.

NEWSPAPERS

The *International Herald Tribune* is published jointly by the Washington Post and The New York Times and printed in Bologna for distribution throughout Italy. You can also find a condensed version of *USA Today*. Besides these two, you can find newspapers from all over the world at almost any newsstand.

FOOD STORES & MARKETS

As mentioned above in the section on outdoor markets, the best places to get your fresh fruit, cheese, salami, ham, turkey, and bread for a picnic would be at any of the markets mentioned above in this section under *Outdoor Markets*. If you can't make it to one of these, here's a list of some small *Alimentaris* and wine stores from which you can get all you need.

Campo dei Fiori, *Open Air Market, Piazza Campo dei Fiori. Open 6am–2pm.*

You can get salamis, cheeses, breads, and fruit here. A few stores on and around the Via Sistine.

Piazza Vittorio Emmanuele, *Open 7am–2pm. Closed Sundays.*

You can find many specialty food items here, especially cheeses, breads, and salamis.

One small store is on Via Laurina. Another small store, near both entrances to the Borghese Gardens, is in the middle of the Via Della Croce.

ALIMENTARI

These are small shops that serve up Italy's famous salamis, meats, cheeses, and breads for you to snack on or take on a picnic. I've listed some of my favorites that are dispersed all over the city, but you only need to find one closest to your hotel for a culinary treat.

Via Principe Amadeo 61 (Termini). *Next to Fiorino Hotel.*

Valeria Basconi, Via Firenze 53 (Via Nazionale). *Near Hotel Alda.*

Salumeria, Via Sardegna 20 (Via Veneto/Trevi Fountain).

Via degli Avignonesi 25 (Via Veneto/Trevi Fountain)

Via Laurina 36 (Piazza di Spagna) – *Meats, cheeses, breads*

Via Laurina 39 (Piazza di Spagna) – *fruits and vegetables and wine*

Via di Ripetta 233A (Pantheon/Navona) – *large meat, cheese, bread, and wine store.*

Via della Scrofa 100 (Piazza Navona/Pantheon) – *meats and cheeses. If you want some prosciutto this small shop will have it cut by hand for you in the window for all to see.*

Via della Scrofa 32 (Piazza Navona/Pantheon)– *hot and cold take out of pastas and souffles as well as salami, cheese and wine.*

WINE

Antica Bottigleria Placidi, *Via del Croce 76, Tel. 679-0896. Expensive. All credit cards accepted. Closed Sundays.*

Opened in 1860, until a few years ago this was an old fashioned, ancient really, wine store selling local vintages directly from large vats.

You would walk past the huge wooden doors and into the cool, dark, and damp store lined with shelf upon shelf of wine and oil, and it would seem as if centuries had been erased. Now it's a yuppified fern-filled wine bar.

They actually have plants in the vats where once I was served some of the choicest vintages. Not that it's all that bad, for a faux wine bar, they do serve palatable side dishes. I just wish they had kept the vats in use.

INTERESTING LITTLE SHOPS

Check out **Cartolerie**, the perfect places to buy unique school supplies for the kids, or yourself, such as pens, notebooks, stationary, pencils, etc. I've been using foreign made notebooks bought in these shops for my journal entries for over six years. They're all over town.

Try also: **Ai Monestari**, *Piazza delle Cinque Lune 76*. A tiny shop of monk-made products including my favorite, **L'Amaro Francescano di Assisi** liqueur.

Another fun place is **Terecotte Persiane**, *Via Napoli 92. Tel. 06/488-3886. Open 10:00am–1:30pm and 3:30pm–8:00pm.* Eclectic mix of terra cotta figures, tiles, masks, planters and post boxes. Located in a small courtyard, the place is packed with everything terra cotta you can imagine. Even if you don't want to buy, come and browse.

16. CULTURE & ARTS

FROM ETRUSCANS TO THE RENAISSANCE

Italy is perhaps best known for its great contributions to painting and sculpture; and many art lovers have described the country as one vast museum. Italy gave birth to such world renowned artists as Giotto, Donatello, Raphael, Michelangelo, Leonardo da Vinci, and Botticelli, known all over the world.

The oldest works of art in Italy are those of the **Etruscans**, and they date back to the 9th century BC. This mysterious society's main cities and art centers were in the middle of the peninsula, between Rome and Florence, mainly in the province now know as Tuscany (the region was named after them ... Etruscans ... Tuscany). In Tarquinia, Volterra, Cerveteri, and Veio, the Etruscans have left behind magnificent temples, sculptures, and bronzes as well as other fascinating testimonies to their presence. The best museum collections of Etruscan art coverd in this guide are Rome's **Etruscan Museum** and Florence's **Archaeological Museum**.

Italy is also known as being a repository of ancient Greek art. During the time of the Etruscans, the Greeks established colonies in the south of modern-day Italy. Magnificent ruins of temples exist today in some of these Greek colonies: **Syracuse**, **Agrigento**, and **Taormina** in Sicily; and **Paestu** and **Coma** in Campania. There are good collections of Hellenic art in the **National Museum of Naples**, and in the museums in Palermo, Syracuse, Reggio Calabria, Paestum, and Taranto (see my *Italy Guide*, Open Road Publishing).

After the Greeks and Etruscans, the Roman Empire left its lasting impression all over Italy. There are still roads, bridges, aqueducts, aches, and theaters built by the Romans. The most extensive excavations have been made at the **Forum** in Rome, at **Ostia** near Rome by the beach, and at **Pompeii** and **Herculaneum**, the cities that the volcanic **Mount Vezuvious** buried. For a first-hand, up-front feel of what life was like in the Roman Empire, don't miss these sites.

After the fall of the Roman Empire, the Byzantine Empire ruled many parts of the southern and eastern regions of Italy. This period left behind many churches, with their glorious mosaics, like those of the 6th century in **Ravenna** near the east coast; as well as the morbid-but-can't-miss site of the **catacombs** outside of Rome.

Then the Renaissance came. This artistic period, meaning "rebirth," began in Italy in the 14th century and lasted for two hundred years. The Renaissance left us an extensive array of churches, palaces, paintings, statues, and city squares in almost every city of Italy. The main cities of Florence, Rome, Venice, Milan, and Naples have most of the treasures and beauty of this period, but smaller towns like **Ferrara** and **Rimini** also have their share. The best museums for viewing Renaissance art are the **Uffizzi Gallery** and **Pitti Palace** in Florence, as well as the **Vatican** and **Borghese Galleries** (in the Borghese Gardens just outside the walls) in Rome.

After the Renaissance, **baroque art** became fashionable. And Rome, more than any other Italian city, contains a dazzling array of churches, paintings, and statues recalling the splendor of such famous artists as Bernini, Borromini, and Caravaggio of the late 16th and 17th centuries.

RENAISSANCE PAINTING

In Italy (with France and Germany soon following suit) during the 14th and 15th centuries, the Renaissance was a period of exploration, invention, and discovery. Mariners from all over Europe set sail in search of new lands. Scientists like **Leonardo da Vinci** studied the mysteries of the world and the heavens. Artists found the human body to be a marvel of mechanics and beauty (but had to secretly study it, as Michelangelo did, lest the Church condemn them for heresy). This was undoubtedly one of Italy's most exciting periods in the history of artistic and scientific advancement.

Many consider the birthplace of Renaissance art to be Florence. It seemed to start with a young painter named **Masaccio**, who began introducing many bold new ideas into his painting. He made his paintings vibrantly interesting by drawing each person completely different from another, as well as making each person as realistic as possible. In conjunction with his ability to express the human form, Masaccio used combinations of colors to give the impression of space and dimension in his landscapes. Now every art student studies how brown makes objects appear closer, and blue makes them appear in the distance.

Paolo Uccello, another Florentine, worked at the same time as Masaccio. A mathematician as well as an artist, he expanded on the mechanical and scientific issues of painting rather than on the human and psychological ones.

One of his paintings, *The Battle of San Romano*, circa 1457, celebrated the victory of Florence over Siena some 25 years earlier, and is a brilliant study in **perspective**. His depiction of objects, men, and horses all help to accentuate the sense of real perspective he was trying to achieve. One technique he used, which is now part of any good art school's curriculum, is **foreshortening**. In the left foreground is a fallen soldier with his feet facing the front of the picture. To give this figure a proper perspective, Uccello had to shorten the perceived length of the body, an extremely difficult task, and one not usually seen in other artists' previous works. In conjunction, Uccello drew roads, fields, etc., going back into the painting, to give the impression of distance.

But most definitely three of the most famous Renaissance artists were **Raphael**, **Leonardo da Vinci**, and **Michelangelo**. Raphael was mainly known for his paintings of the Madonna and Child, from which our concept of the Mother of Jesus is largely based. But all of his paintings reflect a harmony that leaves the viewer with a warm feeling.

Leonardo da Vinci is most well known for his *Mona Lisa*, painted in Tuscany in 1505-06 and now hanging in the Louvre, but he was also a versatile architect and scientist as well. Leonardo studied botany, geology, zoology, hydraulics, military engineering, anatomy, perspective, optics, and physiology. You name it, he did it – the original Renaissance Man!

Another versatile artist of the Italian Renaissance, and definitely its most popular (he was always being commissioned to paint or sculpt all the wealthy people's portraits) was Michelangelo Buonarroti. Although he considered himself chiefly a sculptor – he trained as a young boy to become a stone carver – he left us equally great works as a painter and architect. As a painter he created the huge **Sistine Chapel** fresco, encompassing more than 10,000 square feet in area. As an architect he helped complete the designs for **St. Peter's**, where his world renowned statue, *La Pieta*, currently resides.

RENAISSANCE SCULPTURE

Besides painting and architecture, **Michelangelo Buonarroti** was also the pre-eminent sculptor of the Renaissance. By the age of 26 he had carved *La Pieta*, his amazing version of Virgin Mary supporting the dead Christ on her knees; and was in the process of carving the huge and heroic marble *David*. He also created the memorable **Medici tombs** in the Chapel of San Lorenzo, Florence. His greatest but lesser known work is his majestic *Moses* designed for the tomb of Pope Julius II. Today this great statue can be viewed at the basilica of **San Pietro in Vincoli** in Rome.

Ironically, even though Michelangelo was commissioned to create many works by the Vatican, he had learned his amazing knowledge of the human anatomy by dissecting cadavers in his home town of Florence as a young man, a crime punishable by death and/or excommunication at the time.

During the Renaissance there were many other sculptors of note, but Michelangelo was truly the best. One of the others was **Lorenzo Ghiberti**, who died a few years before Michelangelo was born. For 29 years he labored to produce ten bronze panels, depicting Biblical episodes, for the doors of the Baptistery of Florence. Michelangelo was said to have been inspired to become a great artist because of these beautiful bronze doors.

MUSIC

Italy also has a great tradition in music. Even today, Italian folk music has made a resurgence, mainly because of the theme song for the *Godfather* movie series. Can't you just hear it playing in your head right now?

Besides the folk music and Gregorian chants, Italy is best known for its opera. If you need to hear the shrill explosion of an *aria*, try to get seats for a performance at **Teatro del Opera** in Rome or **La Fenice** in Venice (addresses and phone numbers are listed on the next page).

Italian Opera

Italian opera began in the 16th century. Over time such composers as Gioacchino Rossini, Gaetano Donizetti, and Vincenzo Bellini created **bel canto** opera – opera that prizes beautiful singing above all else. Singers were indulged with *arias* that gave them ample opportunity for a prominent display of their vocal resources of range and agility.

Rossini, who reigned as Italy's foremost composer of the early 19th century, was a master of both melody and stage effects. Success came easily, and while still in his teens he composed the first of a string of 32 operas that he completed by the age of 30. Many of these are comic operas, a genre in which Rossini excelled, and his masterpieces in this form are still performed and admired today. Among them is one you probably recognize (even I know this one): *The Barber of Seville* (1816).

Rossini's immediate successor as Italy's leading operatic composer was **Donizetti**, who composed more than 70 works in the genre. A less refined composer than Rossini, Donizetti left his finest work in comic operas, including *Don Pasquale* (1843) and *Lucia di Lammermoor* (1835).

Although he lived for a shorter time than either Rossini or Donizetti and enjoyed a far briefer career, **Bellini** wrote music that many believe surpassed theirs in refinement. Among the finest of his ten operas are *La sonnambula* (The Sleepwalker, 1831), *Norma* (1831), and *I Puritani* (The Puritans, 1835), all of which blend acute dramatic perceptions with florid virtuosity.

From these roots came Italy's greatest opera composers of all times, **Puccini** and **Verdi**. Giacomo Puccini lived from 1858-1924 and composed twelve operas in all. Considered by many to be a close second to Verdi in skill of composition, Puccini's work will remain alive because of his enduringly popular works such as *Madama Butterfly* and *La Boheme*. Even though Puccini was the fifth generation of musicians in his family, he was mainly influenced to pursue his career after hearing Verdi's still popular *Aida*.

Giuseppe Verdi lived from 1813-1901, and is best know for his operas *Rigoletto* (1851), *Il Trovatore* and *La Traviata* (both 1853), and what could be the grandest opera of them all, *Aida* (1871). Verdi composed his thirtieth and last opera *Falstaff* at the age of 79. Since he mainly composed out of Milan and many of his operas opened at La Scala opera house in that city, today a **Verdi museum** has been established there to honor his work.

Opera, Music, Drama, & Ballet Festivals

As the birthplace of opera, Italy offers visitors a variety of choices during the operatic seasons, which are almost year-round. In the summer months there are wonderful open-air operas presented at the **Terme di Caracalla** (Baths of Caracalla) in the center of Rome near the main train station from July to August, at the **Arena** in Verona from July to August, and at the **Arena Sferisterio** in Macerata in July.

Two of the most spectacular festivals for Italian performing arts are the **Maggio Musicale Fiorentino** with opera, concerts, ballet, and drama performances in Florence from May to June, and the **Festival of Two Worlds** with opera, concerts, ballet, drama performances and art exhibits in Spoleto from mid-June to mid-July.

MAJOR OPERA HOUSES

Teatro dell'Opera, Piazza D. Gigli 1, 00184 Roma. Tel. 06/481-601, Fax 06/488-1253

Teatro La Fenice, Campo S. Fantin 1977, 30124 Venezia. Tel. 041/521-0161, Fax 041/522-1768

Teatro Comunale, Corso Italia 16, 50123 Firenze. Tel. 055/27791 or 2729236, Fax 055/2396954

If you wish to obtain tickets to opera performances, concerts, ballet, and other performances you can either write directly to the theater in question or ask your travel agent to obtain the ticket for you. Currently there is no agency in the US authorized to sell concert and/or opera tickets, so this is the only way. When you are in Italy, your hotel should be able to assist you in obtaining tickets for performances in their city.

REGIONAL & NATIONAL FOLK FESTIVALS

Despite the encroachment of the modern world, the traditional festivals and their accompanying costumes and folk music have survived surprisingly well all over Italy. In many cases they have been successfully woven into the pattern of modern life so as to seem quite normal. Despite all possible modern influences these festivals (both secular and religious) have preserved their distinctive character.

One of the more famous secular festivals is the **Calcio in Costume** in Florence. This violent festival pits different sections of town against one another to see who can earn bragging rights for the year. The Piazza della Signorina is turned into a veritable battleground for a game that is a cross between boxing, soccer, rugby, and martial arts. The old colorful Renaissance costumes are still worn during the festival.

With Italy the home of the Catholic church, religious festivals also play a large part in Italian life. Particularly interesting are the processions on the occasion of **Corpus Christi**, **Assumption**, and **Holy Week**. In Italy, holiday times such as Easter and Christmas have not lost their religious intent as they have in most other places. Commercialism still takes a back seat to the Almighty in Italy.

The items below marked by an asterisk are the ones you simply cannot miss. Plan your trip around them.

JANUARY

- **New Years Day**, *Rome*: Candle-lit processional in the Catacombs of Priscilla to mark the martyrdom of the early Christians
- **January 5**, *Rome*: Last day of the Epiphany Fair in the Piazza Navona. All throughout the piazza a fair filled with food stands, candy stands, toy shops opens to the public. Lasts a week. A must see.

FEBRUARY/MARCH

- **1st half of February**, *Agrigento*: Almond Blossom Festival. Song, dance, costumes, fireworks.
- **Both Months**: *Venice*: Carnival in Venice with costume sand masks, with street mimes, music, and fireworks. A fun time.
- **19 March**, *Many places*: San Giuseppe (St. Joseph's day)

MARCH/APRIL

During March or April, *Rome* celebrates the Festa della Primavera (Spring Festival).

- **1 April**, *San Marino*: Installation of Regents
- **Palm Sunday**, *Many places, particularly Rome and Florence*: Blessings of palms, with procession

- **Wednesday before Easter**, *Many places, particulary Rome*: Mercoledi Santo (lamentations, Miserere)
- **Thursday Before Good Friday**, *Many places, particularly Rome and Florence*: Washing of the Feet, burial of the sacraments
- **Good Friday**, *Many places, particularly Rome and Florence*: Adoration of the Cross. *Taranto*: Procession of the Mysteries (Solemn procession with many beautiful period costumes).
- **Easter Saturday**, *Many places, particularly Rome and Florence*: Lighting of the Sacred Fire
- **Easter Day**, *Rome*: Papal blessing; *Florence:* Scopplo dei Carro ("Explosion of the Cart" – A pyramid of fireworks is set off in the Cathedral square to commemorate the victorious return of the first Crusade.

MAY
- **1 May**, * *Florence*: Calcio in Costume (historical ball game – A Must See; Can't Miss This One)
- **During May**, *Florence*: Maggio Musicale (Music festival of May)
- **Ascension**, *Florence*: Festival of the Crickets. A lot of fun. You get to take home a cricket in a small cage. Something the Chinese do too, but hey, when in Italy ...; *Sassari (Sardinia)*: Cavalcata Sarda (mounted procession)

JUNE
If you're in *Venice*, don't miss the Biennale art exhibition.
- **Mid-June**, *Many places*: Corpus Domini (Ascension processions)
- **June 23-24**, *Rome*: Vigilia di San Giovanni Battista (St. John's Eve, fireworks, eating of snails, song competition)
- **June 29**, *Rome*: Santi Pietro e Paulo (feast of Saints Peter and Paul); *Genoa*: "Palio Marinaro dei Rioni." Rowing race in ancient costumes.

JULY
- **July 19-26**, *Rome*: Festa de' Noantri folklore festival of old Rome in Trastevere, Rome's oldest habitable section, which includes a colorful procession, folk dances, songs, carnival floats, and fireworks. Everybody gets real worked up for this. A must see.
- **Third Saturday in July (from that night to Sunday)**, * *Venice:* Festival of Redentore on the Grand Canal. Procession of Gondolas and othe craft commemorating the end of the black plague epidemic of 1575

AUGUST
- **During August**, *Venice*: Nocturnal Festival on Grand Canal
- **During August/September**, *Venice*: Film Festival
- **15 August**, *Many places*: Assumption (processions and fireworks)

SEPTEMBER/OCTOBER

- **First Sunday in September**, *Venice*: Traditional competition on the canal between two-oar racing gondolas preceded by a procession of Venetian Ceremonial boats from the time of the Venetian Republic.
- **September 7**, *Florence*: Riticolone (nocturnal festival with lanterns)
- **October 1**, *San Marino*: Installation of Regents

NOVEMBER/DECEMBER

- **November 22**, *Many places*: Santa Cecilia (St. Cecilia's day)
- **December 25**, *Rome*: Papal blessing
- **Mid-December to mid-January**, Many places: Christmas crib (Nativity Scenes)

CRAFTS

Hundreds of thousands of skillful Italian artisans are the heirs of a 2,000-year tradition of craftsmanship. Their products – fashioned of leather, gold, silver, glass, and silk – are widely sought by tourists. Cameos made from seashells, an ancient Italian art form, are as popular today as they were in the days of the Roman Empire. The work of Italian artists and artisans is also exported for sale in the great department stores of France, Germany, the United Kingdom, and the United States.

Italian clothing designers are world famous, especially for precise tailoring, unusual knits, and the imaginative use of fur and leather.

The best place to see Italian artisans at work is in the glass blowing factories of Venice. There you'll be amazed at how easily they can manipulate molten balls into some of the most delicate, colorful, and beautiful pieces you've ever seen. Each chapter in this book highlights specific traditional crafts by region.

LITERATURE

Perhaps Italy's most famous author/poet is **Dante Aligheri**, who wrote the *Divine Comedy*, in which he describes his own dream-journey through Hell *(l'Inferno)* Purgatory *(Purgatorio)*, and Paradise *(Paradiso)*. At the time it was extremely controversial, since it is a poem about free will and how man can damn or save his soul as he chooses, which was contrary to church teachings. Even today it sparks controversy since it seems apparent that Dante's description of Purgatory is actually describing the life we all lead on earth, and shows his belief in reincarnation.

Two other notable Italian writers (you should remember these for quality cocktail party conversation) are **Petrarch**, famous for his sonnets to Laura, a beautiful girl from Avignon who died quite young, and is known as the "First of the Romantics;" and **Boccaccio**, the Robin Williams of his time (except he wrote, not performed) his famous *Decameron*, a charming and sometimes ribald series of short stories told by ten young people in a span of ten days – sort of the Chaucer of Italy.

Among contemporary Italian writers, **Umberto Eco** stands out on his own. You may know two of his books that have been translated into English: *The Name of the Rose* and the more recent *Foucault's Pendulum*. If you are looking for complex, insightful, intriguing, and intellectual reading, Eco's your man. Last but not least, one Italian writer whom children all over the world should know is **Calo Collodi**, who wrote *Pinnochio*.

17. SPORTS & RECREATION

There are many different sporting activities to participate in and around Rome, since the city is only 15 miles from the beach and 65 miles from great skiing country. Below is a list of possible activities:

AMUSEMENT PARK

For people with a lot of money in their pockets, there is a permanent amusement park, **Luna Park**, in EUR. To get there take the Metropolitana on Linea B to the EUR stop. EUR stands for *Esposizione Universale Romana*, a grandiose project sponsored by Mussolini as a permanent exhibition to the glory of Rome. The park is to your left as you enter EUR along the Via Cristoforo Colombo.

BICYCLING

Reckless Roman drivers can make biking on the city streets dangerous if you're not careful, and especially if you're a young North American used to the defensive drivers in the States and Canada.

But you can rent bicycles at many different locations (see *Getting Around Town*) and take them for a trip through the **Borghese Gardens** (see *Seeing the Sights*, above).

BOATING

Rowboats can be rented at the **Giardino del Lago** in the Villa Borghese. You can also rent dinghies at **Lago di Bracciano** and **Lido di Ostia** (see Chapter 18, *Rome Area Excursions*).

BOWLING

There are two particularly good bowling alleys *(bocciodromi)* in Rome. Unless you have your own car, both of these places are far outside of the old walls of the city and thus rather difficult to get to except by taxi.

• **Bowling Brunswick**, *Lungotevere Aqua Acetosa, Tel. 396-6696*, and
• **Bowling Roma**, *Viale Regina Margherita 181, Tel. 861-184.*

GOLF

There are a variety of 18 hole and 9 hole courses all around Rome:
• **L'Eucalyptus Circolo del Golf**, *Via della Cogna 3/5, 04011 Aprilla. Tel. 06/926-252. Fax 06/926-8502.* Located 30 km from Rome, this is an 18 hole par 72 course that is 6,372 meters long. It is open all year except on Tuesdays. They also have a small executive course, driving range, pro shop, tennis courts, swimming pool, guest quarters, and a restaurant/bar.
• **Golf Club Torvalaianica**, *Via Enna 30, 00040 Marina di Ardea. Tel. 06/913-3250. Fax 06/913-3592.* Located 25 km from Rome this is a 9 hole par 31 course that is 2,208 meters long. It is open all year except Mondays. They have a driving range as well as a restaurant/bar.
• **Golf Club Castel Gandolpho**, *Via Santo Spirito 13, 00040 Castelgandolpho. Tel. 06/931-2301. Fax 06/931-2244.* This is an 18 hole par 72 course near the Pope's summer residence that is 5,855 meters long. It's open all year except on Mondays. They have a driving range, carts, pro shop, swimming pool, and a restaurant/bar.
• **Circolo del Golf di Fioranello**, *Via della Falcognana 61, 00134 Roma. Tel. 06/713-8080 or 731-2213. Fax 06/713-8212.* Located 17 km from the center of Rome, this is an 18 hole par 70 course that is 5,417 meters long. It is open a year except for Wednesdays. They also have a driving range, pro shop, swimming pool, and a bar/restaurant.
• **Macro Simone Golf Club**, *Via di Marco Simone, 00012 Guidonia. Tel. 0774/370-469. Fax 0774/370-476.* Located 17 km from Rome, this is an 18 hole par 72 course that is 6,360 meters long. It is open all year except for Tuesdays. They also have an 18 hole executive course, driving range, pro shop, swimming pool, tennis courts, massage room, sauna, gymnasium, and an excellent restaurant and bar.
• **Golf Club Parco de' Medici**, *Viale Parco de' Medici 20, 00148 Roma. Tel. 06/655-33477. Fax 06/655-3344.* Located 10 km outside of the city center, this is an 18 hole par 72 course that is 5,827 meters long. It is open all year except on Tuesdays. They also have a driving range, swimming pool, tennis courts, and a restaurant/bar. This is the course most accessible and nearest the city center.
• **Circolo del Golf di Roma – Acqua Santa**, *Via Appia Nuova 716 or Via Dell'Aquasanta 3, Roma 00178, Tel. 06/780-3407. Fax 06/7834-6219.* Located 11 km from Rome, this is an 18 hole par 71 course that is 5,825 meters long. It is open all year except on Mondays. They have a driving range, putting green, swimming pool, and a restaurant/bar.

• **Olgiata**, *Largo Olgiata 15, Roma 00123, Tel. 06/378-9141. Fax 06/378-9968.* Located 19 km from the center of Rome, in a housing development similar to many golf courses in the U.S. At Olgiata there is an 18 hole par 72 course that is 6,396 meters long and a 9 hole par 34 course that is 2,968 meters long. The course is open all year except on Mondays. They have a driving range, pro shop, swimming pool and a bar/restaurant.

RIVER TRIPS

In July and August you can take a river trip through central Rome. The trips are organized by the **Amici del Tevere**. Check the journal *This Week in Rome* for details, available in most hotels.

SWIMMING

The major outdoor pool in Rome is at the **Foro Italico** (*Tel. 396-3958*), open June to September. An indoor pool at the Foro Italico is open November to May.

The best beach is at **Lido di Ostia**, less than an hour west-northwest of Rome. The beaches are clean and large. They have plenty of *cabanas* to rent where you can change you clothes, and there are some excellent seafood restaurants where you can leisurely eat, sip wine, and enjoy the beautiful Italian summers.

TENNIS

The following public courts require reservations:
• **Circolo Montecitorio**, *Via Campi Sportivi 5, Tel. 875-275*
• **EUR**, *Viale dell'Artigianato 2, Tel. 592-4693*
• **Foro Italico**, *Tel. 361-9021*
• **Tennis Belle Arti**, *Via Flaminia 158, Tel. 360-0602*

18. ROME AREA EXCURSIONS

I've planned some fun excursions for you: **Tivoli Gardens**, **Castel Gandolfo**, **Frascati**, **Ostia Antica**, **Lago di Bracciano** and **Cervetri**.

TIVOLI GARDENS

Modern day **Tivoli**, about 23 miles east of Rome, has about 45,000 inhabitants. On the **Aniene**, a tributary of the Tiber, and overlooking Rome from its place on the **Sabine hills**, this town is where the wealthy Romans built their magnificent summer villas. The three main attractions are **Villa Adriana** (Hadrian's Villa), **Villa d'Este**, and **Villa Gregoriana**.

The **Villa Adriana's** main attraction is its huge grounds, where you and lizards can bask in the sun. There are plenty of secluded spots to relax or enjoy a picnic on the grass. The building itself was begun in 125 AD and completed 10 years later, and was at the time the largest and most impressive villa in the Roman Empire. From his travels **Hadrian**, an accomplished architect, found ideas that he recreated in his palace. The idea for the **Poikile**, the massive colonnade through which you enter the villa, came from Athens. And the **Serapeum** and **Canal of Canopus** were based on the Temple of Serapis near Alexandria, Egypt.

The **Villa D'Este's** main draw is its many wonderful fountains. The villa itself was built on the site of a Benedictine convent in the mid-16th century. The **Owl Fountain** and **Organ Fountain** are especially beautiful, as is the secluded pathway of the **Terrace of the Hundred Fountains**. If you make it out to Tivoli, these gardens and their fountains cannot be missed, especially at night during the months of May through September when they are floodlit.

The **Villa Gregoriana** is known for the **Grande Cascata** (the Great Fall), which is a result of Gregory XVI diverting the river in the last century to avoid flooding. The park around the cascade has smaller ones as well as grottoes. This is the least interesting of the three villas.

The addresses and hours of the three villas are:

- **Villa Adriana**, *Bivio Villa Adriana, 3.5 miles southwest of Tivoli. Open Tuesday–Sunday, 9:30am–1 hour before sunset. Closed Mondays. Small fee required.*
- **Villa D'Este**, *Viale delle Centro Fontane. Open Tuesday–Sunday, 9:30am to 1.5 hours before sunset. May–September also open 9–11:30pm with the garden floodlit. Closed Mondays. Small fee required. Sundays free.*
- **Villa Gregoriana**, *Largo Sant'Angelo. Open Tuesday–Sunday 9:30am to 1 hour before sunset. Closed Mondays. Small fee required. Sunday free.*

ARRIVALS & DEPARTURES

By Car

Take the Via Tiburtina (SS5). The Villa Adriana lies to the right about 3.5 miles before the town.

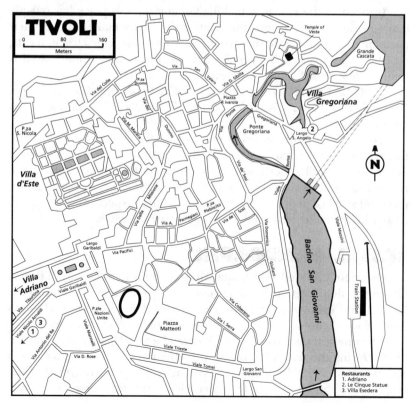

By Train
From Stazione Termini the trip takes about 40 minutes.

WHERE TO EAT

Tivoli simply abounds with restaurants, many offering a magnificent panoramic view of Rome. Here are some of my suggestions.

1. ADRIANO, *(near Hadrian's Villa), Via di Villa Adriana 194, Tel. 0774/529-174. Closed Sunday nights. All credit cards accepted. Dinner for two L130,000.*

Basically at the front of the entrance to Hadrian's Villa, this restaurant attached to a hotel has a beautiful garden terrace. They make excellent *crostini di verdure* (fried dough with vegetabales in side), *raviolini primavera con ricotta e spinaci* (ravioli with spring vegetables, spinach and fresh ricotta), *tagliata di coniglio alle erbette* (rabbit with herbs) and more. The prices are a little rich for my blood, especially with the L6,000 for *coperto* (just sitting down and ordering).

2. LE CINQUE STATUE, *Largo S Angelo 1, Tel. 0774/20366. Closed Fridays. Dinner for two L110,000. All credit cards accepted.*

In front of the entrance to Villa Gregoriana this place has outside seating where you can enjoy the local cuisine. They make many of their pastas in house so they're sure to be fresh. They also specialize in meats, especially the *maialino* (baby pork) and *abbacchio* (lamb) *arrosto* as well as their *verdure fritte* (fried vegetables).

3. VILLA ESEDRA, *(near Hadrian's Villa), Via di Villa Adriana 51, Tel. 0774/534-716. Closed Wednesdays. Dinner for two L70,000. All credit cards accepted.*

You can get some interesting anitpasti like the *insalatine di pesce* (small fish salad), then you can move on to their pastas, which are all made in house, and are all superb, especially the *spaghetti all'amatriciana* (with tomatoes, cream and spices) and the *penne all'arrabiatta* (with tomatoes, galric oil and hot pepper). The meats are a little suspect, so you may get away with a less expensive bill if you only try the pastas.

CASTEL GANDOLPHO

Beautifully located above **Lake Albano**, about 15 miles east of Rome, **Castel Gandolpho** is the summer residence of the Pope. From up at the Castel Gandolpho, you can enjoy a wonderful view of the wooded slopes that fall swiftly down into the murky waters of a volcanic crater.

The one real sight to see is the **Palazzo Papal** (Papal Palace), built in 1624. During the summer months when the Pope is in residence, every Sunday at noon His Eminence gives an address in the courtyard of the palace. No permit is required to enter. First come, first servedis the rule.

ARRIVALS & DEPARTURES

By Car

Take the Via Appia Nuova (SS7) for about 30 minutes.

By Train

From Stazione Termini, it's about 35 minutes. From the station you will have to take a local taxi up to the Castel, unless you feel adventurous and want to walk the three kilometers uphill. Just follow the signs on the side of the road.

WHERE TO EAT

ANTICO RISTORANTE PAGANNELLI, *Piazza A Gramsci 4, Tel. 06/936-0004. Closed Tuesdays. Dinner for two L90,000. All credit cards accepted.*

This restaurant with a nice view of the lake has been in existence since 1882, and they still serve all the traditional dishes made with produce from the local countryside. They make a wonderful *strozzapreti all'amatriciana* (pasta with tomatoes, cream and spices), *risotto al'erbe* (rice dish with herbs), *maialino arrosto* (roast baby pork), *bracciole di cinghiale* (roast boar "arms"), and other savory dishes. Rumor has it that the Pope even has stopped in once of twice.

FRASCATI

Frascati, roughly 14 miles southeast of Rome. This town's wine is world famous, and something you should not miss. The ambiance of this hill town is magnificent.

Frascati is a great place to stay while visiting Rome if you can't stand the urban hustle and bustle. Since it's only 30 minutes and $5 away, Frascati's relaxing pace, scenic views, quaint little wine shops, excellent local restaurants, and winding old cobbletstone streets should be seriously considered as an alternative to downtown Rome.

Since this is still primarily an excursion, I've listed the restaurants first and hotels second for this beautiful town – even though I hope some of you will opt to stay here and enjoy Frscati's many charms.

ARRIVALS & DEPARTURES

By Car

Take the Via Tuscolana (SS215) up to the hill town (25 minute drive).

By Train

From Stazione Termini, board a local train that leaves every forty minutes or so from Track 27. The ride lasts a little over 35 minutes. Cost L4,500.

CONSIDER FRASCATI!

Even though I spent 8 years living in Rome, and have grown to love it, the city can be a bit overwhelming both for a first time visitor and the Roman veteran. It's large, congested, noisy, polluted and challenging while also being one of the most beautiful, charming cities filled with some of the world's most well-known sights and prized artistic treasures. Prices at most hotels and restaurants seem to have gone through the roof.

So if you are someone who would rather not experience the hectic pace of a big city, but you still want to see all that Rome has to offer, stay in **Frascati.** *This quaint, charming, quiet, little hill town is the perfect place to get away from it all while still having access to everything. The town is only 35 minutes away by train (the fare is L4,500) and the trains run every 45 minutes or so until 10:00pm. Granted there might be a concern if you want to take a nap in the middle of the afternoon, but that is what the* **Borghese gardens** *are for. Bring a picnic lunch and take a little siesta in the shade in one of the prettiest and peaceful gardens in any city in the world.*

In Frascati, you'll be able enjoy many good restaurants, sample the fine local wines from quaint little wine stores that are located all over the city. They serve you glasses or carafes from huge vats. You'll also be able to savor the ambiance of an ancient medieval town, with its cobblestone streets and twisting alleys. Here you'll be able to gaze out your windows and see lush valleys below, instead of looking out onto another building as you would probably do in Rome. And if you come in October, you'll be able to experience a wine festival of bacchanalian proportions.

So if you are used to the calm serenity of country life, but still want to experience the beauty that Rome has to offer, Frascati may be your answer.

WHERE TO STAY

1. ALBERGHO PANORAMA, *Piazza Carlo Casini 3, Frascati 00044. Tel. 06/942-1800 or 941-7955. 9 rooms, two with bath. Double with bath L85,000; Single with bathj L75,000. Double without bath L75,000; Single without bath L65,000. L15,000 for an extra bed. L30,000 for all meals. No credit cards accepted.* **

Situated in the centro storico with a beautiful panoramic view of Rome, this is a small but comfortable hotel for those on a budget. Say hi to the proprietress, Laura, for me. The view from the hotel is stunning.

2. BELLAVISTA, *Piazza Roma 2, 00044 Frascati. Tel. 06/942-1068 or 942-6320. Fax 06/942-1068. 13 rooms all with bath. Double L130,000-160,000. Breakfast L10,000. All credit cards accepted.* ***

You have room service, TV in your room, and a hotel bar, as well as a nice view of the valley. The rooms are clean and comfortbale as befits a good country three star. The building is quite quaint, and old but restored perfectly for your comfort. I love the high ceilings in the rooms, making them feel much larger.

3. HOTEL FLORA, *Via Vittorio Veneto 8 00044 Frascati. Tel. 06/941-6110. Fax 06/942-0198. 33 rooms only 30 with bath. Double L150,000; Single L120,000. Breakfast L12,000. All credit cards accepted.* ***

An old hotel decorated with style, located in a central position in Frascati. Much better amenities than the Bellavista, but not as good a view. Located a little ways outside of town, this hotel is set in a wonderfully tranquil environment. A good place to stay.

4. PINNOCCHIO'S, *Piazza del Mercata 20, Tel. 06/941-7883. Fax 06/941-7884. Single L80,000 (Double used as a single); Double L130,000. Seven rooms all with bath, mini-bar, and TV. No credit cards accepted.* **

Large comfortable rooms with gigantic bathrooms. Upstairs from the restaurant, so you can grab yourself a snack until late in the evening. The office is in the restaurant so you'll need to enter there to get your key.

Perfectly located on the central market square. A sight you have to see while in Frascati and a great place to get some fruits, vegetables (you can even get fresh bags of mixed salad), meats, and cheeses. The place is alive with bargaining and local greetings.

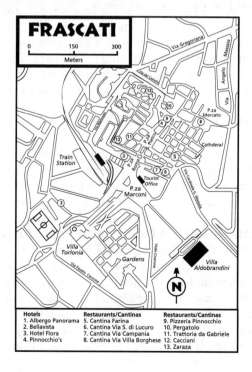

FRASCATI

Hotels	Restaurants/Cantinas	Restaurants/Cantinas
1. Albergo Panorama	5. Cantina Farina	9. Pizzeria Pinnocchio
2. Bellavista	6. Cantina Via S. di Lucuro	10. Pergatolo
3. Hotel Flora	7. Cantina Via Campania	11. Trattoria da Gabriele
4. Pinnocchio's	8. Cantina Via Villa Borghese	12. Cacciani
		13. Zaraza

WHERE TO EAT/WINE BARS

Some of the wine bars are so small and so nonchalant about the tourist trade that they don't even have names. Also many of the places do not have telephones. One of the owners explained to me, *"Why should we have telephones when we can walk over and talk in person?"* That makes sense, since Frascati is such a small intimate little town.

Don't be put off by this casual hill town attitude, since the ones without names or phones are some of the best places to visit. Enjoy.

5. CANTINA FARINA, *Vini Propri, Via Cavour 20. No Telephone.*

A real wine bar, not a fern infested one. With a tile floor, collapsible wooden tables and chairs and great wine served from vats, here you can get a real taste for how the Italians enjoy life. Located near a school, so it can get periodically noisy during the day.

6. CANTINA VIA SEPULCRO DI LUCURO, *Via Sepulcro di Lucuro 6. No Telephone.*

Located just off the main road (Via Catone), this place has a small area for seating outside separated from the rest of the world by large planters. The inside is quite cool, like a wine cellar. Just inside the door is an antique wine press that they still use during the pressing season. Inside or out you'll get some of the best wines Frascati has to offer here.

7. CANTINA VIA CAMPANIA, *Via Campania 17. No Telephone.*

Just down the road from the wine bar listed above, this place has one and a half of its four inside walls covered with wine vats, and the rest of the space taken up with strange looking tools used in the wine trade, as well as large empty bottles that you only wish you could take home with you ... full. The owner is quite friendly and if it's not too crowded will sit down and chat. Great wine. Wonderful atmosphere.

8. CANTINA VIA VILLA BORGHESE, *Via Villa Borghese 20. No Telephone.*

Small wine store filled with large 1,000,000 liter barrels called *botte*, and 500,000 liter barrels called *mezza botte*. Each cask is numbered and initialed with the vineyard it came from. Not very scenic atmosphere and no tables to sit at, but they will sell you a bottle of their finest for only L2,000. That's $1.50 for an excellent bottle of Frascati wine.

9. PIZZERIA/BIRRERIA PINNOCCHIO, *Piazza del Mercato 20, Tel. 06/941-6694 or 942-0330. Dinner for two L55,000.*

A large statue of Pinnocchio advertises this superb restaurant in Frascati's quaintest and most vibrant square (it's actually a triangle). There is outside seating with large planters separating you from the pace of this market-dominated piazza. Inside you'll find tiled floors and wood panelling giving the place a nice rustic flair. They serve great *canneloni ai quattro formaggi* (with four cheeses), as well as great Roman staples such as *amatriciana, carbonara, and vongole.*

For seconds try their *scampi alla griglia* (grilled shrimp) which is reasonably priced at only L16,000. If you find you've lingered too long over your Sambuca, Pinnocchio's has some wonderful rooms upstairs.

10. PERGATOLO, *Via del Castello 20, Tel. 06/942-04-64. L13,000-Cold plate with wine and bread; L20,000-First course of pasta, pizza, or meat, second course of the cold plate with wine and bread.*

Wild and fun atmosphere, a little on the touristy side with singers serenading the diners. You can either enjoy or ignore it in this large and spacious restaurant that has a deli counter displaying all the available meats, cheeses, breads, salamis, etc., that you'll be served. There are roaring fires behind the counter where your meats are all prepared.

If you've come to Frascati for the day or the week, this is one place you have to try, just for the fun of it. Say hi to the beautiful manager Tiziana for me.

11. TRATTORIA/PIZZERIA DA GABRIELE, *Via Solferino 5. No telephone. No credit cards. Dinner for two L35,000.*

You ladies will love the charming part owner Rapaaele. He looks like something out of a movie with his piercing dark eyes and sultry glances. You can get pizza until 1:30am at wonderfully inexpensive prices. Just off the main piazza, this is a fun place to come in the late evening. Try their *pizza can salsiccia* (with sausage) or *con porcini* (mushrooms). I asked them to put both together, with extra cheese, and the pizza came out wonderfully.

12. CACCIANI, *Via Alberto Diaz 13, Tel. 06/942-0378. Closed Mondays. Holidays January 7-15 and 10 days after ferragosto. Dinner for two L110,000. All credit cards accepted.*

One of the most famous restaurants in this region. It has a beautiful terrace that offers a tranquil and serene atmosphere. For starters, try the *crostini con verdure* (baked pastry appetizer filled with vegetables). Then try the home-made *fetuccine alla romana* (made with tomatoes, chicken and spices) or *spaghetti con le vongole verace* (with clams in a hot oil and garlic sauce). For the entré try the *fritto misto di carne* (mixed fried meats) the *saltimbocca*, or any of their grilled fish.

13. ZARAZA, *Viale Regina Margherita 21, Tel. 06/942-2053. Closed Mondays and the month of August. Dinner for two L70,000. Visa accepted.*

Traditional *cucina romana* where you can get *bucatini al'amatriciana* (pasta with tomatoes, cream and spices), *gnocchi al ragu* (potatoe dumplings with tomato-based meat sauce), *capaletti in brodo* (pasta shaped like little hats in soup), *trippa alla romana* (tripe with a tomato-based sauce) *abbacchio al forno* (grilled lamb), as well as some other Roman specialties such as *spaghetti all'amatriciana* and *penne all'arrabiata* (with a hot spicy tomatoe based sauce), as well as *lombata di vitello* (grilled veal chop) and *misto arosto* (mixed roast meats).

A simple rustic atmosphere with a few tables outside offering a limited view of the valley below. Inside tables are located in the basement of (but seperate from) the Albergho Panorama hotel. It's warm and inviting in the winter, with the heat from the kitchen, the brick pillars, the whitewashed arched walls, and the friendly family service.

SEEING THE SIGHTS

If you've driven, you've seen the lovely scenic route to Frascati along the old **Appia Antica**, past the Catacombs and ruined tombs. The town is perched halfway up a hill, and on a clear day you will have splendid views of all of Rome and its scenic countryside.

Besides the great views, the wine, and the chance for some relaxation, Frascati has a wealth of villas and spacious parks that were formerly residences of princes and popes. One of these residences, **Villa Aldobrandini**, sits just above the town, and has a magnificent garden in which you can find solitude. To enter the villa's grounds you need to first get a free pass from the **Aziendo di Soggiorno e Tourismo**, in Frascati's Piazza Marconi. *The hours are Monday–Friday 9:00am–1:00pm.*

Besides the beauty of its old villas, many of which were damaged in Allied bombings because the Germans had taken over the town for their headquarters, Frascati's draw is the fine **white wine** that bares its name. All wines seem to lose a special *qualcosa* when they travel, so if you are a wine lover, do not miss out on this chance to drink Frascati's wine directly at the source.

To enjoy this succulent nectar, there are old, dark wine stores, with heavy wooden tables and chairs located all over town. At one of these you can sip and enjoy this unspoiled and inexpensive wine, the way the natives have been doing it for centuries. The **Cantina Vanelli**, just off Piazza Fabro Filzi, is a prime example of one such wine store, and a fine traditional location to sample Frascati's produce. Just ask for a *bicchiere di vino* (glass of wine). An alternative to the cramped quarters of these wine stores but with quite a bit less atmosphere would be to sit at one of the sidewalk cafés offering superb views along with great wine.

Frascati is the perfect place to wander through, getting lost in the alleys, side streets, steps leading nowhere, and winding roads (all cobblestoned). If you follow the sporadically placed yellow signs that say *Ferario Pedonale,* you'll be guided through all the major sights and sounds of this hill town. One distinguishing feature is that there seem to be more *alimentaris* (little food stores) per person than in any other city I've ever seen.

If you are fortunate enough to be in Frascati in the fall, specifically during the month of October, the town celebrates a **wine festival** of pagan proportions that lasts several days and nights. Come out to witness and partake in the debauchery, but please do not drive back to Rome afterwards – take the train.

LAGO DI BRACCIANO

Bracciano, 26 miles north northwest of Rome, is a place to visit if you desperately need to go swimming or entertain the kids for a while. There are sights to see in the main town, with its imposing castle, but the distance and time to get here, and lack of adequate restaurants, make it a destination only if you feel the need to swim in fresh water. **Ostia Lido** is closer and much more easily accessible if you want to go swimming.

One of the best sights on the way to Bracciano, whether by car or train (since the train follows the roadway) is a still functional ancient **Roman aquaduct** that slices through lush green fields. When you get to the town Bracciano, you need to drive or walk down the hill to get to the **lake**. It's about a 15 minute walk and a three minute drive.

The lake is about 22 miles in circumference, and its shoreline boasts the town of **Bracciano**, standing high above the lake; the picturesque village of **Trevignano**; and the popular resort of **Anguillara**. The shores of the lake, planted with pine and olive groves, make pleasant picnic spots and swimming areas. Bracciano seems dominated by the **Castello Orsini**, the castle of the former landlords of the town. The structure, completed around 1485, is a magnificent example of a private Rennaissance castle. It has a polygonal shape accompanied by five slender circular towers rising from it. Many rooms open to public still display the original frescoes and contain some quite good Etruscan relics and a fascinating collection of arms and armor. *Tel. 902-4003. Open Tuesday to Sunday 10:00am–Noon and 3:00pm–6:00pm in the summer, and Tuesday – Sunday 9:00am–Noon and 3:00pm–5:00pm in the winter. Admission L7,000.*

While at Bracciano you can also rent dinghies and paddle out on the water. There's not much to do or see, and the beach space is relatively limited, so try to come during the week and not on the weekends.

ARRIVALS & DEPARTURES

By Car

Drive about 45 minutes up the Via Cassia (SS2) to Madonna di Bracciano, then take route 493 to the lake.

By Train

From Stazione Ostiense it takes about 1 and a quarter hours and costs L8,400. In Rome, take the metro to the Piramide stop, and walk through the underpass at the "Ple Partigiani" exit to the Ostiense station. Buy your ticket at this station.

WHERE TO EAT

In all honesty I cannot recommend any of the restaurants in Bracciano, but if you haven't prepared a picnic lunch or didn't buy supplies in the town to bring down to the beach area, there are plenty of little bars and cafés lining the main road around the beach, and a few floating restaurants you might brave.

CERVETRI

Cervetri used to be the Etruscan capital of **Caere**, which the Romans at one point overran on their rise to power long before the Roman Empire. But Cervetri is not known today for the town of the living, but the towns of the dead the Etruscans built. These **necropoli** are large circular mounds of tombs laid out in a pattern of street like houses in a city.

Today their round roofs are densely covered with grasses and wild flowers. Inside they have been furnished with replicas of household furnishings carved from stone. Most of the original artifacts are in the **Villa Giulia Museum** or the **Vatican Museums** in Rome. *The site is open Tuesday to Sunday 9:00am–4:00pm. Admission L6,000.*

After viewing the necropolis you can settle down among the mounds and have a picnic lunch, and imagine what life would be like during that time. After sightseeing you can return to the town by taxi, or by car if you have one, and take in the limited sights the little town has to offer. From the crowded main piazza you can climb steps to a **museum** with a lovely medieval courtyard.

ARRIVALS & DEPARTURES

Cervetri is about 28 miles west northwest of Rome.

By Car

A 45 minute drive up the Via Aurelia (SS1), which will give you a more scenic view, or the Autostrada A12, which connects to the 'beltway' around Rome by route 201.

By Train

From Stazione Termini it takes 1 hour and 10 minutes; from Roma Tiburtina it takes 50 minute to get to Cervetri-Ladispoli. Once in the town, to reach the **Necropolis** you can grab a local taxi, or take the two kilometer walk along a quiet little road. There are signs on the road to guide you where you're going. If in doubt stay to the right at the fork in the road.

WHERE TO EAT

DA FIORE, *near Procoio di Ceri, Tel. 06/9920-4250. Closed Wednesdays. Dinner for two L60,000. No credit cards accepted.*

A simple little local *trattoria* in the open country not far from the ruins and only four kilometers from the Via Aurelia. They make great pastas like *penne al funghi* (with mushrooms) *al ragu* (with tomatoe and meat sauce) or *con salsiccia* (with sausage), as well as grilled meats and their famous *brushetta* (garlic bread as an appetizer) and pizza – all cooked in a wood burning oven.

OSTIA ANTICA & LIDO DI OSTIA

Ostia Antica

Founded in the fourth century BC, **Ostia Antica** feels about as far away from Rome as you can get. You get the sensation that the clock has been turned back nearly 2,000 years here. But actually it is only 15 miles southwest of the city, a mere 45 minutes by subway (don't take your car or you'll defeat the purpose of relaxation).

This city was once the bustling port of Ancient Rome, but today it is calm and serene, and it is only busy with quiet. It is well preserved despite having been subject to repeated attacks by pirates and hostile navies. The only invasions it undergoes now are from packs of marauding Italian school children, on their cultural outings, rampaging through its archaeological excavations – the main reason to come here (see below).

ARRIVALS & DEPARTURES

By Car

Take the Via del Mare (SS8) for about 25 minutes.

By Metro & Train

Buy a metro ticket and take Linea B to the Magliana station, and catch the train to Ostia Antica or continue to Lido di Ostia (the beach). It takes about 45 minutes from Stazione Termini. You'll have to pay a new fare (L3,000) to take the beach train, since the Metro and the train systems are different animals.

WHERE TO EAT

Consider a picnic lunch. All the other restaurants are by the beach, so if you're heading that way, see the listings under Lido di Ostia below.

IL MONUMENTO, 18 *Piazza Umberto I, Tel. 06/565-0021. Closed Mondays. Holidays Aug 15 - Sept 15. Dinner for two L90,000. Credit cards accepted.*

A simple seafood restaurant with quaint outside seating on the main piazza. Try the *spaghetti "Monumento"* with seafood and shrimp, as well as the *spaghetti con cozze* (with muscles) either in their light white sauce or their spicy red sauce. For seconds try any of the fish, which they either bake in the oven or grill on an open fire.

SEEING THE SIGHTS

You enter the excavations in Ostia at the **Porta Romana** from which you follow the **Decumanus Maximus**, the old city's main street. You will encounter the well-preserved old **Theater**. From here you overlook the **Piazzale dei Corporazione** (Corporation Square), a tree-lined boulevard once filled with over seventy commercial offices of wine importers, ship owners, oil merchants, or rope makers. The well-preserved laundry and wine shop should be visited. These offices are tastefully decorated with mosaic tiled floors representing the trades of each location (If you will not have a chance to visit Pompeii, this will give you the taste and feel, on a smaller scale, of that famous city). The chief commodity was corn, but there were also such imported luxuries as ivory (depicted by an elephant).

Farther down the Decumanus Maximus you arrive at the **Capitolium**, a temple dedicated to Jupiter and Minerva, located at the end of the **Forum**. The **insulae** (apartment blocks) are of particular interest since they are often four or five stories high. This is where the regular people and smaller merchants lived. Only the most wealthy of the merchants were able to build themselves villas. The *insulae* were well lighted, had running water, and had a means for sanitation (i.e., garbage removal) on each floor.

Two private home of interest that should be visited are the **House of the Cupid and Psyche**, which is west of the Capitolium, and the **House of the Dioscuri**, which is at the southwest end of town.

The site is open daily 9:00am–6:00pm in summer, 9:00am–4:00pm in winter. Admission L10,000.

Lido di Ostia

Lido di Ostia is the beach about four kilometers from the ruins of Ostia Antica. Take the same route that you took to the ruins but continue on a little farther either by car or by train (see *Arrrivals & Departures* above for more details). This is a perfect place to visit after a tough day of walking through the buildings and necropoli of the Old City.

Treat yourself to a seaside celebration. There are rafts to rent, umbrellas to use, *cabanas* to change in, restaurants to go to, and hotels to stay at if you get to tired and don't want to get back to Rome. Lido di Ostia is a typical Italian beach and it's close to Rome. But don't go on the weekend unless you like mobs of people.

WHERE TO STAY

If you find you've lingered over the wine and the seafood a little too long, here are some hotel suggestions:

ROME AIRPORT PALACE HOTEL, *Viale Romagnoli 165, Lido Di Ostia. Tel. 06/569-2341. Fax 06/569-8908. 260 rooms, 230 with bath. All credit cards accepted. Double L320,000; Single L200,000.* *****

Don't let the name fool you, this place is quiet and it is also close to the beach. Also it's the only five star deluxe hotel in the area. They have everything you could need or want like a bar, restaurant, reading room, air conditioning, and more.

SATELLITE PALACE HOTEL, *Via delle Antille 49, Lido Di Ostia. Tel. 06/569-3841. Fax 06/569-8908. 283 rooms all with bath. All credit cards accepted. Single L200,000; Double L320,000. Air conditioning.* ****

Even though the star rating is one below it's cousin just around the corner, the Rome Airport Palace Hotel, the service and prices are exactly the same. They even have more, like a disco, swimming pool, audio video equipment, a sauna, a solarium, and so on, so I don't know why they don't have that last and final deluxe star.

HOTEL KURSAAL 2000, *Via F D'Aragona 10, Lido Di Ostia. Tel. 06/567-0616. Fax 06/567-0547. 38 rooms, 8 suites, all with bath. All credit cards accepted. Double L125,000; Suite L250,000.* ***

A good deal in a very tranquil location right near the beach. They have their own piano bar and restaurant so you don't have to stray too far at night. The rooms are all air conditioned, clean and tidy, and each has the necessary amenities to make this a three star hotel.

HOTEL RIVA, *Piazzale Mageliano 22, Lido Di Ostia. Tel. 06/562-2231. Fax 06/562-1667. 15 rooms all with bath. Single L105,000-115,000; Double L118,000-148,000. All credit cards accepted.* ***

Located near the beach, this is a good but not great three star hotel that overlooks the sea in the front and has a tranquil garden in the back. You also have prompt room service, air conditioning, a good restaurant and a small but comfortable bar.

WHERE TO EAT

LA CAPANNINA DA PASQUALE, *Lungomare Vespucci 156, Tel. 06/567-0143. Closed Mondays. Holidays in November. All credit cards accepted. Dinner for two L110,000.*

A little expensive but the location is supreme, especially the outside seating right on the sea. They have a superb antipasto table which could serve as your whole meal if you're not too hungry. Their pastas and rice dishes are also good since many of them have been home-made at the restaurant. Try the *risotto ai frutti di mare* (rise with seafood ladled over the top). They are known for their seafood dishes so try anything *al forno* (cooked over the grill), with their wonderfully grilled potatoes. The service is stupendous, as it should be based on the price.

CHIARALUCE, *Via Ponte di Tor Boacciana 13, Tel. 06/569-1302. Closed Wednesdays. No credit cards accepted. Dinner for two L60,000.*

A little off the beaten track with tranquil outside seating. This is a small local place that prides itself on making superb food. They make a great *saute di vongole* (sauteed clams) as well as *spaghetti con vongole* (with clams), and a huge mixed fried seafood platter (*frittura mista*). They also make perfectly grilled fish that goes well with their excellent house wine. The food is very good here.

PECCATI DI GOLA, *Corso Regina Maria Pia 19, Tel. 06/560-1233. Closed Mondays. No credit cards accepted. Dinner for two L70,000.*

On a street parallel to the beach, this is (surprise) another great fish restaurant that also serves well prepared meat dishes. You can watch through the glass partition as the cooks make each dish. If you're looking for light fare try their *insalata di mare* (mixed seafood salad).

TRE PULCINI, *Viale della Pineta di Ostia 30, Tel. 06/562-1293. Closed Mondays. Dinner for Two L110,000. All credit cards accepted.*

A simple family run place with mama Antonietta in the kitchen and Renato in the restaurant. Here you'll experience some true down home Italian cooking. Try their *saute di cozze e vongole* (sauteed muscles and clams), *zuppa di pesce* (fish soup), or their *fritto misto* (mixed fried seafood). You can also get some home-made *gelato* (ice cream) as dessert which is made daily by the daughter Cristina. You can enjoy all of this either outside on the balcony or in the air conditioned comfort of the interior.

VILLA IRMA, *Corso Regina Maria Pia 67, Tel. 06/560-3877. Closed Tuesdays. Holidays December 20-30. Dinner for two L 150,000. All credit cards accepted.*

Super expensive but superb restaurant, some say the best in Ostia. You can enjoy the ambiance of the patio or the comfort of air conditioning inside while you dine on the wonderfully prepared seafood dishes. Anything here on the grill (*alla griglia*) or fried (*fritta*) is great. The service is four-star perfect. The place to come if you want to be treated like royalty.

19. POMPEII, HERCULANEUM, & CAPRI

If you have any free time while in Rome, try to visit the two ancient cities of **Pompeii** and **Herculanuem**. They are truly a major wonder of the world: two cities trapped in time by a devastating volcanic eruption. What more could you ask for?

If that's not enough, I've also included in this chapter an excursion to the beautiful **Isle of Capri**, a Mediterranean paradise for beach fans and water sports enthusiasts alike.

POMPEII & HERCULANEUM

Two thousand people died and thousands more lost their homes when **Vesuvius** erupted in 79 AD, and submerged **Pompeii**, **Herculaneum**, and **Stabiae** with lava. The lava created an almost perfect time capsule, sealing in an important cross-section of an ancient civilization for many centuries.

ARRIVALS & DEPARTURES

Since these ancient towns are a good 150 miles away from Rome, and could easily take three hours each way, consider a tour to see the ruins.

By Tour
Contact one of the following tour operators:
• **American Express**, *Piazza di Spagna 38, Tel. 6764*
• **Appian Line**, *Via Vittorio Veneto 84, Tel. 474-1641*
• **CIT**, *Piazza della Repubblica 68, Tel. 479821* (they'll help you find your own tour guide.)

By Car
Take the Autostrade A2 to Naples, then the S18 to the S70.

By Train

From Stazione Termini to Napoli Centrale, then go one floor below the Central Station to the Circumvesuviana station for a local high speed train to Ercolano (Herculaneum) or Pompeii Scavi (3 1/2 to 4 hours total journey). Purchase one of the inexpensive maps available so you can find your way through the two ruined cities.

Pompeii

Before the catastrophe, **Pompeii** was an old established city with a diverse population of about 25,000 that reflected successive waves of colonization. By 80 BC, it was a favorite resort of wealthy Romans.

Although the ruins were discovered in the 16th century and rudimentary excavations began in 1763, systematic excavations did not get under way until 1911. Since then only about three fifths of the site has been freed from the death grip of the lava.

Strolling through this dead city is quite ominous. You can easily imagine yourself living here. Many pieces of regular life remain: the walls are covered in graffiti, ranging from erotic drawings to political slogans, since a local election was taking place when the eruption occurred. There are also abundant frescoes depicting mythological scenes in the wealthier homes, as well as frescoes indicating what form of work the owners of the house partook in.

Some of the best homes to see are the **House of the Faun** and the **House of the Vettii**, both in the residential area north of the Forum. Other homes of interest are the **House of the Melander** (located to the east of the Forum), the **Villa of the Mysteries** (located to the west of the main town), and the **House of Pansa** (located to the north of the Forum) that also included rented apartments.

Also in evidence in the remains are symbols of the cult of Dionysos. But this cult was only one of many that flourished in the city. The **Temple of Isis** (to the East of the Forum) testifies to the strong following that the Egyptian goddess had here. The public **Ampitheater**, in the east of the city, should not be missed. There are locations on the stage area that if a whisper is spoken, even a person standing at the top-most part of the seating area can hear it clearly. Other attractions are the footprints left in time, the mummified bodies trying to shield themselves from the lava, and more. Everything about Pompeii is a wonder to behold.

Gates to the site open year round 9:00am to 1 hour before sunset. Admission L10,000.

Herculaneum

Seventeen miles northeast of Pompeii is the smaller town of **Herculaneum**. At the time of the eruption it had only 5,000 inhabitants, compared to the 25,000 in Pompeii, had virtually no commerce, and its industry was solely based on fishing. The volcanic mud that flowed through every building and street in Herculaneum was different from that which buried Pompeii. This steaming hot lava-like substance settled eventually to a depth of 40 feet and set rock-hard, sealing and preserving everything it came in contact with. Also the absence of the hail of hot ash that rained down on Pompeii, which smashed its buildings, meant that many of the inhabitants of Herculaneum were able to get away in time, and that complete houses, with their woodwork, household goods, and furniture were preserved.

Although Herculaneum was a relatively unimportant town compared with Pompeii, many of the houses that have been excavated were from the wealthy class. It is speculated that perhaps the town was like a retirement village, populated by prosperous Romans seeking to pass their retirement years in the calm of a small seaside town. This idea is bolstered by the fact that the few craft shops that have been discovered were solely for the manufacture of luxury goods.

Archaeologists speculate that the most desirable residential area was in the southwest part of town which overlooked the ocean in many different housing terraces. Here you will find the **House of the Stags**, famous for its beautiful frescoes, sculpted stags, and a drunken figure of Hercules.

Farther north you can find the marvelously preserved **House of the Wooden Partition**. It is one of the most complete examples of a private residence in either Pompeii or Herculaneum. (Remember that this town was recently discovered which allowed for better preservation efforts, unlike Pompeii which was discovered in the 16th century) Near this house to the north are the **Baths**, an elaborate complex incorporating a gymnasium and assorted men's and women's baths.

Gates to the site open year round 9:00am to 1 hour before sunset. Admission L10,000.

CAPRI

Capri is an island geared completely for the reaping of tourist dollars. That doesn't mean that it is not beautiful, like the **Blue Grotto**, but remember that in the summer the population of Capri fluctuates perhaps more than any other island in the world. This increase is a result of many tourists from the mainland and all over the world, and temporary residents who summer on the island. In winter, life reverts to the dreamy pace that has been so characteristic of Capri over the centuries. So if you want to see a relatively pristine part of paradise unsoiled by rampant tourism, try to visit in the winter months. Many tourist stores and restaurants will be closed, but you'll have the island almost to yourself.

ARRIVALS & DEPARTURES

By Tour

Since this beautiful island is over 125 miles away from Rome, and could easily take three hours each way, I recommend taking a tour to see the beauty of the place. Contact one of the following tour operators:

• **American Express**, *Piazza di Spagna 38, Tel. 6764*
• **Appian Line**, *Via Vittorio Veneto 84, Tel. 171-1611*
• **CIT**, *Piazza della Repubblica 68, Tel. 479821* (they'll help you find your own tour guide.)

By Car

Take the Autostrade A2 to Naples down to the ferry or hydrofoil docks (they only run in the summer). Go to the Mole Beverello to catch the ferry or hydrofoil (tourist cars are not allowed on the island, so you'll have to leave it in Naples. Not a good idea.)

By Train

From Stazione Termini to Napoli Centrale takes about 2 hours and 30 minutes. Then take a taxi to Molo Beverello in the harbor to catch the ferry or hydrofoil to the island.

WHERE TO STAY

1. QUISISANA E GRAND HOTEL, *Via Camerelle 2, 80073Capri, Tel. 081/ 837-0788. Fax 081/837-6080. 143 rooms, 15 suites all with bath. All credit cards accepted. Double L330,000-550,000; Single L225,000-325,000.* *****

An ultra-luxurious hotel with swimming pool, health club, tennis courts, sauna, a great restaurant, as well as excellent views of the whole island. Here you'd be staying in the lap of luxury. The rooms are large and comfortable and have all the amenities you could expect: mini-bar, TV, air conditioning, room service, hairdryers and more. If you have the money, this is a great place to stay.

2. EUROPA PALACE HOTEL, *(Anacapri) Via Capodimonte, 80071 Capri. 081/837-0955. Fax 081/837-3191. 93 rooms all with bath. Double L270,000-460,000; Single L180,000-250,000. All credit cards accepted.* ****

They have an outdoor pool as well as a covered swimming pool, a health club, a weight room, a sauna, a private beach, a sun room, a piano bar, a great restaurant with a scenic view and almost everything you could

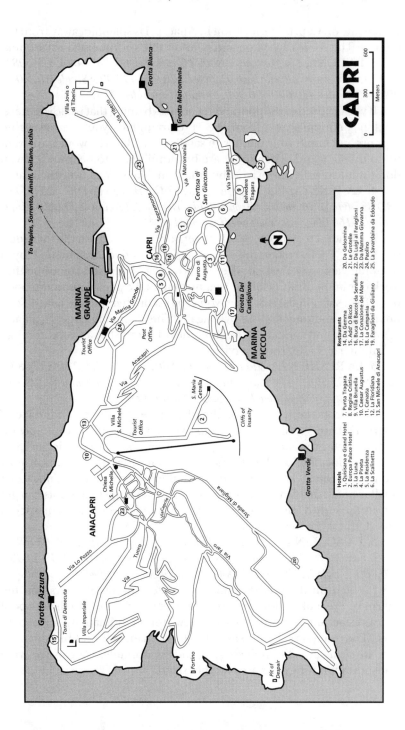

want while on Capri. The location in Anacapri is splendid, away from the crowds. The rooms are large and comfortable with spotless bathrooms.

3. LA LUNA, *Via Matteoti 3, 80073 Capri. Tel. 081/837-0433. Fax 081/ 837-7459. 50 rooms all with bath. Double L220,000-430,000; Single L165,000-200,000. Suites 430,000-550,000. Breakfast included.* ****

If you get tired of the pool and the topless bathing that is allowed here, or the panoramic view from the restaurant/bar, you can always go upstairs and numb your mind with satellite TV. But why would you want to do that in Capri, when there are beautiful sights to be found? If you don't want to walk they have a bus that can take you all over the island.

4. LA PINETA, *Via Tragara 6, 80073 Capri. Tel. 081/837-0644. Fax 081/837-6445. 36 rooms all with bath. Double L170,000-290,000; Single L80,000-160,000. All credit cards accepted.* ****

If you want to gain weight, then get back in shape all in the same day, stay here. Their restaurant serves superb food complimented by a stunning view over the sea. After you've gorged yourself you can either work out in the health club or weight room, take a few laps in the pool, or go for a swim in the sea. Then you can rest on their private beach, soak up the sun, and then do it all over again. The rooms are large, clean and comfortable and contain all the amenities of a four star: air conditioning, TV, mini-bar, radio, room service, etc.

5. LA RESIDENZA, *Via F Serena 22, 80073 Capri. Tel. 081/837-0833. Fax 081/837-7564. 114 rooms all with bath. All credit cards accepted. Single L170,000-200,000; Double L260,000-320,000.* ****

The second largest hotel on the island (the Quisisana e Grand Hotel is larger), here you'll find everything you could want for your stay on Capri: a good restaurant with a great view, a pool with scenic guests, a hotel bar, location on the sea, clean and comfortable rooms, transport around the island, and more. But if you want the romantic intimacy of a smaller hotel, this is not the place to stay. It's so large that guests can get lost in the crowd. But if you want anonymity for you and your special friend, this is a good choice.

6. LA SCALINATELLA, *Via Tragara 10, 80073 Capri. Tel. 081/837-0633. Fax 081/837-8291. 30 rooms, 2 suites, all with bath. Double L350,000-580,000; Single L230,000-350,000. All credit cards accepted.* ****

Located on the sea, this small intimate little hotel offers you the charm you're looking for when you think of Capri. They also have a pool and a restaurant that offers perfect views for an intimate dining experience. The rooms are slightly small, but this enhances the intimate appeal; they are clean, eclectically decorated, and comfortable. They also provide transportation for guests around the island.

7. PUNTA TRAGARA, *Via Tragara 57, 80073 Capri. Tel. 081/837-0844. Fax 081/837-7790. 16 rooms all with bath. Double L280,000-400,000; Suite L380,000-520,000. Breakfast included. All credit cards accepted.* ****

A prime, elegant, intimate hotel. With only 16 rooms every guest is a treasure to the proprietors. They offer small serene rooms, many with excellent views. They are located on the sea and have a weight room, sauna, and thermal baths for your pleasure. Then in the evening you can either enjoy their disco or bar, or go for a walk into Capri.

8. REGINA CRISTINA, *Via F Serena 20, 80073 Capri. Tel. 081/837-0744. Fax 081/837-0550. 55 rooms all with bath. Double L160,000-400,000; Single L130,000-180,000. All credit cards accepted.* ****

Located on the sea, this hotel offers all the basic amenities of a four star hotel. It's quiet, they have a pool, transportation for guests, but there's something missing – charm. The rooms are fair sized, somewhat clean, and comfortable, but – again – no charm. Maybe it's the surly staff, or that things look a little in disarray.

9. VILLA BRUNELLA, *Via Tragara 24, 80073 Capri. Tel 081/837-0122. Fax 081/837-0430. 18 rooms all with bath. Double L300,000. All credit cards accepted.* ****

You can enjoy the sea by the view from the restaurant or from the small local beach a few meters away. A small hotel with its own piano bar and cocktail lounge, the rooms are relatively small but they have the necessary air conditioning, TV, mini bar, etc. The bathrooms are okay-sized but immaculately clean. Located a little way outside of Capri, it's only a short walk to get into the center of town.

10. CAESAR AUGUSTUS *(Anacapri), Via G. Orlandi 4, 80071 Capri. Tel. 081/837-1421. Fax 081/837-1444. 58 rooms, 4 suites all with bath. Double L100,000-350,000; Single L60,000-150,000; Suite L350,000. Breakfast L15,000. All credit cards accepted.* ***

This is *La creme de la creme* of the three stars on Capri. The rooms are large with well appointed bathrooms. They have a pool that seems to attract some of the best bathing beauties around, and the hotel also has a stupendous view of the sea and parts of Capri. The only thing really missing is a restaurant, but you're within walking distance of Anacapri so you can sample the many restaurants there.

11. CANASTA, *Via Campo di Teste 6, 80073 Capri. Tel. 081/837-8298. Fax 081/837-8933. 17 rooms all with bath. Double L120,000-200,000; Single L90,000-110,000. All credit cards accepted.* ***

A quaint little three star that has all the amenities and charm of many of the four stars without the exorbitant prices. Located on the sea, this is a small romantic hotel that only lacks a restaurnat so guests don't have to go out for dinner. With the restaurant, this place would be a four star.

12. LA FLORIDIANA, *Via Campo di Teste 16, 80073 Capri. Tel. 081/ 837-0166. Fax 081/837-0434. 36 rooms all with bath. Double 125,000- 240,000; Single L60,000-120,000; Suite 380,000. Breakfast L30,000. All credit cards accepted.* ***

An intimate three star with a good restaurant that has a fantastic view. Some of the quiet rooms share this same view of the sea. In the evenings you can sit sipping a room service cocktail from your plain but attractive room and reflect on the beauty that is Capri. Since you're right on the sea your bathing opportunities abound.

13. SAN MICHELE DI ANACAPRI, *Via G Orlandi 3, 80071 Capri. Tel. 081/837-1427. Fax 081/837-1420. Double L140,000-200,000; Single L100,000-120,000. Breakfast included. All credit cards accepted.****

Oh my, what a view. Located on the edge of a cliff, almost all the rooms have the most spectacular view you could find anywhere. The excellent restaurant and swimming pool share the same scenery. It doesn't have the intimacy of a smaller hotel, but it has worlds of charm. The rooms are large and comfortable and bathrooms are immaculate.

WHERE TO EAT

14. DA GEMMA, *Via Madre Serafina 6, Capri, Tel. 081/837-0461. Closed Mondays and November. Dinner for two L50,000. All credit cards accepted.*

In the hot summer months, come here to enjoy the cool air-conditioned comfort and great food. Even though Gemma is no longer around to run the place, her family continues the tradition of classic Italian food with just enough flair to make them unique and interesting. They are famous for their *spaghetti alla vongole* (with clam sauce) and the *"fritto alla Gemma"* (fried food alla Gemma with mozzarella and zucchini and other vegatables).

15. ADD' 'O RICCIO, *Locanda Gradola, Via Grotta Azzurra 4, Tel. 081/ 837-1380. Open all week. Closed for holidays November 10 - March 15. Dinner for two L110,000. All credit cards accepted.*

Come here for the food as well as the beautiful terrace overlooking the water, the rocks, and the Grotta Azzurra (Blue Grotto). They make a superb *risotto al mare* (seafood rice dish) and grilled or baked fish.

16. BUCA DI BACCO DA SERAFINA, *Via Longano 35, Tel. 081/837- 0723. Closed Wednesdays and November. Dinner for Two L80,000. All credit cards accepted.*

This is a small pizzeria *trattoria* with the wood burning oven the center of attention in the place. As you guessed, they make great pizzas. Try one of their specials, loaded with mozzarella and ricotta cheeses. They also make great pasta dishes, including a *pennette alla peperoni* (small tubular pasta in a tomato and sausage sauce). Since they're on Capri, they also serve a variety of seafood dishes for good prices.

17. LA CONAZONE DEL MARE, *Via Marina Piccola 93, Tel. 081/837-0104. Only open for dinner. Holidays November to March. Meal for two L110,000. All credit cards accepted.*

Located at the small marina with a beautiful terrace overlooking everything. The perfect place to enjoy a meal and watch the people go by. You can get a variety of food here, including toast (bruschetta) loaded with mozzarella, tomatoes and olive oil, as well as a scrumptious club sandwich. Any of their *antipasti di mare* (seafood appetizers) are superb. Try their *spaghetti con pomodor e basilico* (with tomatoes and basil) or their *spaghetti ai frutti di mare* (with seafood). For seconds they have a great selection of fresh fish, either grilled, cooked in the oven, or *all'aqua pazza* (in crazy water, i.e. boiled).

18. LA CAMPANINA, *Via delle Botteghe 12, Tel. 081/837-0732. Closed Wednesdays and November to Easter. Dinner for two L140,000. All credit cards accepted.*

A fine family run, upscale, but rustic establishment. You'll enjoy the air conditioning in the heat of the summer. Try their linguine *ai frutti di mare* (with seafood) and their *coniglio "alla tiberiana"* (rabbit stewed with tomatoes and spices). Here you'll get peasant fare for a princely sum.

19. FARAGLIONI DA GIULIANO, *Via Camarelle 75, Tel. 081/837-0320. Closed Mondays and Nover 15 to March 15. Dinner for two L110,000. All credit cards accepted.*

You can enjoy the traditional cooking either in air conditioned comfort inside or out on their terrace overlooking the street. They make a good *risotto alla pescatore* (rice with seafood), *spaghetti ai frutti di mare* (with seafood) and any of their grilled fish dishes, especially the sole.

20. DA GELSOMINA, *(Anacapri) Via Belvedere Migliari, Tel. 081/837-1499. Closed Tuesdays and January 20-31. Dinner for two L70,000. All credit cards accepted.*

Off the beaten path, and quite a hike from Anacapri or Capri, but it's worth the journey. Great peasant food served on a beautiful veranda overlooking the ocean and the lights from Capri below. Try their *spaghetti alla cozze* (with muscles) or their great antipasto table for primo. Then sample their great *coniglio alla cacciatore* (rabbit with a tomato, brandy, and mixed spices – you have to try it).

21. LE GROTELLE, *Via Arco Naturale 5, Tel. 081/837-5719. Closed Thursdays and December 1 - January 3. Dinner for L 100,000. All credit cards accepted.*

Out in the middle of a virtual nature preserve, from the terrace you have a spectacular view of the sea, the stars, and nature. Here you get typical local fare like *pasta e fagioli, ravioli alla caprese*, and fish either fried or grilled. If you sit inside, these delicious smells permeate the rooms making your meal all the more enjoyable.

22. DA LUIGI AI FARAGLIONI, *Strade dei Faraglioni, Tel. 081/837-0591. Open only for dinner. Dinner for two L120,000. All credit cards accepted.*

The best terrace in Capri. Out on a small peninsula off the island, you can try some wonderfully prepared seafood dishes like *sauté di vongole* (sautéd clams), or *pomodoro "alla Luigi"* (with mozzarella e basil) or *pizza "Monacone"* (filled with vegetables). Come for the romantic view (remember to reserve a spot) and stay for the food.

23. DA MAMMA GIOVANNA, *(Anacapri) Via Boffe 3/5, Tel. 081/837-2057. Closed Mondays and the ten days after Christmas. Dinner for two L80,000. All credit cards accepted.*

Located in the heart of Anacapri, this is a small, quaint, local trattoria that makes great pizzas as well as grilled or oven cooked meats and fish. They have a terrace from which you can watch the night pass as you sip your dry house wine and enjoy the food.

24. PAOLINO, *Via Palazzo a Mare 11, Tel. 081/837-6102. CLosed Mondays and January 15 to Easter. Dinner for two L120,000. All credit cards accepted.*

They've got old stoves and other cooking devices for the bases of the tables, which lends the place a nice down to earth touch that seems to go well with their sky high prices. Try their *ravioli alla caprese, spaghetti con pomodoro*, or *rucola e gamberi* for primo. For seconds try any of their seafood on the grill.

25. LA SAVARDINA DA EDOARDO, *Via Lo Capo Tiberio 8, Tel. 081/837-6300. Closed November to March. Dinner for two L75,000. All credit cards.*

You can only get here on foot, but it's worth the hike. Some of the best food on the island as well as some of the best prices. The terraces looks out over lemon and other fruit trees making the meal quite tranquil. They make great *fiori di zucchine fritte* (fried zucchini flowers) and *conniglio alla cacciatore* (rabbit cooked in tomatoes, brandy, and spices). A nice place to come for a change of pace.

SEEING THE SIGHTS

To get to the town of Capri after you've made it to the **Marina Grande**, the main harbor on the island, take the funicular (kind of like a trolley rising up the mountain). From here you can enjoy a memorable view from **Piazza Umberto I** over the **Bay of Naples**. You can walk – granted it's a long way – northeast to the ruined **Palace of Tiberius**, and along the way enjoy the breathtaking views.

The Palace is perched on an imposing hilltop from which the Emperor is said to have thrown his enemies (and if you've read any Roman history this is probably true). *Open daily 9:00am until 1 hour before sunset. Admission L5,000.* On the south edge of town is the **Certosa di San**

Giacomo, a 14th century Carthusian monastery now largely in ruins, as well as the **Parco Augusto** that offers you fine views to the south of the island. *Both are open 24 hours.*

From here you can follow a road that leads to the **Marina Piccola** (small harbor). From the harbor southeast along the shoreline you can venture a dip in the water from the rocks (in the summer of course).

My favorite part of the island is the town of **Anacapri**. It is perched high up on a rocky plateau, its flat-roofed buildings obviously Moorish in style. Here you can find the 18th century **Church of San Michele** (*open daily 7:00am–7:00pm*) and the **Villa San Michele**, which is known for its beautiful gardens and vast collection of classical sculpture. *Open summer 9:00am–6:00pm, winter 10:00am–3:00pm. Admission L12,000.* From Anacapri you can walk or take a chair lift up to **Monte Solaro**, which has amazing views over the entire island and toward another Island, **Ischia**

Finally, the famous **Grotta Azzura** or **Blue Grotto**. To get there you have to take a motorboat from Marina Grande, then transfer to rowboats to enter the grotto. The silver-blue color of the water is caused by refraction of light entering the grotto from an opening beneath the surface. I know it seems cheesy and touristy, but if you've made it this far, the Blue Grotto really is worth seeing. *Open 24 hours. Boat trips from Marina Grande go from 9:00am–6:00pm.*

Walking is by far the best way of getting about the island, but horse-drawn carriages and buses operate, the latter linking Capri and Anacapri, and Marina Grande and Marina Piccola. And if you're walking during the summer months, remember to rest frequently; the hills can be steep. Bring along some water to prevent dehydration.

20. FLORENCE

A visit to Italy is not complete without a trip to **Firenze** (**Florence**), one of the most awe-inspiring cities in all of Europe. The Renaissance reached its full heights of artistic expression here, where countless master artists, writers, inventors, political theorists and artisans lived and learned their craft - Michelangelo being only the best known outside of Italy. But I'll wager you've also heard of Leonardo da Vinci, Dante, Petrarch, Machiavelli, Giotto, Raphael and many other learned and talented Florentines.

Strolling through the cobblestone streets of Florence, it's like your walking in an art history book come to life. The sights, smells, and sounds of this wonderful medieval place have got to be experienced first-hand. So read on, and I'll guide you through the amazing, lovely city of Florence!

REBIRTH OF ART & SCIENCE IN FLORENCE

*Florence, rather than Rome, was the cradle of the Italian **Renaissance**. This rebirth of classical knowledge soon gave way to new creativity in art and literature, and Florentines led the procession. **Dante's** magnificent poetry made the Tuscan dialect the official language of Italy. **Francesco Petrarch** composed his lovely sonnets that still live today, and **Giovanni Boccaccio** wrote his Decameron Tales here. **Niccolo Machiavelli**, another Florentine, set down his brilliant, cynical observations on politics.*

***Giotto** was the first of many immortal Florentine painters and sculptors. **Michelangelo** worked by day on the city's fortifications and by night on his paintings and statues. **Ghiberti** labored almost a lifetime on the doors for the Florentine Baptistery. Many other great artists studied or worked in Florence, among them **Leonardo da Vinci, Donatello, Raphael,** and **Luca della Robbia**.*

TRY NOT TO MISS THESE PLACES!

After spending all your time and money to come to this Renaissance paradise, there are a few sights you that if you don't see you can't really say you've been to Florence. The first of which is hard to miss: the **Duomo** with its campanile and baptistery. The next is a gem of Medieval and Renaissance architecture, the **Ponte Vecchio** with all its gold shops. And if you miss Michelangelo's **David** in the Accademia you shouldn't show your face back in your home town. That work of art is as close to sculpted perfection as any artist will ever achieve.

And then there is the art collection in the **Uffizzi Gallery**. To actually do this museum justice you may need to spend close to one day wandering through its many rooms. And don't forget to sample the *panini* at **Nerbone**, a small local eatery inside the **Mercato Centrale** that serves the most succulent boiled meat sandwiches, prepared right in front of you.

There are countless other wonderful sights to see and places to go in Florence. Walking the streets is like walking through a fairy tale. But if you haven't seen the items above, you haven't been to Florence.

ARRIVALS & DEPARTURES

By Bus

There are many different bus companies in Italy, each serving a different set of cities and sometimes the same ones. Buses should be used only if the train does not go to your destination since traffic is becoming more and more of a problem in Italy.

The most convenient bus company in Florence is located directly next to the train station in **Piazza Adua**, called **LAZZI** *(055/215-154)*. They have over 50 arrivals and departures a day to and from a variety of different locations like Pisa, Lucca, Prato, and Pistoia.

By Car

If arriving in Florence from the South, for speed you will probably be on the **A1** (**E35**). If you were looking for a more scenic adventure, you would be on the **Via Cassia** which you take all the way from Rome. If arriving from the North in a hurry, you would also take the **A1** (**E35**), but if in no rush you would probably take the **SS 65**.

Sample trip lengths on the main roads:
- **Rome**: 3 1/2 hours
- **Venice**: 4 hours
- **Bologna**: 1 1/2 hours.

If you need to rent a car while in Florence, please refer to the *Getting Around Town* section of this chapter, below.

By Train

The station, **Santa Maria Novella**, is located near the center of town and is easily accessible on foot to most hotels. The **tourist information**

office in the station *(Tel. 055/278-785)* is open daily from 7:00am to 10:00pm and is your first stop if you don't have a reservation at a hotel. The **railway office**, at the opposite end of the station from the tourist information office is your destination to plan your trip from Florence. You need to take a number to get information.

The wait can be quite long, but it is entertaining watching Italians become completely confused about having to take a number, wait in a queue, and actually do something in an organized fashion. First your average Italian will attempt to assert his Latin ego to an information officer, whether they are serving someone else or not, get rebuffed, attempt to do it again with another information officer, get rebuffed again, finally look at the machine spitting out numbers and the directions associated with it, stare as would a deer trapped in an oncoming car's headlights, turn and glare at the long line formed since they attempted their folly, then ultimately strut out of the office without getting the information they need. I've seen it happen too many times!

There are **taxis** located just outside the entrance near the tourist information office as well as **buses** that can take you all over the city.

Sample trip lengths and costs for direct *(diretto)* trains:
- **Rome**: 2 1/2 hours, L35,000
- **Venice**: 3 1/2 hours, L27,000
- **Bologna**: 1 hour, L15,000.

GETTING AROUND TOWN

By Bicycle & Scooter

There is one reputable company in Florence to get either motorbikes or bicycles:
- **Noleggio dell Fortezza** *(two locations),Corner of Via Strozzi and Via del Pratello, Open 9:00am to 8:00pm, the 15th of March to 31st of October; and Via Faenza 107-109r. Tel. 055/283-448.* **Scooter prices**: *1 hour L9,000/ half day L20,000/ 1 day L38,000.* **Bicycle prices**: *1 hour L3,000/ half day L8,000/ 1 day L15,000.*

By Bus

There is no need to go by bus in Florence unless you're going up to Fiesole. But if you need to, first get information from the booth at the Piazza della Stazione across the piazza from the station itself. Here they can give you all the information you need to go anywhere you want to go. A ticket costs L1,400 and is reusable within an hour.

At all bus stops, called **fermatas**, there are signs that list all the buses that stop there. These signs also give the streets that the buses will follow along its route so you can check your map to see if this is the bus for you. Also, on the side of the bus are listed highlights of the route for your convenience. Nighttime routes (since many of them stop a midnight) are indicated by black spaces on newer signs, and are placed at the bottom of the older signs. In conjunction, the times listed on the signs indicate when the bus will pass the *fermata* during the night so you can plan accordingly.

Riding the bus during rush is very crowded, so try to avoid the rush hours of 8:00am to 9:00am, 12:30pm to 1:30pm, 3:30 to 4:30pm, and 7:30pm to 8:30pm. They have an added rush hour in the middle of the day because of their siesta time in the afternoon.

By Car

Renting a car is relatively simple, as things go in Italy, but it is somewhat expensive. You can rent a car from a variety of agencies all over Florence. All prices will vary by agency, so call for an up-to-date quote.

• **Budget**, *Borgo Ognissanti 134r, Tel. 055/29.30.21 or 28.71.61.*
• **Euro Dollar**, *Via il Prato 80r, Tel 055/238-24-80. Fax 055/238-24-79.*
• **Avis**, *Borgo Ognissanti 128r, Tel 055/21-36-29 or 239-8826*
• **Avis**, *Lungarno Torrigiani 32/3, Tel 055/234-66-68 or 234-66-69*
• **Hertz**, *Via Maso Finiguerra 33, Tel. 055/239-8205. Fax 055/230-2011*
• **Maggiore**, *Via Maso Finiguerra 11r, Tel. 055/21-02-38*

Most companies require a deposit that amounts to the cost of the rental, as well as a 19% VAT added to the final cost, which can be reimbursed once you're home (see Chapter 7, *Basic Information*). A basic rental of a Fiat Panda costs L120,000 per day, but the biggest expense is gasoline. In Italy it costs more than twice as much per gallon as it does in the States.

Also if you're adventurous enough to think of renting a car, remember that the rates become more advantageous if you rent for more than a week.

By Moped

Since Florence is so small, the areas in Tuscany I'm recommending quite close together, and the drivers are not quite as crazy as Romans, a moped (50cc) or *vespa* (125cc) is one of the best ways to get around and see the countryside. But this isn't a simple ride in the park. Only if you feel extremely confident about your motorcycle driving abilities should you even contemplate renting a moped.

Rentals for a moped (50cc) are about L40,000 per day, and for a 125cc (which you'll need to transport two people) about L70,000 per day. Some companies you can rent even bigger bikes, but I would strongly advise against it. You can also rent the cycles for an hour or any multiples thereof.

• **Firenze Motor**, *Via Guelfa 85r. Tel 055/280-500. Fax 05/211-748. Located in the Centro section to the right of the station and north of the Duomo.*

By Taxi

Taxis are the best, and also the most expensive, way to get around Florence if you're tired of walking. They are everywhere, except on the streets designated for foot traffic only, so flagging one down is not a problem. But since they are so expensive I wouldn't rely on them as your main form of transportation. Also have a map handy when a cabby is taking you somewhere. Since they are on a meter, they sometimes decide to take you on a little longer journey than necessary. And also watch out for the fly by night operators that don't have a licensed meter. They will really rip you off.

The going rate as of publication was L3,500 for the first 2/3 of a kilometer or the first minute (which usually comes first during the rush hours), then its L300 every 1/3 of a kilometer or minute. At night you'll also pay a surcharge of L3,000, and Sundays you'll pay L1,000 extra. If you bring bags aboard, say for example after you've been shopping, you'll be charged L500 extra for each bag.

There are strategically placed cab stands all over the city.

SUGGESTED ITINERARY

DAY ONE

Morning

Walk to the **Accademia** and see Michelangelo's *David*. Also take in other works by the master here.

Lunch

Walk back to the **Piazza San Lorenzo** where there is a daily market. Go to **Nerbone's** in the **Mercato Centrale** for lunch. Try one of their amazing *Panini* (boiled beef or pork) served on a Panino roll. They'll ask whether you want some juice placed on the roll. Tell them *si* (yes); it makes it much tastier. Order either a beer or a glass of wine and sit at one of the tables directly in front of Nerbone's.

After your meal, wander through the two story market. Check out the different cuts of meat the Italians use in their recipes. Upstairs is the vegetable and fruit market, where you can buy some healthy snacks for later.

Afternoon

Wander through the San Lorenzo Market until about 2pm. Then head to the nearby **Piazza Duomo**. Admire the bronze doors on the belfry, the simplicity of the baptistery, and the expanse of the church. Take the time to go all the way up top of the dome.

Late afternoon, if needed, take a little siesta. If you're not tired, head to the **Piazza della Signoria** and admire the statues in the Loggia. Also go into the **Palazzo della Signoria** and admire the staircase that leads to their museum. This was the residence of the Medici until the Palazzo Pitti was made available. If you're interested, go upstairs and pay the fee to see the inside.

Just outside of the Piazza dell Signoria is the **Uffizzi Gallery**, which you'll be visiting tomorrow. Check to see if there is a long line since this will indicate how early you'll have to get here.

Now make your way to the **Ponte Vecchio** over the river Arno. Make sure you stop in the middle of the bridge and, if you're with a friend, take each other's photo with the river as a background. Follow the bridge over to the other side of the Arno. From here we're going to the **Pitti Palace** and the **Boboli Gardens**. It costs L10,000 to get in to admire the beautiful artwork, the building, and the peace and tranquillity of the gardens. If you bought some snacks at the Mercato Centrale, you may want to take the time to have a brief picnic in the gardens. When you leave, check out the store **Firenze Papier Mache** in the piazza.

Evening

Return back to your room to freshen up and get ready for dinner. Tonight we're going to a wonderful local place called **La Bussola** *(Via Porta Rossa 58, Tel. 293-376)*. You can either sit at the counter and have a simple meal of pizza or sit in the back and soak up all the ambiance and romance of Florence. Try their *Spaghetti alla Bolognese* and their tortellini alla panna.

After dinner, wander over to the **Piazza Santa Maria Novella** and stop at the **Fiddler's Elbow** for a pint. This place has an authentic Irish Pub atmosphere, great people, and fun times. If dancing is your desire, try the **Space Electronic** nearby *(Via Palazzuolo 37, Tel. 292-082)*.

DAY TWO
Morning

Get to the Uffizzi Gallery early so you can beat the lines. You'll probably spend all morning here.

Lunch

For lunch, try **Buca Lapi** *(Via del Trebbio 1, Tel. 213-768)*, a quaint basement restaurant between the Duomo and the train station and near Piazza Santa Maria Novella. There are old travel posters plastered all over the walls and ceiling, and the tables surround the cooking area. It's sometimes closed for lunch, but go take a look see. Try their *cinghiale con patate fritte* or their *pollo al cacciatore con spinache*.

Afternoon

Remember the church in the piazza where the Fiddler's Elbow was last night? We're going there now (Chiesa di Santa Maria Novella). Some of the frescoes on the walls were painted by Michelangelo. While we're in this area of town, check out the store **Il Tricolore** *(Via della Scalla 32)*, just off the piazza. This is an Italian Army/Navy store. Actually it is the official outlet for the police and military in Florence, where you can buy a variety of items like pins, hats, shirts, badges, etc. that you can take home as gifts.

Next stop: the place where Michelangelo is buried, **Chiesa di Santa Croce**. They have a leather shop associated with the church. It's a good place to find inexpensive gifts.

Late Afternoon

From here, we're going up to the **Piazzale Michelangelo** to watch the sun set. Remember to take your camera and high speed film to catch all the light possible. You'll get some of the best shots of Florence from up here. Afterwards, sit and savor the ambiance as long as you want. On the way back into town stop at the **Il Rifrullo** *(Via San Niccolo 55, 213-631)* to get a pint of beer or glass of wine. At night this is an isolated and relaxing place to come and soak up the Florentine evenings.

Evening

For dinner tonight we're going to the **Tredici Gobbi** ("13 hunch-backs") located on Via Porcellana. Situated down a small side street near the Arno, you can enjoy a combination of Italian and Hungarian cuisine. The walls are covered with paintings traded by artists for a filling meal.

For an after diner drink, wander over to the nearby **Excelsior Hotel** and go up to their roof deck. Enjoy a *Sambuca con tre mosce*. From this roof, you'll have a beautiful view over all of Florence as it lines the Arno.

WHERE TO STAY

I've listed the hotels in this section by expense, and have also noted where each hotel is located by district. First, I've described each district, to help you decide which part of Florence you'd like to rest your weary head after a long day of sightseeing!

Centro Storico

The **Centro Storico** is the very heart of Florence. Anywhere you stay, shop, eat, or drink will be relatively expensive, since this is the prime tourist area of Florence. In this area you have the **Duomo** dominated by Brunelleschi's huge dome; the **Baptistery** next door with its beautiful bronze doors; the **Piazza della Signoria** with its copy of Michelangelo's *David* and, under the cobble stones, Bronze age relics proving that

Florence is centuries older than anyone ever thought; the **Uffizzi Gallery** with it many art treasures; the **Ponte Vecchio** which was built in 1345 and used to house butchers, blacksmiths, green-grocers, tanners and leather workers but is now home to with its many gold shops; the **Piazza della Repubblica** that once was the site of a Roman Forum; the **Jewish ghetto**; the **Mercato Nuovo** or Straw Market with its many fine examples of Tuscan craftsmanship; and the Fifth Avenue of Florence, the **Via Tornabuoni**, where it even seems expensive to windowshop.

Centro

This section is north of the Duomo and west of the Via Tornabuoni, and is home to many reasonably priced hotels, restaurants, and stores. Here you'll find the **Mercato of San Lorenzo**, a huge daily outdoor clothing market, and the **Mercato Generale**, Florence's main food market. The train station is also located here.

Santa Croce

This is the area of Florence in which Michelangelo played as a child before he was sent to the country to live with a stone carver, from whom he learned the fundamentals for his amazing ability to carve figures from slabs of marble. Located to the east of the Centro Storico and the Centro sections of Florence, Santa Croce is more of an authentic, residential, working class neighborhoodand seems far from the maddening crowds, even though it's just around the corner from them. The church that gives this area its name, Santa Croce, is home to the graves of Michelangelo, Galileo, and other Italian greats.

This is also the area in which Florentines come to dine at regular Tuscan restaurants or some of the newer restaurants offering nouvelle cuisine. The area is also home to another food market, the **Mercato Sant'Ambrogio**, located in the Piazza Ghiberti. There is also a prime picnic location, not nearly as nice as the Boboli Gardens but still a respite from the crowds, in the Piazza Massimo D'Azeglio.

Oltrarno

Oltrarno, literally "the other side of the Arno," is home to many of Florence's artisans, leather workers, etc. It is looked upon as a city unto itself since it wasn't encompassed into the walls of Florence until the 14th century . Most of the beautiful architecture was destroyed during World War II, not only by the Germans but also by the Allied bombings. Thankfully both sides spared the Ponte Vecchio, The Duomo, and the other great pieces of architecture on the other side of the river.

Also spared was the **Palazzo Vecchio** (also known as the **Medici Palace**) and the **Boboli gardens**, where Michelangelo first began his serious artistic training with the support of the Medici family. Beyond these sights and the artisans shops, the only other place to visit is the **Piazza Santo Spirito** that boasts its 15th century church with the unfinished facade by Brunelleschi. The piazza is also home to a small fresh **produce and flower market** every morning.

THE FIVE BEST HOTELS IN FLORENCE

Best one star hotel: **ALBERGO FIRENZE**
Best two star hotel: **HOTEL LA SCALETTA**
Best three star hotel: **HOTEL HERMITAGE**
Best four star hotel: **HOTEL TORRE DI BELLOSGUARDO**
  – There's no better hotel in Florence!.
Best five star hotel: **EXCELSIOR HOTEL**

Expensive

HOTEL CONTINENTAL, *Lungarno Acciaioli 2, 50123 Firenze. Tel. 055/282-392. Fax 055/283-139. American Express, Diners Club, Mastercard and Visa accepted. 48 rooms all with private bath. Single L 270,000; Double L350,000; Penthouse suite L630,000. Breakfast L25,000.* ****
Centro Storico District.

If only I could afford the penthouse suite I would be in heaven. One rung below that fantasy is the hotel's superb terrace with breathtaking views of the Arno and the Ponte Vecchio. I mean breathtaking since they're basically right on top of the old bridge. You can't go wrong with the location, the ultra-modern rooms, the exquisite service. At the Continental you can truly live the experience of being in Renaissance Florence with all the modern amenities to keep you happy.

EXCELSIOR HOTEL, *Piazza Ognissanti 3, 50123 Firenze. Tel. 055/264-201. Fax 055/210-278. Toll free number in American 1-800-221-2340. American Express, Diners Club, Mastercard and Visa accepted. 200 rooms all with private bath. Single L290,000-340,000; Double L420,000-490,000' Suite L800,000-L1,300,000. Continental breakfast L26,000. American breakfast L41,000.* *****
Centro District.

Directly across from its sister, The Grand Hotel CIGA, both of these hotels are run by the Ciga organization. Some rooms in this hotel are decorated similarly to those in the Grand Hotel, but the size and decor of the rooms here varies widely – but they are all of the highest standard. I mean, this is the Excelsior. The best feature of this hotel is its roof garden/restaurant where you can have your meal or sip an after dinner drink, listen to the piano player, and gaze out at the splendor that is Florence. You don't have to stay here to enjoy the view; just come for dinner.

GRAND HOTEL CIGA, *Piazza Ognizzanti 1, 50123 Firenze. Tel. 055/ 288-781. Fax 055/217-400. Toll free number in American 1-800-221-2340. American Express, Diners Club, Mastercard and Visa accepted. 106 rooms all with private bath. Singe L360,000-400,000; Double L510,000-580,000; Suite L900,000-1,600,000. Continental breakfast L26,000. American breakfast L41,000.* ****
Centro District.

Aptly named, this hotel is wonderfully quiet, even though it is on a main thoroughfare, and extremely elegant. Housed in a pale yellow and gray palazzo, the reception rooms have all been restored to their former brilliance. Each bedroom has beautiful neo-classic furniture and elegant decorations and frescoes. More pleasant and comfortable than the Excelsior since its modernization, but remember to go to the Excelsior for their roof-bar restaurant.

HOTEL TORRE DI BELLOSGUARDO, *Via Roti Michelozzi 2, Firenze. Tel. 055/229-8145. Fax 055/229-008. 16 room all with bath. Single L250,000; Double L330,000; Suites L430,000-530,000. All credit cards accepted.* ****
Oltrarno District.

If you have the money, this is the place to stay in Florence – you'll feel like you stepped back in time to the Renaissance. Simply the best view of the city from anywhere around the city. Their grounds are filled with gardens, olive trees where horses graze, an open lawn in front, and a pool with a bar – all overlooking the magnificent city of Florence below.

The rooms are in an old castle that was once the small English language school, St. Michael's, that catered to 100 students. So you can imagine that with only sixteen rooms the size of your accommodations are quite large; and the interior common areas are like something out of a movie script, with vaulted ceilings and arches, as well as staircases leading off into hidden passages. You're a short distance outside of the old city walls but you'll get romance, peace, and tranquillity. The hotel is so magnificent that you have to reserve well in advance, since they are booked solid most of the glorious spring, summer, and fall months. I can't say enough about the view. If you aren't already in love, you'll find it or rekindle it in this wonderful hideaway.

HOTEL LUNGARNO, *Borgo S Jacopo 14, 50125 Firenze. Tel. 264-211. Fax 055/268-437. American Express, Diners Club, Mastercard and Visa accepted. 66 rooms all with private bath. Single L210,000-L275,000; Double L280,000-L390,000; Junior Suite L360,000-L540,000.* ****
Oltrarno District.

An excellent location right on the river, only a few meters from the Ponte Vecchio, and situated down a quaint, Florentine side street with some great restaurants and food shops a few stores away. Even though most of the hotel is modern, it is a quaint establishment. The lounge just off the lobby offers a relaxing view of the river and the Ponte Vecchio. An ancient stone tower is part of the hotel, with a great penthouse suite, in the old tower. If you want the atmosphere of the tower, specify this upon making your reservation. Some of the rooms have terraces overlooking the river, which makes for a perfect place to relax after a tough day of sightseeing. Get a confirmation to ensure you will be staying exactly where you want.

VILLA CORA, *Viale Machiavelli 18-20, 50125 Firenze. Tel. 055/229-8451. Fax 055/229-086. American Express, Diners Club, Mastercard and Visa accepted. 47 rooms all with private bath. Single L280,000-380,000; Double L400,00-600,000; Deluxe Double Room L500,000-700,000; Suites L700,000-1,800,000. A full buffet breakfast included.* *****

Oltrarno District.

You'll find this extravagant and ornately decorated hotel that was once a nineteenth century palazzo on a residential street that curves up to the Florentine hills. It is truly magnificent with its chandeliers, statues, bas-relief covered walls, gilded mirrors and staff that will wait on you hand and foot. If you want to stay in the lap of luxury and are willing to pay for it, this is the place for you. There is a poolside restaurant, Taverna Machiavelli, where you can eat and relax after a hard day's touring. Another important feature is the rooftop terrace garden, offering excellent views of Florence. And the rooms are superb, stupendous, *fantavolosso* – think of an adjective and the rooms will surpass it!

Moderate

HOTEL HERMITAGE, *Vicolo Marzio 1 (Piazza del Pesce), 50122 Firenze. Tel. 055/287-216. Fax 055/212-208. Mastercard and Visa accepted. 29 rooms all with private bath. Single L120,000-160,000; Double L190,000-240,000. Breakfast included.* ***

Centro Storico District.

Only steps from the Ponte Vecchio but located above the tourist noise, this 20 room *pensione* is on the top three floors of an office building and is reached by a private elevator. It has the most wonderful roof terrace, complete with greenery and flowers and a wonderful view of the rooftops of Florence, as well as the Arno and the Ponte Vecchio. That's where you can start your day, since they serve breakfast up there in good weather.

The rooms are not that large but the ambiance and the location make up for it, as does the spacious terrace and common areas. The staff speaks a variety of languages. For a three star the prices are great.

HOTEL LA SCALETTA, *Via Guicciardini 13, Firenze. Tel. 055/283-028. Fax 055/289-562. Mastercard and Visa accepted. 12 rooms, 11 with* *private bath. Single L80,000: Double L125,000; Triple L165,000; Quad L185,000. Breakfast included.* **

Centro Storico District.

No ifs, ands, or buts about it; this is the best place to stay in Centro Storico. But you have to reserve your rooms well in advance. Let's say at least 4-5 months before you go, to guarantee you'll get a room overlooking the garden! Yes, yes there's no air conditioning, but it's not needed. This building seems to suck up the cold air in the summer and retain the warm in the winter. Why can't we create buildings like this back home?

You should stay here because of the large rooms, the location, and the incomparable terrace that overlooks all the best sights of Florence. Relaxing on the terrace alone or with your fellow guests after a day on the town makes this stay sublime. And let's be serious, the prices are dirt cheap for the quality offered. But these prices won't last forever; they've already put air conditioning in three rooms, and when all are complete, they may get their three star rating which will send their prices through the terrace, just like it did with La Scalinetta di Spagna in Rome.

HOTEL APRILE, *Via della Scala 6, 50123 Firenze. Tel. 055/216-237. Fax 055/289-147. American Express, Mastercard and Visa accepted. 29 rooms, 25 with private bath. Single L75,000-90,000; Single with bath or shower L125,000-140,000; Double L120,000-150,000; Double with bath or shower L165,000-195,000. The first price listed above is without breakfast the second is with breakfast.* ***

Centro District.

On a quaint side street of Piazza Santa Maria Novella that has plenty of shops, bars, cafés, and other hotels, this is a delicately decorated three star with all necessary amenities. Try to get a room that overlooks the quiet courtyard garden, so when you open the windows you can escape the onslaught of the moped noise.

HOTEL LOGGIATO DEI SERVITI, *Piazza SS. Annunziata 3, 50122 Firenze. Tel. 055/289-593/4. Fax 055/289-595. American Express, Diners Club, Mastercard and Visa accepted. 29 rooms all with private bath. Single L110,000-170,000; Double L190,000-240,000; Suite for 2 L300,000-500,000. Breakfast included. L80,000 for an extra bed.* ***

Centro District.

Located in a 16h century loggia that faces the beautiful Piazza della SS Annunziata. The interior common areas consist of polished terra cotta floors, gray stone columns, and high white ceilings. Rooms are pleasant and comfortable and generally filled with antique furnishings. All designed to make you feel like you just walked into the 17th century, and it works. But they do have the modern amenities necessary to keep us weary travelers happy, especially the air conditioning in August. If you want to feel as if you're a part of history, stay here and you'll love it.

CLASSIC HOTEL, *Viale Machiavelli 25, 50125 Firenze. Tel. 055/229-3512. Fax 055/229-353. American Express, Mastercard and Visa accepted. 20 rooms all with private bath. Single L120,000; Double L170,000; Triple L200,000. Breakfast included. Without breakfast take off L10,000 per room.* ***

Oltrarno District.

Located in a quaint little old palazzo outside the old city walls, here you can get a taste of Florentine life without the constant clamoring of mopeds riding past your bedroom window. Piazzale Machiavelli is an exclusive address and this hotel shows it. The lush garden in the rear (there's a glassed-in section for winter guests) is your breakfast location as well as your mid-afternoon slumber spot, and there's a small bar just off the garden for evening drinks.

Your rooms are palatial, with immense ceilings and clean bathrooms. Each room is furnished quite differently. Some have antique furniture, others have newer but sill attractive pieces. The diversity lends a spot of charm. I would recommend this gem to anyone that likes to tour and then escape the hectic pace of the city. One minor note, they do not have air conditioning, but when I was there on a 90 degree day each room was very cool. These old palazzi were built to keep cool in the summer and remain warm in the winter. Don't ask me how, it just works.

Inexpensive

HOTEL SOGGIORNO BRUNORI, *Via del Proconsolo 5, Firenze. Tel 055/289-648. No credit cards accepted. 9 rooms, 1 with private bath. Double L62,000-78,000; Triple L87,000-110,000; Quad L110,000-138,000.* *

Centro Storico District.

Leonardo (the thick heavy set guy) and Giovanni (the thin witty one) will do anything to make your stay at their hotel more pleasurable. Call a taxi, book train reservations, etc. You name it they'll do it. The rooms aren't spectacular but there are some with balconies that overlook the busy street and give you some decent views.

But look at the prices. They are continuing to upgrade the facilities but as they do all is still very accommodating here. If you call for a reservation and they don't have a room for you, they'll put you in touch with other places with similar prices just to keep you happy.

ALBERGO FIRENZE, *Piazza Donati 4 (Via del Corso), Firenze. Tel. 055/268-301. Fax 055/212-370. No credit cards accepted. 60 rooms, 35 with private bath. Single L50,000-60,000; Double L74,000-86,000; Triple L100,000-115,000. Breakfast included.* *

Centro Storico District.

This is two different hotels. One is new, the other's left in a time warp from the 1950s. My recommendation is based on the new section, so call in advance to get your reservations. Even though this place doesn't have air conditioning, it shouldn't be a one star. The lobby is all three star, as are the rooms in the new wing. Room 503 caught my fancy since it has a great view of the Duomo from the bed. So when you wake up in the morning, open your eyes, and there's the Duomo right in front of you.

Besides the beauty and comfort of the new wing, the lobby and breakfast area is of a much higher standard than any other one star I've been in. It's beautiful and its inexpensive. They speak English, so make sure you tell them that you want to stay in the new wing.

HOTEL UNIVERSO, *Piazza Santa Maria Novella 20, 50123 Firenze. Tel. 05/281-951. Fax 055/292-335. 45 rooms, 31 with bath. Single L60,000-100,000; Double L90,000-110,000; Triple L110,000-130,000; Quad L149,000-179,000; Quint L187,000-227,000.* **

Santa Croce District.

A double on this picturesque square for only L110,000 with bath cannot be beat, except in August since they do not have air-conditioning. Simple and basic in style, you also get a 10% discount in the off-season. The rooms are not spectacular but they are convenient and comfortable. Remember to request a room with bath and, if you don't like noise, one that faces away from the piazza. Great location and great prices.

ISTITUTO GOULD, *Via dei Serragli 49, 50125 Firenze. Tel. 055/212-576. Fax 055/280-274. No credit cards accepted. 25 rooms, 20 with private bath. Single L40,000; Double L30,000 per person.* *

Oltrarno District.

If you don't have your own bath here you're still okay, since you only have to share two toilets and two showers with four other rooms. The office is on the ground floor and there are limited office hours (9:00am–1:00pm and 3:00pm–7:00pm) but they give you your own key so you can go in and out as your please. A rarity in Florence for one-stars. The rooms, on the second and third floors scattered all over the place, are quite large. My single easily should have been a double. In your search here you'll find an immense common room with comfortable chairs and a quaint little terrace overlooking some rooftops in the rear, a great place to relax.

The best part of your stay is that the Istituto Gould is a home for wayward children (their quarters are far removed from your own and the kids I met seemed just to want to practice their English and play soccer), and your payment goes to assist in their care and well-being. They separate the more mature budget travelers from the younger crowd, so the late night adventures of the younger set don't keep us old folks awake.

PENSIONE SORELLE BANDINI, *Piazza Santo Spirito 9, 50125 Firenze. Tel 055/215-308. Fax 055/282-761. No credit cards accepted. 13 rooms, 5 with private bath. Double (for one or two people) L110,000-140,000 Triple L150,000-186,000; Quad L184,000-232,000. Breakfast included.* *

Oltrarno District.

Usually occupied by art students from a variety of different American universities, you can usually find a room before May and after June. And what a place this is! The maze of staircases, floors, passageways intertwining with balconies, and the look of the rooms makes you feel as is you've suddenly found yourself in a medieval castle. If you can get one of the rooms with a bath, stay here for the balcony and the prices. The balcony extends around two sides of the palazzo, offering you some great vistas of Florence.

The rooms are all large, and as mentioned the clientele are mostly of university age, which makes it fun for geezers like me. Breakfast is served to all. Only dinners go to the students, but like the cats do, you too can sneak in if you want to try.

WHERE TO EAT

Tuscan Cuisine

During the Renaissance, Florence and Tuscany experienced a burst of elaborate cuisine, much the result of Catherine de Medici importing a brigade of French chefs, but today that type of cuisine has given way to more basic fare. Tuscan cooking has its roots in the frugal peasant fare that was the result of the region being agriculturally poor for so many centuries. The food is simple but healthy, with the emphasis on fresh ingredients which accentuates the individual tastes of each dish.

Grilled meats are a staple of the Florentine diet, with *Bistecca alla Fiorentina* rivaling anything Texas could dream of producing. The Florentines tend to over-salt their vegetables and soups, but you can ask for them to be prepared *senza sale*, without salt, and no one will be insulted at all. You'll also find beans and olive oil prominently used in many dishes, as well as many types of game that populate the hills of Tuscany. And if you like cheese, my favorite is the full flavored *pecorino* made from sheep's milk.

Tuscany is not really known for their pasta dishes, but they do make an excellent *Pasta alla carrettiera*, a pasta dish with a sauce of tomato, garlic, pepper, and parsley. If you want a simple, filling, healthy meal, you'll find one in Tuscany. Just don't expect some extravagant saucy dish. For that go to France.

Tuscan Wines

Tuscany is known for its full bodied red wines, especially its **Chianti**. There are plenty of wine cellars and *enoteche* (wine bars) in every Tuscan city for you to sample the regional offerings. Some Tuscans say that their food is so bland so that they can enjoy the wine with their meals more. Whatever the reason, you'll love sampling the different varieties.

Most Italian wines are classified by the type of grape used and the district from which the wines are produced. Some of the best wines come with a **DOC** (*Denominazione di Origine Controllata*) label that indicates the wine comes from a specially defined area and was produced according to specific traditional methods. If the label reads **DOCG** (G stands for *Garantita*) the wine will be of the highest quality, guaranteed.

The best wines are called *Classico*, which means they come from the oldest part of the production zone. If the wine is a Chianti Classico red you'll find a black rooster label on the neck of the bottle that designates such a wine. There are also *Riserva* and *Superiore*, which indicates that the wine has been aged for quality.

From the Chianti region you should try the following red wines: **Castello di Ama**, **Castello di Volpaia**, and **Vecchie Terre di Montefili**. Outside the region try some **Rosso delle Colline Luchesi** from the hills around Lucca, **Morellino di Scansano** from the hills south of Grossetto, and **Elba Rosso**, made on the island of Elba.

Some whites you might enjoy are a dry **Montecarlo** from the hills east of Lucca or a dry **Bolgheri** from the coast. The red wines mentioned above also have some excellent white wines to complement them.

Some of these wines may a bit pricey in restaurants so you may want to buy them at a store and sample them back in your hotel room or on a picnic. At restaurants, in most cases the house wines will be locally produced and of excellent quality, so give them a try.

THE BEST DINING IN FLORENCE

LA BUSSOLA, *Via Porta Rossa 58, 50123 Firenze. Tel. 055/293-376. Visa and Mastercard accepted. Closed Mondays. Dinner for two L90,000.*

NERBONE, *Mercato Centrale. No telephone. No credit cards accepted. Meal for two L10,000.*

BUCA LAPI, *Via del Trebbio 1, 50123 Firenze. Tel. 055/213-768. American Express, Diners Club, Visa and Mastercard accepted. Closed Sunday for dinner and Mondays. Dinner for two L70,000*

TREDICI GOBBI *(13 Hunchbacks), Via Porcellana 9R. Dinner for two L100,000. Credit cards accepted.*

ZI ROSA, *Via dei Fossi 12, 50123 Firenze. Tel. 055/287-062. American Express, Diners Club, Visa and Mastercard accepted. Closed Thursdays and Friday for lunch. Dinner for two L55,000.*

TRATTORIA MOSSACCE, *Via del Pronconsolo 55, 50122 Firenze. Tel. 055/294-361. No credit cards accepted. Closed Sundays. Dinner for two L65,000.*

Expensive

TREDICI GOBBI *(13 Hunchbacks), Via Porcellana 9R. Dinner for two L100,000. Credit cards accepted.*

Centro District.

Mainly Florentine cuisine, with a little Hungarian dishes added for spice. A moderately priced restaurant with some pricey dishes, which are mostly the excellent *Bistecca Fiorentina* and other beef dishes. The pasta is average. One endearing quality is the thicker spaghetti used which gives the pasta an exotic texture. The atmosphere is sophisticated and superb.

Tredici Gobbi's walls are crammed with paintings received in payment from impoverished Florentine artists in exchange for the restaurants fine food. If you are captivated by one, it is usually for sale. After enjoying your *Bistecca*, soaking up the delightful atmosphere, and admiring the many paintings, it's time for the dessert cart. These well-presented delicacies and a steaming cup of café will round out an excellent meal.

LA BUSSOLA, *Via Porta Rossa 58, 50123 Firenze. Tel. 055/293-376. Visa and Mastercard accepted. Closed Mondays. Dinner for two L90,000.*

Centro Storico District.

You can get superb pizza in this pizzeria/ristorante/tavola calda, as well as pasta. The waiters and ambiance of this place is like something out of a movie set, especially in the back. They have a marble counter where you sit and watch the pizza master prepare the evening's fare in the wood heated brick oven. Or, if you're into the formal dining scene, try the back with tablecloths, etc. Wherever you sit the food will be excellent.

For pasta, try the *capricciossa, quattro formaggi,* or the *tortellini all panna.* You can get any type of pizza you want here. Even ask to mix and match ingredients. The pizza master is more than willing to accommodate. You won't need to leave too large of a tip since they tack on a *coperto* of L9,000.

MAMMA GINA, *Borgo S Jacopo 37, 50125 Firenze. Tel. 055/239-6009, Fax 055/213-908. American Express, Diners Club, Mastercard and Visa accepted. Closed Sundays. Dinner for two L 85,000.*

Oltrarno District.

A very small place with great food. I tried their *tortellini all crema* with apprehension since I do not believe that Florentines know how to make good pasta, and was pleasantly surprised. Then I had the *petti di pollo alla griglia* (chicken breasts o the grill). You might also try the *Penne strascicate alla Fiorentina* (a meat and tomato based pasta) and the *petti di pollo al cogna can funghi* (chicken breast cooked in cognac with mushrooms ... it gives it kind of a cacciatore taste).

Moderate

BUCA LAPI, *Via del Trebbio 1, 50123 Firenze. Tel. 055/213-768. American Express, Diners Club, Visa and Mastercard accepted. Closed Sunday for dinner and Mondays. Dinner for two L70,000.*
Centro District.

One of the very best restaurants Florence has to offer. On a small street, down in the basement of an old building, Buca Lapi treats you to the food of a lifetime (and the spectacle of a lifetime too). There is a small open kitchen surrounded on two sides by tables from which you can see all the food being prepared. The decor is bizarre in a fun way, with travel posters covering the walls and ceiling.

Try the *spaghetti al sugo di carne e pomodoro* (with meat and tomato sauce) for starters, then try either the *pollo al cacciatore con spinache* (chicken cooked in tomato-based spicy sauce with spinach) or the *cingulae con patate fritte* (wild boar with fried potatoes). A superbly intimate restaurant with wonderful culinary and visual experiences.

DA GANINO, *Piazza dei Cimatori 4, 50123 Firenze. Tel. 055/214-125. All credit cards accepted. Closed Sundays. Dinner for two L75,000.*
Centro Storico District.

The best place to sit in the summer is at the communal outside wooden benches hedged in by flower pots. The two rooms inside are made to look rustic with their wooden paneling and yokes hanging from the walls but the marble topped tables give away the fact that they're faux, not real. Nonetheless the somewhat pricey food is still great, especially when eaten in the secluded piazza. Try the *Petto di pollo alla crema di limone* (chicken breast with cream and lemon sauce) or the *conniglio e verdure fritte* (fried country hare and vegetables). You have to try hare at least once before you leave Italy, so it might as well be here.

TRATTORIA COCO LEZZONE, *Via dei Parioncino 26, 50123 Firenze. Tel. 055/287-178. No credit cards accepted. Closed Saturdays and Sundays in the Summer and Tuesdays for dinner. IN the winter closed Sundays and Tuesdays for dinner. Dinner for two L75,000.*
Centro District.

Located in what was once a dairy, Coco Lezzone's long communal tables contrast sharply with the white tiled floors. Despite the strange decor, Florentines pack themselves in to enjoy the authentic Tuscan cuisine. The portions are pleasantly large, the meats are amazingly good, especially the *arista al forno* (pork loins on the fire). Also try the *Piccione* (pigeon) cooked over the grill; don't worry, they're farm raised – they don't go out to the piazza and catch the dinner. Where else will you be able to eat pigeon?

TRATTORIA MOSSACCE, *Via del Pronconsolo 55, 50122 Firenze. Tel. 055/294-361. No credit cards accepted. Closed Sundays. Dinner for two L65,000.*
Santa Croce District.
Great prices for great food. The meats are especially exquisite, especially the *osso bucco*. Try the *ribollita* as a beginner. I suggest you sit all the way in the back around the "L" of a dining area so you can sit in front of the small open kitchen and watch the cooks prepare your meal. That alone makes this restaurant a lof of fun. It's basically a place for locals but they accept the occasional tourist in their midst.

TRATTORIA ANGIOLINO, *Via Santo Spirito 36, 50125 Firenze. Tel. 055/239-8976. Mastercard and Visa accepted. Closed Mondays. L60,000.*
Oltrarno District.
A large and vibrant local *trattoria* that serves basic Tuscan fare. You'll love the wood stove in the middle of the room, as well as the wrought-iron light fixtures an he full hams hanging in the entranceway. This place is definitely rustic. If you come in the winter try to get a seat in the back where you can watch the action in the open kitchen. In the heat of the summer that wouldn't be such a good idea. The food is your basic peasant fare at peasant prices. Try the *tortellini alla panna* (cheese stuffed pasta in a cream sauce) or the *taglietelli con funghi* (pasta with mushrooms), then the *Lombata di vitello* (veal chop roasted) or the ever present *bistecca all fiorentina*.

OSTERIA DEL CINGHIALE BIANCO, *Borgo San Jacopo 43, 50125 Firenze. Tel. 055/215-706. Mastercard and Visa accepted. Closed Tuesdays and Wednesdays.*
Oltrarno District.
Wild game is the specialty here as befitting a place named The White Boar, so get ready to enjoy some fine peasant dishes. I tried the wild boar cold cuts but liked the assorted salamis of Tuscany better. The chicken breast cooked with ham and cheese was not Italian, but it was great. I like the wrought-iron motif that dominates the place, especially the the old cooking pot hanging from the ceiling.

Inexpensive
ZI ROSA, *Via dei Fossi 12, 50123 Firenze. Tel. 055/287-062. American Express, Diners Club, Visa and Mastercard accepted. Closed Thursdays and Friday for lunch. Dinner for two L55,000.*
Centro District.
Intimate little pizzeria with great food at superb prices. If you like pizza, *crostini* (sandwiches), or *calzone* you'll will fall in love with this place. All the food is prepared quickly and with the best of care. Try the pizza con *salame piccante* (with spicy salami), *calzone con salsiccia* (with sausage) or the *crostini con mozzarrella e rucola* (with two types of cheese). All are

baked to excellence. After a few sips of wine you'll be in the mood to try another delicacy from their oven.

NERBONE, *Mercato Centrale. No telephone. No credit cards accepted. Meal for two L10,000.*

Centro District.

In operation since 1872, this small food stand in the Mercato Centrale serves the absolutely best boiled pork, beef, or veal sandwiches for only L3,500. They're simply called *panini* and your only choice of meats is what they have boiled for the day. The sandwich is just the meat, the bread, and some salt, but it is amazing. They take the boiled meat out of the steaming hot water, slice it right in front of you, ladle it onto the meat, pour a little juice over it for flavor (they usually ask if you want this ... say yes), sprinkle it with a little salt, and voila, the best lunch you'll have in Florence.

You can stand at the counter and sip a glass of wine or beer, or take your meal to the small seating area just across the aisle from Nerbone. They also serve pasta, soups, salads, etc., but everyone comes here for their terrific *panini*.

SEEING THE SIGHTS

The sights of Florence are fascinating, incredible – add your own superlatives after you've seen them! The sights below are numbered and correspond to the *Florence Sights* map.

1. Statue of David at the Academia

Via Ricasoli 60. Open 9:00am–2:00pm Tuesday–Saturday. Sunday 9:00am–1:00pm. Admission L10,000.

Granted the **Accademia** is filled with a wide variety of paintings by artists from the Tuscan school of the 13th and 14th centuries, but the museum's main draw is a must-see for you in Florence, Michelangelo's perfect *David*. Michelangelo finished sculpting this wonderful statue at the age of 25 in the year 1504, after four years of labor. It was originally in front of the Palazzo della Signoria, but was replaced with a substitute in 1873 to protect the original from the elements.

Leading up to the David are a variety of other works by Michelangelo, most unfinished. These are called *The Prisoners,* since the figures appear alive and to be trapped in stone. These were destined for the Tomb of Pope Giulio II, but Michelangelo died before he could bring the figures to life. Also included in this wonderful exhibit of Michelangelo's sculptures is the unfinished *Pieta*. Many art critics have spent their entire lives comparing this Pieta with the more famous one in St. Peter's in Rome. Comparing these two works, you can see how Michelangelo's worked progressed through the years.

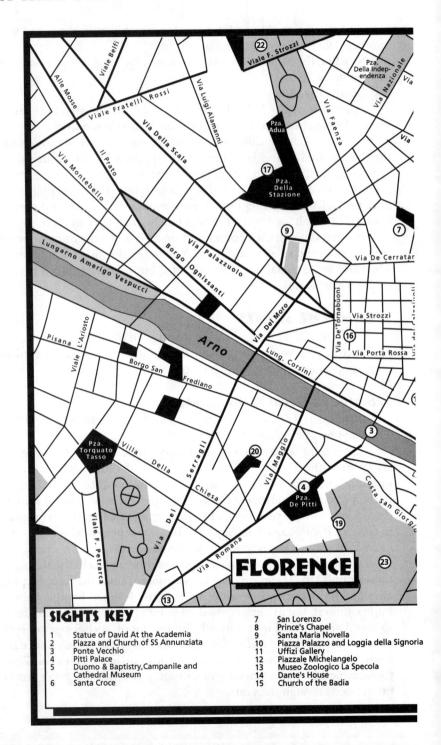

SIGHTS KEY

1	Statue of David At the Academia	7	San Lorenzo
2	Piazza and Church of SS Annunziata	8	Prince's Chapel
3	Ponte Vecchio	9	Santa Maria Novella
4	Pitti Palace	10	Piazza Palazzo and Loggia della Signoria
5	Duomo & Baptistry,Campanile and Cathedral Museum	11	Uffizi Gallery
		12	Piazzale Michelangelo
		13	Museo Zoologico La Specola
6	Santa Croce	14	Dante's House
		15	Church of the Badia

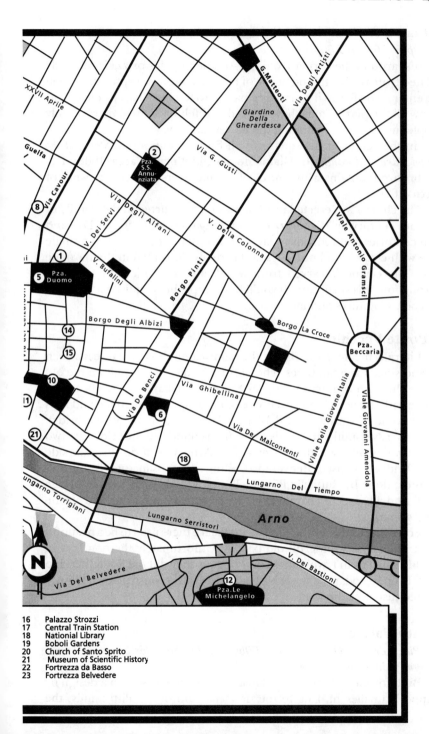

Via XXVII Aprile

Via Guelfa

Via Cavour

G. Matteotti

Via Degli Artisti

Giardino Della Gherardesca

② Pza. S.S. Annunziata

Via G. Gusti

Viale Antonio Gramsci

⑧

Via Dei Servi

Via Degli Alfani

V. Della Colonna

① V. Bufalini

⑤ Pza. Duomo

Borgo Pinti

Borgo Degli Albizi

Borgo La Croce

Pza. Beccaria

⑭

⑮

Via De Benci

Via Ghibellina

Viale Della Giovane Italia

Viale Giovanni Amendola

⑩

⑥

Via De Malcontenti

㉑

⑱

Lungarno Del Tiempo

Lungarno Torrigiani

Lungarno Serristori

Arno

N

Via Del Belvedere

⑫ Pza.Le Michelangelo

V. Dei Bastioni

2. Piazza & Church of SS Annunziata

Open 7:00am–7:00pm.

Just around the corner from the Accademia, this piazza is relatively isolated from the hustle and bustle of Florence's tourist center, and when you enter it you feel as if you walked back into Renaissance Florence. This is how all the piazzas must have looked and felt back then, no cars, only people milling around sharing the Florentine day.

In the center of the square you'll find the equestrian *Statue of the Grand Duke Ferdinando I* by **Giambologna** and **Pietyro Tacca** (1608). The two bronze fountains with figures of sea monsters are also the work of Tacca (1629).

The church was erected in 1250, was reconstructed in the middle of the 15th century by **Michelozzo**, and was again re-done in the 17th and 18th centuries and remains today as it was then. The interior is a single nave with chapels on both sides and is richly decorated in the Baroque style. The ceiling is carved from wood and is wonderfully intricate. Throughout this small church you'll find simple but exquisite bas-reliefs, frescoes, sculptures and more.

3. Ponte Vecchio

Literally meaning *Old Bridge*, the name came about because it's been around since Etruscan times. The present bridge was rebuilt on the old one in the 14th century by **Neri di Fiorvanti**. Thankfully this beautiful bridge with its shops lining each side of it was spared the Allied and Axis bombardments during World War II. Today the shops on the bridge belong to silversmiths and goldsmiths. In the middle of the bridge are two openings that offer wonderful views of the Arno. On the downstream side of the bridge is a bust of **Benvenuto Cellini**, a Renaissance goldsmith and sculptor, done by Raffaelle Romanelli in 1900. At night on the bridge you'll find all sorts of characters hanging out, sipping wine, and strumming guitars.

From the Ponte Vecchio to the Pitti Palace there used to be a beautiful street lined with wonderful old palazzi. Unfortunately the bombers in World War II didn't avoid these buildings as they did the Ponte Vecchio itself. Even so, today the street is filled with lovely reconstructed buildings erected just after the war.

4. Pitti Palace

Piazza dei Pitti. Open 9:00am–2:00pm Tuesday–Saturday. Sunday 9:00am–1:00pm. Admission L10,000.

Built for the rich merchant **Luca Pitti** in 1440, based on a design by Filippo Brunalleschi. Due to the financial ruin of the Pitti family, the construction was interrupted until the palace was bought by **Eleonora da Toledo**, the wife of Cosimo I.

It was then enlarged to its present size. Currently it is divided into five different museums: **The Palatine Picture Gallery**, famous for its Raphaels and its Titian and Rubens; **The Silver Museum** that houses Lorenzo di Medici's vases; **The Costumer and Porcelain Museums**; **The Gallery of Modern Art**, which exhibits paintings by Tuscan artists that are similar to French impressionists; and **The Museum of Precious Stones**.

This is another wonderful place to come if you're tired of looking at all that religious art in the Uffizzi and elsewhere. Even though some of the Medici clan were elected Pope, their taste in art was more secular in nature, so you'll find a good complement of both religious and secular works.

5. Duomo & Baptistery, Campanile, & Cathedral Museum

*All located at the Piazza del Duomo. Hours: **Duomo** - Church open 7:00am–7:00pm. Entrance to the dome open Monday–Saturday 10:00am – 5:00pm. Admission L6,000. **The Baptistery** – Open Monday – Saturday 1:00pm–6:00pm andx Sunday 9:00am–1:00pm. **The Campanile**– Open 9:00am–5:00pm, Summer 8:30am–7:00pm. Admission L6,000. **Cathedral Museum** (Museo dell'Opera del Duomo) – Open 9:00am–6:00pm Tuesday–Saturday. Until 7:30pm in the summer. Holidays open 9:00am–1:00pm.*

Duomo

When you're in Florence the one sight you have to see is the **Duomo**, Florence's cathedral. It was consecrated in 1436 by Pope Eugenio IV as **Santa Maria del Fiore** (Saint Mary of the Flowers), and that is still its official name, but everybody calls it "The Duomo." It was started in 1296 by Arnolfo di Cambio on the spot where the church of Santa Reparata existed. After di Cambio's death in 1301, the famous Giotto took over the direction of the work, but he dedicated most of his attention to the development of the Bell Tower (*Campanile*).

When Giotto died in 1337, Andrea Pisano took over until 1349 (he didn't die, he just moved on to other projects). By 1421 everything else was finished except for the dome, which **Brunelleschi** had won a competition to design and build. It took 14 years just to build the gigantic dome. Over the years, slight modifications and changes have been made, and in 1887, the current facade of the Duomo was finished by architect **Emilio de Fabris**.

The interior of the Duomo is 150 meters long and 38 meters wide at the nave and 94 meters at the transept. There are enormous gothic arches, supported by gothic pillars, which gives the interior a majestic quality. The dome is 90 meters high and 45.5 meters in diameter and is decorated with frescoes representing the Last Judgment done by Giorgio Vasari and Federico Zuccari at the end of the 16th century. In the niches of the pillars supporting the dome are statues of the Apostles.

The central chapel is home to the **Sarcophagus of San Zanobius** that contains the saints relics. The bronze reliefs are the work of Lorenzo Ghiberti (1442).

When you've finished wandering through and admiring the art and stained glass windows, you can go up to the top of the Duomo and get some great views of Florence. The way up is a little tiring, but the magnificent photo opportunities are fabulous. Don't miss these views!

The Baptistery

Definitely considered one of the most important works of art in the city, the **Baptistery** was built on the remains of a paleo-Christian monument, as well as an early Roman monument. The Baptistery was dedicated to Saint John the Baptist, the patron saint of Florence and was built in the 10th and 11th centuries. Up until 1128, it was the cathedral of Florence. That's why they built the Duomo; this small structure just didn't reflect the stature of the city of Florence.

Its shape is octagonal and is covered with colored marble. On the pavement by the Baptistery you'll find the signs of the Zodiac taken off of oriental textiles in the 13th century. Inside is the tomb of Giovanni XXIII by Donatello and Michelozzo in 1427. Next to the altar, you'll see the *Angel holding the Candlestick* by Agostino di Jacopo in 1320. To the left between the Roman sarcophagi is the wooden statue *Magdalen* by Donatello in 1560.

But the bronze paneled doors by **Ghoberti** and **Andrea Pisano da Pontedera** are the true masterpieces of the Baptistery. The door that is open to the public is the **Southern Door**, created by Andrea Pisano da Pontedera and is of least interest. The east and north doors are far more beautiful and intricate. Michelangelo described the east door as "the door to paradise." On it you'll find stories of the Old Testament, beginning as follows from the top left hand side:

• Creation of Adam; original sin; expulsion of Adam and Eve from Paradise
• Stories of Noah and the universal deluge (strangely enough some of these panels were almost lost in the flooding of 1966)
• Jacob and Esau; Rachel and Jacob; Isaac blesses Jacob
• Moses receives theTen Commandments on Mount Sinai
• The battle against the Philistines; David and Goliath.

From the top right hand side:
• Adam works the soil; Cain and Abel at work; Cain kills Abel

• Three angels appear to Abraham; Abraham sacrifices Isaac
• Joseph meets his brothers in Egypt; Stories of Joseph
• Joshua crosses the Jordan river; The conquering of Jericho
• Solomon receives the Queen of Sheba in the Temple.

The Campanile

Giotto died while he was attempting to complete the **Campanile**, but after his death **Andrea Pisano** and **Francesco Talenti** both scrupulously followed his designs until its completion. The only part they left out was the spire that was to go on top, which would have made the Campanile 30 meters higher than its current 84. The tower is covered is colored marble and adorned with bas-reliefs by Andrea Pisano and Luca della Robbia and Andrea Orcagna. Sculptures by Donatello, Nanni di Bartolo, and others used to be in the sixteen niches but are now in the Cathedral Museum.

Cathedral Museum (Museo dell'Opera del Duomo)

This is the place where many pieces of artwork that used to be in the Cathedral or the Campanile are now located. This was mainly done to help preserve them from the environment and the onslaught of hordes of tourists. Most of the items are statues and bas-relief work. The most famous ones to keep an eye out for are *St. John* by **Donatello**, *Habakkuk* by Donatello, *Virgin with Infant Jesus* by Arnolfo, and *Choir Gallery* with many scenes by Donatello.

6. Santa Croce

Piazza Santa Croce. Open 8:00am–12:30pm and 3:00pm–6:30pm.

The church of **Santa Croce** sits in the Piazza Santa Croce, surrounded by ancient palazzi renowned for the architecture. The one opposite the church is the **Palazzo Serristori** by Baccio D'Agnolo in the 16th century. Facing the church on the right hand side at #23 is the **Palazzo dell'Antella** built by Giulio Parigi in the 17th century.

The frescoes on the facade were created in only 20 days by 12 painters working non-stop. In the center of the square is a statue of **Dante Aligheri**, he of *Divine Comedy* fame, sculpted by Enrico Pazzi in 1865. This is a wonderfully ornate yet simple church belonging to the Franciscan Order. Consturction was begun in 1295 but its modern facade was created in 1863 by Nicolo Matas. It has a slim bell tower whose Gothic style doesn't seem to fit with this modern exterior. The interior, on the other hand, fits perfectly with the simple stonework of the bell tower.

Initially the walls inside had been covered with exquisite frescoes created by Giotto but these were covered up by order of Cosimo I in the 16th century. What remains is a basic monastic church that conveys piety and beauty in its simplicity. Of the many Italian artistic, religious, and political geniuses that lie buried beneath Santa Croce, the most famous has to be that of **Michelangelo** himself.

Besides the beautiful bas-reliefs, exquisite sculptures, and other works of art in Santa Croce you can find an excellent and inexpensive **leather school** *(Scuola del Cuoio)*. To get there go through the sacristy and you'll end up in the school that was started by the monks more than three decades ago. Here you'll find all kinds of leather goods for sale in what was once cells for the monks. The prices and selection are good even if the atmosphere is completely touristy *(Tel. 244-533, Tuesday–Saturday, 9:00am– 12:30pm and 3:00pm–6:00pm. American Express, Mastercard, and Visa accepted).*

7. San Lorenzo

Piazza San Lorenzo. Open Monday–Saturday 9:00am–Noon and 3:30pm– 5:00pm.

One of the most ancient basilicas in Florence. The architecture is the work of **Filippo Brunelleschi**, done from 1421-1446, but the church was finished by his pupil **Antonio Manetti** in 1460. The facade was never completed even though Michelangelo himself submitted a variety of designs for its completion.

The interior is made up of three naves with chapels lining the side walls. In the central nave at the far end are two pulpits that are the last two works of **Donatello** who died in 1466 after completing them. You'll find plenty of works by Donatello in this church, including:

• The stucco medallions in the Old Sacristy that represent the *Four Evangelists*
• The stucco medallions in the Old Sacristy that are *Stories of Saint John the Baptist*
• The terracotta *Bust of Sant Laurence* in the Old Sacristy
• The bronze doors with panels representing the *Apostles and Fathers of the Church* in the Old Sacristy.

8. Princes' Chapel

Piazza San Lorenzo. Open 10:00am–1:00pm and 3:00pm–7:00pm Monday, Tuesday, Thursday through Saturday. Sunday 10:00am– Noon. Wednesdays closed.

Just around the corner from the church of San Lorenzo, this octagonal building's construction was begun in 1604 on a design by Prince Giovanni dei Medici. It houses the tombs of a variety of Medici princes from which it gets its name. It is of interest to many tourists because of the tombs in the New Sacristy which were created by Michelangelo himself.

The Tomb of Lorenzo, Duke of Urbino (created by Michelangelo) has a statue of the duke seated and absorbed in meditation as well as two reclining figures that represent Dawn and Dusk. On the opposite wall is the *Tomb of Giulano, Duke of Nemours* (also created by Michelangelo) which shows a seated duke replete in armor, ready for action, as well as two reclining figures that represent night and day. Another Michelangelo work in the New Sacristy is the unfinished *Madonna and Child.*

If you like Michelangelo's sculpture but want to avoid the crowds that congregate at the museum that houses the David, this is the place to come.

9. Santa Maria Novella

Piazza Santa Maria Novella. Open 7:00am–Noon and 3:30pm–5pm Monday–Saturday and Sunday 3:30pm–5:00pm.

Built in 1278 by two Dominican friars, **Fra Ristoreo** and **Fra Sisto**, the church was created in the Gothic style with green and white marble decorations that are typically Florentine in character. The church was completed in 1470. To the left and right of the facade are tombs of illustrious Florentines all created in the same Gothic style as the church.

The interior of the church is in a T shape with the nave and aisles divided by clustered columns that support wide arches. Down the aisles are a variety of altars created by **Vasari** from 1565 to 1571.

As a young artist, Michelangelo worked on many of the frescoes as commissioned by his teachers. This is where he got his initial training that helped him create the now famous frescoes in the Sistine Chapel in Rome.

You can spend hours in here admiring the magnificent frescoes done by many Florentine artists including **Domenico Ghirlandaio** (Chapel of High Altar), **Giuliano da San Gallo** (Gondi Chapel), **Giovanni Dosio** (Gaddi Chapel), **Nardo di Cione** (Strozzi Chapel) and more. And if you're tired of sightseeing and need a little break, Florence's best pub, The Fiddler's Elbow, is in the piazza outside the church.

10. Piazza, Palazzo, & Loggia della Signoria

Piazza della Signoria

This piazza, with the Palazzo, the Loggia, the fountain, the replica of the statue of David, and more is incomparable in its beauty. Over the centuries great historical and political events, as well as the lives of average Florentines, have been worked out here.

Today the square is the site of the annual event, **Calcio in Costume** (soccer played in period garb), where the different sections of the city vie for dominance in a game that is a cross between soccer, rugby, and an all-out war. This annual contest used to be played in the square of Santa Croce but was moved here during modern times. If you are in Florence during June, when the event covers three of the weekends in that month, you definitely have to try and get tickets. The entire piazza is covered with sand, and stadium seats are put up all around the makeshift field. A truly memorable experience.

In the small square on the left is **Ammannati's Fountain** with the giant figure of *Neptune*. He's commonly called *Biancone* (Whitey) by the locals because of his bland appearance. Giambologna created the equestrian statue representing *Cosimo I dei Medici* on the left of the square.

Palazzo della Signoria – Palazzo Vecchio

Piazza della Signoria. Open Monday–Friday 9:00am–7:00pm, and Sunday 8:00am–1:00pm. Admission L10,000 for upstairs galleries.

The most imposing structure in the square is the **Palazzo Signoria**. It is 94 meters past the fortified battlements to the top of **Arnolfo's Tower**. The entire structure is rather severe, but at the same time elegant. Its construction began in the late 13th century but took hundreds of years to finish. It was once the home of **Cosimo de Medici** and other members of the Medici family before the Pitti Palace was completed.

In front of the building on the platform at the top of the steps, ancient orators used to harangue the crowds, and for this reason this section of the building is called *Arringhiera* (The haranguing area). Located here are several important sculptures including the *Marzocco* (a stone copy of the original which sits in the National Museum, a lion which symbolizes the Florentine Republic); *Judith and Holofernes* created by Donatello in 1460, which is a record of the victory over the Duke of Athens; the copy of Michelangelo's *David* (the original is in the Accademia), and *Hercules and Cacus* created by Baccio Bandinelli.

Above the main door is a frieze with two lions and a monogram of Christ with the inscription *Rex Regum et Dominus Dominantium* (King of Kings and Lord of Lords), which records the time that the Florentine republic elected Christ as their King in 1528. The inscription used to read as follows *Jesus Christus Rex Florentinei Populi S P Decreto Electus* (Jesus Christ elected by the people King of Florence) but was changed in 1851.

The interior is mainly filled with artwork glorifying the Medici family that ruled Florence and much of Italy for centuries. So if you're need a break from religious art and all those paintings of the Madonna and Child, this is the respite you've been asking for. Everything is elaborate and ornate, as befitting the richest family in the world at that time.

You enter through the courtyard which was designed by Michelozzo in 1453. The elaborate stucco decorations on the columns and frescoes on the arches were added in 1565 on the occasion of the wedding between Franscesco dei Medici and Joan of Austria. The fountain is the center of a *Graceful Winged Cupid* was done by Verrochio in 1476. From here most of the art to see is upstairs, so either take the staircase up or use the elevator. What follows is a description of the important works to see in each room:

Hall of the Five Hundred - Salone dei Cinquecento

The most splendid and artistic hall in Florence. It was designed for public meetings after the Medicis had been thrown from power. When Cosimo I regained the family's control over Florence, he had the hall enlarged and used it for his private audiences. On the wall opposite the entrance you'll find three large magnificent paintings by Baccio D'Agnolo, Baccio Bandinelli and Giorgio Vassari: *The Conquest of Siena; The Conquest of Porto Ercole; The Battle of Marciano*. On the wall across from this you'll find: *Maximilian Tries to Conquer Livorno; The Battle of Torre San Vincenzo; The Florentines Assault Pisa*. Underneath these painting you'll find sculptures by Vincenzo de Rossi representing *Hercules Labors*.

The ceiling is divided into 39 compartments with paintings by Giorgio Vasari that represent *Stories of Florence and the Medici*. The coup de grace is in the niche of the right wall at the entrance. Here you'll find Michelangelo's unfinished work, *The Genius of Victory*, which was designed for the tomb of Pope Julius II. If you only have a little time, spend it here. This rooms is magnificent.

Study of Francesco I de Medici

Here you'll find the work of many of Florence's finest artists crammed into as small a space as imaginable. The walls and even the barrel shaped ceiling are covered with paintings, and niches are filled with a variety of bronze statues. Elaborate and ostentatious.

Hall of the Two Hundred - Salone dei Duecento

It is called thus since this is where the Council of two hundred citizens met during the time of the Republic for their important decisions. The walls are adorned with tapestry, the ceiling is ornately decorated, chandeliers hang low, and statues and busts adorn any free spot. The center of the room is occupied by the seating used by the Council of 200.

Monumental Quarters - Quartieri Monumentali

These are a series of rooms that get their names from a member of the Medici family. Each are elaborate in their own right, filled with paintings, sculptures, frescoes, and more. From here you'll find many more interesting rooms and paintings as you explore, both on this floor and the one above, but this is the bulk of the beauty in the Palazzo Signoria.

The Loggia della Signoria
In the Piazza, on the right of the Palazzo, is the expansive and airy **Loggia della Signoria**, a combination of Gothic and Renaissance architecture. It was built by Benci di Cione, Simone Talenti and others during the years 1376–1382. At either end of the steps are two marble lions, one of which is very old, the other made in 1600.

Underneath the arch are some wonderful sculptures: *Persius* by Cellini in 1553 under the left hand arch; *The Rape of the Sabines* by Giambologna in 1583 under the right arch; *Hercules and the Centaur* by Giambologna in 1599 under the right arch also. There is also *Menelaus supporting Patroclus* and a few other less important works. All of them, since they are open to the elements and pollution, have been stained and discolored, but all are excellent studies in human anatomy.

11. Uffizzi Gallery

Piazza del Uffizzi. Open Tuesday to Saturday 9:00am–7:00pm and Sunday 9:00am–1:00pm. Admission L10,000.

The building housing the **Uffizi Gallery** was begun in 1560 by Giorgio Vasari on the orders of the Grand-Duke Cosimo I. It was originally designed to be government offices, but today holds the most important and impressive display of art in Italy, and some would say the world. The gallery mainly contains paintings of Florentine and Tuscan artists of the 13th and 14th centuries, but you'll also find paintings from Venice, Emilia, and other Italian art centers as well as Flemish, French, and German works. In conjunction there is a collection of numerous ancient sculptures.

These fabulous works of art were collected first by the Medici family, then later by the Loraine family. After the Gastone, the last of the Medici, the last inheritor, Anna Maria Luisa donated the entire Gallery to the Tuscan state in 1737 so that the rich collection gathered by her ancestors would never leave Florence. Not everything would go as planned, since in the 18th century some pieces were stolen by Napoleon's marauding forces, but most of these were later ransomed for their return. Some items were damaged in the great flood of 1966, and still others were damaged in 1993 when a terrorist car bomb ripped through parts of the Gallery. Even with all these occurrences, the Uffizzi is still one of the finest galleries in the world.

It's collection is so rich and so vast that it has caused some tourists to grow queasy, feel faint, and generally feel ill. A medical study has determined that some people become completely overwhelmed with the large amount of artistic beauty and cannot handle the input; while others postulate that it is the abundance of religious paintings, mainly of the

Madonna and child, that make people disoriented by the constant repetition of the same theme. Whatever the reasons for the symptoms, if you start to feel queasy, don't be shy to ask for a place to rest.

It is interesting to see, as you enter the Uffizzi, the statues of Cosimo the Elder and Lorenzo the Magnificent, as well as several busts of the rest of the Medici rulers, since when they ruled most Florentines despised their despotic ways. But now they are immortalized in time because of the philanthropic gesture of their last heir. Anyway, it would be virtually impossible to list all the paintings and sculptures exhibited, so let me make a list of those that you absolutely must see if you visit the gallery:

- *Madonna of the Pomegranate* - Botticelli - Room X
- *Self Portraits of Titian, Michelangelo, Raphael, Rubens, Rembrandt and more* - Third Corridor
- *Madonna of the Goldfinch* - Raphael - Room XXV
- *Holy Family* - Michelangelo - Room XXV
- *Venus of Urbino* - Titian - Room XXVIII
- *Young Bacchus* - Caravaggio - Room XXXVI
- *Portrait of an Old Man* - Rembrandt - Room XXXVII
- *Portrait of Isabelle Brandt* - Peter Paul Rubens - Room XLI

12. Piazzale Michelangelo

From this piazza you have a wonderful view of the city of Florence dissected by the river Arno. Remember to bring your camera for the best public view of the city. The best private view is from the Hotel Torre di Bellosguardo, but if you want to see it you have to stay there and it's in the high price range. At the center of the Piazzalle Michelangelo is a monument to **Michelangelo** dominated by a replica of the statue of *David*. Round the pedestal are four statues that adorn the tombs of famous Medicis which Michelangelo created.

If you don't want to walk up the steep hill to the Piazza, take bus number 13 from the station.

13. Museo Zoologico la Specola

Via Romana 17. Closed Wednesdays. Open Sundays 9:00am–1:00pm, and all other days 9:00am–12 noon.

This is an outing for the entire family, especially little boys. They have vast collection of stuffed animals from all over the world, some extinct, as well as bugs, fish, crustaceans, and more. Unfortunately some ignorant tourists have started using a hollowed out elephant foot as a trash can.

You won't believe the extent of this collection, and that's just the animals. The best part of the exhibit are the over 500 anatomical figures and body parts that were made in very life-like colored wax between 1175 and 1814. Every part of the body has been preserved separately and in whole body displays. They even left the hair on the female bodies to make them look more realistic. One exhibit you may not want your kids to see is the part on reproduction, which gets pretty graphic. That room is at the end so you can march ahead and steer your loved ones into another room.

The other stuff is very tame. The last room has miniature wax scenes that are completely realistic depcitions of the toll taken by the Black Death (the Plague). One particular tiny image of a rat pulling on a dead man's intestine is quite intense. Look at these pieces as art, not the anatomy tools they were used for, and you'll appreciate them as much as the many art students I encountered sketching the wax figures.

The Boboli Gardens

Located behind the Pitti Palace. Open 9am until one hour before sunset.

Hidden behind the Pitti Palace is your respite from the Florentine heat and its hectic pace. Began in 1549 by Cossimo I and Eleanor of Tudor, the gardens went through many changes, additions, and alterations before they reached their present design. Among its many pathways and well-placed fields, the **Boboli Gardens** are the only true escape from the sun, humidity, and crowds that swarm through Florence in July and August. If you are inclined to walk in a calm, peaceful garden, far from the bustling crowds, or if you wish to enjoy a relaxing picnic, the Boboli is your place.

In the groves and walks of the Boboli you can find many spots to sit and enjoy a picnic lunch, or you can simply enjoy the platoons of statuary lining the walks. Some of the most famous works here include: *Pietro Barbino Riding a Tortoise*, commonly called Fat Baby Bacchus riding a turtle (you'll find reproductions of this statue in almost every vendor's stall in Florence); a Roman amphitheater ascending in tiers from the Palazzo Pitti, designed as a miniature Roman circus to hold Medici court spectacles; and *Neptune's Fountain* at the top of the terrace, created in 1565 by Stoldo Lorenzi.

From this fountain a path leads to the adorable **Kaffeehaus**, a boat-like pavilion that offers a fine view of Florence and drinks to quench your thirst. Keep going up until you reach the **Ex Forte di Belvedere**, which offer magnificent views of all of Florence, and Cypress Alley, lined with statues of many different origins.

La Limonaia

Even if you are not looking for it, you can't miss the **Limonaia**, a room 340 feet long and 30 feet wide that became the 'hospital' for all the devastated works of art during the Flood of '66 (see story below).

Originally used to house the Boboli Gardens' lemon trees during the winter months, this room, many experts felt, was the savior of the Florentine masterpieces, because of its insulation from the Florentine humidity. Most of the art treasures from the disastrous flood of '66 were brought here to be rehabilitated. I guess you could say that all art lovers can be thankful that the Medicis, who built the Boboli Gardens and the Limonaia, had a passion for lemons.

Porta Romana

This garden stretches seemingly forever, and it hides some of the best green spaces at its farthest corners, near Florence's **South Gate** (**Porta Romana**).

NIGHTLIFE & ENTERTAINMENT

Florence is definitely not known for its nightlife like Rome or Milan are. Local Florentine activities usually include some form of late night eating and drinking at a restaurant that stays open late. Heated dancing and wild debauchery don't seem to part of the Florentine make-up.

Here are some places to go if you get that itch to be wild; the numbering follows the restaurants on the *Florence Restaurants* map.

THE RED GARTER, *Via de Benci 33r, Tel. 055/234-4904. Serve Heineken, McFarland, Guiness, margaritas and an any other drink you could want. Open 8:30pm - 1:00am. Happy hour 8:30pm - 9:30pm.*

A raunchy, wild and fun-filled place with live music in the back and a bar up front. Their pitchers cost L24,000-30,000, Liters L14,000-18,000, and half-pints L7,000-10,000. A place to come and be wild. Why else would they serve pitchers?

IL FAUNO, *Via Cavour 89. Tel 055/471-682. Open 5:00pm - 2:00am. Happy hour 5:00pm - 10:00pm.*

Yes, they have a loooong happy hour (five hours). Enjoy the half-priced drinks in a not so authentic Irish pub. Fiddler's is where the ex-pats hang out, so if you're into a pseudo Irish time, and want to save some bucks give this place a try. If it's no good, after happy hour, hop over to Fiddler's.

THE FIDDLER'S ELBOW, *Piazza Santa Maria Novella 7R, Tel. 055/215-056. Open 3:00pm- 1:15pm every day.*

If you want to wallow in a true Irish pub outside of Ireland, you've found it. They serve Harp, Kilkenny, Guiness and some Inch's Stonehouse Cider. A pint costs L7,000, a half-pint L4,000 and the lovely Irish and English bartenders will gladly serve you a shot or two of your pleasure. There is no food served, and there is seating outside but no service for the tables.

But to actually feel as if you're in Ireland, step into the air conditioned comfort, sit among the hanging musical instruments, belly up to the dark wooden bar, eye yourself in the mirror, and have a pint. For snacks (you have to pay for them), they have peanuts, salami sticks for the Italians, and four types of Highlander Scottish potato chips (they call them crisps): Roast Beef Taste, Cheddar & Onion, Caledonian Tomato, and Sea Salt. If you want to be a part of the ex-pat community here in Florence this is one of the places to go. They also have bars in Rome and Venice. Mr. Fiddler has really become a businessman.

IL RIFRULLO, *Via San Niccolo 55, Tel. 055/213-631. Large beer L5,000, small beer L3,000, Crepe L5,000. Open from 8:00am to midnight.*

Located in the centro, this is a charming and relaxing place where you can enjoy a drink in the garden in the summer, in front of the fireplace in the winter, or up at the bar whenever you please. The atmosphere in the front room is all pub, in the back room all *taverna*, and in the garden, all party. They have a bar set into ancient struts that hold up the building; the tables are under an overhead canopy. They serve Whitbread Pale Ale, Campbells Scotch Ale, Stella Antois (Belgian) and Leffe (and Belgian Double Malt on tap), as well as some of the largest and most scrumptious crepes around.

SPACE ELECTRONIC, *Via Palazzuolo 37, 50123 Firenze. tel. 055/292-082. Fax 055/293-457.*

The largest and loudest discotheque in the city. They've had videos playing here before anybody knew what videos were (I remember), and they continue to be the trendsetters when it comes to club antics. What they are into now I'll keep quiet, so maybe you'll come check them out. They play all sorts of music, so no one is left out. A fun place.

HARRY'S BAR, *Lungarno a Vespucci 22, 50123 Firenze. Tel. 055/239-6700. American Express, Mastercard and Visa accepted. Closed Sundays.*

Based on the famous Harry's Bar in Venice (see the Venice Section in this book), but with no business connections (Italians obviously have different trademark laws than we do), this is now the place to find the best burgers in Florence. They also mix some strong drinks in the evening, so if you have nothing to do and just want to get out of the hotel room, pop in here.

DUBLIN PUB, *Via Faenza 27r. Tel. 055/293-049. Closed Mondays. Open from 5pm to 2:00am*

A true Irish pub, dark and dingy and open only at night. They serve Kilkenny, Harp, Guiness for L7,000 a pint and L4,000 a half pint; as well as some Bulmers Cider. A hopping nightlife spot with true Irish ambiance. I prefer Fiddler's Elbow, but they're close enough together that you can try them both. This one is near the outdoor San Lorenzo Market and the Mercato Centrale.

Movies in English

Try **Cinema Astro**, P*iazza San Simone (near Santa Croce; closed July 10–August 31 and Mondays. Ticketc cost L8,000.* There's a student discount on Wednesdays for L6,000. There are films in English here every night. Either call for the schedule or stop by and pick one up.

There's also a movie poster listing the films playing at Cinema Astro just inside the **Fiddler's Elbow** pub (see above in this section).

SPORTS & RECREATION

Balloon Rides in Tuscany

Contact **The Bombard Society**, *6727 Curran Street, McLean VA 22101-3804, US, Tel. 800/862-8537, Fax. 703/883-0985. In Virginia or outside, Tel. 703/448-9407; you can call collect.* Call for current price and information about the most spectacular way to view the most spectacular scenery in the world.

Bicycling

Florence is the perfect city to explore on a bicycle and there are a few rental places available.
• **Free Motor**, *Via Santa Monaca 6-8, Tel. 055/295-102, in the Oltrarno area.*
• **Motorent**, *Via San Zanobi 9, Tel. 055/490-113, in the Centro area.*
• **Sabra**, *Via Artisti 8, Tel. 055/576-256, in the Oltrarno area.*

Golf
• **Circolo Golf dell'Ugolino**, *Via Chiantigiano 3, 51005 Grassina, Tel. 055/320-1009. Fax 055/230-1141.* Located 9km from Florence this is a par 72, 18 hole course that is 5,728 meters long. Open all year round except on Mondays. They have tennis courts, a swimming pool, a pro shop, a nice bar and a good restaurant.
• **Poggio de Medici Golf & Country Club**, *Via San Gavino 27, 50038 Scarperia. Tel. 055/83-0436/7/8. Fax 055/843-0439.* Located 30km from Florence this is a 9 hole, par 36, that is 3,430 meter long course, open all year round except for Tuesdays.. They have a driving range, putting green and a club house with snacks and drinks.

Swimming

There are three public pools in Florence:
• **Piscine Bellariva**, *Lungarno Colombo 6, Tel. 677-521, located outside the city.*
• **Piscine Costoli**, *Viale Poali, Tel. 055/669-7444, located outside the city.*
• **Piscine Pavoniere**, *Viale degli Olmi, Tel. 055/367-506*

Tennis

• **Associazione Sportiva**, *Viale Michelangelo, Tel. 055/681-2686*

SHOPPING

Antiques

Many of the better known antique stores have been located in the **Via dei Fossi** and **Via Maggio** for years, but there are some interesting little shops in the **Borgo San Jacopo** and the **Via San Spirito**, all located in the **Oltrarno** section of Florence across the river.

When shopping for antiques in Florence, there is one important thing to remember: the Florentines are excellent crafts people and as such have taken to the art of antique fabrication and reproduction. How can they do this legally? Under Italian law, furniture made from old wood is considered an antique. These products can be exported. But if you find a 'real' antique by American standards, it is usually stamped so that it cannot be taken out of the country.

Artisans

If you want to see some of this fabrication and reproduction work, as well as genuine restoration in progress, you need venture no further than across the river to the **Oltrarno** section. In these narrow streets you'll find small workshops alive with the sounds of hammers and saws, intermingled with the odors of wood, tanning leather, and glue. When I lived in Florence this was my favorite area to come to. Watching someone creating something out of nothing has always been a relaxing adventure, and besides, not many tourists even venture into these tiny alcoves of Florentine culture.

Some of the most well known shops are located in the **Via Santo Spirito**, **Viale Europa**, **Via Vellutini**, **Via Maggio** and the **Via dello Studio**. Strangely enough, on these same streets are your reputable antique shops. How convenient to have the fabricators and reproducers next door to the 'legitimate' antique dealers.

Books & Newspapers in English

BM Bookshop, *Borgo Agnissanti 4r, Tel 055/294-575. American Express, Mastercard and Visa accepted. Open Winter: Monday 3:30pm-7:30pm, Tuesday-Saturday 9:00am-1:00pm and 3:30pm-7:30pm. Open Summer: 9:30am-1:00pm and 3:30pm-7:30pm daily.*

An extensive collection of English language books in both hardcover and paperback. This is also one of the meeting places for the English-speaking community in Florence. Located in the *Centro* area.

English Bookstore Paperback Exchange, *Via Fiesolana 31r, Tel 247-8154. American Express, Diners Club, Mastercard and Visa accepted. Open Monday-Saturday 9:00am-1:00pm and 3:30pm-7:30pm. Closed in August. Closed Mondays November–February.*

The unofficial English speaking expatriates meeting place, this store has the largest and best priced selection of English-language paperbacks in Florence. It's the Florentine equivalent of the *Economy Bookstore* in Rome. You will get paid for any used paperbacks you want to get rid of, or they'll credit the amount to any purchases you want to make. Located in the *Santa Croce* section of Florence.

Libreria Internazionale Seeber, *Via Tornabuoni 68r, 055/215-697. Mastercard and Visa accepted.*

This is a quaint old fashioned bookstore that's been around since the 1860s to serve the expatriate community. An entire room is devoted to foreign books, not all of which are in English. Even if you can't find what you want, this is a fun place to browse.

Cartoleria - Stationary Stores

L'Indice Scrive, *Via della Vigna Nuova 82r. Tel. 055/215-165. Mastercard and Visa accepted.*

A wide variety of stationary products and unique pens are featured in this store. Most of the items are hand-made, including the diaries, ledgers, guest books, desk sets. etc. A great place to get a gift for someone back home.

Il Papiro, *Piazza Duomo 24r, Tel. 055/215-262. Credit cards accepted.*

If you like marbleized paper products, this is the store for you. You can get boxes, notebooks, picture frames, pencil holders, basically anything you could imagine. The prices are a little high but that's because of the great location and high quality products.

Markets

The markets in Florence are all hustle and bustle, especially in the high tourist season. But despite the crowds you can have a great time browsing and shopping. And of course, the prices are sometimes close to half what they are in stores. Remember to bargain if you want something.

Mercato Centrale, *immediately north of Piazza San Lorenzo, near the Duomo, open Monday–Saturday, 7am–1pm, 4–7:30pm.*

This is Florence's main food market for wholesale and retail fish, fresh meat, vegetables, cheeses, oils, breads, and many other delicacies. The meat and fish section is on the ground floor, with a few vegetable stands thrown in, but if you're into healthy food, make your way upstairs to their fruit and vegetable market. The aroma is enough to make you want to come back every day you're in Florence. Try to find some *caciotta* (sheep's milk cheese) and *finocchiona* (salami flavored with fennel) because they are an exquisite local delicacy. This is the best place to shop for your picnic supplies. A must see while in Florence. The market itself is surrounded by the large clothing market of San Lorenzo.

When you visit the Mercato Centrale, don't think of leaving without getting a sandwich at **Nerbone's** (see review above in *Where to Eat*). In operation since 1872, this small food stand serves the absolutely best boiled pork, beef, or veal sandwiches, for only L3,500. They're simply called panini and your only choice of meat is what they have boiled for the day. The sandwich is just the meat, the bread, and some salt, but it is amazing. You can stand at the counter and sip a glass of wine or beer, or take your meal to the small seating area just across the aisle.

Mercato di San Lorenzo, *located near the Duomo, open Monday–Friday, 7am–2pm, Saturdays and holidays 4–8 pm.*

This is the largest and most frequented street market in Florence, and it completely dominates the church of San Lorenzo and its piazza, as well as spilling into most adjacent streets. You can find everything from shoes to pants, T-shirts, belts, and much more, most at prices close to half of what you would pay in a store. Both Florentines and tourists come here looking for bargains. Again, remember to bargain, because once a merchant marks you as a tourist the price quoted is usually higher than that quoted to Italians.

Mercato Nuovo, *located in the Logge del Mercato Nuovo off the Via Por San Maria near the Piazza del Signoria, open daily 9am–5pm.*

This is the famous Straw Market. They sell traditional products made from straw but also exquisite leather products, ceramics, linens (like table clothes and napkins), statues, and other hand-made Florentine crafts.

Mercato Delle Piante, *located in the Piazza della Repubblica in front of the Central Post Office, open Thursday 7am–1pm.*

This beautiful flower market can calm any soul. Even if you do not want to buy any plants, simply walk through the many different flowers and enjoy the sights and smells.

Mercato dell Pulci, *located in the Piazza dei Compi about four blocks north of the church of Santa Croce, open Tuesday–Saturday, 8am–1pm, 3:30pm–7pm, and the first Sunday of each month from 9am–7pm.*

This is Florence's famous flea market. If you want antiques and junk at obviously trumped up prices, come here. They think tourists will pay anything for a true Italian antique – so remember to bargain. The next market, Mercato di Sant'Ambrogio, is located just to the east of this market.

Mercato di Sant'Ambrogio, *located in the Piazza Lorenzo Ghiberti between the Via Dell' Agnolo and the Borgo La Croce, open weekday mornings.*

This is another of Florence's food markets. It has a less hectic and more intimate atmosphere than the larger Mercato Centrale. Also a good place to sit at their lunch counter, try some food, and settle down with a nice cappuccino.

Mercato delle Cascine, *located in the Cascine park along the Arno river on the outskirts of Florence to the west, just off of the Piazza Vittorio Veneto, open Tuesdays, 7 am–1pm.*

This is like a huge outdoor department store. For sale are mainly clothing and household products, but even if you're not going to buy anything, this is an interesting insight into Italian culture and society.

Picnic & Food Supplies

If you can't make it to the **Mercato Generale** or the **Mercato di Sant'Ambrogio** for your Boboli Gardens or day trip picnic supplies, here's a small list of food stores from which you can get almost everything you want. The perfect amount of meat for a sandwich would be *mezzo etto*, and same goes for your cheese. Also, at most bars you can order a sandwich to go if you're too lazy to make your own sandwich, as well some *vino* or *birra* to take with you.

Alimentari, *Via Luigi Alimani #6.*

Located right next to the train station. Actually it's housed in the same building but the entrance to this place is outside. A perfect place to pick up a snack before you go on a day trip.

Vera, *Piazza Frescobaldi 3r, Tel 055/215-465. No credit cards accepted.*

Located in the Oltrarno section of Florence, this store is a food connoisseur's delight. It is indisputably Florence's best stocked food store, conveniently located close to the Boboli Gardens. It has the best fresh cheeses, salamis, hams, roasted meats, freshly baked breads, olive oil, soups and salads. If you want fresh fruit you're also in luck – but not here, in the store across the street.

Alimentari, *Via Arione 19r, 055/214-067. No credit cards accepted. Closed Wednesday afternoons.*

Located in the Centro area of Florence near the Piazza San Trinita, this is your basic Italian grocery store. There's a sandwich counter from which you can have the sandwich of your choice made with a wide variety of meats (try the *prosciutto*), cheeses (get some of the fresh buffalo-milk *mozzarella*), salamis, and fresh bread. You can also get *vino* to go here. If you want to eat or enjoy a glass of Chianti at the bar, upside-down barrels serve as seats.

Cibreo Alimentari, *Via del Verrocchio 4, 50122 Firenze. Tel. 055/677-298.*

A deli-type store in the Santa Croce area that is associated with the Cibreo restaurant in the same area. They sell authentic and fresh local delicacies for take-out.

Vino e Olio, *Via dei Serragli 29r, Tel. 055298-708. No credit cards accepted.*

You can find any type of wine or olive oil you could dream of in this store. Since it is slightly expensive you may not want to get your wine for the picnic here, but it is a great place to buy gifts for friends at home. If you don't want to carry them with you on the rest of your trip, the owner will arrange to have them shipped to wherever you choose.

Alessi Paride, *Via delle Oche 27-29r, Tel. 055/214-966. Credit cards accepted.*

This store is a wine lover's paradise. They have wines from every region of Italy and there's one room entirely of Chianti. This store may also be a little expensive for picnic supplies, but you can get any manner of wine imaginable here, as well as selected liquors, chocolates, marmalades, and honeys.

PAPIERMACHE & POLICE SURPLUS!

*One store you simply cannot miss is the small studio/gallery of the artist Bijan, **Firenze of Papier Mache, Piazza Pitti 10, 50125 Firenze, Tel. 055/230-2978, Fax 055/365-768.** He makes some beautiful masks covered with intricate sketchings of famous paintings, as well as beautiful anatomical forms all from papiermache. Even if you don't buy anything, simply browse and savor the beauty of his work. Since the shop is near the Palazzo Pitti, one of your 'must see' destinations while in Florence, there's no reason why you shouldn't stop here.*

__Il Tricolore__, Via della Scala 32, is a moderately priced Italian army navy store, with a few American items thrown in. You can get Caribinieri (Italian military police) hats, T-shirts, knives, pins, badges, jackets, bags, etc., all from the Italian police or military services. Some items they can't sell to you since they are official army and/or police issue, but the stuff you can buy will make some great gifts for yourself or others.

PRACTICAL INFORMATION

Bank Hours & Changing Money

Banks are open Monday to Friday, 8:30am–1:20pm and 3pm–4pm, and are closed Saturdays, Sundays and national holidays. You'll need your passport when changing money or travelers checks at a bank as well as at a hotel or foreign exchange office *(ufficio di cambio)*.

You'll find the best rates at banks and *cambio*. To get the most for your money try to avoid changing it at the American Express office or at a hotel.

Business Hours

Shops are generally open 9am–1pm and 3:30pm or 4pm to 7pm or 7:30pm, although some in the *Centro Storico* area stay open all day to cater to the tourists. And an even more accommodating gesture towards the almighty dollar is that some stores even open on Sundays. I can remember when nothing was open in Florence on a Sunday except the restaurants.

In the winter, most shops are closed on Monday morning, except the food stores which close on Wednesday afternoon. (Why? Who knows?) In the summer, some stores close all day Saturday, but remain open on Monday morning. The rules change constantly.

Church & Synagogue Ceremonies in English
- **St. James**, American Episcopal Church, *Via Rucellai 9, Tel. 055/294-417.* Located in the *Centro* section of Florence.
- **St. Marks**, Church of England, *Via Maggio 16, Tel. 055/294-764.* Located in the *Oltrarno* section of Florence.
- **Synagogue**, *Via L.C. Farini 4, Tel. 055/245-251/2.* Located in the *Santa Croce* section of Florence.

Consulates
- **British Consulate**, *Lungarno Corsini 2, Florence, Tel. (055) 284-133*
- **United States Consulate**, *Lungarno Amerigo Vespucci 38, Florence, Tel. (055) 239-8276*

If you're Canadian, Irish, or another nationality, you'll need to contact your embassy in Rome (see our *Rome* chapter, *Practical Information* section).

Local Festivals & Holidays
- **January 1**, New Years Day
- **April 25**, Liberation Day
- **Ascension Day**
- **Easter Monday**, Cricket Festival with floats and many little crickets sold in cages. Kids love this festival. You won't be able to bring the crickets back to the states though.
- **May 1**, Labor Day
- **Month of May**, Iris Festivals
- **May and June**, *Maggio Musicale Fiorentino*
- **Mid-June to August**, *Estate Fiesolana*. Music, cinema, ballet and theater
- **Three Weekends in June**, *Calcio in Costume*
- **June 24**, St. John the Baptist's Day celebrated with fireworks
- **August 15**, *Ferragosto*
- **First Sunday in September**, Lantern Festival
- **November 1**, All Saints Day *(Ognissanti)*
- **December 8**, Conception of the Virgin Mary *(Immacolata)*
- **December 25 & 26**, Christmas

Laundry

After you're on the road for a few days, and especially if you're going to be on the road for quite a while, you're definitely going to need to do some laundry, quickly, easily, and cheaply. If you're staying at a four star hotel don't bother reading this because you've already sent your clothes down to be starched and pressed by the in-house staff.

For the rest of us, we need to find a good coin operated laundry, and in Florence they have just the thing. Actually, there are four of them, all branches of the same outfit, plus one lone entrepeneur.

• **Wash & Dry**, *Open seven days a week from 8:00am to 10:00pm. Last wash allowed in at 9:00pm. General number 055/436-1650. L6,000 for wash, L6,000 for dry, L2,500 for detergent. At the following locations:* **Via dei Serragli 87/R** *(in the Oltrarno);* **Via della Scala 52/54R** *(by the train station) – has air conditioning;* **Via dei Servi 105/R** *(by the Duomo) – has air conditioning;* **Viale Morgagni 21/R** *(Quite a ways away from the tourist center. You'll probably never get out this far).*

• **Laundrette**, *Via del Guelfa 33. Open seven days a week from 8:00am to 10:00pm. Wash L5,000, Dry L3,000, Detergent L5,000.*

Postal Services

The **central post office** in Florence *is at Via Pietrapiana 53-55, in the Santa Croce section of town*; but stamps can be bought at any tobacconist (store indicated by a T sign outside), and mailed at any mailbox, which are red and marked with the words *Poste* or *Lettere*. You can send duty free gift packages (need to be marked "gift enclosed") home to friends or relatives as long as the cost of the gift(s) in the package does not exceed US$50.

If you need to mail a package of material which you brought with you on you trip, you need to mark the package "American goods returned."

Tourist Information & Maps

• **Information Office**, *Via Manzoni 16, Tel. 055/247-8141.* Located in the Santa Croce area of Florence. Provides city maps, up-to-date information about Florence and the Province of Florence, which includes museum hours, event, and bus and train schedules.

• **Information Office**, *at the Train Station, Via Stazione 59r. Open 7am to 10pm. Tel. 055/278-785.* They can book hotel rooms for you here. You have to pay the first night's stay in advance plus a fee of L10,000 for a deluxe hotel, L6,000 for a four-star, L5,000 for a three-star, L4,000 for a two star, and L3,000 for a one star. There's an attached form that you need to fill out so that they can find just the room for you.

• **American Express**, *Lungarno Guicciardini 49, Tel. 055/288-751.* Located in the *Oltrarno* section of Florence. You don't need to be a card holder or be in any way related to American Express to ask for assistance.

Tour Operators

• **American Express**, *Via Dante Aligheiri 22r, Tel. 055/50981.* Located in the *Centro Storico* section of Florence.

• **Wagon-Lit**, *Via del Giglio 27r, Tel 055/21-88-51.* Located in the Centro section of Florence.

• **World Vision Travel**, *Via Cavour 154/158r. Tel 055/57-71-85. Fax 055/582-664; and Lungarno Acciadi 4. Tel. 055/29.52.71. Fax 055/215-666.*

• **CIT**, *Via Cavour 56-59, Tel. 055/294-306.* Located in the Centro section of Florence.

21♦ VENICE

City of Canals & Bridges

Venice is one of the great cultural centers of Europe, and as such attracts tens of thousands of tourists each year. It serves as the capital of the province of Venice (**Venezia**) and the **Veneto region**, which includes the towns of **Padua, Verona,** and **Vicenza.**

The historic center of Venice that everyone comes to see is built on a group of islets and mudbanks in the middle of **Laguna Veneta**, a crescent-shaped lagoon separated from the **Adriatic Sea** by a barrier of narrow islands and peninsulas. The modern city covers the whole 90 mile (145 km) perimeter of the lagoon and includes ten principal islands, in addition to those of the mother city and two industrial boroughs of **Mestre** and **Marghera** on the mainland.

The main core of Venice includes the islands of **La Giudecca** with its floating cafés and restaurants; **San Giorgio Maggiore**, with its famous 16th century church of the same name; and **San Michele** with its famous cemetery. Other islands include the **Lido**, a resort built in the 19th century, with casino, hotels, and beaches; **Murano**, noted for its glass-works; **Burano**, famous for its lace; and **Torcello**, site of the remains of the **Santa Maria Assunta** cathedral. Venice is separated from the sea by natural and artificial breakwaters, but flooding is common from November through March of each year, so if you visit then, remember to bring some galoshes.

Because of this water, Venice is world renowned as a city of canals and bridges. These facilitate internal transportation and have a beauty and charm that draw countless visitors each year. Chief among these arteries is the **Grand Canal**, which starts at the railway station at **Piazza Roma** and ends at **Piazza San Marco** (**St. Mark's Square**). Altogether there are more than 200 canals, which are literally the streets and avenues of Venice. Crossing the waterways are about 400 bridges, the most famous of which is probably the **Rialto** with its many shops, and the daily market near its base in the **San Polo** section. Other well known bridges include the **Scalzi,** the **Accademia**, and the infamous **Bridge of Sighs**, which leads from the upper story of the **Doges' Palace** to the republic's prison. It's called the Bridge of Sighs because centuries ago prisoners went over it sighing in trepidation of their torture and death.

Within the Venetian islands, canals, and lagoons, commodities move by barges and tugs, while passenger movement is primarily by *vaporetti* (water buses). The world-famous black *gondolas*, propelled by professional gondoliers, are narrow with high prows and sterns and are used mainly for short canal passages. Now they are mainly the vehicles of merchants, politicians, and especially tourists.

ARRIVAL & DEPARTURES

By Bus

When arriving by bus you have to disembark at Piazza Roma, then either walk or catch some form of water transport to your destination. The main local bus service is **ACTV** *(Tel. 041/528-7886)*. They have a tourist office in Piazza Roma where you can get maps, tourist information about Venice, and reserve bus seats to a variety of different cities in the region including Mestre, Padua, Mira and Treviso.

By Car

If you arrive in Venice by car, be prepared for long waits near **Piazza Roma** before you can deposit your automobile for the duration of your stay. One of the beauties of Venice is that it is automobile free. The only way to get to Venice by car is through the mainland town of **Mestre**, then over the bridge (made by Mussolini) to the parking lots around the Piazza Roma. Once you get rid of your car, you can either walk to your destination or hop on the *vaporetto* at the Piazza Roma stop on the canal. You will also be able to catch water taxis or gondolas from this location.

Sample trip lengths on main roads:
• **Padua**: 50 minutes
• **Bologna**: 2 hours
• **Florence**: 4 hours
• **Rome**: 6 hours.

If you want to rent a car, try **Avis**, *Piazza Roma 496/H, 041/522-5825* or **Hertz**, Piazza Roma, 496/E, *041/528-4091*.

By Train

Arriving by train is the most convenient way to get to Venice. The **Stazione di Santa Lucia** is located on the northwestern edge of the city. From here you'll need to either walk to your hotel through the maze of medieval streets, take a *vaporetto* (a water bus), hire a water taxi, or go in style (and expense) in a gondola. All of these transportation services are located on the canal directly in front of the train station.

The **tourist information office** *(041/719-078)*, on the left, and hotel information *(041/715-016)*, on the right, are located side by side near the front entrance of the station. If you need a hotel reservation get in the right line. If you just want information about upcoming events in Venice, a map, etc., get in the left line.

Sample trip lengths and costs for direct *(diretto)* trains:
• **Padua**: 45 minutes, L4,000
• **Bologna**: 1 1/2 hours, L15,000
• **Florence**: 3 1/2 hours, L27,000
• **Rome**: 5 hours, L56,000.

VISIT VENICE OFF-SEASON IF YOU CAN

Because of the crowds and the tacky commercialism that comes with them, Venice is definitely a place to visit in the off-season. You'll share the city almost completely with the locals, and you'll be able to stay in a much better hotel since all accommodations virtually cut their rates in half during the off-season. You'll also miss the stench that sometimes seeps its way from the canals during the heat of July and August. And by coming in the off-season you may be lucky enough to be in Venice during one of their rare snow storms that blanket the city with a powdery decoration, turning a gorgeous city into a magical one.

ORIENTATION

Venice is conveniently broken up into six **sestieri**, or sections, and the houses are numbered consecutively from a point in the center of each section, making finding specific locations an adventure in and of itself. The six *sestieri* are:

• **Cannaregio**, where the Jewish Ghetto is located; not too many tourists here.
• **Santa Croce**, along with San Polo is still considered the 'other side of the canal,' even though the Rialto bridge was built back in 1588 to connect this section of Venice with the more influential San Marco section.
• **San Polo**, site of the famous food market near the foot of the Rialto bridge that is open every morning except Sunday and Monday.
• **San Marco**, which is the cultural and commercial center of Venice and the location that most tourists never leave.
• **Dorsoduro**, where you can have a relaxing meal on the **Zattere**, the series of quays facing the island of **La Guidecca**, and watch the sun go down.

• **Castello**, the location of the **Arsenale**, where many of Venice's ships have been built.

GETTING AROUND TOWN

By Vaporetti – Water Buses

The least expensive way to travel around Venice and the most efficient is via a **vaporetti**. If you're staying longer than a week you may want to invest in a **Carta Venezia** pass, which enables you to take the *vaporetti* for one-third the regular fare. You can buy these at most tobacconists, the same place you buy your stamps. Some of the *vaporetti* may be quite crowded so be prepared to act like a sardine sometimes.

The main lines are as follows:

• **Accelerato No. 1** – Stops at every landing spot on the **Grand Canal**. Obviously this one takes a little time.

• **Diretto No. 2** – Fastest way to get from the **train station** and **Piazzale Roma** to **Accademia**, **Rialto**, and **San Marco** stops. Often very crowded and as their name suggests, *diretti* are direct trips.

• **Diretto No. 4** – Summer time *vaporetto* that basically follows the same path as the No. 2.

• **Motoscafo No. 5** – The circle line that travels in both directions around the periphery of Venice and to the smaller islands around Venice, **Isola San Michele** and **Murano** (see Day Trips & Excursions section of this chapter for more details). A great ride in and of itself for you to see the peripheral areas of Venice from the water.

• **Vaporetto No. 12** – Goes to **Murano, Burano,** and **Torcello**, all smaller islands around Venice (see Day Trips & Excursions section of this chapter for more details); departs from the **Fondamenta Nuove** stop just across from the Isola San Michele.

• **Vaporetti 6 & 11** – Goes to the resort of **Lido** and leaves from the **Riva Degli Schiavoni** stop to the east of Piazza San Marco.

By Traghetti – Gondola Ferries

At many points along the Grand Canal, basically near many of the regular *Vaporetti* stops, you can cross by using the inexpensive public gondola ferries called **traghetti** that are rowed by pairs of gondoliers. The times for each varies for each departure based on whether the gondoliers have enough passengers.

In these boats there is standing room only, which causes you to unlearn everything you've ever been taught about boat etiquette. You'll be packed in with crowds of locals, workmen, business people with their briefcases, art students, and others while you're poled along.

By Gondola

Gondolas are privately operated boats operated by professional **gondoliers**. This is the most delightful way to admire Venice at a leisurely pace. Granted they are expensive (a half hour ride costs over $50) but they're still fun and romantic if you're so inclined. There are only a little over 400 licensed gondoliers in Venice and the licenses, though theoretically open to everyone, are in practice restricted to the sons (not the daughters) of gondoliers.

If you are going to hire a gondola, take one with a specific destination in mind, like going to a specific restaurant or specific site instead of just asking the gondolier to pole you around for a while. Even though gondoliers are trained to take you to the prettiest places for your money, by bringing you to a specific destination you and gondolier become part of the Venice of old, because in the not so distant past gondolas were the main form of transportation for all the elite Venetians when they went out to dinner or the opera.

You can also hire a gondola for *serenate* (group rides in which the gondolas feature an accordionist and a singer) at night. These rides can be very expensive, but if it's your honeymoon or a special occasion who cares?

Remember to bargain with the gondolier for each ride, whether it's a regular trip or a *serenate*. Their prices are not set in stone.

By Water Taxi

There are plenty of **water taxis**, but they too are extremely expensive. If you don't want to be part of the maddening crowds, however, this is the quickest way to get from point A to point B. If you want to get picked up at a certain place at a certain time, *call 523-2326 or 522-2303*.

By Foot

Let's be serious. Venice is comparable in size to New York City's Central Park, so it's possible for you to walk anywhere you want, as long as you're not in a hurry, or worried about getting lost. I've done that plenty of times when I forgot to bring my map with me, but I usually found some out-of-the way shop or café to enjoy on my journeys.

The true beauty of this city is the absence of cars or buses. The streets are the way they should be, designed for walking. This fact alone makes life in Venice seem calmer and more serene than anywhere else. Many Venetians are proud of the fact that throughout their entire lives they have never owned an automobile. Not having owned one for more than six years now, I can understand their pride.

WHERE TO STAY

If you are unable to make suitable reservations prior to arriving in Venice, you should stop by the train station and consult with their friendly, multi-lingual **hotel finders service**, *Santa Lucia Train Station, Tel. 041/715-016*. They'll book you a room based on your specifications: for example,you can request a double with bath in the Desoduro section. During the summer high season you may not have much of a choice, but at least you'll get a room.

Venice is very popular all over the world, so if you want to stay in the perfect place, please reserve at least six months or more in advance. Most of the lower budget hotels in Venice subscribe to the service at the station. In the same office space, but not the same entrance is the **general information office** for tourists *(Tel. 041/522-6356)*, where you can get maps, directions, and all sorts of necessary information if you're in a bind.

Hotels are listed by expense, and I have also noted each hotel's *vaporetto* (water taxi) stop and it's district. I've described each district below, to help you decide where in Venice you'd like to stay.

THE FIVE BEST HOTELS IN VENICE
Best one star hotel: **ANTICO CAPON**
Best two star hotel: **HOTEL CAMPIELLO**
Best three star hotel: **HOTEL FLORA**
Best four star hotel: **HOTEL DANIELI**
Best five star hotel: **HOTEL CIPRIANI**

San Marco

Directly in the center of Venice, **San Marco** is the commercial and tourist center. Most people that visit Venice hardly ever leave this section of the city. For good reason. If you only have a little time, even the most seasoned traveler will be able to find everything s/he desires right here.

The **Piazza San Marco** is the center of this stage, where people vie with pigeons for space. The most frequently followed path is from this piazza down the busy main tourist shopping street to the **Rialto Bridge**. You can find everything you'll need right here: history, architecture, restaurants, cafés, shops, sights, fun, and many people.

Castello

This part of town offers the perfect chance to escape from the tourist hordes and discover the real Venice. There are plenty of quiet residential neighborhoods here, where old Italian ladies chat with each other from windows overhead while putting out their laundry to dry. If you're looking to shop this isn't the section of Venice for you, but there are some excellent and relatively inexpensive restaurants. Avoid the Riva degli Schiavoni to find the best prices for restaurants.

Castello is home to the **Arsenale** (where many of Venice's boats have been made) and the **Giardini Publici** (Public Gardens), which are a great place to come and relax.

Santa Croce & San Polo

For purposes of clarity we have combined these two geographically connected sections of Venice into one. Still considered to be "the other side of the canal," even though the **Rialto bridge** was built back in 1588 to connect these two sections with the more influential San Marco. Beyond the area around the Rialto, you can find small little pizzerias that serve great good for an excellent price.

There are also plenty of tiny artisan's shops along with your regular touristy stores. **Campo San Polo** is the second largest in Venice and is a center for social life in these two neighborhoods. This is a great area just to roam through the back streets and discover the secrets of Venice.

Dorsoduro

If you want to try and get away from it all while in Venice, this section of the city is great. There are few stores but many real Venetian sights. You'll find artisans, locals buying fruit from a boat that comes daily from the mainland, as well as ritzy hotels and museums. The best place in this section is the **Zattere**, "rafts" that are home to a variety of different and excellent restaurants. Eating on the water, looking out over the island of La Guidecca, you will be amazed at the beautiful sunsets over the island.

Cannaregio

This section in the north of the main island is where the **Jewish ghetto** is located. This was the first place in Europe that Jews were isolated from the rest of the population and have it named a ghetto. Three of the synagogues in the main square of the tiny island (which comprised the first ghetto) are worth seeing. Here you'll find some of the tallest buildings in Venice, because once the Jewish population started to increase, the only place they could find more space was to build up.

Compared to the rest of Venice the place looks a little run down, but the place is alive with local shoppers buying their supplies for the day, with beautiful side streets and canals away from it all.

Expensive

HOTEL GRITTI PALACE, *Campo Santa Maria del Giglio, Venezia. Tel. 041/794-611. Fax 041/520-0942. American Express, Diners Club, Mastercard and Visa accepted. 96 rooms all with bath. Single L290,000-548,000; Double L371,000-742,000.* *****
Vaporetto Stop – *Santa Maria del Giglio;* **San Marco District.**

Definitely a top-notch, high-class, deluxe hotel, with lots of local charm. You are treated like royalty, since many of their guests actually are. Located in a fifteenth century palace that still looks and feels like a private residence, you'll find Murano chandeliers everywhere as well as Burano lace table linens. There's really no words to describe the splendor of this place. Enjoy a night here if you're not worried about spending the equivalent of a monthly car payment. Or if you only want to feel like royalty for a little while, simply have a drink at their bar on the canal or enjoy a fine dinner at their lovely adjacent terrace restaurant. If you want romance, this is your place in Venice.

HOTEL DANIELI, *Riva degli Schiavoni 4196, Venezia. Tel. 041/522-6480. Fax 041/520-0208. American Express, Diners Club, Mastercard and Visa accepted. 235 rooms all with bath. Single L240,000-480,000; Double L350,00-700,000. Suites L1,158,000-2,698,000.* *****
Vaporetto Stop – *San Zaccaria;* **Castello District.**

First opened in 1882 with only 16 rooms, the Danieli has expanded to encompass many surrounding buildings. The lobby, which is built around a Gothic courtyard, with its intertwining staircases and columns is spectacular. You feel as if you're in a castle. The largest hotel in Venice as well as the most romantic. The best place for breakfast, lunch, or dinner in all of Venice is their rooftop dining room which has an exquisite view of the Lagoon. If you can't afford to stay here, at least romance yourselves with a dinner or light lunch.

HOTEL GABRIELLI SANDWIRTH, *Riva degli Schiavoni 4110, Venezia. Tel. 041/523-1580. Fax 041/520-9455. American Express, Diners Club, Mastercard and Visa accepted. 100 rooms all with bath. Single L120,000-295,000; Double L180-470,000. Closed mid-November to mid-March. Breakfast included.* ****
Vaporetto Stop – *San Zaccaria;* **Castello District.**

Located in a Gothic palace with a beautiful rose garden in its center where you can take a drink from the bar. You can also roast in the sun on the roof terrace that overlooks the lagoon while enjoying your drink. This is the place to come for luxury on the lagoon. The best views are over the water. You don't have to worry about noise, since this is a bit off the main tourist track. All the rooms are tastefully decorated with antiques, chandeliers, and the ever-present roses. A less expensive option for luxury travel.

CARLTON EXECUTIVE HOTEL, *Santa Croce 578. Tel. 041/718-488. Fax 041/719-061. 122 rooms all with bath. All Credit cards accepted. Single L140,000-210,000; Double L205,000-325,000. Breakfast L20,000 extra.* ****

Vaporetto Stop – *San Stae*; **Santa Croce District.**

A little off the beaten path, but the calm serenity makes up for that. As you can see, this is quite inexpensive for a four star hotel in Venice. A good opportunity to live in luxury for less. Their little garden is a perfect place to relax after a tough day of vacationing.

HOTEL CIPRIANI, *Fondamenta San Giovanni 10, La Guidecca, Venezia. Tel. 041/520-7744. Fax 041/520-3930. American Express, Diners Club, Mastercard and Visa accepted. 98 rooms all with bath. Single L 340,000-680,000; Double L495,000-990,000.* *****

Vaporetto Stop – *Zitelle*; **Dorsoduro District.**

This exquisite hotel occupies three beautiful acres at the east end of La Isola del Guidecca. There is a swimming pool, saunas, Jacuzzis, a private harbor for yachts, a private launch to ferry guests back and forth from the center, an American-style bar with every drink imaginable, and two superb restaurants. Sixty rooms overlook the lagoon, while many others look out over the pool.

This hotel is probably as close to heaven on earth as you'll find in Venice. There are even private suites that can be rented by the week which have their own butler assigned to them. If you can't afford to stay here, simply come out and enjoy a drink by the pool.

Moderate

HOTEL FLORA, *Calle Larga 22 Marzo 2283A, Venezia. Tel. 041/520-5844. Fax 041/522-8217. American Express, Diners Club, Mastercard and Visa accepted. 44 rooms, 43 with bath. Single L125,000-195,000; Double L165,000-260,000. Breakfast included. Closed November through January.* ***

Vaporetto Stop – *San Marco;* **San Marco District.**

The garden setting, where breakfast and afternoon drinks are served in the summer, is dominated by an old well and several old pieces of statuary. This area, the breakfast room service, and the general ambiance lend an old fashioned sense of hospitality to this hotel. A great place in the thick of things where you can still feel you've gotten away from it all. To get to the rooms, some of which are very small, you go up a painted stairway that is something to behold. The best rooms are those that overlook the serene garden. A good deal for its location and charm.

HOTEL SAN STEFANO, *Campo Santo Stefano 2957, Venezia. Tel. 041/520-0166. Fax 041/522-4460. Mastercard and Visa accepted. 11 rooms and with bath. Single L80,000-150,000; Double L130,000-200,000; Triple L200,000-250,000. Breakfast included.* ***

Vaporetto Stop – *San Angelo*; **San Marco District.**

There are TVs in every room, as well as phones and hairdryers, and air conditioning available for L10,000-15,000 extra. Located on the colorful local Campo Santa Stefano close to the Accademia and Piazza San Marco, this hotel is a good place for its price. Many rooms have a view onto the square, but if you're a light sleeper don't ask for one of these since it can get noisy at night. The *campos* in Venice are the locals' gathering place in the evenings, which makes your stay more colorful, but if you face the Campo it will be nosiy at night. There is also a charming little garden patio for unwinding after a day of being a tourist. A good choice for anyone who wants to come to Venice.

HOTEL CAMPIELLO, *Campiello del Vin 4647, Venezia. Tel. 041/520-5764. Fax 041/520-5798. American Express, Diners Club, Mastercard and Visa accepted. 16 rooms, 15 with bath. Single L55,000-120,000; Double L120,000-170,000.* **

Vaporetto Stop – *San Zaccharia*; **Castello District.**

A friendly, quiet, and clean hotel located just behind the Riva degli Schiavoni. Consider this hotel if you like luxury on a budget. It is inexpensive, near everything, yet still on a quiet little canal. You can't ask for more. The rooms are all clean and quiet and the assistance you get from the owners is stupendous. They actually seem to like us tourists.

HOTEL SAN CASSIANO, *Calle della Rosa 2232, Venezia. Tel. 041/524-1768 Fax 041/721-033. American Express, Mastercard and Visa accepted. 35 rooms all with bath. Single L65,000-198,000; Double L85,000-283,000.* ***

Vaporetto Stop – *San Stae*; **Santa Croce/San Polo District.**

Located in a Gothic palazzo on the Grand Canal, with its own dock from which you can arrive or depart by water taxi. At this same dock area they have a few tables where you can sit and enjoy the passing boats on the canal and feel completely free of the thundering herds of tourists. The rooms are all elegantly furnished with antiques, and there are chandeliers everywhere. The building seems a little down on its luck but that makes the stay quaint and romantic. They have *USA Today* available every morning so you can keep abreast of news at home.

ACCADEMIA VILLA MARAVEGIE, *Fondamenta Bollani/Marevegie 1058, Venezia. Tel. 041/521-0188. Fax 041/523-9152. American Express, Diners Club, Mastercard and Visa accepted. 27 rooms, 25 with bath. Single L65,000-130,000; Double L110,000-200,000; Triple L225,000. Breakfast included.* ***

Dorsoduro District.

This is a perfect spot for post-touring relaxation. This impressive 17th century villa, formerly the Russian consulate, is surrounded by beautiful gardens and is just off the Grand Canal. There is a patio with chairs and tables and many plants on one side of the villa facing the Grand Canal.

The inside is simply beautiful, and its amazing that you can find a room here for so cheap. You also have an upstairs tea-room as well as breakfast room that overlooks a flower garden. All the rooms are large, save number 8 which is a tiny single. Obviously because of the location and ambiance, reservations are sometimes necessary over a year in advance!

Inexpensive

ALBERGHO DONI, *Calle del Vin 4656, Venezia. Tel. 041/522-4267. No credit cards accepted. 13 rooms none with bath. Single L45,000-55,000; Double L55,000-85,000. Extra bed L35,000. Breakfast included. Closed December 20 through March 15. **

Vaporetto Stop – *San Zaccaria*; **Castello District**.

Located just off the Riva Schiavoni and near Piazza San Marco and the church of San Zaccaria, this little hotel is a gem in a prime location. The views from the rooms overlook either a beautiful canal usually filled with gondolas or a small garden in the rear. The rooms are larger than would be expected and the prices are good. You can have your breakfast taken off of your bill for an extra L10,000 which will make it even a more pleasant stay. A perfectly romantic and serene place to stay for those on a low-budget. Close to my favorite restaurant in all of Venice, the Rivetta. A hangout for all the gondoliers whose boats are in the canal in front of the hotel. The perfect place for budget travelers, but book well in advance.

ANTICO CAPON, *Campo Santa Margherita 3004B, Venezia. Tel. 041/ 528-5292. No credit cards accepted. 7 rooms, all with bath. Single L50,000- 77,000; Double L62,000-100,000. **

Dorsoduro District.

A super deal in the best local area in Venice. The Campo Santa Margherita and its environs have everything you'll need while staying in this tourist-plagued city. Most mornings there is a small market selling fruit, vegetables, and fresh fish in the piazza. You'll also find places for pizza, pastries, a supermarket, an Irish Pub, a laundry, and more. The hotel is directly in the middle of all this Venetian life, and three of the rooms face this hustle and bustle while the other four face the uninspiring rear. The rooms are large but the bathrooms are quite small. The shower is located above the toilet.

If you've been to Venice before and disliked the crowds, this is the place for you to stay. It is truly a respite from insanity. The perfect antidote for the crowds of Venice.

LOCANDA MONTIN, *Fondamenta di Borgo 1147, Venezia. Tel. 041/ 522-7151. Fax 041/520–0255. American Express, Diners Club, Mastercard and Visa accepted. 9 rooms none with bath. Single L35,000-45,000; Double L65,000-85,000; Triple L95,000. (No Stars)*

Vaporetto Stop – *San Toma*; **Dorsoduro District.**

Conveniently located just off the Piazza Santa Barbara, the hotel is entered through a huge, local restaurant. If you're too tired to go out to eat, just go downstairs and enjoy great Italian food in their huge restaurant. Eclectic furnishings, but everything is clean and comfortable. Perfect for low budget travelers. Two rooms have teeny tiny balconies covered with flowers that overlook the canal. Perfect for budget travelers.

ALBERGO BERNARDI-SEMENZATO, *Calle del Oca, SS. Apostoli 4363-4366, Venezia. Tel. 041/522-7257. 041/522-242. Credit cards accepted. 15 rooms, 7 with bath. Single without shower L32,000-L58,000; Double without shower L45,000-70,000; Double with shower 65,000-98,000. Breakfast L7,000 extra.* *

Vaporetto Stop – *Ca' D'Oro*; **Cannaregio District.**

This place has changed quite a bit in the last few years. It's now a super renovated, extremely clean, and wonderfully inexpensive little hotel in a great location. They even have a roof terrace that overlooks Venetian rooftops for you sun worshippers, or those of you that wish to grab a quiet drink at the end of the evening. Getting up there is kind of rough, and the clothes lines can get in the way, but for a one star to have a roof deck in Venice, ignore it.

If you are a budget traveler, this is the time to stay here. They're in the process of putting in air conditioning and TVs in the rooms in hopes of getting upgraded to a two star by 1998. If they do everything right, they'll end up a three star instead. So enjoy them while you can, because the prices are going to shoot through the roof soon.

WHERE TO EAT

When applicable, each restaurant reviewed below also lists the closest water taxi *(vaporetto)* stop.

Venetian Cuisine

Venice is not generally known for its cuisine, especially reasonably priced cuisine, but they do know how to prepare some great seafood dishes. The seafood usually comes placed over a bed of *risotto* (rice), and even though pasta is not used as often as in other regions of Italy, the Venetians make really good *spaghetti alla vongole* (clams) or *alla cozze* (mussels). Another favorite is the *zuppa di pesce* (fish soup),which mixes together every kind of fish that could be found at the market. You can't go wrong with fish here, except maybe on Sundays and Mondays when the *pescheria*, the seafood market at the Rialto, isn't open, which means your fish won't be fresh, but, (gasp) horrors, one or two days refrigerated.

Honestly, eating most anywhere in Venice you won't get the bang for your buck that you'd get somewhere else in Italy. Most of the restaurants have been created to cater specifically to the tourists and as such they charge ridiculously high prices. Even the natives go to the mainland to find themselves a good inexpensive meal. But with this word of warning, you can also find some great little pizzeria that cater to the local population. I'll list some later in this section.

THE BEST RESTAURANTS IN VENICE

AL BACARETO, *Calle Crosera 3447, Venezia. Tel. 89-336.*

ALLA RIVETTA, *Ponte S Provolo 4625, Venezia. Tel. 528-7302.*

HOSTERIA DA FRANZ, *Fondamenta San Isepo 754, Venezia. Tel. 522-0861 or 522-7505.*

AL MASCARON, *Calle Lunga Santa Maria Formosa 5225, Venezia. Tel. 522-5995.*

TAVERNA "CAPITAN UNCINO" *(Captain Hook), 1501 Campo San Gaicomo del'Orio.*

TRATTORIA/PIZZERIA ANTICO CAPON, *Piazza Santa Margherita 3004, Tel. 041/528-525.*

POSTE VECHIE, *Pescheria 1608, Venezia. Tel. 721-822.*

SAN TROVASO, *Fondamenta Priuli 1016, Venezia. Tel. 520-3703.*

TRATTORIA ALTANELLA, *Guidecca Calle delle Erbe 270. Tel. 041/522-7780.*

Regional Wines

You'll probably recognize many of the white wines from this region, especially the **Friuli** wines, such as **Pinot Brigio** and **Pinot Bianco**, and the incomparable **Soave's** which can be found in your stores at home. The reds are not so recognizable except for the **Cabernet**, and they're not nearly as good as the reds from the Chianti region around Florence. But then again, not many reds can compare to a Chianti.

Expensive

HOSTERIA DA FRANZ, *Fondamenta San Isepo 754, Venezia. Tel. 522-0861 or 522-7505. American Express, Mastercard and Visa accepted. Closed Tuesdays and in January. Dinner for two L180,000.*

Vaporetto Stop – *Giardini;* **Castello District.**

Located in a tranquil neighborhood area of Venice, way off the beaten path, this is a fantastic culinary adventure. Owned by Gianfranco Gasperini, the menu offers many Venetian dishes, especially seafood like *antipasto ai crostacei* (crustacean antipasto) and *gamberetti con salsa al curry* (baby shrimps in a curry sauce). Their rice dishes are also exquisite. Try either the *risotto di pesce* (rice with fish) or *ai frutti di mare* (with mixed seafood). For seconds your mouth will water anticipating the grilled fish, the delicately fried shrimp or mixed seafood dish. Expensive but world renowned. Take a water taxi here and back since it is quite a hike.

POSTE VECHIE, *Pescheria 1608, Venezia. Tel. 721-822. American Express, Mastercard and Visa accepted. Closed Tuesdays. Dinner for two L100,000.*

Vaporetto Stop – *Rialto*; **Santa Croce/San Polo District.**

Huddled in the corner of the vast *pescheria* fish market (hence the address), and located near the old post office (hence the name). To get here, follow a private wooden bridge that leads to this old converted inn with low ceilings and dark wooden beams. They are known for perfectly prepared fish, especially the grilled variety, and a bountiful antipasto table. In the summer you can dine in the splendid garden that has vines and leaves hanging overhead. Try their *risotto di pesce* (rice with seafood for two people), then try their exquisite *sogliola ai ferri* (grilled sole).

DO MORI, *Fondamenta del Ponte Piccolo 558, La Guidecca, Venezia. Tel. 522-5452. No credit cards accepted. Closed Sundays. Dinnfer two L85,000*

Vaporetto Stop – *Guidecca*; **Dorsoduro District.**

The plain ambiance inside doesn't reveal the excellence of the cooking. They have a superb *zuppa di pesce* (fish soup) or *zuppa di verdure* (vegetable soup) as well as a great *frittura di pesce* (mixed fried seafood). The best place to eat all this is not in the local hangout inside but on the water outside. If you want a peaceful respite from the tourist hordes, take the *vaporetto* over and enjoy.

LA LINEA D'OMBRA, *Punta della Dogana-Zattere 19. Tel. 041/528-5259. Credit cards accepted. Closed Sunday nights and Wednesdays. Dinner for two L160,000.*

Vaporetto Stop – *Santa Maria Della Salute*; **Dorsoduro District.**

This is a traditional Venetian restaurant: they serve lots of fish dishes, but they also try to be creative with their cooking. Inside is where all the locals and interesting people sit, but outside on their terrace you get great views of the Canal looking towards La Guidecca. A great place to watch the sun set. You'll find light cream sauces covering their salmon, and you'll find spaghetti mixed with shrimp and zucchini. But you'll also find a mixed fried seafood extravaganza if you can't make up your mind. Come for the food, stay for the view. Extremely romantic.

Moderate

AL BACARETO, *Calle Crosera 3447, Venezia. Tel. 89-336. American Express, Mastercard and Visa accepted. Closed Saturdays for dinner and Sundays. Dinner for two L75,000.*

Vaporetto Stop – *San Samuele*; **San Marco District.**

Located on the corner of Salizzada San Samuele, this authentic neighborhood *trattoria* serves excellent Venetian dishes. There are a few tables outside from which you can not only enjoy your meal but revel in the sights and sounds of the local neighborhood. The seating inside is warm, with a dark wooden beamed ceiling where you'll notice many local customers indulging in their favorite meal.

You can get their specialty *Fegato alla veneziano* (calf's liver sautéed with onions) or any of their great seafood dishes for seconds. Then try their *risotto pesce* (rice mixed with seafood) or the *zuppa di pesce* (fish soup) for starters.

RISTORANTE AL BUSO, *Ponte di Riallo 5338, Tel. 041/528-9078. Dinner for two L 65,000. Credit cards accepted.*

Vaporetto Stop – *Rialto*; **San Marco District**.

Located right beside the Rialto bridge down on the water by the Grand Canal. It only has a few tables set outside for the great canal-side views, but its worth the wait. Your red jacketed waiters will serve from the nearby restaurant with a variety of appetizing meals. Their pizza and pasta are both good and inexpensive. To be Venetian for the night, try their *pizza ai frutta di mare* (seafood pizza) or the *spaghetti con pesce* (with seafood). Then for *doppo* (seconds), try the grilled sole, a wonderful finish to any meal.

ALLA RIVETTA, *Ponte S Provolo 4625, Venezia. Tel. 528-7302. American Express, Mastercard and Visa accepted. Closed Mondays. Dinner for two L55,000-60,000.*

Vaporetto Stop – *San Zaccaria*; **San Marco District**.

Tucked away at the foot of a bridge this place is largely overlooked by tourists since many people don't bother to look down as they cross the canal. A hangout for some of the gondoliers as a drinking hole (they have a bar that faces onto the small canal where the gondoliers park their craft) and for many of the locals because of the food, location, and prices.

Their menu is in four languages so you'll be able to order what you desire, but here are some suggestions: *antipasto di pesce* (seafood antipasto), then the *spaghetti alla bolognese* (with veal, cream and tomatoes), and finally either the *fritto misti di mare* (mixed fried seafood) or the *cotolette alla milanese* (breaded veal cutlet). The atmosphere is all Venetian and the menu is from all over Italy. Enjoy both together.

ARCIMBOLDO, *Calle dei Furlani 3219, Venezia. Tel. 86-569. No credit cards accepted. Closed Tuesdays. Dinner for two L60,000.*

Vaporetto Stop – *Riva Degli Schiavoni;* **Castello District**.

Located on a small canal, off the beaten path near the Scuola di San Giorgio degli Schiavoni. You'll love the local flavor and quiet ambiance of the outside seating. Hardly a tourist around, save for yourself. Try their exquisite *scampi al curry* with rice pilaf and any of their grilled meats. A wonderful place to get away from it all. But bring your map – this is a tough one to find.

CORTE SCONTA, *Calle del Pestrin 3886, Venezia. Tel. 522-7024. American Express, Mastercard and Visa accepted. Closed Sundays and Mondays. Dinner for two L70,000.*
Vaporetto Stop – *Arsenale;* **Castello District.**
Located near the Piazza San Giovanni in Bragora, this restaurant has a plain decor but interesting patrons. Their menu changes with the tide, i.e., whatever the catch is that day, but they always seem to have a well stocked but diverse *fritture mista di mare* (mixed fried seafood). Since this is a very popular, high end local restaurant, reservations are required.

AL MASCARON, *Calle Lunga Santa Maria Formosa 5225, Venezia. Tel. 522-5995. No credit cards accepted. Closed Sundays and mid-December to mid-January and 15 days in August. Dinner for two L70,000.*
Castello District.
Located near Santa Maria Formosa and SS Giovanni e Paolo, this is a rough and plain bar/*trattoria* with a truly rustic atmosphere. You can get great boiled or roasted vegetables as an appetizer or a side dish. If you don't mind a wait, order the *pennette al pesce spada* (small noodles with a sauce of swordfish), then for seconds any of their fish on the grill.

TAVERNA "CAPITAN UNCINO" (Captain Hook), *1501 Campo San Gaicomo del'Orio. Tel. 041/72-19-01. Credit cards accepted. Closed Wednesdays. Open until midnight. Dinner for two L65,000.*
Vaporetto Stop – *Riva di Biasio;* **Santa Croce/San Polo District.**
Exquisite food in a local restaurant on a beautiful piazza, completely off the beaten path. You'll want to buy the colored glass fishnet floats hanging from the ceiling, as well as the other implements of the sea hanging around. As long as there is no soccer game of importance being played, they don't turn the TV on that sits in one corner. Even so, watching a soccer game with frenzied Italians can add to the ambiance. The seafood is great. I like the *spaghetti alla vongole* (with clams) and their *frittura di scampi e calamari* (deep fried shrimp and squid).

SAN TROVASO, *Fondamenta Priuli 1016, Venezia. Tel. 520-3703. American Express, Mastercard and Visa accepted. Closed Mondays. Air conditioned. Dinner for two L65,000.*
Vaporetto Stop – *Accademia or Zattere;* **Dorsoduro District.**
If they put you in the side room or upstairs with the locals, you feel as if you entered a heated discussion since everyone seems to be talking at once. Couple this with the clatter of pans and the occasional dropped glass or plate from the kitchen and this place has a great local feel to it. And the food is great, otherwise the locals wouldn't come, right? Try either the *Spaghetti Newburg* (with shrimp, tomato sauce, and cream) or the *spaghetti alla carbonara* (with ham, cream and egg). For secondo they have plenty of reasonably priced meats and fish. Take your pick, they're all good.

Inexpensive
TRATTORIA/PIZZERIA ANTICO CAPON, *Piazza Santa Margherita 3004, Tel. 041/528-525. Credit cards accepted. Dinner for two L50,000.*
Vaporetto Stop – *Ca' Rezzonico*; **Santa Croce/San Polo District.**
Located right next to and below the great one star hotel of the same name, this is a perfect place to enjoy the life of a Venetian Piazza. Sit under the awnings or in the sun, but enjoy some good pizza or *crostine* (sandwiches). The *crostino con funghi, prosciutto, e mozzarella* (with mushrooms, ham, and mozzarella) is great, as is the *crostino al inferno* (literally translated it means hell's sandwich. It has tomatoes, mozzarella, hot salami, mushrooms, and *pepperoncini* and is quite tasty, if a little spicy).
LA ZUCCA, *Calle del Megio 1762, Venezia. Tel. 011/521-1570. Credit cards accepted. Closed Sundays. Dinner for two L50,000.*
Vaporetto Stop – *San Stae*; **Santa Croce/San Polo District.**
Zucca means pumpkin, and you guessed it, their specialty pasta in the winter is pumpkin pasta. Surprisingly enough, it is rather delicious, especially with a cream sauce. They also have fresh fish, chicken, and salads but not too much red meats. So if you're a supreme carnivore, this healthy menu will discourage you. The owners and staff all have this radiant glow, which is what eating healthy food will do to you. Enjoy a small table outside or one of their inside tables with views of the canal. You won't regret it.
PIZZERIA ALLE ZATTERE, *Zattere ai Gesuati 795, Venezia. Tel. 041/520-4224. Credit cards accepted. Closed Tuesdays. Dinner for two with only pizza L40,000.*
Vaporetto Stop – *Zattere*; **Dorsoduro District.**
This a favorite local pizzeria near the Campo San Agnese, not only for its many varieties of pizza but also for its excellent view of Guidecca island from the pizzeria's tables on the Zattere's floating rafts. A perfect place to eat when the sun sets. You can get almost any type pizza here, including *margherita* (with sauce and cheese), *verdure* (with grilled vegetables), and I would imagine they could put any topping on you ask for. Give it a try. They oblige me here by putting extra cheese, salami (they didn't have pepperoni), and a sprinkle of oregano on mine. There are also seafood salads and seafood pastas from which to choose.

SEEING THE SIGHTS
Some people say that Venice is dead, that it is really only a museum of itself, but that's what makes it perfect for tourists. Everywhere you look you see something so beautiful, so awe inspiring that Venice at times seems like a living amusement park. I guess that is probably why this was the late Walt Disney's favorite city.

Medieval in layout and design, this city built on pilings in a marshy lagoon has everything you could imagine for a vacation, except, during high season, reasonable prices. You can find exquisite churches, beautiful synagogues, pristine *palazzi*, spacious *piazze*, magnificent museums, deserted islands only a *vaporetto* ride away, skilled crafts people blowing glass or making masks right in front of you, superb restaurants, relaxing hotels, and so much more.

The Quiet Side of Venice

During the summer months Venice is literally crammed with tourists, and at some point you'll need to take a break from them. If you're in need of a little solitude, basically anywhere away from Piazza San Marco, the Piazzale Roma, and the Rialto Bridge you can find a more serene experience.

And as you're walking (or taking the *vaporetto* then walking) to these isolated areas, don't be afraid of getting lost. You'll always find your way back, every place in Venice is perfectly safe virtually all day and all night long, and you'll also find some charming piazza or café that will seem as if it hasn't been touched by a single tourist. So strap on your walking shoes and get going.

Cannaregio – This section in the north of the main island is where the Jewish ghetto is located. Three of the synagogues in the main square of the tiny island are worth seeing. Here you'll find some of the tallest buildings in Venice, because once the Jewish population started to increase, the only place they could find more space was to build up. Compared to the rest of Venice the place looks a little run down, but the neighborhood is alive with local shoppers buying their supplies for the day, and beautiful side streets and canals away from the big crowds.

Castello – There's not much to see or do in this section of Venice, but they do have some of the best restaurants. In and around the **Arsenale** you'll find real Venetian neighborhoods, with grandmas chatting at each other from window sills above the canals, children playing in the narrow streets, and life peacefully devoid of the rumble of tourist crowds.

Dorsoduro – By simply walking from the Accademia to the Piazzale Roma in a meandering fashion you'll wander through some of the best neighborhoods that offer a taste of local color. You'll find artisan's shops, lovely houses, and of course narrow medieval streets and calm canals. And for food, wine, and a calming atmosphere, you can sit for hours on the *Zattere*. Literally meaning rafts, these open air restaurants are anchored off the eastern edge of the Dorsoduro and face the Isola della Guidecca. Try one of these restaurants for a real treat. It is an experience you'll cherish, especially if you stay long enough to see the sun go down. The glow is magnificent.

Isola della Guidecca – This a thriving neighborhood where everybody seems to know everyone else. If you're interested in gondolas, here you'll find the main gondola repair shop on the **Rio del Ponte Lungo**. This is a great place just to walk, watch, and listen.

BUY A MAP IN VENICE

*Venice is one big interconnecting alleyway with little to no address organization or structure. Sometimes street names are repeated in different districts of Venice and many times there are no street signs on the walls. Venice is confusing to get around and the only way I was able to before I figured out the city was to buy a map. I reccomend the **F.M.B. Piante di Citta** with its ugly orange/yellow cover for L8,000.*

---

1. Accademia

Located in Campo della Carita, Dorsoduro. Tel 522-2247. Open Monday–Saturday 9am–7pm in the summer and 9am–4pm in winter. Sunday and holidays 9am–1pm. Vaporetto – Accademia.

Five hundred years of unequaled Venetian art are on display at the **Accademia**. The collection began in 1750 when the Republic of St. Mark's decided to endow the city with an academy to feature local painters and sculptors (*Accademica di Pittori e Scultori*). The original academy occupied the current Port Authority building located by the gardens of the royal palace overlooking the harbor of St. Mark's.

During the French occupation of 1807, the collection was moved to the School and Church of the Carita (in Campo della Carita) as well as the former monastery of the Lateran Canons. Since then it has grown and expanded immensely and is a must-see for anyone visiting Venice who is interested in art.

There are far too many excellent paintings and sculptures to list them all, but these are the ones you should definitely discover on your own:

- *St. George* – Montegna (Room 4)
- *The Madonna degli Alberelli* (Madonna among the little trees) – Giovanni Bellini (Room 5)
- *The Tempest* – Giorgione (Room 5)
- *The Miracle of the Slave* – Jacopo Tintoretto (Room 10)
- *Banquet in the House of Levi* – Veronese (Room 10)
- *The Pieta* – Titian (Room 10) The last work of this famous artist before his death
- *Legend of St. Ursula* – Vittore Carpaccio (Room 21)
- *Detail of the Arrival of The Ambassadors* – Vittore Carpaccio (Room 21)
- *Presentation at the Temple* – Titian (Room 24)

2. Arsenale

Open 9:00am–Noon and 3pm–7pm Monday–Saturday. **Vaporetto** – *Arsenale.*

The **Arsenale** is an imposing group of buildings, landing stages, workshops, and more from which the Venetian Navy was built. It was also the shipyard for the Venetian fleet. Begun in 1100, it has been continually enlarged over the years. Surrounded by towers and walls, the Arsenale has an imposing Renaissance entrance created by Giambello in 1460. In the front of the entrance is a terrace with statues that symbolize the victory of the Battle of Lepanto. At the sides are four lions, the symbol of the Venetian city state.

Inside you'll find the **Naval History Museum** with its collection of relics and trophies of the Italian Navy as well as Venice. There is a wonderfully detailed model of the last *Bucintoro*, the vessel in which the Doge of Venice celebrated the "Wedding of the Sea" between Venice and the sea by throwing a ring into the Adriatic.

This is a great place, not only since you have to trek through real Venetian neighborhoods to find it, but also because of its impressive collection of armaments, models, relics of modern craft used in World Wars I and II. Kids especially seem to like the displays.

3. Doges Palace - Palazzo Ducale

Located in St. Mark's Square (Piazzetta San Marc o), San Marco. Tel. 522-4951. Open Monday–Sunday 8:30am–7pm in the summer and 8:30am–2pm in the winter. **Vaporetto** – *San Marco.*

Another must-see while in Venice. To view it all will take the better part of a day if you perform a thorough inspection. Finished in the 1400s after being started in the 9th century by the Doges Angelo and Giustiniano Partecipazio, this was the seat of the government, the residence of the **Doge**, Venice's supreme head of state. The flamboyant Gothic style was mainly created by a family of skilled Venetian marble craftsmen, the **Bons**. It is still a joy to behold despite the devastation by fire in 1577 of one of the building's wings. Since then it has been rebuilt in its original form. It has a double tier of arcading and pink and white patterned walls which gives the building a delicate open air feeling.

Everywhere you roam in this building you will be amazed by the combination of styles and the ornate style in which they were prepared. As you enter you will pass through the **Porta della Carta**, created by the Bon family, with its flamboyant Gothic style. You'll see the statue of *Doge Frascari kneeling before the winged lion* and the statue of a woman seated at the tallest spire that represents Justice. After passing through you'll enter the courtyard of the Palace, which has a pair of imposing bronze wells in

SIGHTS KEY

1 Accademia
2 Arsenale
3 Doges Palace (Palazzo Ducale)
4 Frari (Santa Maria Gloriosa de Frari)
5 Gesuati (Santa Maria del Rosario)
6 Gesuiti (Santa Maria Assunta)
7 Jewish Ghetto
8 La Guidecca

9 Grand Canal
10 Madonna dell'Orto
11 Redentore
12 Rialto Bridge
13 Salute (Santa Maria della Salute)
14 San Giorgio Maggiore
15 Santi Giovanni e Paolo (San Zanipole)
16 Santa Maria Formosa
17 Guggenheim Museum
18 Bridge of Sighs

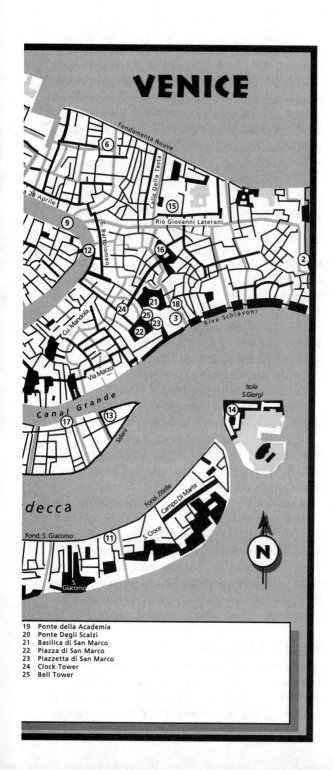

VENICE

Fondamenta Nouve

Calle Della Testa

a 28 Aprile

S. Bartolomeo

Rio Giovanni Laterani

C.u. Mandola

Riva Schiavoni

Via Marzo

Canal Grande

Saleri

Isola
S.Giorgi

decca

Fond. Ziteile

Campo Di Marte

S. Croce

Fond. S. Giacomo

S. Croce

Fond. S. Giacomo

S.
Giacomo

N

19	Ponte della Academia
20	Ponte Degli Scalzi
21	Basilica di San Marco
22	Piazza di San Marco
23	Piazzetta di San Marco
24	Clock Tower
25	Bell Tower

the middle. The one closer to the Poscari Portal is by Alfonso Alberberghetti (from 1559) and the other is by Niccolo del Conti in 1556. Stand here a moment and soak in the typically blended Venetian style of architecture, where they combine Gothic with Renaissance. Also enjoy the countless archways, the exquisite sculptures, and inspiring staircases.

One such staircase is *The Staircase of the Giants*, so named because of the two colossal statues of Mars and Neptune on either side of the landing made by Sansovino and his pupils. The new Doges were officially crowned on the landing at the top of the stairs.

You will also find some of the most beautiful plaster relief ceilings, marble relief fireplaces, paintings, sculptures, tapestries, medieval weapons rooms and ancient dungeons anywhere in Europe.

4. Frari - Santa Maria Gloriosa de Frari

*Campo dei Frari, San Polo. Tel. 522-2637. Open Monday–Saturday 9:30am–Noon and 2:30pm–6pm. Sun open 2:30pm–6pm. **Vaporetto** – San Toma.*

This Romanesque-Gothic style Franciscan church contains tombs of many famous Venetian figures. The church was begun by Franciscan monks in 1250 from a design by Nicola Pisano and was later made a little more ornate by Scipione Bon, a member of the famous Venetian family of sculptors in 1338. It was finally finished in 1443. I guess the monks didn't have much money, so they took their time completing it.

Today the unadorned facade is not much to look at but is beautiful in its simplicity. It is divided into three sections by pilaster strips surmounted by pinnacles. Over the central portal are statues attributed to Alessandro Vittorio in 1581. There is a Romanesque bell tower that is the second largest in Venice after that of St. Mark's.

The interior is as simple and as equally beautiful as the exterior. It is laid out in a Latin cross with single aisles set off by twelve huge columns. The main draw for this simple church is the tomb of the grand master Titian, who died of plague in 1576. There are two works by Titian featured inside, *Assumption of the Virgin* done in 1518 hanging over the main altar, and *Pesaro Altarpiece* done in 1526, depicting the Virgin with members of the Pesaro family over the second altar. Another work to note is the statue of *St. John the Baptist* by Donatello in the altar of the first chapel.

5. Gesuati - Santa Maria del Rosario

*Fondamenta delle Zattere, Dorsoduro. **Vaporetto** – Accademia or Zattere.*

This church was erected between 1726 and 1743 for the Dominican friars, and was built over a 14th century monastery called "Monastery for the poor Gesuati." *Gesuati* are Jesuits, by the way. The exterior is simple and tasteful in the basic Classical style. This elliptical shaped church has no aisle, making it seem larger than it really is, and contains superb frescoes on the ceiling of the dome by GB Tiepolo.

The first altar contains the *Virgin in Glory with Three Saints*, a masterpiece done in 1747 by Tiepolo. The second altar has a work by GB Piazzetta, *St. Dominic*, done in 1739. The third altar has the *Crucifixion* created by Tintoretto in 1741.

6. Gesuiti - Santa Maria Assunta

Campo dei Gesuiti, Cannaregio. **Vaporetto** – *Fondamenta Nuova.*

This grandiose church was given to the Jesuits (Gesuiti) in 1656, but it was built in the 12th century. It was remodeled between 1715 and 1730 with a Baroque facade designed by Fattoretto. It contains the statues of the 12 Apostles by Penso, the Groppellio brothers, and Baratta.

This is a single-aisled church laid out in a Latin Cross Style and is decorated with a variety of colored marble inlays. The main draw to this church are two outstanding paintings: the *Assumption of the Virgin* by Jacopo Tintoretto and the *Martyrdom of St. Lawrence* by Titian.

7. Jewish Ghetto

Near the train station, Cannaregio. Guided tours of the synagogues available every hour on the hour from 10am–4pm, and Sunday 10am–Noon. Tours not available Saturday and holidays. **Vaporetto** – *San Marcuola.*

This was the first Jewish Ghetto in Europe. The word itself, ghetto, originated in Venice. The location was established by Ducal decree in 1516 and remained an enforced enclave for the Jews in Venice until 1797, with Napoleon's victory over the Republic. The Jews were moved here originally from the section of the city known as La Guidecca (see below) so the government could keep an eye on them.

Here you'll find five synagogues, three of which are open to the public: **Sinagoga Grande Tedesca**, **Sinagoga Spagnole**, and **Levantina**. The small museum, **Museo Ebraica** *(Tel. 71-53-59) in the Campo del Nuovo Ghetto*, the main square in the ghetto, contains information about the five centuries of Jewish presence in Venice.

8. La Guidecca

Vaporetto – *Guidecca.*

This populous suburb was once the neighborhood set aside for the Jews of Venice prior to their move to the Jewish Ghetto in 1516 – hence its name, which roughly means *The Jewish Area*. A brief excursion here is a wonderful respite from the hectic pace of tourist Venice. You'll find real Venetian neighborhoods, top-of-the-line hotels along the **Fondamenta**

Zitelle, abandoned factories, and more. There are not many sights to see, but you can take a relaxing stroll without running into hardly any tourists.

9. Grand Canal

The **Grand Canal** is shaped like a large upside down "S" bisecting the city. It is almost 2 1/2 miles long, 15 feet deep, and ranges anywhere from 100 to 150 feet across. Usually calm and serene, the canal has become more and more menacing and rough since the introduction of huge ocean liners docking close by.

Lining this wonderful waterway are tremendous old buildings, palaces, and homes dating from every time period and epitomizing every architectural style. You'll also see small canals thrusting off into the darkness, and beautiful gateways and entrances blackened by and beginning to be covered by the water. The best way to see the canal is to take the *vaporetto* around a few times and simply enjoy the view.

10. Madonna dell'Orto

Campo Madonna dell'Orto, Cannaregio. Open 9am–5pm. **Vaporetto –** *Madonna dell'Orto.*

This is a simple little church that contains the remains of **Jacopo Robusti**, known as **Tintoretto**, who was buried here in 1594. There are also some exquisite works by the grand master himself, **Titian**. These paintings are in the choir: *Last Judgment, Adoration of the Golden Calf, Moses Receiving the Tablets of the Law.* The tomb of Tintoretto is marked by a simple stone plaque and is just to the right of the choir.

11. Redentore

Campo Redentore. Open 9am–5pm. **Vaporetto –** *Redentore.*

Built between 1577 and 1592 by Andrea Palladio and Antonio Da Ponte, as part of a thanksgiving for the end of another of the many plague epidemics that struck Venice. Across Europe more than a third of the population died because of the plagues.

A huge staircase leads up to the facade and the entrance to the church. Inside you'll find the same simple harmony as the outside as well as a magnificent Baroque altar adorned with bronzes by Campagna. In the sacristy you'll find *Virgin and Child* by Alvise Vivarini, *Baptism of Christ* by Veronese, *Virgin and Child with Saints* by Palma the Younger, and a variety of works by Bassaro.

12. Rialto Bridge

One of the best places to view the traffic along the **Grand Canal** and all its charm. This is the oldest of the three bridges spanning the canal and was originally made of wood. It collapsed in 1440 and was rebuilt in wood but still remained rather unstable, so in the 16th century the Doges decided to build a more stable bridge. Michelangelo himself submitted a design for the bridge but a local boy, Antonio Da Ponte, was awarded the contract to design and build the bridge. The bridge was finished in 1592. The Rialto spans 90 feet and is 24 feet high. There are 24 shops lining the bridge separated by a double arcade from which you can walk out onto the terraces and get those superb views for which it is richly famous.

Every morning, except Sunday on the San Polo side of the Rialto, the **Fish** and **Vegetable market** is held. A sight that should not be missed while in Venice, especially the **Pescheria** (Fish Market).

13. Salute - Santa Maria della Salute

Campo delle Salute. Open 9am-5pm. **Vaporetto** *- Salute.*

One of the sights you'll see from St. Mark's square across the canal is this truly magnificent church. Adorned with many statues sitting atop simple flying buttresses, this octagonal church is topped with a large dome, and a smaller one directly above it. It was erected as thanksgiving for the cessation of a plague that struck Venice in 1630. During its construction it had a variety of mishaps like the foundation sinking, the walls being unable to support the dome, and other simple engineering problems like that.

Inside are six chapels all ornately adorned. On the main altar you'll find a sculpture by Giusto Le Court that represents *The Plague Fleeing The Virgin*. The church is replete with Titian's work, including *The Pentecost* to the left of the third altar, *Death of Abel* on the sacristy ceiling, *Sacrifice of Abraham* in the sacristy, *David and Goliath* on the sacristy ceiling, and an early work *St. Mark and The Other Saints* over the altar in the sacristy.

14. San Giorgio Maggiore

Isola San Giorgio Maggiore. Open 9am-12:30pm and 2:30pm-6:30pm. **Vaporetto** *- San Giorgio.*

On an island just off the tip of La Guidecca, this magnificent church by Palladio can be seen and admired from St. Mark's Square, but you should go out and visit because the view of the lagoon and the city from its bell tower are priceless and unforgettable.

The church's white facade makes it stand out wonderfully from the ochre and brown colored monastery buildings surrounding it. It was finished in 1610 by Scamozzi from the plans of the master Palladio. The facade is distinctly his, with its three sections divided by four Corinthian columns. In two niches between the columns are statues of *Sts. George* and *Stephen,* and on either side are busts of *Doges Tribuno Mommo* and *P Zini* all by Giulio Moro. The bell tower we mentioned earlier was erected by Benedetto Buratti from Bologna (a city known at the time for its many towers) in 1791 to replace an older one that collapsed in 1773.

The interior is simple yet majestic. It has a single aisle and is shaped like an inverted Latin cross. Three works to admire are: *Crucifix* by Michelozzo in the second altar on the right, and *Last Supper* and *Shower of Mana* by Tintoretto at the main altar.

15. Santi Giovanni e Paolo - San Zanipolo

Campo Santi Giovanni e Paolo, Castello. Open 9am–5pm. **Vaporetto** – *Rialto or Fondamenta Nuova.*

Started by the Dominican monks in 1246, **Santi Giovanni e Paolo** was not finished until 1430, probably due to lack of funds just like their Franciscan counterparts when they were building Santa Maria Gloriosa dei Frari. Like that church, it contains the tombs of many well-known Venetian citizens. The church's style is known as Venetian Gothic with its combination of Gothic and Renaissance styles. Unfortunately, the facade was never finished, but it is still beautiful in its simplicity.

The inside is filled with monuments, sculptures, and paintings depicting a large number of Doges and their families. Don't miss the magnificent 15th century Gothic window by Bartolomeo Vivarini.

16. Santa Maria Formosa

Campo Santa Maria Formosa, Castello. Open 9am–5pm. **Vaporetto** – *Rialto or San Zaccaria.*

This church was starting to be rebuilt in 1492 (when Columbus sailed the ocean blue) and has two 16th century facades and a 17th century belfry. It is in the shape of Latin cross and has no aisles. The walls are covered with wonderful works by such artists as Vivarini and Palma the Elder. A simple, small church that sits in a part of Venice that most tourists never find. The piazza is filled with the sights and sounds of true modern day Venetian life.

17. Guggenheim Museum

Palazzo Venier dei Leoni, Dorsoduro 701, Calle Cristoforo. Tel. 520-6288. Open March–October, Wednesday–Monday 11am–6pm and Saturday 11am–9pm. Closed Tuesday Admission L10,000. **Vaporetto** – *Accademia.*

This is a magnificent 20th century art collection developed by the intriguing American heiress and art aficionado Peggy Guggenheim. It is exhibited in Ms. Guggenheims old home, where she lived until her death in 1979. Here you'll find all the 20th century movements including cubism, surrealism, futurism, expressionism, and abstract art. There are works by Dali, Chagall, Klee, Moore, Picasso, Pollock and many others.

18. The Bridge of Sighs

From the canal side of Ponte della Paglia you can look directly at this covered bridge connecting the Doges Palace and Prigione Nuovo (New Prison). It was built in the 17th century to transport convicts from the palace to the prison to face their punishment. The name presumably derives from the sighs of prisoners as they crossed the bridge.

19. Ponte Della Accademia

The least attractive and most modern bridge in Venice, it is one of three that traverses the Grand Canal. It is a metal and wood construction that seems to fit, but not quite, with the fairy tale images all around it. It's as if a pioneer style bridge was placed in Snow White's scenes at Disneyland.

Nothing magnificent to see but convenient to use to go from San Marco to the Accademia.

20. Ponte Degli Scalzi

Also known as the **station bridge** since it is right near the station, this is the first bridge you'll cross if you're walking from the station to St. Mark's. But don't walk – take the *vaporetto*. A simple, single span bridge made of white Istrian stone, it was erected in 1934 to replace a metal bridge built in 1858. The bridge is approximately 130 feet long and 23 feet above water level.

21. Basilica di San Marco

Piazza San Marco. Open 9:30am–5:30pm. **Vaporetto** *– San Marco.*

The church is so large and magnificent that a day's adventure is normal for an art and architecture lover.

The building was built to house the remains of the republic's patron saint, St. Mark, as well as to glorify the strength of Venice's sea power. The structure was begun in 829, a year after St. Mark's remains were brought back from Egypt. By 832 the church had all its main structures and by 883 it was fully decorated. Its beauty was slightly marred in 976 from a fire that was set in the Doges Palace. Then in 1000 the church was demolished because it was not grand enough. The church we know and love today was started in 1063 and was originally a Byzantine plan. It was finished in 1073 and then for centuries it was adorned with superb mosaics, precious marbles, and war spoils brought back by merchants, travelers, and soldiers, so that today the church is a mix of Byzantine, Gothic, Islamic and Renaissance materials.

It is magnificent inside and out. A description of all the art and architecture in this incredible place would fill another book, so you might want to hire a local tour guide or purchase one of the local guide books inside the church specifically for the Basilica.

22. Piazza San Marco

Vaporetto – San Marco.

When the Basilica of St. Mark and the Doge's Place were being erected, the grassy field in front of them was filled in and paved (around 1172-1178). On either side of the pavement, elegant houses were built with arcades running the length of them. Many were taken over by government magistrates, called *Procurati*, which gives these buildings their name today, *Procuratie*. In 1264 the square was repaved with bricks in a herringbone pattern. Then in 1723 it was paved again with gray trachyte and white marble.

The square is 569 feet long, 266 feet at the side of St. Mark's, and 185 feet long at the side facing St. Mark's. The piazza is alive with orchestra music being played by competing cafés and is wonderful place to stroll and people watch. You won't find many Venetians here, unless it's the off-season.

23. Piazzetta di San Marco

Vaporetto – San Marco.

Directly in front of the Doges Palace, this little piazza blends into the larger Piazza San Marco and is sometimes lumped together with it. Originally it was a market place for food stuffs, but in 1536 the Doge mandated that it remain clear for public executions. The two columns at the dock (one with the *Lion of St. Mark* atop and the other with a statue of *St. Theodore*) were brought back from the Orient in 1125 and erected in 1172. Here you'll find some peaceful but expensive outside cafés.

24. Clock Tower

*Piazza San Marco. Tel. 523-1879. Admission L5,000. **Vaporetto** – San Marco.*

Facing St. Mark's, the **Clock Tower** is directly on your left. No, it's not the tall brick structure in the middle of the piazza; that's the Bell Tower). It was built between 1496 and 1499, and the wings were added from 1550-1506. Above the tower is an open terrace upon which stands a bell with two male figures on either side that hammer the bell to indicate the time. These figures have been performing their faithful service for over 500 years and as a result have taken on a dark weather-beaten appearance. Because of this, they are called the Moors.

Beneath the terrace that houses these figures is the symbol of Venice, a golden winged lion. Below the lion is a niche that contains a statue of the Virgin and Child that has been attributed to Alessandro Leopardi sometime in the early 1500s. The clock, just below this, in addition to just telling the time, also indicates the changing of the seasons, the movements of the sun, as well as the phases of the moon.

25. The Bell Tower

Piazza San Marco. Tel. 522-4064. Open 9:30am–10pm. Admission L6,000.
Vaporetto – San Marco.

Built over old Roman fortifications, the **Bell Tower** has been added to off and on since 888. It withstood floods and earthquakes, but it finally gave in to less than perfect craftsmanship. On July 14, 1902, it collapsed but was reconstructed and re-opened to the public in 1912. It is the most convenient place to get a birds-eye view of the city and the lagoon. (The next best place is the bell tower of the church of San Giorgio Maggiore). An elevator can take you to the top where there are five bells that toll on special occasions.

In the past a cage used to jut from the wall on the piazza side that would occasionally contain criminals to be exposed to the elements as punishment. This practise was abolished in the 16th century. Another tradition was to stretch a rope between the tower and the Doges Palace and have an acrobat walk the span.

NIGHTLIFE & ENTERTAINMENT

THE FIDDLER'S ELBOW, *3847 Cannaregio (near Ca' d'Oro Vaporetto stop). Tel. 041/523-9930. Open from 5:00pm - 1:30am. Closed Wednesday but not in the summer.*

Come here for a taste of old Ireland. You'll find Harp, Guiness, and Kilkenny on tap (Pint L7,000 half pint L4,000), as well as almost any other drink you can imagine. The Irish lads and lassies behind the bar will serve you up proper, so enjoy a pint or two for the homeland (well, their homeland anyway). The meeting place for Anglophiles in Venice.

THE GREEN PUB, *Campo San Margherita 3053A, Tel. 041/520-1993. Pints inside: Harp L6,500; Guiness and Kilkenny L7,000. Pints outside: Harp L7,500; Guiness, Kilkenny L8,000.*

Great outside seating on the perfect piazza in Venice, but it's usually packed so get here early and try to stay late. They also have small snacks like sandwiches and *tramezzini*.

EL SOUK PUB, *Accademia 1056A, Tel. 041/520-0371. Pint of Tennents L5,000.*

A real nightclub/harem atmosphere, with a small dance floor to work off some of the drinks. Located right near the Accademia (take the Accademia's vaporetto stop). To get here, start at the vaporetto stop and go down the road to your right. Take your first right and El Souk will be on your right hand side after a few paces. It's not really a pub. It's more of a disco, so if you want a pint and a conversation, go to one of the two above.

SPORTS & RECREATION

For recreation, you'll have to go to the island of **Lido**, where you'll find golf, bicycling, horseback riding, tennis and of course, swimming. But I am averse to mentioning Lido, since It really doesn't seem to it into the whole atmosphere of Venice. Why? It was built only recently so the architecture has nothing in common with the beauty of Venice, and most importantly on Lido they allow cars and buses, so that tranquil feeling you get while in Venice leaves instantly when you arrive on Lido. But if you're in need of some sporting fun, go to it.

To get to Lido, take vaporetto no. 6 or no. 11.

Bicycling

Having a leisurely bicycle ride on Sundays is a favorite pastime of the people on Lido. To rent a bike, tandem, or tricycle, *contact Giorgio Barbieri at Via Zara 5, Lido. No phone number.*

Golfing

• **Circolo Golf Venezia**, *Via del Forte, 30011 Alberoni. Tel. 041/731-1333/ 731-015. Fax 041/731-339.* Located 10 km from Venice, this is an 18 hole, par 72, 6,199 meters long course. It's open year round except on Mondays. They have a driving range, pro shop, bar and restaurant.

• **Ca' Amata Golf Club**, *Via Postioma di Salvarosa 44, 31033 Castelfranco Veneto. Tel. 0432/721-833. Fax 0432/721-842.* Located 30 km from both Venice and Padua, this is a nine hole, par 36 course that is 3,311 meters long. Open from February to December and closed Mondays. This place has a driving range, pro shop, putting green, restaurant and swimming pool.

• **Ca' Della Nave Golf Club**, *Piazza della Vittoria 14, 30030 Martellago. Tel. 041/540-1555. Fax 041/540-1926.* Located 12km from Venice on the mainland, this is an 18 hole par 72 course that is a challenging 6,380 meters long. It is open year round except on Tuesdays. They have a putting green, pro shop, tennis courts, restaurant and bar.

Horseback Riding

If you want to go riding, you'll have to pay a kings ransom to rent a horse from the **Venice Riding Club** *at Ca'Bianca on the Lido, Tel. 765-162.* They have an indoor riding school and paddock with fixed and competitive fences and a variety of competition horses for hire.

Swimming

Your choices are the pools at the **Excelsior Hotel** and the **Hotel des Bains** where you can purchase very expensive daily or seasonal tickets; and the public beaches are at **San Nicolo** and **Alberoni** at both the north and the south ends of **Lido**. The rest of the beaches are private and attached to hotels for the use of their guests.

Tennis

There are tennis courts for rent at the **Lido Tennis Club** *(Via San Gallo 16, Tel. 760-954)*, and from the **Tennis Union** *(Via Fausta, Tel. 968-134)*. Court time is expensive.

SHOPPING

Books & Newspapers in English

Most newsstands in Venice will carry a variety of different international newspapers and magazines. The most current newspaper will most probably be *The International Herald Tribune*, which is a joint venture between The Washington Post and The New York Times and is printed all over Europe. If you can't seem to find a paper, simply go into one of the better hotels and they should have some available for sale. Or if they don't have any, they can surely tell you where to find one.

As for books, listed below are a few bookstores that have English language titles available.

Libreria Pio X, *Studium Veneziano, Calle di Canonica 337, San Marco. Tel 522-2382. Credit cards accepted.*

A religious as well as a general style bookstore near the Ponte della Canonica that also is well stocked with English language books. In conjunction they have many books about Venetian history, architecture, and literature so if you want to bone up on your knowledge of Venice, this bookstore can be of assistance. Everything is laid out in an organized fashion so browsing is easy. I have to mention this because sometimes, here in Italy, some things are not as organized as we expect.

Libreria Internazionale San Giorgio, *Calle Large XXII Marzo 2087, San Marco. Tel. 38-451. Credit cards accepted.*

There is an excellent selection of travel and information books about Venice and other parts of Italy. You'll also find a selection on art, architecture, and history, but only a small section of paperback literature. There also some interesting posters and postcards.

Glass Products

Venice has been making glass products for more than 1,000 years. The glass blowing furnaces were moved in 1292, for fire safety reasons, to the five islands of **Murano** (see *Day Trips & Excursions* below) which are five minutes north of Venice by *vaporetto*. To make sure you're not getting a reproduction or something of inferior quality, always check to see if the letters **VM** are stamped on the bottom of the glasswork. The VM *(Vetro Murano)* is the mark for quality Venetian glass.

All over Venice you'll find these silly glass animals and figurines and you can bet they are not of the highest quality. Yes, they're cute, and I bet your kids go ga-ga over them, but you can find some great glass on Murano. Two of the five major manufacturers on Murano have shops in Venice (**Salviati** and **Venini**) but the rest sell only from the island of Murano. Here's the place to get some fine glass pieces at great prices.

Lace Products

The small island of **Burano** (see *Day Trips & Excursions* below) has been producing intricate hand-made lace work for centuries. Mary Tudor got her wedding gown made on the island. Since that time the style has been widely copied and some say the French make a better lace now, but an excursion to the island to see how the stuff is made is a fun trip.

Masks

Venice is home to one of the world's best **carnivals** (**Carnevale** in Italian), designed for everyone to sow their wild oats before the fasting begins for Lent. The merriment generally begins in February or March and lasts for several weeks before it culminates on **Shrove Tuesday** (**Mardi Gras**), the day before Lent begins on Ash Wednesday. Also, in its history Venetians sometimes wore masks during daily life, allowing men to court and cavort with impunity and women to be able to walk around unchaperoned and meet their secret lovers undetected. Since masks are part of their history, which continues today in the **Carnevale**, Venetians have become quite adept at preparing masks of all kinds.

There are all sorts of traditional masks, many taken from the 16th century *Commedia Dell'Arte*, and any of these masks would make for a great wall ornament or Halloween costume. The craftsmen carve wooden molds from which they make plaster casts – basically negative images of the mask – which are then layered with papiermache to shape the masks. There are plenty of stores where you can watch the mask makers at work.

Paper Products

Venice has been popular for their decorative paper goods for centuries, specifically the marbelling effect they produce for the cover of books, desk blotters, pencils, pens, and many other items. When wandering around the back streets of Venice you will surely stumble upon a small shop making and selling their own versions of marbelized paper products.

Shoes

Now why would shoes be popular in a city that does not allow cars? Because the Venetians have to walk everywhere. Venetians consume the most shoes per capita than anywhere else in the world. Even though Florence, Rome, and Milan all have great shoes, most of the prices in Venice are slightly less expensive.

Markets

The **Erberia** (Vegetable Market) and the **Pescheria** (Fish Market). *Vegetable market is open Monday through Saturday 8:00am to 1:00pm; the fish market is open Tuesday through Saturday 8:00am through 1:00pm.*

The natives and the restaurants of Venice find their daily produce, cheese, fish, meats, and breads in the large Campo and the adjoining streets near the Church of San Giacomo di Rialto and at the base of the Rialto bridge. It is a bustling, crowded, fun adventure just to go there to buy something. By actually going to market with the Venetians you feel almost a part of them since you're sharing one of their truly unique daily experiences.

Look for the *Pescheria* on your map, since that is where most of the fun is located. You'll see a six foot swordfish sliced to perfection for restaurants and home buyers, as well as witnessing a young Venetian peel shrimp faster than you could eat them. Also most stands sell snails. Notice how the persistent buggers attach themselves to the sides of the ladle when the proprietor scoops them out to be weighed. They are only delaying the inevitable transformation into a delectable butter and garlic antipasto. But you have to admire their persistence. A fun place.

Campo San Barnaba, Dorsoduro. *Open Monday and Tuesday, and Thursday through Saturday 9:00am to 1:00pm and 3:30pm to 7:30pm, and Wednesday 9:00am to 1:00pm.*

Located right of the Piazza Santa Margherita, this is a quaint open air floating market where you can mainly buy fresh vegetables.

Campo San Margherita, Dorsoduro. *Open Monday, Tuesday, and Thursday through Saturday from 9:00am to 1:00pm and 3:30pm to 7:30pm.*

A few stalls inter-dispersed around the piazza sell fruits, vegetables, and fish. Not nearly as grand as the Rialto market but one to enjoy nonetheless. This square has to be the best example of true Venetian life there is. Besides the market, come for the mothers playing with their children, the small local shops, and relaxing seating on some of the benches in the square. Don't miss Campo San Margherita.

Calle Regina 2328A. A local pastry factory. Walk by and savor the tantalizing smells that emanate from their open door. You can't go in, but you can watch from the doorway as they prepare the pastries for the shops on the island. But the smell is what brings me back here time after time.

Picnic Supplies
    The best place to get picnic supplies is at the **Rialto bridge market** at the base of the bridge on the San Polo section side, which is held every morning except Sundays and Mondays (see *Markets* just above).

PRACTICAL INFORMATION

Bank Hours & Changing Money
    Banks in Venice are open Monday through Friday from 8:30am to 1:30pm. Very few re-open in the afternoon, and the few that do only open from 2:45pm to 3:30pm. *Cambi* (money exchanges) follow store hours, which are generally 9:00am to 12:30pm and 4:00pm to 7:30pm Monday through Saturday.
    If you're really desperate, the **American Express** office stays open in the summer months from 8:00am to 8:00pm. *They are located at Salizzada San Moise 1471, San Marco, Tel. 520-0844.*

Business Hours
    Store hours are generally 9:00am to 12:30pm and 4:00pm to 7:30pm Monday through Saturday. But as is the Italian way, there are many exceptions to the rule. Some stores stay open a half an hour later, some close a half and hour earlier, so don't depend on the stores being open when you want them to be.
    Food stores generally close on Wednesday afternoons. Also stores in the main tourist areas generally stay open during the traditional siesta hours and most stores do not close for August as they do almost everyhwere else in Italy. The Venetians are willing to make the necessary sacrifices to get as much of our money as they possibly can.

Consulates
• **United Kingdom**, *Dorsoduro 1051, near the Accademia, Tel. 522-72-07*
• **United States**, *Largo Donegani 1, Milan, Tel. 01/652-841*
• **Canada**, *Via Vito Pisani 19, Milan, Tel. 01/669-74-51. For emergencies 01/ 66-98-06-00*
• **Australia**, *Via Borgogna 2 , Milan, Tel. 01/76-01-33-30*

Mailing Services
    The **main post office** is located *at Salizada del Fontegho dei Tedeschi 5554, near the Rialto. Tel. 528-6212 and 520-4143.* Open Monday–Saturady 8:15am–6:45pm. Stamps are sold at *tabacchi* all over town.
    Venice's **postal code** is *30124.*

Laundry Services
• **Lavaget**, *Cannareggio 1269, Tel. 71-59-76, on the Fondamenta Pescaria.* Located near the station. L15,000 for three kilos of clothes, soap and dry included. Open Monday–Friday 8:30am–12:30pm and 3:00pm–7:00pm. Drop off clothes and pick up later in the day.

Local Festivals & Holidays
• **January 1**, *Primo dell'Anno* (New Years Day)
• **April 25**, *Festa Del Liberazione* (Liberation Day)
• **February**, the two weeks before Lent is **Carnevale**, a time of riotous celebration where costumes are worn both day and night, and grand balls and celebrations occur frequently.
• **March**, First Sunday after Ascension day; anybody piloting an oar powered craft can take part in *La Vogalonga*, the "long row." Participants set off at 9:30am from the Bacino di San Marco and follow a marathon-like course around Venice and its islands. Rowers usually return between 11:00am and 3:00pm
• **May 1**, *Festa del Lavoro* (Labor Day)
• **August 15**, *Ferragosto* (Assumption Day)
• **September**, First Sunday in September is the *Regata Storica*, the historic regatta. The races are preceded by a magnificent procession on the Grand Canal of period boats manned by Venetians in historic costumes. A spectacle to behold. On par with the Palio in Siena.
• **November 1**, *Ognissanti* (All Saints Day)
• **November 21**, *Festa della Madonna della Salute*, which originated as a time of thanks for being spared from the Plague which at one point had decimated over 3/5's of Venice's population. Celebrated on two floating bridges built across the Grand Canal from the Giglio to the Dogana.
• **December 8**, *Festa dell Madonna Immacolata* (Immaulate Conception)
• **December 25**, *Natale* (Christmas)
• **December 26**, *Santo Stefano* (Saint Stephen's Day)

Most stores in Venice take a one or two month vacation in or around Christmas time.

Tourist Information & Maps
• **Ente Provinciale per il Turismo** (three different locations): *Piazza San Marco 71C, Tel. 522-6356; Piazzale Roma, Tel. 522-7402; Sant Lucia Train Station, Tel. 715-016.* They also have an excellent hotel finders service here that comes in real handy if you don't have reservations when you arrive.

• **American Express Travel Service**, *San Marco 1471, Tel. 520-0844.* You don't have to be a card member to get assistance here. A great private travel service.

Tour Operators
• **American Express Travel Service**, *San Marco 1471, Tel. 520-0844.* Same as above. Ask for details on various Venice and area tours, since they change periodically.
• **CIT**, *San Marco 4850, Tel. 528-5480*
• **Wagons-Lit/Cook Travel**, *San Marco 289, Piazzett Leoncini, Tel. 522-3405*

DAY TRIPS & EXCURSIONS: THE OUTER ISLANDS OF VENICE

The first three islands mentioned here can all be seen in a three to four hour period. To get to any of them, buy a round-trip ticket for L7,500 *at vaporetto booth #12 at the Fondamente Nuova.* After you have finished your lunch or dinner at one of the fine restaurants on **Torcello** (your last stop) simply stamp your ticket in the yellow machine before boarding the *vaporetto* and you'll be on your way back to Venice.

If you start in the morning around 9:00am and go first to **Murano**, then **Burano**, and then **Torcello**, you will have worked up a powerful hunger. The same goes if you start the trek at 3:00pm or so, after your lunch in Venice. By the time you get to Torcello, you'll be dying to sample their excellent food in a restaurant with wonderful outdoor seating.

To go to just one of the islands, simply purchase a single ticket for L4,000, and stamp it as you leave and again on your return.

MURANO

Located 3/4 of a mile northeast of Venice, **Murano** is a lagoon town that is spread among five little islands. It has a relatively quiet and uncrowded feel to it, especially around dinner time, when all the tourists have returned to the crowds of Venice.

Murano today is what Venice must have been like fifty years ago before international tourism really took off. In Venice every door and building front has been turned into a shop, café, or restaurant for tourists. Here it may only be one out of every four. There are small café's and restaurants dotting the canal-scape, so if you're in the need for a drink, some coffee, a little ice cream or any type of snack, you'll have it. The island group is roughly divided in half by a relatively large canal that is spanned by one bridge, the **Ponte Longo**.

ARRIVALS & DEPARTURES

Take *Vaporetto* 5 or 12 from the Fondamenta Nuove. It takes about five minutes.

SEEING THE SIGHTS

Murano is the perfect place to just stroll around and explore. You feel as if you've entered a time warp as you go down certain streets. Make sure you go off the beaten path. Everything is small enough that it's impossible for you to get lost. This island chain is world-renowned for its **glass blowing** industry, which dates back to 1291 when the furnaces were banned from Venice as a precaution against fire and espionage. At its height in the 16th century, Murano had 37 glass factories and a population of 30,000. Today the population is only a little under 8,000.

What used to be the closely guarded secret of glass blowing is today common knowledge, but Murano glass is still in demand all over the world because of the skilled artisans that prepare the fine works.

And that's what we've come to Murano to see, a glass blowing exhibition. There are number of factories dotting the island group, but the two below are the most interesting:

• **Mazzega SRL**, *Diondamenta Da Mula 147, 31041 Venzia/Murano, Tel. 041/736-888. Fax 041/739-079.* Located directly at the base of the Ponte Longa.

• **Civam**, *Viale Garibaldi 24, Venezia Murano30141, Tel. 041/739-323. Fax 041/739-323.* Located where the boat lets you off from Venice. Don't go right there, since the other one is actually better; but first simply walk around the island to explore.

Other recommended sights include:

• **Museo dell'Arte Vetraria**, *Fondamenta Giustinian and Fondamenta Manin. Tel 739-586. Open Monday, Tuesday, Thursday and Saturday 10:00am–4:00pm, Sun 9:00am–12:30pm. Closed Wednesdays.* This is the Glass Museum.

• **Santi Maria e Donato**, *Campo San Donato. Open 8:00am - noon, 4:00pm - 7:00pm.*

Also check out the **glass factories** on Fondamenta dei Vetrai, three of which offer glassblowing exhibitions.

BURANO

Located 5 1/2 miles northeast of Venice, **Burano** occupies four tiny islands that are inhabited mainly by fishermen and lace seamstresses. It was first settled in the 5th and 6th centuries by refugees from Altinum fleeing Attila's Huns. Even though it is mainly known for the traditional art of lace making, which the women of the town have been handing down to their daughters for centuries, Burano is also a great place to unwind from the hectic pace of Venice.

The brightly colored houses on the island give it the air of an Italian opera set – a perfect background for some excellent photographs. You'll also find plenty of green space in which to relax. Burano and Torcello (our next destination) have more grass than all of the island chain of Venice proper combined. So for those of you that can get tired of looking at concrete and marble, coming here will be your needed respite.

There are also plenty of little cafés and *gelaterias*, and *trattoria* to quench a hunger or thirst.

ARRIVALS & DEPARTURES

Take *Vaporetto* number 12 from Fondamenta Nuove. It takes about 35 minutes. You'll first stop at Burano.

WHERE TO EAT

1. TRATTORIA AI PESCATORI, *Via Galuppi 371, Tel. 041/730650. Closed Wednesdays and January. All credit cards accepted. Dinner for two L140,000.*

Here you can get great lagoon cooking, which means of course, seafood. Located in the center of the island with a terrace you can enjoy in the summer, this is a nice but expensive local place. Try any of their pasta with fish, like *Spaghetti ai frutti di mare* (with the fruits of the sea) and any of their grilled or fried fish. The name of the place means Fisherman's Trattoria, so fish is the best here.

SEEING THE SIGHTS

Take a look at the lace school and satisfy your curiosity about the inner workings of the lace business. The school is **Consorzio dei Merletti**, *located in the Palazzo dell Podesta in the Piazza B. Galuppi. Tel. 730-034. Open Monday–Saturday 9:00am–6:00pm, and Sunday 9:00am–4:00pm.*

The other interesting sight on Burano is the **Church of San Martino**, *Piazza B. Galuppi,* with its leaning tower. It's no Pisa, but still intriguing nonetheless.

TORCELLO

Located six and a half miles northeast of Venice, **Torcello** is one of the most fascinating spots in the venetian Lagoon. The island was settled between the 5th and 7th centuries by the first wave of refugees from the barbarian hordes. It got its name from the tower (*Torcello* means little tower) from which the bishop of Altinum saw his vision of how to make his people safe.

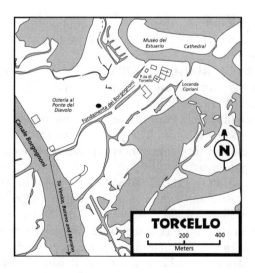

Now just a solitary village on a lonely island, it was once a flourishing center of commerce and culture whose greatness dimmed as that of Venice grew. Since the 18th century, Torcello has been nearly deserted, with a population today of only about 100 people. All that remains of this long ago splendor is a group of monuments that face out onto the scenic but grassy central piazza.

Most of the land that remains has either been abandoned or has been cultivated, mainly for wine. After you've seen the few sights and walked the few hundred meters of town, the only thing left to do is satisfy your hunger at one of the exquisite outdoor restaurants. Eating, drinking, and making idle conversation is the main activity here. That's why Hemingway liked it so much.

ARRIVALS & DEPARTURES

Take vaporetto number 12 from Fondamenta Nuove. It takes about 45 minutes. You'll stop at Murano, Mazzorbe, and Burano first. After you get off the boat you'll have a little walk beside a canal that has no shops, stores, houses, restaurants or cafés (how amazing!).

SEEING THE SIGHTS

• **Cathedral**, *Santa Maria Assunta. Tel 730-084. Open 10:00am–12:30pm and 2:00pm–6:30pm. Closes 2 hours earlier in the winter.*
• **Museo dell'Estuario**, *Santa Maria Assunta. Tel. 730-761. Open Tuesday–Sunday 10:30am–12:30pm and 2:00pm–4:00pm. Closed Mondays.*

WHERE TO EAT

If you make it to Torcello, you really should try at least a small meal at one of these places:

LOCANDA CIPRIANI, *Tel. 730-150 or 73.54.33. American Express accepted. Open mid-March–October. Closed Mondays and Tuesdays. Dinner for two L160,000.*

An offshoot of Harry's Bar with the same high prices. This used to be a haunt of Hemingway's too. The place serves traditional dishes like grilled meats and fish. The atmosphere is pleasant, especially the seating in the terrace garden area.

OSTERIA AL PONTE DEL DIAVOLO, *Via Chiesa 10/11. Tel 730-401 or 730-441. American Express and Visa accepted. Open for lunch only. Closed on Thursdays and in January Dinner for two L140,000.*

This restaurant has a relaxing outdoor seating area and serves Venetian specialties like *Tagliatelli con gli scampetti* (tagliatelli pasta with little shrimps). They also make exquisite grilled fish and meats. A high end restaurant that serves great food in a peaceful and calm environment.

SAN MICHELE

If you like cemeteries, you should come here to pay your respects to the graves of Ezra Pound, Igor Stravinsky, and Frederick Rolfe. Otherwise, you may want to skip this stop altogether. The island is located half a mile north of Venice.

This is the strangest cemetery you'll ever see. Why? You can't bury anybody below ground here since its all water, so all they do is stack them one on top of each other and put them in long rows so you can come pay your respects. The island actually is quite scenic and very peaceful, with it's organized paths and beautiful tall trees. Not quite the place to have a picnic, but a place to go that I guarantee you not many tourists visit frequently. Its nothing like the cemetery in Genoa that looks like a little town, but it's still an experience.

ARRIVALS & DEPARTURES

Take *Vaporetto* 5 from Fondamenta Nuove. It takes 5 minutes.

INDEX

TRAVEL NOTES

Tuesday —
   Got to hotel ≈ 11:00 - walked up &
Around
St Peter in chains
Coloseum
Constantine arch
St Ignatio (trompe l'oeil

TRAVEL NOTES

TRAVEL NOTES

TRAVEL NOTES

TRAVEL NOTES

TRAVEL NOTES

TRAVEL NOTES

TRAVEL NOTES

TRAVEL NOTES

TRAVEL NOTES

TRAVEL NOTES

FROM THE PUBLISHER

Our goal is to provide you with a guide book that is second to none. Please remember, however, that things do change: phone numbers, prices, addresses, quality of food served, value, etc. Should you come across any new information, we'd appreciate hearing from you. No item is too small, so if you have any recommendations or suggested changes, please write to us.

Have a great trip!

Open Road Publishing
P.O. Box 20226
Columbus Circle Station
New York, NY 10023

OPEN ROAD PUBLISHING
Your Passport to Great Travel!

Going abroad? Don't leave home without an Open Road travel guide to one of these great European destinations:
France Guide, $16.95
Italy Guide, $17.95
Paris Guide, $12.95
Portugal Guide, $16.95
Spain Guide, $17.95
London Guide, $13.95
Holland Guide, $15.95
Austria Guide, $15.95
Rome Guide, $14.95
Israel Guide, $16.95

And if you're traveling abroad to Latin America & the Caribbean, Asia, or the Middle East:
Central America Guide, $17.95
Costa Rica Guide, $16.95
Belize Guide, $14.95
Honduras & Bay Islands Guide, $14.95
Guatemala Guide, $16.95
Southern Mexico & Yucatan Guide, $14.95
Bermuda Guide, $14.95
China Guide, $18.95
Hong Kong & Macau Guide, $13.95

Forthcoming 1996-1997 foreign guides: Greek Islands, Turkey, Ireland, Czech & Slovak Republics, Moscow, Vietnam, Japan, Thailand, Philippines, Mexico, Bahamas, Kenya, and more!

Closer to home, check out Open Road's US travel guide series:
Las Vegas, $12.95
Disney World & Orlando Theme Parks, $13.95
America's Most Charming Towns & Villages, $16.95
Florida Golf Guide, $19.95
San Francisco Guide, $14.95

Forthcoming 1996-1997 US guides: Hawaii, Colorado, California Wine Country, New Mexico, Alaska, Arizona, Texas, Boston, and more!

To order any guide directly from us, send a check or money order to:
Open Road Publishing, P.O. Box 20226, Columbus Circle Station, New York, NY 10023. Orders must include the price of each book, plus $3.00 for shipping/ handling for the first book and $1.00 for each book thereafter.